I0892136

The Louisiana Populist Movement, 1881–1900

THE LOUISIANA POPULIST MOVEMENT 1881–1900

Donna A. Barnes

LOUISIANA STATE UNIVERSITY PRESS BATON ROUGE

Published by Louisiana State University Press
Copyright © 2011 by Louisiana State University Press
All rights reserved
Manufactured in the United States of America
First printing

DESIGNER: Michelle A. Neustrom
TYPEFACE: Minion Pro, text; Berthold Baskerville Book, display
TYPESETTER: Thomson Digital, Inc.
PRINTER: McNaughton & Gunn, Inc.
BINDER: Dekker Bookbinding

LIBRARY OF CONGRESS CATALOGING-IN-PUBLICATION DATA
Barnes, Donna A., 1954–
The Louisiana populist movement, 1881-1900 / Donna A. Barnes.
p. cm.
Includes bibliographical references and index.
ISBN 978-0-8071-3727-7 (cloth : alk. paper)
1. Louisiana—Politics and government—1865–1950. 2. Populism—Louisiana—History—19th century. 3. Social movements—Louisiana—History—19th century. 4. Louisiana—Social conditions—19th century. I. Title.
F375.B27 2011
976.3'05—dc22

2010029104

The paper in this book meets the guidelines for permanence and durability of the Committee on Production Guidelines for Book Longevity of the Council on Library Resources.

To the memory of
Theresa Burleson Barnes,
beloved mother of six

Contents

Tables

Preface and Acknowledgments

WHAT CONDITIONS ARE FAVORABLE to the emergence and growth of social movements? This has been one of the central questions posed by social scientists interested in social movements. This book tackles this broad question by exploring the dynamics of the Louisiana Populist movement during the late 1800s. The Louisiana Populist movement was part of the broader southern Populist movement, which was essentially an agrarian revolt by small farmers. In its early years this revolt consisted primarily of self-help, economic strategies developed and implemented by a newly formed organization known as the Farmers' Alliance. By 1892, however, the Alliance had shifted its focus to politics. The Alliance served in many southern states as a "bridge" organization to a newly established third party, the People's Party. Once formed, the People's Party largely displaced the Alliance as the primary vehicle for collective protest.

There were several factors that drew my attention to the southern Populist movement. First, this movement was one of the largest social movements in American history. In the South, the Farmers' Alliance had approximately three million members at its peak in 1891. In many southern states, this membership became the major recruiting pool for the People's Party and helped make it one of the largest third-party challenges in American political history. Another factor drawing my attention to this movement was my interest in the responses of small farmers to the transformation of southern agriculture in the post–Civil War era. This era was typified by the increased commercialization of agriculture, as well as the revolutionary shift away from a slave-based labor system in the production of cotton. The final factor influencing my interest was my concern about the temporal bias that currently exists in the field of social movements. Case studies have been strongly tilted in favor of contemporary movements of the post–World War II era. If we are to better understand the factors conditioning the emergence and growth of social movements, we need to move beyond studying movements in the same time period.

Readers might be curious as to why I chose to focus on the Populist movement in Louisiana. To a certain extent, it was a pragmatic decision. The primary historical materials available to researchers of the southern Populist movement can quickly become overwhelming. Dozens of Populist newspapers are available in various state archives, as well as numerous daily and weekly newspapers with articles and editorials about the Populist movement. The research process is made all the more challenging by the fact that the Populist movement varied significantly from state to state. It is not a movement that lends itself easily to broad generalizations.

The primary reason, however, that I chose to focus on Louisiana Populism goes back to the early 1980s, when I was doing research for a book on late nineteenth-century agrarian protest in Texas. I discovered that while agrarian protest among small farmers in Texas was growing and its organizational manifestation, the Farmers' Alliance, was thriving during the late 1880s, the protest movement among small farmers in the adjacent state of Louisiana was relatively anemic. It struggled to spread beyond a limited number of parishes in the northern and central part of the state. While the Alliance had recruited close to 50 percent of farmers in Texas, in Louisiana the rate was half of that—about 25 percent of farmers.[1] Furthermore, the Alliance-affiliated organization in Louisiana, the Louisiana Farmers' Union, served as a weak bridge to the People's Party, the final organizational manifestation of the agrarian revolt.

The lackluster agrarian protest in Louisiana was puzzling to me because census data clearly showed that the state's agricultural sector had levels of distress comparable to those in Texas. It was all the more puzzling because the Louisiana Farmers' Union merged with the vibrant Farmers' Alliance in Texas in 1887, prior to the explosive growth of the latter organization. Why had the protest movement among small farmers in Louisiana fared relatively poorly?

While social scientists have tended to focus upon the emergence and growth of successful social movement organizations, much can be learned from studying mobilization efforts that fail, or at least have very limited success. The relatively poor mobilization record of the Louisiana Farmers' Union provided an excellent opportunity to explore factors impeding successful mobilization.

Other research endeavors, however, interrupted my intentions to pursue this research opportunity. More than a decade later, I belatedly returned to my interest in the challenges that undercut the efforts to build a successful Populist movement in Louisiana. My interest was further piqued by discovering that little had been written on Louisiana Populism. The last extensive treatment of the Populist movement in Louisiana was in William Hair's book, *Bourbonism and Agrarian Protest,* published four decades ago.

The objectives of this study of the Louisiana Populist movement are twofold. The first objective is to contribute to the historical understanding of the southern Populist movement by shedding light on its struggles to mobilize small farmers in Louisiana into a force for change. On a number of important points, the conclusions of my study differ from those of other studies of the Populist movement. Hopefully, my different interpretation of key aspects of the movement will invite discussion and, thereby, contribute to the ongoing scholarly debate about nineteenth-century Populism. The second objective is theoretical: to reflect on the Populist movement in Louisiana using social movement theories and to demonstrate the advantages of utilizing all three of the leading theories, rather than depicting them as competing theories or selectively employing one or the other of the theories. Too often, social movements are explored through discrete studies of shifting political opportunity, mobilization challenges, or framing issues. While such studies certainly have their value, what is missing is an examination of the dynamic relationships among these important factors. Such relationships, it will be shown, were important to both the development and the demise of the Populist movement. Furthermore, the theoretical objectives of the current study include an attempt to demonstrate that the leading social movement perspectives can be expanded in ways that address some of the major criticisms that have been leveled against these perspectives.

With both historical and theoretical objectives, it can be difficult to appease two divergent audiences: historians and social scientists. Historians will expect to find a richly detailed account of the Louisiana Populist movement. Most social scientists will be primarily interested in the analysis of the Populist movement and the theoretical relevance of the case study, perhaps regarding any richly detailed historical description of the movement as excessive. Aware of these two different audiences, I have striven for balance. This entailed providing enough historical details to give a good sense of movement dynamics, but avoiding a finely detailed historical description of the movement so that attention could be directed to an analysis of Louisiana Populism.

OTHER SCHOLARLY WORK ON POPULISM

It is appropriate at this point to address, at least briefly, other work on the southern Populist movement and to note how my account complements or differs from this work. Historical writings on Populism abound. An exhaustive review of those writings is outside the scope of this work. But no contemporary work on Populism can ignore historian Lawrence Goodwyn's seminal work, *Democratic Promise.* He correctly depicted the Farmers' Alliance and the People's Party as "sequential expressions" of the same movement, and he recognized that the early cooperative strategies of the Alliance were the primary impetus to its successful mobilization.[2] This was a much needed corrective to the neglect of the cooperative strategies by earlier historians, such as Richard Hofstadter who claimed that cooperative strategies incorporating an "awareness of the exactions of middlemen" emerged for the first time among farmers during the New Deal.[3] My account of the cooperative strategies of the movement is largely consistent with Goodwyn's, with the important distinction that I give much more emphasis to the inherent structural limitations of the cooperative strategies. His slighting of structural limitations is evidenced in his discussion of the "incomplete Alliance organizing effort" in Louisiana, which avoided any mention of strategy limitations and also completely ignored the mobilization challenges created by the structure of agriculture in that state. Instead, he focused almost exclusively on allegations of poor leadership.[4]

Another important aspect of Goodwyn's influential work on Populism was his distinction between genuine Populism and the free-silver "shadow" movement. He strongly criticized earlier historical writings on Populism by John Hicks and Richard Hofstadter,[5] which he argued confounded the political tenets of Populism with the shadow movement of free silver. My account of the political phase of the Populist movement concurs with his view that there was a crucial difference between the tenet of free silver and the full slate of financial demands of the Alliance. However, I disagree with his contention that free-silver advocates came to control the People's Party through duplicitous means. My account emphasizes the diversity of interests within the People's Party, a diversity that was obvious from the moment of its inception. To be sure, the Alliance was a very important organization that the People's Party was dependent upon to garner southern support. But the People's Party was not solely a political extension of the Alliance. In fact, the Alliance was largely absent from the founding convention of the People's Party. Furthermore, I argue that the diversity of interests within the People's Party, which Goodwyn found problematic, was essential to a political party seeking reform within a "winner-takes-all" electoral system. Alliance mobilization in and of itself was not a sufficient base for a viable national political party.

On a final note, my analysis of the decline of the Populist movement differs from Goodwyn's. While he primarily stressed the role of the free-silver shadow movement in that decline, I adopt a more eclectic explanation that emphasizes the disfranchisement process in many southern states, as well as a critical factor totally overlooked by Goodwyn: a serious challenge to the Populist analysis of the root causes of the agricultural depression.

In regard to the Populist movement in Louisiana, the only major account is found in William Hair's book, *Bourbonism and Agrarian Protest.* On many matters, this book contains an excellent description of the Populist movement in Louisiana. But as an historical work, it understandably does not reflect on Populism from the perspective of social movement theory. It is also very limited in terms of its explanation and insight into a number of important events and issues in the state Populist movement, such as the limits of the early self-help cooperative strategies, the challenges facing the jute boycott, the factors propelling the movement's shift to politics, and the tension between free silver and fiatism within the Louisiana movement. Furthermore, the present study challenges Hair's broad depiction of Louisiana Populists as seeking "genuine political equality" for blacks.[6]

While the Populist movement has generated intense scholarly interest among historians, it has been relatively neglected by sociologists. To my knowledge, no other sociologist has explored southern Populism through the lens of contemporary social movement theory. The best-known sociological analysis of the movement, Michael Schwartz's *Radical Protest and Social Structure: The Southern Farmers' Alliance and Cotton Tenancy, 1880–1890,* was written before major advances in social movement theory and, therefore, utilized none of the contemporary theories of social movement emergence and development. While Schwartz's work has been rightfully influential, especially in regard to his analysis of the structure of the cotton tenancy system, it suffers from several limitations. First, it focused only on the Alliance phase of the Populist movement up to 1890 and did not follow that movement through its crucial post-1890 political phase. Second, it put forth an analysis of the Alliance's cooperative strategies that entailed an overly optimistic stance in regard to the potential of those strategies to reshape the agricultural economy. Third, it blamed oligarchic leadership for the Alliance's shift to politics in 1890, arguing that the shift was the result of planter conservatism. Such an explanation, however, conflicts with the decidedly non-conservative demands of Alliance leaders in the 1890–1892 period following the shift to politics.

The only other book-length treatment of the Populist movement by a sociologist is Scott McNall's excellent book, *The Road to Rebellion,* which focused on the Populist movement in Kansas. This work examined the Populist movement through the conceptual lens of class, exploring the class structure of nineteenth-century Kansas and its relevance to the farmers' movement. McNall made no reference to contemporary theories of social movement in his discussion of Populism. Consequently his analysis is quite different from mine, which is couched in terms of social movement theory. However, his analysis shares an important focus with mine in that he was very attentive to the roles of both agency and structure—agency as represented in the choices that people make in terms of protest tactics and movement ideology, and structure as represented by the constraints placed on the movement by the existing economic and political forces of the times. In discussing agency and structure, he cogently argued that "each deserves its due in a disentangling of the development and ultimate decline of the Farmers' Alliance and the Populist movement."[7]

In sum, while the works of Goodwyn, Hair, Schwartz, and McNall have much to recommend them to those interested in the Populist movement, none of these scholarly writings examined the movement through the lens of social movement theory. I hope that by using such a lens to probe the dynamics of the Louisiana Populist movement, my work will contribute to the ongoing discussion about the rise and fall of the movement.

POPULISM THROUGH THE LENS OF SOCIAL MOVEMENT THEORY

The major theoretical insight that is demonstrated by the present study of the Louisiana Populist movement is that the explanatory power of social movement theory is enhanced when the three leading theories—the

Resource Mobilization, Political Process, and Framing theories—are employed together, rather than being depicted as competing theories. Using an eclectic theoretical approach, a number of analytical insights into the Louisiana Populist movement are gleaned. Some of the more important of these insights are highlighted below.

One major finding of this research project is that the emergence and early growth of the Louisiana Farmers' Union was largely a product of the coalescence of three factors: enhanced political opportunity unleashed by the end of Reconstruction; the development of a diagnostic frame that effectively countered the overproduction explanation for the agricultural depression; and the development of a strategic frame focused on self-help cooperative tactics that initially held out hope to small farmers of economic salvation. A second major finding concerns the limitations of the self-help strategic frame and the consequences of those limitations for the movement. Self-help strategies were most appropriate for small farmers who owned the land on which they toiled and who could survive without crop-lien loans. Unfortunately, such farmers were a minority of Louisiana's rural population. Therefore, the strategic frame limited the effectiveness of the Louisiana Farmers' Union in mobilizing tenant farmers and agricultural wage laborers.

Another major finding concerns mobilization challenges after the self-help strategic frame faltered. At this point, a faction within the Louisiana Farmers' Union pushed for a strategic shift into electoral politics. However, given that the limited utility of its self-help strategy had curtailed mobilization in many parishes, the Farmers' Union was not an adequate organizational base from which to mobilize voters. It was largely absent in the alluvial cotton and sugar parishes and was almost completely missing from the only large urban center in the state—New Orleans. Therefore, the foray into electoral politics was in auspicious in that it required mobilizing support in order to exercise political leverage, but without an adequate organizational base through which to reach most voters.

Once the Populist movement shifted its attention to politics, Louisiana Populists also struggled with identity framing, which entails constructing identities that create an effective sense of "us" versus "them" and move people to collective action. The most important identity frame in Louisiana during the late 1800s was "white" versus "black." The Democratic Party capitalized on this frame by promoting a powerfully effective white supremacy ideology that characterized any fracture in white political unity as a calamitous threat. The difficulties in challenging the powerful racial identify-frame played a major role in undercutting the Populist movement in Louisiana.

When the shift to politics eventually resulted in a third party, the People's Party, leaders of the third-party movement in Louisiana initially promoted the full reform slate of that movement. However, beginning in 1895, they shifted their emphasis to the free-silver issue. This study argues that this shift was largely the result of a pragmatic, strategic framing decision motivated by the desire to compete successfully in the winner-takes-all electoral system.

Finally, this research project argues that the collapse of the Louisiana Populist movement is best explained by insights drawn from all three of the leading social movement theories: Mobilization was undercut by the success of the state disfranchisement campaign in decimating the voter base of the movement. Political opportunity for the movement contracted sharply as a result of disfranchisement and political decisions over delegate allotment to state nominating conventions and seat allotment in the state legislature. A bitter strategic framing dispute within the People's Party between the free-silver fusion and anti-fusion factions debilitated the movement, and an economy recovery that began late in 1898 called into question the credibility of its diagnostic framing of the agricultural depression. In regard to identity framing, the movement floundered as occasional efforts by leaders to surmount the prevailing white supremacy identity frame competed with increasingly commonplace efforts to appeal to voters with racist rhetoric.

BOOK STRUCTURE

Chapter 1 discusses the three major social movement perspectives within sociology today—the Resource Mobilization, the Political Process, and the Framing perspectives. It also explores some of the major criticisms of these theoretical perspectives and seeks to demonstrate that these criticisms can be addressed through adjustments to the perspectives. The importance of borrowing from each of the major theoretical perspectives to explain dynamics within the Louisiana Populist movement, as well as the utility of adjustments to those perspectives, is illustrated through generous use of examples from the Populist movement.

Chapters 2 through 9 present the details, chronologically, of the case study of the Louisiana Populist movement. Chapter 2 discusses the years 1865–1880, preceding the emergence of large-scale agrarian protest among small farmers in Louisiana. These years are probed because it is important to gain an understanding of the period preceding the birth of a social movement in order to understand the conditions giving rise to the movement and to better understand the timing of its emergence. Chapter 2 also discusses the structure of the agricultural economy in Louisiana, which had a major effect on the Populist movement in that state. Chapter 3 covers the experiences of the Louisiana Farmers' Union from 1881 through 1889. The challenges facing the farmers' movement during these years are discussed and then analyzed through the prism of social movement theory. Chapter 4 discusses the emergence and development of the Colored Farmers' Alliance, as well as the difficulties of mobilizing an effective biracial coalition between black and white small farmers in Louisiana. In chapter 5, the shift within the Louisiana Farmers' Union to political strategies is discussed. Attention is given to the reasons for this shift and the challenges facing the small farmers' movement after the shift. Chapter 6 focuses attention on the efforts in Louisiana to mobilize support for a newly formed third party, the People's Party, in the state election campaign of 1892. Chapter 7 discusses the mobilization processes, political opportunity, and frame disputes surrounding the national election campaign of 1892 and the election campaigns of 1894. Chapter 8 focuses on the pivotal state election campaign of 1896, especially in terms of the effect of state-level political opportunity on the viability of the Populist movement. The presidential election campaign of 1896 is examined in chapter 9, with particular attention given to the crisis created by partial fusion between the Democratic Party and People's Party. The major post-1896 factors in the demise of the Louisiana Populist movement, as well as the Populist movement nationally, are also explored. The concluding chapter provides an analytical summary of the key insights gleaned from the present study of the Louisiana Populist movement.

ACKNOWLEDGMENTS

Many people have earned my gratitude for assisting me in the research on which this book is based. I owe thanks to the National Endowment for the Humanities, which awarded me a summer stipend during one of the summers when I immersed myself in the archives and examined countless reels of microfilmed newspapers. The Interlibrary Loan staff at the University of Wyoming also deserves special thanks. They were very helpful in locating and obtaining microfilmed documents relating to my case study. It was a pleasant surprise how far I was able to go in my exploration of Louisiana history from the confines of my office in Laramie, Wyoming.

I would also like to thank the University of Wyoming and its Department of Sociology, both of which awarded me research grants. These internal grants funded my trips to the Louisiana State Archives and to the Hill Memorial Archives at Louisiana State University. These trips enabled me to examine pertinent historical documents that were non-circulating.

Finally, I would like to thank my husband Richard Machalek for his tolerance of my frequent expressions of exasperation and anxiety during various stages of this project. His support and encouragement were enormously appreciated. I would also like to acknowledge my sons Travis and Max who graciously accepted that the work-home balance that I had achieved since their entry into the world had to tilt a bit while I researched this book and worked my way through several written iterations of the manuscript.

The Louisiana Populist Movement, 1881–1900

1

Louisiana Populism

Through the Lens of Social Movement Theory

IN THE 1880S AND 1890S, a spirit of revolt engulfed the agricultural parishes of northern Louisiana. Hardy Brian, one of the leaders of this revolt, had grown weary of the failure to achieve economic and political reform. In the aftermath of the state elections of 1896, which were riddled with fraud, he called upon farmers to assemble in the state capitol and take control of the state government by force if necessary. Major newspapers in the state warned that nine thousand farmers were preparing to answer his call to arms. A boat equipped with weaponry and munitions for these farmers was allegedly anchored in waiting along the banks of the Mississippi River near the capitol. The state government was reportedly quickly organizing paramilitary units to defend the capitol.[1]

Not since Reconstruction had Louisiana confronted such a dangerous political crisis. Tempers cooled, and the siege never materialized. But the political tone of the times continued to be that of passionate disagreement about what, if any, economic and political reforms were needed. Hardy Brian held on to his intense antipathy toward the Democratic Party, given that it had foiled all major efforts at reform. His antipathy is reflected in his caustic comment upon learning that the Democratic governor of Louisiana was going on an extended vacation out West: "If the Indians will only scalp him, they will be gratefully remembered by our people."[2]

The agrarian revolt that swept the small farm parishes of northern Louisiana would become part of a larger movement of the times, the Populist movement. While there has been relatively little research on the Populist movement in Louisiana, the Populist movement in general has generated significant scholarly interest over the last half-century. This book seeks to contribute to our knowledge of the Populist movement with new research on the experiences of the Populist movement in Louisiana. Importantly, the book strives to weave the historical details of the movement with analytical insights from social movement theory.

Social movement scholarship within the field of sociology is guided by three leading social movement perspectives: the Resource Mobilization, the Political Process, and the Framing perspectives. The present study strives to contribute to social movement scholarship in two ways. First, while the three leading social movement theories are at times depicted as competing perspectives, it is the contention of the present study that social movement research is best served by an eclectic theoretical approach—one that borrows concepts and insights from all of the leading theoretical perspectives. Such an approach allows for a more complex and comprehensive understanding of social movements. Exploring either political opportunity, mobilization processes, or framing in isolation ignores other potentially crucial aspects of social movement formation and development. Second, each of these leading perspectives has faced growing criticism since the late 1990s. Some of the criticisms are highly relevant to the present study. By exploring the nature of these criticisms, the theoretical framework used to study social movements can be refined and a better understanding of the dynamics of the Populist movement in Louisiana becomes possible.

This chapter is structured as follows. The first section provides an introduction to the three leading perspectives on social movements and a discussion of major criticisms that have been leveled against these perspectives. The intent of this section is not to exhaustively describe every criticism that has been lodged against the leading perspectives, but rather to focus on those criticisms that are most relevant to the study of the Populist movement. The second section seeks to demonstrate that these criticisms do not necessitate a rejection of the currently dominant theoretical perspectives on social movements. Rather, the leading perspectives can take these criticisms into account and emerge stronger for doing so.

LEADING SOCIAL MOVEMENT PERSPECTIVES: PERSISTENCE AMID GROWING CRITICISM

The Resource Mobilization perspective argues that the mobilization process through which aggrieved populations organize and seek to reach their goals should be the central focus of any social movement theory. When the Resource Mobilization perspective was initially proposed in the 1970s, it represented a major shift of attention. Most research on social movements at that time focused on individuals and their grievances, often arguing that individuals who participated in movements were psychologically stressed and not acting rationally. The Resource Mobilization perspective, in contrast, directed attention to social movement organizations (SMOs) that attempted to gather the resources necessary for collective protest. It argued that the level of resources mobilized for protest was the key factor in the rise and fall of social movements.[3]

The Resource Mobilization perspective also called for greater attention to the dynamics within SMOs and a close examination of how these dynamics affected the viability and strength of social movements. Furthermore, it drew attention to the relationship among different SMOs within a movement, as well as the relationship between movements and emergent counter-movements, and argued that attention to those relationships would yield a better understanding of the rise and fall of social movements.[4]

The Resource Mobilization perspective expanded over time to incorporate other important insights. It stressed the role of informal social networks in successfully recruiting participants to the movement. It also emphasized the rationality of movement participants and the importance of persuading potential participants that movement strategies would bring about benefits that outweighed the costs of participation.

In regard to the Political Process perspective, the writings of scholars such as Peter Eisenger, Michael Lipsky, Doug McAdam, Sidney Tarrow, and Charles Tilly have firmly established the importance of studying the effects of the broader political system on the opportunities for effective collective action.[5] Studies of the political system's impact on social movements have tended to focus on *changes* in political structure or power relations that account for the timing of a social movement's emergence and its development over time. Other social movement scholars, particularly those that seek to explain differences in social movement emergence and development among states or nations, have focused on the effects of institutional political structures on social movements.[6]

Whether examining static or dynamic features of the political system, the argument of the Political Process perspective remains the same: social movements are shaped by the political environment in which they occur, and analyses of movements need to be attentive to political structure and shifts in political opportunities associated with that structure. McAdam, one of the early advocates of this perspective, argued that to a large extent political opportunity was affected by the political alignment of groups within the larger political environment. In discussing shifts in political opportunity, he stated that "*any* event or broad social process that serves to undermine the calculations and assumptions on which the political establishment is structured occasions a shift in political opportunities."[7]

In regard to the Framing perspective, it arose in the 1980s in response to the downplaying by contemporary theorists of the role of grievances in the emergence of social movements. These theorists had reasoned that grievances were always present and, therefore, were not useful when trying to explain the variant aspects of social movement formation and development. While Framing theorists accepted the argument that grievances in and of themselves were not an adequate explanation for the emergence and development of social movements, they challenged the notion that grievances were unimportant. Instead, they stressed that the social construction of grievances was a crucial task confronting social movement leaders. Grievances had to be defined in such a way that the legitimacy of the status quo was effectively challenged. Otherwise people might explain their troubles on the basis of perceived personal faults or by reference to the impersonal forces of nature or fate. Neither of these types of explanations would produce protest movements.[8]

In their early work within the social constructionist perspective, David Snow, E. Burke Rochford, Steven Worden, and Robert Benford stressed the importance of frames to social movements. Frames were defined as shared understandings of the world that legitimate and motivate collective action. They also focused attention on the framing *process,* whereby groups of people work to create frames that successfully recruit social movement participants.[9]

The Resource Mobilization, Political Process, and Framing theories on social movements were initially developed in the 1970s and 1980s. Though very widely used, they have increasingly come under fire. Consequently, there is at present "a good deal of theoretical turmoil among analysts of social movements."[10] Three of the major criticisms that have been lodged against these perspectives are highly pertinent to the present study of the Populist movement and will, therefore, be discussed at length. These criticisms are: the leading perspectives inappropriately have a strong structural bias and neglect the importance of "agency"; they neglect the role of emotion in social movements and inappropriately juxtapose rationality and emotion; and they give inadequate attention to the important geospatial aspects of social movements. Each of these criticisms is discussed, respectively.

The first major criticism relates to the role of structure and agency in social movement theories. Critics have argued that the Resource Mobilization, Political

Process, and Framing theories are overly structural in their approaches. While they concede that these perspectives have guided an enormous amount of excellent research, they complain that these leading perspectives have skewed social movement research in the direction of a strong structural bias. That is, the leading perspectives have encouraged a focus on factors that are relatively stable over time and largely outside the control of social movement leaders and participants.[11] For example, social networks are often depicted as key mobilizing structures that influence social movement recruitment. However, such networks are usually depicted as an external "given" to which the social movement has to adapt. Rarely is attention given to the possibility that social movement leaders and activists might create their own mobilizing structures or take an active role in expanding existing social networks used for recruitment purposes.[12]

In regard to the Political Process perspective, political opportunity is typically conceived as the political environment that provides potential movement participants with the incentive (or disincentive) to engage in collective action by influencing their perceptions of the likelihood of the success or failure of such action. It is often described with a structural metaphor, as an opening or closing window of opportunity that favors or disadvantages a social movement. While political opportunity can shift over time, such shifts are typically depicted as the result of factors external to the movement rather than the result of action on the part of movement participants. Jeff Goodwin and James Jasper argue: "The main blind spot we see among process theorists is a failure to recognize or incorporate the insights of cultural constructionism of the last twenty years."[13] Instead, work in the tradition of the Political Process perspective has tended to depict political opportunity as an external "given" to which movement participants respond, with little attention given to the choices that movement leaders make and the effect of those choices on the political processes affecting social movement dynamics.

With respect to the Framing perspective, critics argue that it too often results in scholars merely describing key grievances and discussing the root causes of those grievances (diagnostic frames) or describing the strategies that a social movement adopts to address those grievances (strategic frames). Often missing from accounts of framing is attention to the role of agency, or choice, in social movements. Critics stress that social movement leaders and activists have choices when deciding what strategies to employ in an effort to achieve their goals. That is, strategies are not fully determined structurally.

Rather, choices about strategic action have to be made. Yet, critics argue, the important role of agency in the decision-making process is slighted by the leading social movement perspectives, and this neglect has distorted our understanding of social movement dynamics.[14]

Finally, some critics have contended that the Framing perspective deflects attention from a fuller analysis of the role of culture and agency in social movement formation. They argue that social movement scholars need to pay more attention to broad cultural meanings, not simply social movement frames. Movement frames are typically too narrowly conceived to reflect the myriad ways in which culture can affect social movements. Whether individuals support, or fail to support, a movement is strongly affected by the extent to which the movement's positions on major issues resonate or align with their experiences and beliefs. While this insight was present in some of the early scholarship on framing, such as in the seminal work of David Snow, it has not received sufficient attention in subsequent research on framing.[15]

The second major criticism of the leading social movement perspectives is that they ignore emotional dimensions of protest activities.[16] To a large extent, the inattention to emotion was a direct reaction against pre-1970s social movement theories that equated emotion with irrationality and often depicted emotional social movement participants negatively. For example, Neil Smelser likened the beliefs of protestors to magical beliefs, claiming that protestors disregarded the many steps involved in an effective solution and pushed for simplistic, short-circuited solutions. Eric Hoffer depicted movement participants as fanatics who desperately needed to believe in the movement's ideology to compensate for the lack of meaning in their personal lives. Similarly, William Kornhauser argued that the activism of social movement participants was motivated by deep-seated psychological needs, such as the need to overcome alienation.[17]

This early tradition of treating emotion as derivative of some type of psychological need or problem began to receive intense criticism in the 1970s at the same time that the new, and now dominant, social movement perspectives were beginning to emerge. As a result, these new perspectives ignored the role of emotion altogether. Social movement participants were presented as highly rational individuals who carefully weighed the cost of participation against the benefits. They were depicted as individuals who strategically chose to pursue political goals outside of the normal, institutionalized channels of political influence. Grievances, and the emotional reactions to those grievances, were viewed as constants and, therefore, incapable of contributing to a better understanding of the highly variable nature of social movement emergence and development.[18]

By the late 1990s, some social movement scholars were calling attention to what they perceived as a false juxtaposition of emotion and rationality. They argued that the either-or approach to emotion and rationality failed to recognize that social movement dynamics could be significantly affected by both emotion and rationality. They also objected to emotions being depicted as inherently irrational. As Jeff Goodwin, James Jasper, and Francesca Pollenta succinctly put it: "While the earlier theorists had portrayed protestors as emotional to demonstrate their irrationality, the new theorists demonstrated their rationality by denying their emotions."[19]

The critics called for greater attention to the role of emotion in both movement emergence and growth. In the absence of intense emotion, a social movement might never materialize in response to grievances. Without strong emotion, social movements might fizzle, never obtaining a sufficient following to have an impact. Within growing social movements, intense emotions can shape activist preferences and strategic choices. By neglecting emotion, social movement theorists were missing a potent force in the dynamics of social movements.[20]

A final major criticism of leading social movement theories concerns their alleged inattentiveness to geospatial factors. Critics charge that social movement scholarship too often only incidentally mentions the relationship between geospatial factors and movement dynamics. Some social movement scholars worry that the disproportionate attention given to the movements of the 1960s risks distorting our understanding of contentious politics by confining our examination of social movements to a narrow time period. It is as if scholars assume that findings derived from movements of the 1960s will apply to movements in general, regardless of time and place.[21]

Critics charge that the inadequate attention given to the social and historical contexts within which movements emerge has undercut our understanding of social movements. They have called upon researchers to become more sensitive to the unique effects of time and place on social movements. These effects can be wide-ranging, such as collective identity formation, alliance-building, shifts in localized political opportunities, and resource mobilization challenges. All social movements, critics argue, must be properly contextualized or situated in time and place. To do otherwise is to assume improperly that external opportunities or threats are experienced by all social movements in the same manner, independent of the historical epoch in which the movement occurs and its prevailing culture and practices.[22]

Critics who call for more attention to the geospatial aspects of movements are particularly adamant about the effect of place on social identity formation. That is, *where* identities are formed has a strong effect on the salience of different aspects of identity, such as race, class, and gender.[23] In no movement has this been truer than in the Populist movement of the nineteenth century, both in terms of its early Alliance phase and in terms of its subsequent third-party phase. For example, race was central to the identity of small farmers in Louisiana. The centrality of race was in large part due to the fact that blacks were a majority of the population of Louisiana. Fears of "Africanization," or black control over the political affairs of local and state government, were frequently expressed in local newspapers and newspapers affiliated with the Louisiana Populist movement. There is also ample evidence that Populist leaders in Louisiana participated in race-baiting rhetoric during the height of the movement. In contrast, studies of the Populist movement in the adjacent state of Texas have not reported comparable levels of race-baiting rhetoric within the movement.[24]

The growing criticism of the leading social movement theories has begun to attract significant attention from scholars. However, it is the contention of the present study that the current leading social movement theories can be modified to take these criticisms into account. That is, there is no need for a holistic rejection of the dominant perspectives. Rather, these perspectives can be expanded to incorporate the insights of the critics.

Let us turn our attention to the leading perspectives and discuss how each of these perspectives can be tailored to take into account the major criticisms that have been discussed.

Fine-tuning the Resource Mobilization Perspective

The Resource Mobilization perspective can be broken down into distinct components, making it easier to demonstrate how criticisms can be used to modify the perspective to enhance its utility in social movement research. In discussing these different components, particular attention will be given to their significance to the present study of the Louisiana Populist movement.

One of the central tenets of the Resource Mobilization perspective is that potential movement participants rationally weigh the costs of participation against the perceived benefits. For a movement to be successful in its recruitment efforts, its leaders and activists need to convince potential participants that the movement will produce benefits that outweigh the costs of participation. Employment of a highly effective strategy tends to lead to significant growth for a social movement. Conversely, the failure of strategies to achieve limited objectives often leads to demobilization unless new tactics, or the refinement of old tactics, are forthcoming.[25]

It is important to realize that strategic choice is an issue of agency in that movement participants willfully select protest strategies, with their choices having important consequences for the movement. In regard to the small farmers' movement of the nineteenth century, its founding leaders were small farm owners. As will be discussed in detail later, their class status affected their initial choice of self-help, economic cooperative strategies. The early success of these strategies played a major role in mobilizing small farm owners with at least some cash reserves. But the self-help strategies were of little benefit to sharecroppers, who often had little, if any, cash reserves and depended on crop-lien financing. Their financial circumstances prevented their participation in the cash-only, cooperative purchasing strategies. Consequently, recruitment among sharecroppers was much less successful and created a class bias within the Alliance movement, which ultimately undercut the success of its cooperative strategies.

The Farmers' Alliance also chose to restrict its membership to white farmers. This strategic choice was strongly influenced by the white supremacy culture of the times and was driven by the intense emotional context of race relations in the South following the Civil War. The decision to be a whites-only organization had serious consequences, but choosing to be a racially integrated organization would likely have had equally serious consequences. Decisions are made within specific social, economic, and political contexts. To divorce those decisions from the contexts in which they were made is ill-advised.

Structure is as important as agency in terms of movement mobilization. Economic production, for example, can be structured in such a way as to aggregate people or scatter them, with significant consequences for mobilization. It can be structured in such a way that people have a measure of economic autonomy, affording them the opportunity to participate in a social movement, or in such a way that people are structurally constrained in their ability to participate. The racial composition of a community, a component of social structure, can also influence racial attitudes and affect the degree of interest in mobilizing across racial lines and in fostering racial cooperation within a social movement.

It is also important to recognize that the outcome of strategies chosen by movement leaders can be affected by structural conditions. For example, it is ineffective for social movement leaders to focus most of their energies on a campaign to persuade voters of the need for reform if the political system is relatively closed, with either minimal chances for voter input or massive electoral fraud. Ultimately this was a major factor in the downfall of the Louisiana Populist movement, which shifted to politics only to find that its opponents were willing to resort to massive electoral fraud to defeat them at the polls. Therefore, an adequate understanding of the strategic choices of movement leaders, and the consequences of those choices, requires careful attention to both structure and agency.

Critics have correctly pointed out that scholars working within the Resource Mobilization perspective have approached strategic choices through the lens of rationality and, consequently, have neglected the role of emotions in social movements. However, there is no intrinsic reason why the assumption of rationality cannot coexist with greater attention to the role of emotion in social movements. That is, emotion is not inextricably linked to irrationality. Heightened emotion can exist even in the presence of a calculative approach to selecting a strategic course of action. In fact, heightened emotion can be used strategically by social movement leaders and activists to persuade participants to expend more energy on behalf of the movement. Past emotional experiences or heightened emotion may also help explain why movement activists choose one particular strategy over other possible strategies.

In examining historical movements such as the Populist movement, it is possible with the benefit of hindsight to label certain strategies as inherently and fatally flawed. But it is important to remember that strategic choices occur within a complex environment of cultural, social, and political contexts and within a rich emotional context, all of which shape strategic choices. To ignore that complex environment is a mistake.[26] For example, while the leaders of the Louisiana Populist movement may be chided by contemporary scholars for using racist rhetoric, those leaders were fully cognizant of powerful white supremacy culture of the times and the uphill battle they would face if they tenaciously challenged that culture.

Another issue that has garnered considerable attention by scholars working within the Resource Mobilization perspective is the relative importance of indigenous versus external resources for social movement organizations. Some scholars have argued that external resources are crucial in social movements of the disadvantaged. For example, Anthony Oberschall claimed that "a negatively privileged minority group is in a poor position to initiate a social protest movement through its own efforts alone."[27] Similarly, when commenting on whether disadvantaged groups such as farm workers are able to sustain protest movements with their own resources, J. Craig Jenkins and Charles Perrow replied: "We think not. . . . For a successful outcome, movements by the 'powerless' require strong and sustained outside support."[28]

In contrast, other social movement scholars have argued that external resources are not critical to the emergence and development of movements of the disadvantaged. For example, in his work on the contemporary civil rights movement in the United States, Aldon Morris emphasized the importance of resources indigenous to the black community and argued that those resources were sufficient in and of themselves.[29] Some social movement analysts have also noted that external resources can have a dampening effect on protest if external contributors attempt to use their resource contributions to control a movement's espoused ideology or its tactical choices.[30]

The issues of structure and agency are clearly relevant to a discussion of external versus internal resources. It is inappropriate to ignore structural constraints and assume that any group, no matter how poor, has sufficient leverage to mount a successful social movement all on its own. It may well be that the necessity of external resources is in direct proportion to the extent of poverty in the group seeking to mobilize. It is equally ill-advised to ignore the importance of agency and assume that any group with ample resources, no matter what its choice of strategies and ideology may be, can successfully mobilize and reach its goals. Movements can be undercut by squandered resources, strategic missteps, or repression by opponents threatened by strategic or ideological choices.

The issue of internal versus external resources is very pertinent to the southern Populist movement. Undercapitalization was a major problem in the cooperative, self-help tactics of the early years of the Louisiana Farmers' Union (LFU) and helped prompt the shift to politics. Small farmers simply did not have the financial capacity to restructure the marketing and purchasing system in the agricultural sector. Thus, choice or agency entered the picture as farmers engaged in heated discussion about the best strategy for improving economic well-being. Eventually, the choice was made to shift from economic self-help strategies to political strategies. Yet the shift to politics did not abate the need for external resources. Although it is true that numerical strength can influence politics, any attempt to mobilize large numbers of voters is costly. Populist electoral campaigns were often run on a shoestring budget that hampered prospects for victory. The impact of external funding was clearly shown by the dramatic expansion of the Populist press in Louisiana following the massive infusion of funds when wealthy Republican sugar planters fused with the state Populist Party during the 1896 state election. The underside of external resources, in terms of their ideological effects, was apparent as well.

The Resource Mobilization theory can also be modified in terms of its focus on the role of social networks in social movement mobilization. Social networks can serve as recruitment tools when an individual has close friends or family who participate in the movement. Research has found that individuals with links to movement participants are much more likely to be recruited successfully than individuals with no such links. Social networks can also serve to inhibit recruitment when friends and family have strong antipathies toward the movement or key participants in the movement.[31]

When discussing social networks, it is important to recognize that the existence or absence of pre-existing social networks affects the degree of difficulty that movements face in their mobilization efforts. Pre-existing networks create fertile conditions for rapid recruitment. Conversely, the absence of such networks creates significant challenges to the mobilization process. It is also important to recognize that social movement leaders and activists make choices in terms of their decisions to activate or create social networks that foster and maintain commitment to a movement. Therefore, social networks should not be viewed as fixed, pre-existing structural features of society that inevitably favor or doom movement recruitment. Attention needs to be given not only to the structural aspects of pre-existing networks, but also to the role of agency in decisions about whether to expand those networks. Movement leaders can choose to rely solely on pre-existing social networks or they can expend considerable energy on expanding social networks and connecting previously unconnected segments of the population. Movement leaders can limit their mobilization efforts to a particular class, thereby forming a class-specific movement, or they can choose to broaden their appeal to people from different classes. They can ignore race and ethnic minorities when they recruit or can choose to work industriously to recruit across all race and ethnic groups. They can make a concerted effort to transcend racial prejudices or they can succumb to those prejudices.

Populist leaders in Louisiana did all of the above—at times limiting their mobilization efforts primarily to small farm owners, and at other times attempting to broaden their appeal to all of those who struggled mightily to make a living through farming; at times catering to the racial prejudices of the times, and at other times trying to transcend those prejudices and mobilize a biracial coalition for reform. For this reason, unless researchers take a longitudinal approach to studying the Louisiana Populist movement, they risk mischaracterizing it as narrowly appealing to small farm owners alone or as a movement with broader class appeal; as rabidly racist or as a movement that successfully rose above the intense racism of its time. All of these characterizations are true, but at different times in the life of the movement.

The historical record clearly indicates that Populist leaders recognized the importance of social networks and often planned picnics and social gatherings at which Populist leaders spoke. But while there were significant social networks among small farmers in the rural countryside that could be utilized in the generation and maintenance of commitment to the Populist movement, social networks were heavily segregated by race. Populist leaders struggled to build a biracial coalition in the absence of supportive, biracial social networks.

There is no question that biracial unity in addressing the farm crisis in Louisiana was undermined by the weakness of social ties between the white and black communities in Louisiana and the strong undercurrent of racial tension. Blacks in rural Louisiana had good reasons for being distrustful of whites in the backland parishes where Populism thrived. Emotions ran deeply in regard to the racial divide, rooted not only in the legacy of slavery, but also in the scars created by the violence against blacks in the backland parishes during the Reconstruction era.

Louisiana third-party leaders initially attempted to build a biracial political coalition based on the common class interests that transcended race. Both white and black cotton farmers experienced economic problems as crop prices plummeted. Regardless of their race, farm owners struggled to hold on to their land, and tenant farmers struggled against a crop-lien system of financing that created debt peonage.

Racial differences, however, undercut common class interests. Black Louisianans knew that they were highly vulnerable to the ravages of racism and the injustices of a judicial system that did little to hold racist behavior in check. Even if significant economic improvements were to result from the Populist movement, the quality of their lives could be dramatically compromised at any moment by the actions of racist whites. White farmers could dream of purely economic solutions to their problems. For blacks, the picture was more complicated. While their economic problems were serious, their quality of life was compromised every bit as much by racism and a judicial and political system that provided little protection from racism. Therefore, concerns about race impinged, as strongly as class concerns, upon their decision about whether to support the third-party movement.

It is important for social movement scholars to be attentive to the fact that there are multiple structures of domination, and these structures can create cross-pressures that influence movement dynamics. In regard to structure, economic production can be structured in such a way as to aggregate people or scatter them, with significant consequences for movement mobilization. It can be structured in such a way that people have a measure of economic autonomy, affording them the opportunity to participate in a social movement, or in such a way that people are structurally constrained in their ability to participate. The racial composition of a community, a component of social structure, can also influence racial attitudes and affect the degree of interest in mobilizing across racial lines and in fostering racial cooperation within a social movement.

The Resource Mobilization perspective has also called attention to the effect of the internal functioning of SMOs on mobilization, particularly in regard to formalization, hierarchy, and oligarchy. Formalization relates to the extent to which an SMO has established procedures and structures that enable it to perform tasks routinely and to continue functioning smoothly when leadership changes occur. SMOs also vary in the extent to which they adopt an internal hierarchy of authority and in the extent to which that leadership is responsive to the rank-and-file membership.[32]

In regard to the Populist movement, both the Farmers' Alliance and the People's Party were formally structured. There was a clear organizational hierarchy extending from the local to the state to the national level. Rules of representation were spelled out in detail, with explicit formulas used to allocate delegates to local, district, state, and national meetings. Given the size of the movement, formalization of structure was essential. At its peak, the Farmers' Alliance reportedly reached three million members. After the shift to politics and the emergence of the People's Party, organizational structure was largely determined by the nature of political parties in a nation with millions of citizens. Any other structure would have courted chaos and gridlock. Nevertheless, the presence of hierarchy and formalized structures produced a great deal of suspicion among those who perceived the hierarchical, formalized structure as too far removed from the grassroots of the small farmers' movement. Thus, the organizational dynamics that necessitated this type of structure clashed with the desires of at least some of the movement activists who distrusted leaders that they believed were distantly connected to the heartbeat of the grassroots small farmers' movement.

In regard to the issue of oligarchy, it was broached long ago by Robert Michels and resulted in his classic formulation of the so-called iron law of oligarchy. According to Michels, "The principle of organization is an absolutely essential precondition for the political struggle of the masses. Yet this politically necessary principle of organization, while it overcomes that disorganization of forces which would be favorable to the adversary, brings other dangers in its train. We escape Scylla only to dash ourselves on Charybdis. Organization is, in fact, the source from which the conservative currents flow over the plain of democracy, occasioning there disastrous floods and rendering the plain unrecognizable."[33]

In their work, Frances Fox Piven and Richard Cloward embraced Michels's conclusions about the conservative tendencies of organizational leaders, stressing that leaders of SMOs become so preoccupied with organizational maintenance that they curb their former insurgency.[34] Other scholars have disagreed, concluding that the assumption of the inevitability of oligarchy is overly deterministic. Such scholars have argued that a better approach is to investigate the factors that have an impact on whether the policy stances of protest leaders change over time and on whether those changes are in the direction of greater conservatism or radicalism.[35]

The issue of oligarchy is the subject of debate in regard to the Populist movement. While some scholars have concluded that the movement suffered because it became oligarchical,[36] that conclusion is challenged in this study. Without a doubt the insurgency of the Populist movement was tempered, especially after 1894. However, attributing this development primarily to oligarchy is misguided. An alternative explanation is developed in the present study, one that focuses on the role of agency and the strategic choices of movement participants.

Social movement scholars utilizing the Resource Mobilization perspective have also examined the effect on mobilization of the interaction among SMOs in the same social movement. At times, SMOs compete fiercely for members, and in the process harshly criticize their competitor SMOs. This can be a very damaging process. As for the interaction between social movements and counter-movements, McAdam has stressed the importance of tactical escalation when opponents of a SMO undercut the effectiveness of its tactics. Otherwise, the SMO faces demobilization.[37]

Much of what is interesting about the relationships among SMOs falls within the role of agency. That is, SMOs make numerous choices in regard to how to relate to other SMOs. They can choose to form coalitions and cooperate when implementing strategies. Or they can choose to compete for monetary support and members by criticizing the leaders or strategies of other SMOs. Their choices have significant consequences, both in terms of each SMO's viability and in terms of the overall success of the movement.

In regard to the Alliance phase of the Populist movement, the Farmers' Alliance chose to restrict its membership to white farmers. With blacks excluded from membership, a parallel organization for black farmers was formed—the Colored Farmers' Alliance (CFA). The relationship between this organization and the whites-only Alliance was at times cooperative and at times contentious. While some of the inter-organizational tension was due to the culture of racism, there also were structural sources of tension that created conflicts of interest. Therefore, an exploration of the relationship between the CFA and the whites-only Alliance benefits from careful attention to the influence of structure, as well as the influence of agency.

In regard to the third-party phase of the Populist movement, the Farmers' Alliance (with which the LFU was affiliated) became only one among multiple SMOs vying for political influence. It was, however, by far the most influential SMO representing small farmers in the late 1800s, an important distinction in a country that was still heavily agricultural. The Alliance decided to move slowly on the issue of third-party politics and, consequently, was largely absent at the founding convention of the People's Party in 1892. The heterogeneous base of the People's Party, as well as the absence of the Alliance at the founding convention, had significant consequences for the direction of the Populist movement—consequences overlooked or slighted in some studies of the Populist movement, such as in Goodwyn's influential work.[38]

When the Alliance shifted to politics, especially third-party politics, it courted the fierce opposition of the highly organized, well-funded dominant two parties. While there were occasional alliances with those parties, in general such coalitions were temporary concessions to political reality with little genuine regard for the reform principles associated with the Populist movement.

Fine-tuning the Political Process Perspective

In his influential variant of Political Process theory, McAdam focused heavily on the concept of political opportunity, which he defined as the political alignment of groups within the larger political environment that made the political system more or less open in regard to specific social movements. Recently, however, McAdam argued that the "singular preoccupation with opportunity was excessively narrow,"[39] and he called for greater attention to threat as a stimulant to social movement formation and as an important factor in social movement development. He stressed that perceived threats to group interests can act along with shifts in political opportunities as a major factor in the emergence and development of social movements.

The experiences of the Populist movement in Louisiana underscore the wisdom of expanding the Political Process perspective to incorporate more attention to threat. The importance of geospatial factors to perceived political opportunity and threat also needs to be acknowledged. The perceived threat of the African American population can be strongly influenced by the size of the African American population at both the state and local levels. Whites may respond very differently in a state or locality where African Americans represent the majority of voters than in places where they constitute a smaller percentage of the electorate. Furthermore, when examining the choices of social movement leaders and activists, emotional responses to perceived threats also need to be taken into consideration. The response to racist appeals or calls for biracial cooperation might well be mediated by emotional recollections of past conflict or violence between the races. Geographical areas where there is a protracted history of political violence between the races present a unique challenge to any social movement attempting to create a biracial political coalition.

Let us now turn our attention to several aspects of political opportunity or threat that are particularly relevant to the present study: the extent to which the institutionalized political system is open or closed; the degree of stability or instability of elite political alignments; the response of political elites to the social movement; the rule-making and enforcement capacities of the government; and the effect of demographic variables and economic structure on political opportunity.

In regard to the institutionalized features of the political system, they can be more or less open, with openness being a function of the extent to which democratic procedures are firmly ensconced. Social movements, at least reform movements, are more likely to emerge and thrive under conditions of genuine freedom in terms of speech, assembly, and the press than in contexts where those freedoms are restricted or nonexistent. Furthermore, reform movements are facilitated when there is direct voter input in candidate selection, vigorous political party competition in elections, and an honest count in elections.

It is important to recognize that the extent of democracy may fluctuate over time and across locale. In the United States, the democratic process was seriously compromised in some states during the last half of the nineteenth century, the era in which the Populist movement developed. The tainted democratic process was nowhere more evident than in Louisiana, where it undercut efforts of small farmers to build an effective protest movement. Thus, social movement scholars need to be attentive to the geospatial factors affecting political opportunities for protest.

The experiences of Louisiana Populists also powerfully illustrate the importance of recognizing the role of both structure and agency. While the degree to which a political system is opened or closed is a structural issue to a certain extent, it also is affected by agency or choice. That is, the formal rules may dictate democratic procedures, but those in political power may choose to undermine or corrupt those procedures. This was certainly the case in the late 1800s and played a major role in the failure of the Populist movement in Louisiana. While a casual glance at the political system in Louisiana would notice many of the indicators of a democracy—nominating conventions, elections, and suffrage rights for adult males—a more careful examination calls into question the openness of the political system. Planters dominated the political process because of their ability to control the district and state nominating conventions of the Democratic Party, the party that consistently controlled state politics during the time of the Populist movement. Since the number of Democratic votes cast in the previous election determined seat apportionment at nominating conventions, planters wielded their considerable power to orchestrate landslide electoral victories in the black-belt plantation areas of the state. Such victories ensured that they would control the majority of seats at the next nominating conventions, and thereby would control who would be the party nominees for governor and other major state political offices. This created a formidable structural obstacle to early efforts by Populists to achieve reform by fighting from within the Democratic Party. Consequently, the calculus of competing strategy choices available to Populist leaders in Louisiana—to fight for reform within the Democratic Party or through a third party—was strongly influenced by the structure of the electoral process in Louisiana. That is, structure and agency were closely linked.

Another important dimension of political opportunity concerns the degree of stability in elite alignments. Stable elite alignments tend to make it more difficult for movements to mobilize. United opposition is always more difficult to overcome than an opponent experiencing internal divisiveness. Political process theorists have tended to focus on shifts in political alignments as a precursor to the emergence of social movements. Such shifts are depicted as opportune times for social movements to have an impact. It is important to recognize, however, that such shifts can follow the emergence of a social movement, rather than precede it. They can be the result of the strategic and ideological choices of social movements, rather than their precipitator. Thus, political alignments are best viewed through the lens of both structure and agency, with political alliances shifting as a result of choices made largely in regard to economic and political interests.[40]

Elite alignments clearly had significant consequences for the Populist movement. The unraveling and subsequent restructuring of elite alignments were important in terms of its rise, development, and eventual demise. Elite alignments at both the state and national levels were important to the fate of the movement. In Louisiana, the movement received a huge, financial boost from the unraveling of the alignment in state politics between cotton and sugar planters. Traditionally, sugar planters in Louisiana voted Republican in national elections and Democratic in state elections. Their allegiance to the Republican Party in national elections was due to that party's support of a sugar subsidy that buffered the sugar industry from the effects of declining sugar prices. Most sugar planters, however, stayed loyal to the Democratic Party in state elections. This changed in 1896, when the federal sugar subsidy was repealed, with the blessings of Democratic President Grover Cleveland and Louisiana's two Democratic senators. The anger of the sugar planters toward the Democratic Party significantly changed the political environment facing Populists in the 1896 state elections. Wealthy sugar planters formed a political alliance with Populists and contributed large sums of money to the state campaign for the fused Republican-Populist ticket. Populists no longer faced a united, seemingly invincible foe.

The Populist-Republican alignment proved to be a mixed blessing. The infusion of large sums of money into the coffers of the state People's Party resulted in a significant increase in the number of newspapers devoted to the Populist cause, clearly boosting the chances of reaching voters. In this sense, the unraveling of the loyalty of sugar planters to the state Democratic Party represented a favorable shift in political opportunity for Populists. The alignment, however, had a serious downside. Republican Party principles and Populist reform principles did not mesh well, and ideologically the alliance was strained. It was an alliance born purely out of a desperate need to unite against a common and powerful foe: the Democratic Party.

Without question, the most important and controversial shift in political alignment was in the presidential election of 1896, when delegates to the People's Party convention endorsed the presidential nominee of the Democratic Party. The endorsement was heatedly debated within the People's Party, and some scholars have portrayed it as the major factor in the demise of Populism. The endorsement decision, however, is best viewed through the lens of the structure/agency distinction. Delegates to the national People's Party convention had an important decision to make, a matter of agency, but the decision was intricately influenced by the political structure of the People's Party and by the American political party system in general. Some scholars, blessed with the benefit of hindsight, have strongly condemned the fusion decision of 1896. But attention to both structure and agency produces a more nuanced and sympathetic interpretation of that decision.

It is not only important to be attentive to how elites respond to protest, but also to how their response may change over time. The shifting responses of elites, an issue of agency, can be pivotal to the development of a social movement. Such shifts are often the result of the strategies chosen by social movements, and this can change over time. Movements may shift strategies when past strategies prove to be ineffective or when, as a result of the actions of movement opponents, they become less effective over time. Movements also may change their ideologies, becoming more radical or conservative in their rhetoric. Such strategic and ideological shifts often prompt changes in how elites respond to the movement.

Shifts in elite response were definitely crucial to the southern Populist movement. When the small farmers' protest movement switched its focus from self-help cooperative strategies to political strategies beginning in 1890, there was a dramatic change in elite response to the movement. While political elites had previously tolerated the movement, their response shifted to overt hostility. They engaged in character assassination of movement leaders and public ridicule of movement ideology. When those responses seemed insufficiently damaging, they shifted to heavier tactics, such as electoral intimidation and fraud. Nowhere were such tactics more heavily employed than in Louisiana, and they played a major role in the weakness of the Populist movement in Louisiana relative to other southern states.

Another tactic used by elites was temporary political alliances with the Alliance and People's Party. Such alliances effectively directed the potential threat of the Populist challenge into channels where it was more readily controlled by elites. In Louisiana, Democratic Party leaders deflected the mounting agrarian revolt by successfully soliciting a temporary electoral alliance with the Alliance-affiliated LFU in order to block the rechartering of the notorious Louisiana Lottery Company. While the corruption of that company was worthy of attack and an appropriate target of reformers, the electoral alliance between the anti-lottery faction of the Democratic Party and the LFU during the 1892 state campaign blunted the political radicalism of the Populist challenge in Louisiana. At a point when the Farmers' Alliance was serving as a bridge to the newly established People's Party in many southern states and attacking the Democratic Party for its refusal to endorse important reforms, the LFU was calling for an alliance with state Democrats and pleading for a delay in committing to a third-party revolt. Therefore, the third-party phase of the agrarian revolt had an unusually inauspicious start in Louisiana.

The use of temporary alliances was not a tactic used solely by the Democratic Party. As noted previously, the state Republican Party successfully courted fusion with the People's Party in the state elections of 1896. These temporary alignments undercut the Populist movement by making it vulnerable to the charge that loyalty to its reform principles was shallow and ever-shifting. An alliance with the Democratic Party in one state election and an abrupt shift to an alliance with the Republican Party in a later campaign suggested a capricious approach to reform.

While in hindsight it is easy to criticize Populists for their seemingly whimsical choices about political alliances, an appreciation for the difficulty that faced Populist leaders in making such choices is gained when one takes into account the political and economic structures in which those decisions were made. In Louisiana, Populist leaders had a bleak choice. They could remain fiercely loyal to the entire reform platform of the People's Party and go it alone at election time against the powerful sugar and cotton planters. Given the political power of the planters, they would almost certainly lose the election. Or they could compromise and form coalitions in hopes that electoral victory might be possible and that, once in office, there would be a chance to push as a political insider for reform.

It is important to recognize that the response of political elites to a social movement is a dynamic aspect of political opportunity that is movement specific. That is, elites may be neutral or facilitative toward one particular social movement and hostile to another movement occurring during the same time period. For example, during the mid-1890s, politicians of the two dominant parties were significantly more hostile to the monetary reform ideas of the Populist movement than they were to the free-silver reform movement. This differential response played a major role in shaping the subsequent decisions of Populist leaders in regard to monetary reform.

Another important dimension of political opportunity is variation in government rule-making and enforcement capacities. Governments differ in both time and place in terms of what is thought to be within the appropriate sphere of government rule-making, as well as beliefs about the appropriate level of enforcement powers to implement those rules. Rule-making and enforcement capacities are affected by rules and regulations passed by Congress and by decisions of the U.S. Supreme Court about the proper interpretation of the Constitution. Thus, the extent to which government experiences structural constraints in its rule-making and enforcement capacity is influenced heavily by matters of agency. Once again, we find structure and agency inextricably linked. Legislative and judicial choices are made, but once made they can become significant structural constraints on future choices on the part of both the government and social movement leaders attempting to influence the political process.

The issue of governmental rule-making and enforcement capacity is very pertinent to the Populist movement. In the late nineteenth century Congress passed the Enforcement Act and the Ku Klux Klan Act, which established federal jurisdiction and criminal penalties for interference with voting rights. These were important laws since state courts in the South had a reputation for failing to protect the voting rights of blacks. But both of these laws were challenged in the courts, with the challenges eventually becoming U.S. Supreme Court cases. The Court concluded that court cases against citizens who violated the voting rights of other citizens fell within the proper domain of state courts, a ruling that undercut the capacity of the federal government to make and enforce laws relating to voting rights violations by individuals. More specifically, the Court ruled that federal authority was not appropriately activated by the failure of state government to protect citizens' voting rights. Such authority was only appropriately invoked by racially discriminatory state statutes or by voting rights misconduct by public officials.[41]

The weakness of federal capacity to intervene to protect voters against intimidation and threat was a major structural detriment to the Populist movement in Louisiana. It is important to recognize the role of agency as it related to the problems of voting rights violations and electoral fraud. The presence of more federal supervision of elections could have been a major asset to the Populist movement. But during the Alliance phase of the Populist movement, the Farmers' Alliance actively opposed efforts to pass a federal election reform bill to restore integrity to the election process. During the third-party phase of the Populist movement, Populist leaders pushed for an anemic secret-ballot solution to electoral fraud. The absence of effective election reform created an insurmountable obstacle to the success of the Populist movement.

Political Process theory has also focused attention on the effects of demographic variables and economic structure on political opportunity or threat. In his well-known work on the modern civil rights movement, McAdam stressed the effect of demographic shifts of the African American population on political opportunity.[42] Demographic variables played a similarly pivotal role in the Louisiana Populist movement. High percentages of minorities created a strong perception of political threat in the non-minority population and negatively affected attitudes about mobilizing a biracial political coalition. Low percentages of minorities reduced the sense of threat to the point where biracial cooperation was more likely to be considered. It was no coincidence that the Louisiana Populist movement found it most fertile ground in the backland parishes, where the black population was relatively small in size.

The structure of agriculture also played a pivotal role in the Louisiana Populist movement. Commercial agriculture in Louisiana consisted of both sugar and cotton production, with marked differences in the labor force within those two commodity markets. Sugar production was typified by a very small class of elite white plantation owners and a very large class of poor blacks who were wage laborers and worked together in "gangs." Cotton production was characterized by two very different production structures: the alluvial, cotton plantation areas had a small number of relatively wealthy white plantation owners who divided their land into parcels of approximately forty acres to be tilled by black sharecroppers in return for a share of the crop. In contrast, cotton production outside of alluvial plantation areas was characterized by white small farm owners who relied primarily on the labor of family members. As the agricultural depression worsened, many small farmers lost their farms and became either sharecroppers or tenant farmers on the land that they had formerly owned.

The structure of agriculture in Louisiana helped maintain deep race and class divisions that affected the political opportunity for forming a biracial political coalition for reform. Building a coalition between the black wage laborers who toiled on the sugar plantations, the black sharecroppers in the alluvial cotton parishes, and the white small farm owners and tenant farmers in the non-alluvial parishes was a huge challenge facing the Populist movement in Louisiana. It was a challenge that the movement never successfully met.

In examining the role of agency, attention needs to be given to the effects of geospatial factors. These factors can play a pivotal role in why movements make different decisions, depending on the region, state, or locality in which those decisions are made. For example, the racial composition of the population was an extremely important factor that structurally constrained the development of the Populist movement in Louisiana, one of only three states with a black majority in the late 1800s. The fact that blacks outnumbered whites had a tremendously adverse impact on efforts to mobilize widespread support for the Populist movement. The majority-black status intensified the racial threat perceived by whites, many of whom were obsessed with the possibility of whites losing political control of the state. Anything that jeopardized white political unity, and that certainly included the Populist movement, was anathematized. In the adjacent state of Texas, race had a less destructive effect on political opportunity for the movement.[43]

Fine-tuning the Framing Perspective

In addition to resource mobilization and political process, framing activities are another crucial factor affecting movement development. The Framing perspective has made an important contribution to the field of social movements by highlighting the ideational and constructionist aspects of social movements. Critics have argued, however, that the perspective is often applied too narrowly, thereby missing important aspects of culture that affect the development of movement frames. Another criticism has been that framing analysis has a strong cognitive bias, stressing the instrumental aspect of the framing process and neglecting the emotional aspect.[44] These criticisms are taken into account when elaborating upon aspects of the Framing perspective that are of particular importance to the present study: attention to the diagnostic, strategic, and identity framing processes; the effects of frames on mobilization; the dynamics of framing contests; and the relationship between an SMO's frames and existing mainstream culture.

In regard to diagnostic and strategic framing processes, a clear distinction is needed between frames as ideological constructs and framing as a process whereby frames are developed and modified over time. Diagnostic framing refers to the process whereby an SMO determines the root causes of a grievance that afflicts the aggrieved population it is seeking to mobilize. Strategic framing refers to the process whereby SMO activists discuss strategies to address identified grievances and debate which strategies hold the most promise. Social reality is sufficiently complex that there are usually competing views about the causes of a grievance or about which strategy offers the most hope in redressing the grievance. Consequently, the frame selection process is largely one of agency or choice.[45]

The issue of agency in the framing process is highlighted by the notion of framing contests, which refers to disputes over frames. Some factions within a movement or SMO may push for a particular diagnostic or strategic frame, with other factions strongly advocating alternative frames. Such disputes are a ubiquitous feature of social movements, both among SMOs within the same social movement and between SMOs and their opponents.[46] Framing contests were certainly central to the Populist movement and will be discussed at length in the present study.

An analysis of movement framing is best done with a longitudinal approach that can shed light on the continuities and changes in a movement's frame(s). Not only does such an approach permit researchers to detect framing shifts, but it allows for a closer examination of the dynamic relationship over time between diagnostic and strategic frames.

The experiences of the Populist movement illustrate well the importance of both a dynamic, longitudinal approach to framing and agency. Alliance leaders made choices in terms of the strategies that they adopted. They subsequently reflected on the outcomes of their strategy choices and, finding them problematic, proposed new strategic approaches. Two major explanations of the farm crisis in the late 1800s vied for the support of movement participants and both flowed from an anti-monopoly diagnostic frame. The first explanation stressed the existence of an exploitative marketing and purchasing system. The self-help strategies that dominated the early years of the Populist movement, which called upon farmers to undermine or bypass the existing marketing and purchasing system, were inextricably tied to this explanation of the farm crisis. The second explanation of the farm crisis stressed problems within the nation's monetary system. It was tied to the anti-monopoly diagnostic frame because of its structural critique of the redeemable, metal-based monetary system and the financial manipulation of that system by the "money kings." When Alliance leaders fully recognized the limitations of the self-help strategies, they shifted their attention to the monetary system. While there was no need to abandon the anti-monopoly diagnostic frame, there was a major shift in the strategic frame from self-help, economic cooperative strategies to politics because problems with the monetary system were viewed as best addressed by utilizing the political power of a farmers' voting bloc.

In the mid-1890s the focus of the Populist movement would shift again, this time to the demand for free silver. Populist leaders de-emphasized their structural critique of the monetary system in favor of a singular focus on the volume of circulating currency. This led to a de-emphasis of the anti-monopoly diagnostic frame that had been such an essential component of the movement, and the neglect of this frame would play a role in the demise of the movement.

In terms of the effect of diagnostic and strategic frames on mobilization, social movements are often comprised of individuals from diverse socioeconomic backgrounds. This diversity can result in differing economic and political interests. Consequently the relevance or effectiveness of various diagnostic and strategic frames may not be the same for all members of the aggrieved population. This has important implications for mobilization, yet it has not received sufficient attention in social movement research.

In regard to the Populist movement, potential participants in the Alliance phase of the movement were from divergent social class backgrounds, and the chosen frames significantly influenced who was effectively mobilized as participants. There were four groups of farmers from which the small farmer agrarian movement of the late nineteenth century could recruit: (1) farmers firmly ensnared in the crop-lien system of financing, that is, farmers who were perpetually in debt; (2) farmers who were forced to rely on lien financing but were able to pay out at harvest time; (3) farmers who were able to make cash purchases but operated on such a low margin of cash flow that they constantly feared becoming future victims of lien financing; and (4) farmers who made cash purchases and whose cash reserves were ample enough to allow them to fund cooperative enterprises in their rural communities.

The Alliance movement sought to capitalize on the shared interest held by all four of the above groups. With cotton prices falling to $0.09 or less per pound, all cotton farmers were negatively affected and, therefore, could potentially be mobilized in support of a movement that promised economic relief. The diagnostic frame of the Alliance, which incorporated a structural critique of monopolistic forces in the purchasing and marketing systems of agriculture, had the potential to appeal broadly to cotton farmers. However, the strategic frame selected by the Alliance and Alliance-affiliated organizations such as the LFU had significantly different consequences for the four farmer groups. Farmers who depended on crop-lien financing, which included the first two groups, were neglected as a result of the strategies chosen by Alliance leaders. As a result of this neglect, it was difficult to mobilize them.

Viewed through the lens of the structure/agency distinction, Alliance leaders chose a strategic frame from among several possibilities. The leaders selected the strategies that they felt held the most promise for redressing the root causes of the grievances that they had identified. So choices, or agency, played a crucial role. However, once those strategic choices were made, they had a differential impact on farmers from varying socioeconomic backgrounds. The differential impact affected the mobilization process, making it more difficult to attract farmers who depended on crop-lien financing. This would be a major obstacle to mobilization during the Alliance phase of the Populist movement because over time more and more farmers depended on crop-lien financing.

When the strategic frame of the Populist movement shifted from self-help to third-party politics, an even more serious challenge to mobilization arose. The South had been solidly Democratic since Reconstruction ended in the late 1870s. White unity under the banner of the Democratic Party was seen as essential to maintaining the southern way of life. Calling for the desertion of the Democratic Party was heresy. In a compelling statement about the culture of the times, Milford Howard (Alabama's sole Populist congressman) exclaimed: "My own father . . . said that he would rather make my coffin with his own hands and bury me than to have me desert the Democratic Party."[47]

According to Snow, Rochford, Worden, and Benford the most common approach to framing by movement leaders is the process of frame alignment, whereby the frames of an SMO are linked to prevailing values and beliefs of individuals whom the movement is attempting to mobilize.[48] Yet the third-party strategic frame of the Populist movement was a direct challenge to the strong loyalty in the Deep South to the Democratic Party as the party of white unity and white political supremacy. That is, as a strategic frame, it did not represent an alignment with the prevailing belief among white southerners that white political unity under the Democratic Party banner was essential. Therefore, it is not surprising that considerably more intense mobilization challenges were created as a result of this shift in strategic framing.

In regard to identify framing, it is intricately connected to the process whereby SMO leaders actively discuss whom to recruit, how to collectively define the group that they are seeking to mobilize, and how to create a sense of "us" versus "them."[49] Identity framing should always be contextualized by discussing the relationship between identity frames and mainstream culture. Identity frames can be differentiated by the extent to which they depart from existing culture, with some resonating well with generally accepted precepts in the prevailing culture and, therefore, easily diffused. But other identity frames encounter an uphill battle, given that they represent a new identity formation and conflict in important ways with mainstream culture. In their seminal article on frame processes, Snow, Rochford, Worden, and Benford defined frame transformation as occurring when "new values have to be planted and nurtured, old meanings or understandings jettisoned, and erroneous beliefs or 'misframings' reframed."[50] While acknowledging that such frame transformations were very difficult to achieve, their work did not address questions about the conditions under which they was more or less likely to succeed.

In regard to the Alliance phase of the Populist movement of the late nineteenth century, it initially tapped into the existing farmers-as-producers collective identity. Farmers had long viewed themselves as an important vestige of the Jacksonian ideal of small owner-producers who were crucial to the maintenance of democracy. Any framing by the movement along these lines was readily accepted among the rural populace.

However, the collective identity of small farmers was complicated by the class divisions among them—small farm owners versus cash renters and sharecroppers. In regard to identity framing, social movement leaders actively make a choice about whom they seek to mobilize. The social class backgrounds of leaders can affect that choice. The founding leaders of the LFU—all of whom were white, small farm owners—chose to focus on mobilizing white, small farm owners who raised cotton for their major cash crop. Explicit decisions were made about limiting tactics largely to self-help strategies aimed at non-indebted small farmers. The failure to effectively mobilize tenant farmers had serious implications for the movement.

Identity framing during the Alliance phase of the Populist movement was also accompanied by race-based collective identity construction. Most Alliance members strongly opposed letting blacks into their organization. Consequently, attempts by white small farm owners to organize collectively were restricted to same-race endeavors. Eventually a network of southern ministers created a parallel CFA organization. But the extent of cooperation between the CFA and whites-only Farmers' Alliance was minimal, and at times overtly conflictual. The inability to transcend racial differences to create a broad class-based movement seriously affected the ability of white small farmers to implement effective self-help strategies.

The race-based approach to mobilization also had a profound impact on the subsequent development of the third-party phase of the Populist movement. For a brief time period following the creation of the Louisiana People's Party, third-party leaders expanded their identity framing efforts to include people of all races. They experimented with a biracial message that focused on an occupationally based small farmer identity. The emphasis was on the economic struggles of all cotton farmers, regardless of race, because of the plummeting market prices for cotton. But the experiment was short-lived. Populist leaders soon returned to blatantly racist rhetoric, abandoning all effort to court the black vote.

In discussing identity framing, it is important to acknowledge the role of emotion. Intense emotions can shape preferences among social movement participants and strategic choices. This is certainly true for the Louisiana Populist movement. The Reconstruction era that preceded the Alliance phase of the Populist movement was unusually violent in Louisiana. One of the most violent single days during Reconstruction took place on Easter Sunday in 1873 in Colfax, Louisiana, when the Colfax Massacre unfolded. More than a hundred blacks were murdered by whites during a political stand-off at the county courthouse. The violence that surrounded elections in Louisiana during Reconstruction reflected the determination of white Louisianans to maintain political control despite black voting rights and the black majority among eligible voters in Louisiana.[51] Such intense emotions are not easily circumvented. Any discussion of biracial political cooperation elicited recollections of the emotion-laden strife typical of race relations in the state.

In sum, it was hard for Populist leaders to attract support from black farmers while espousing white supremacy rhetoric. It was hard for the leaders to attract and retain the support of white farmers while espousing biracial appeals. It was a no-win situation and played no small part in the failure of the movement.

A FLEXIBLE AND INTEGRATED APPROACH TO SOCIAL MOVEMENTS

Social movement research is best served by an eclectic approach that emphasizes mobilization processes, political opportunity, and framing issues. The value of such an inclusive approach lies in the more complex and comprehensive understanding of social movements that it makes possible. Exploring only political opportunity, mobilization processes, or framing in isolation ignores the other crucial aspects of social movement formation and development. For example, while political opportunity may help shape the timing of a movement's emergence and its development, in and of itself it is not sufficient for explaining social movement dynamics. A shift to an optimal political opportunity environment will be of no avail if, for example, the aggrieved population is isolated with minimal contact with each other, or if most members of that population believe their grievances are rooted in personal failure or in the unavoidable forces of nature.

More is needed, however, than simply combining the components of the major social movement theories to make sure that each gets attention. Rather, social movement research needs to adopt a dynamic, interactive focus that examines the relationships among the key factors affecting movement emergence and growth. Researchers need to be particularly attentive to the compensatory potential that each of these three factors can have. It is possible, for example, that strong mobilization networks and/or a highly effective frame can compensate for a shift toward less favorable political opportunity. That is, an unfavorable shift in political opportunity does not automatically foreclose the possibility of social movement emergence or foretell the doom of a particular social movement organization. Optimal mobilizing structures and successful framing might overcome a disadvantageous political environment.[52]

Conversely, weak mobilization networks might at times be offset by a highly advantageous political opportunity structure or by adopting a frame that merely amplifies values or beliefs already widely present in society rather than threatening those values or beliefs. In contrast, any social movement that adopts a transformative frame that departs significantly from mainstream culture requires extensive mobilization networks to effectively counter the dominant culture. This was certainly true for southern Populism. When it deviated from the accepted culture—in terms of its initial call for black and white political cooperation and its call for a fiatist money supply rather than currency backed by gold and/or silver—it became imperative to have extensive mobilization networks to generate and maintain commitment to its controversial reform demands. Where mobilization networks were weak, support for Populism was weak. Perhaps this factor, more than any other, explains the decision of many national Populist leaders to shift the emphasis to reform demands more consistent with the dominant culture. For this reason, a discussion of resource mobilization benefits tremendously from a discussion of framing.

Indeed, the field of social movement research is poorly served by a search for inflexible theoretical generalizations about the relative importance of a particular factor such as political opportunity to movement emergence or growth. Insisting on such generalizations will lead to a steady production of conflicting conclusions as case studies of various social movements alternately confirm and challenge the generalization. Ultimately, this may well lead to a crisis in the field of social movements as researchers squabble among themselves about what generalizations, if any, have survived case study challenges. A case study, for example, wherein shifts in political opportunity were the key factor in movement emergence might tempt the researcher to argue that such shifts are always crucial to the emergence of social movements. But such a broad generalization is vulnerable when challenged by other case studies that find no evidence of significant shifts in political opportunity prior to movement emergence.

To avoid this quandary, the field needs to move in the direction of a flexible approach wherein the key factors in social movement emergence and growth are identified, with attention directed both to the role of each of these factors and to the relationships among them. Such an approach recognizes that each social movement faces a unique context. While political opportunity, mobilization processes, and framing need to be examined, there is always the potential that the strength of one of those factors will compensate for the weakness or even absence of other factors. An eclectic, flexible approach recognizes the complexities facing social movement formation across a multitude of tremendously variable places and times. Such an approach holds the most promise for providing further insight into the dynamics of social movement emergence and development.

Let us now turn to an exploration of the Populist movement of the late nineteenth century. The focus of our exploration will be the mobilization challenges, political opportunity, and framing issues that faced that movement in Louisiana, with some observations about the relevance of those factors to the Populist movement in general.

2

Backdrop to Populism

IN STUDYING THE EMERGENCE of a social movement, it is important to gain an understanding of the period preceding its formation. Assessing the relevance of various factors in social movement emergence is hampered in the absence of a longitudinal focus. Without knowledge of the preceding era, one cannot determine whether there were structural changes in the economy that affected the nature of grievances or perhaps their interpretation, whether there were shifts in the political opportunity for protest, or if the resources with which to protest improved or deteriorated over time.

With this in mind, this chapter explores features of the agricultural economy and politics of postbellum Louisiana, 1865–1880, which were relevant to the emergence of a protest movement among small farmers. More specifically, it argues that most participants in the agricultural economy of Louisiana experienced economic hardships during the years leading up to the Populist movement. The prospects, however, for translating those hardships into a broad-based protest movement were hampered by several factors. First, prospects were undercut by structural divisions within the agricultural economy. The bifurcation of commercial agriculture between cotton and sugar production and between alluvial and backland crop production presented unique challenges to mobilizing an agrarian revolt in Louisiana. Second, prospects for an agrarian protest movement were weakened by major race and class divisions among those who earned their living through farming. These divisions were reinforced by a population distribution pattern that created black-belt parishes in the alluvial areas of the state. Third, prospects were negatively affected by an unfavorable political climate during the tumultuous years of Reconstruction. Nowhere did violence hamper the political opportunity for dissent during Reconstruction to a greater extent than in Louisiana. Finally, the diagnostic and strategic framing options available to leaders for mobilizing agrarian dissent were constrained during the Reconstruction era. There was a close interplay between political opportunity and framing, with the framing process characterized by constrained agency wherein protest options were limited by the extremely hostile political environment that faced any framing choice that threatened to create political divisiveness among whites.

STRUCTURAL DIVISIONS WITHIN AGRICULTURE

Louisiana was a heavily rural state. Beyond New Orleans, there were no other areas that came even close to being large cities. Shreveport ranked second in size, but in 1880 it had barely 8,000 inhabitants. Only 4 other towns reported more than 2,500 inhabitants. Since economic opportunities were limited both in small towns and in New Orleans, the majority of the state's population lived in the countryside and earned a living farming.[1]

Broadly speaking, the farming parishes of Louisiana can be divided into three types: the alluvial cotton plantation parishes, the alluvial sugar plantation parishes, and the backland cotton parishes. The Populist movement in Louisiana would arise in, and be largely confined to, the latter parishes. It was a movement composed primarily of small white farm owners dependent upon cotton for their livelihood. The structure of the agricultural economy is crucial to understanding the class basis and racial composition of the movement, as well as the geospatial factors that affected the movement. It is to a discussion of this structure that we now turn.

King Cotton in the Alluvial Parishes[2]

Large cotton planters in Louisiana had thrived during the antebellum period. Property values had been among the highest in the South, and Louisiana ranked second in the nation in per capita wealth. This prosperity was in large part due to the state's extensive alluvial lands, which comprised approximately one-third of its soil.[3]

The plantation economy in the alluvial cotton parishes (see map) was severely disrupted by the Civil War. In the aftermath of the war, Louisiana plunged from among the top states in wealth to thirty-seventh in wealth. Much of the wealth loss consisted of the value of the freed slaves. More than in any other southern state, commercial agriculture in Louisiana had depended upon slavery: While the median slaveholding in the South was twenty-three, in Louisiana it was forty-nine.[4]

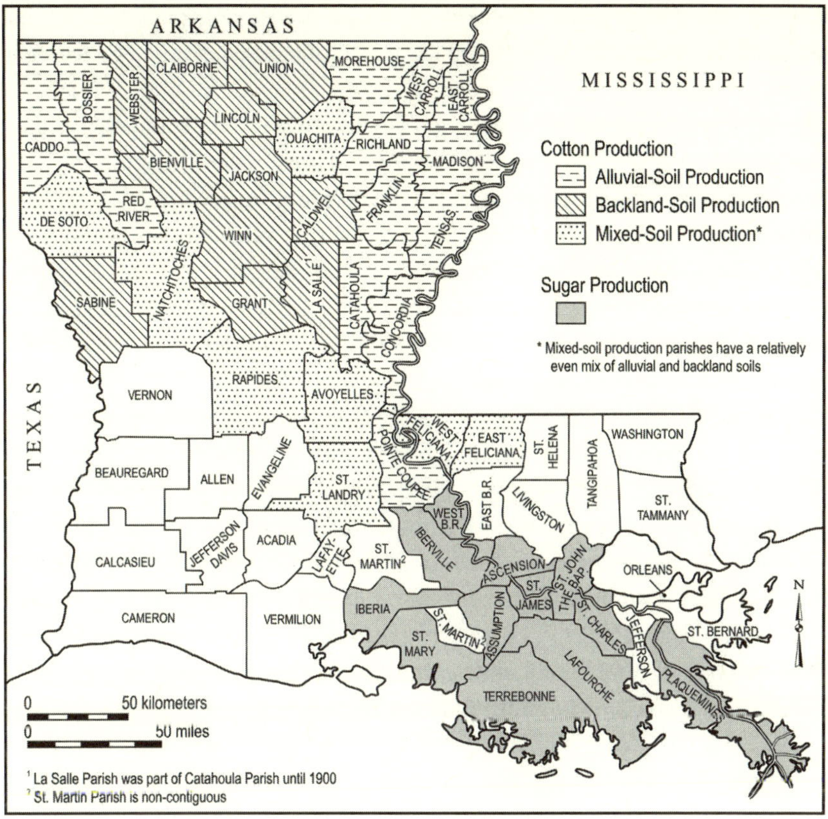

Major Cotton- and Sugar-producing Parishes of Louisiana, 1880

While cotton continued to be the major money crop after the Civil War, cotton plantations faced significant challenges. Much of the levee system had been destroyed, and floods were a major concern. Weeds filled many acres where cotton had once grown. Many plantation homes were in serious disrepair. The value of alluvial land plummeted more than 70 percent, given the amount of work needed to get the land back into production and the uncertainty of how the agricultural labor system would be restructured and how efficient it would be.[5]

In the first few years after the war, cotton planters reluctantly contracted with freedmen primarily as wage agricultural laborers. Bitter feelings and aggressive actions against blacks worsened in the aftermath of the war. The pecuniary value of blacks as slaves had served to protect them, at least to some degree. Now many former slaveholders unleashed their anger and frustrations on the freedmen, blaming them and the free agricultural labor system for their economic woes.[6]

An already bad situation was made worse when floods and caterpillars destroyed much of the cotton crop in 1866 and 1867, exhausting both the cash reserves and credit rating of many planters. Many agricultural laborers received no pay after planters deducted the cost of room and board from their wages, and they believed that planters were attempting to reintroduce slavery.[7]

As a result of their concerns about having a sufficiently docile and cheap labor supply, planters pushed successfully in 1866 and 1867 for laws to maximize their control over the freedmen. These laws, often referred to as the Black Codes, limited the functioning of a free labor market for the freedmen.[8] Given the poor treatment of agricultural laborers and the mentality implicit in the Black Codes, what the freedmen wanted most was economic autonomy. Their greatest desire was for land of their own. Many were upset when it became clear that their expectations of "forty acres and a mule" would not be realized.[9]

Given the freedmen's preferences for a measure of autonomy rather than supervised wage labor and the severe shortage of cash among planters with which to pay wages, by 1868 most cotton plantations were being divided into small units to be farmed independently by tenant farmers. Tenant farmers grew cotton on their assigned acreage in return for a stipulated share of the crop, and thus were often called sharecroppers. In Louisiana, their share varied from one-third to one-half of the crop.[10]

Although sharecropping arguably represented the best of limited alternatives for freedmen who remained in the cotton parishes, it ultimately served to imprison them through the debt bondage that became inseparable from sharecropping. While the freedmen had hoped that growing cotton would provide them with a reliable source of cash, this hope was rarely fulfilled. Since few freedmen had the cash necessary to pay for living expenses until their cotton was harvested, they were quickly drawn into the system of crop-lien financing. In this system, a planter or furnishing merchant financed the sharecroppers—not by lending money, but by advancing supplies and goods in return for a lien on the cotton crop.[11]

Since crop-lien financing played a pivotal role in creating fertile ground for the rise of southern Populism, and also created daunting challenges to the effectiveness of its early protest strategies, it warrants closer attention. The workings of this financing system were essentially the same throughout the South. The merchant advanced the farmer a credit line for the purchase of goods and supplies in return for a lien on his cotton crop. The interest charged for these crop-lien loans was very high. The director of the Louisiana Agricultural Experiment Stations commented: "That [the interest rate] varies very much. From 20 percent up. . . . Frequently they will buy stuff in August, and may pay for it with the picking of the first crop in September or October; and when you calculate the annual interest, it is 200 percent."[12]

To make matters worse, in addition to the interest charged on the credit extended the farmer, farmers using this type of credit were charged "time prices" on purchased goods and supplies instead of the considerably lower prices paid by cash customers. The extent of the markup varied both by the merchant and by the degree of risk perceived in granting a particular farmer a crop-lien loan. But the markup was usually at least 25 percent above the price paid by cash customers.[13]

As a result of their almost universal dependence on crop-lien loans, black tenant farmers often saw the entire profit from the sale of their share of the cotton go toward debt payment. Often they were unable to pay off their debt at harvest time and became deeper in debt with each passing year. They were legally tied to the land in a never-ending effort to pay off their debt and by the absence of realistic employment alternatives.

The prevalence of sharecropping among black farmers was not unique to Louisiana. What was unique was the preponderance of black sharecroppers. In contrast to most southern states, where the majority of sharecroppers were white, in Louisiana more than 70 percent of sharecroppers were black.[14] Any attempt to mobilize sharecroppers in that state would require heavy recruitment efforts in the alluvial cotton plantation parishes where black sharecroppers predominated. Therefore, race would play a pivotal role in the Populist movement that emerged in Louisiana in the late nineteenth century.

While there is no question that there were serious grievances among black sharecroppers, the debt peonage that accompanied sharecropping served as a highly effective form of social control. Economic survival necessitated that freedmen who sharecropped have access to a continuous flow of crop-lien loans. If they behaved in an objectionable way, they risked having their crop-lien credit reduced or cut off entirely. This vulnerability to economic retaliation made black sharecroppers in the plantation parishes very difficult to mobilize for collective protest endeavors, despite their escalating economic desperation when cotton prices started their descent.

The Backland Cotton Parishes

A small-farmer economy characterized the backland cotton parishes of north-central and northwestern Louisiana (see map).[15] The economy of these parishes was decimated by the Civil War. The Confederacy had refused to give waivers from military service to small farmers in contrast to the large planters. Beginning in 1862, when white males between ages eighteen and thirty-five were conscripted into the Confederate Army, women and children had to manage most small family farms. Their management might well have sufficed had it not been for the fact that the backland parishes remained under Confederate control for most of the war, and Confederate troops insisted on provisions of food from local farmers at well below-market prices. To make matters worse, the army paid with Confederate money that was of little value because of serious depreciation. If farmers resisted selling food to the Confederate Army, it was often taken without any remuneration at all.[16]

After the war, small farmers struggled financially. The decline in the cash value of their farms was precipitous. In Winn Parish, for example, where small farms predominated, farms lost more than 60 percent of their value. Furthermore, while large slaveholding had been uncommon in the backland parishes, ownership of one or two slaves was common enough to create a wealth-drain when slaves were freed.[17]

While farmers in the backlands were primarily subsistence oriented prior to the war,[18] many of them had planted at least some acreage in cotton to earn cash. In Winn Parish, for example, about 85 percent of the farmers raised cotton in 1860. In struggling to survive economically after the war, small farmers increased their production of cotton in locales where they had access to markets. In some backland parishes, the increases in cotton production were dramatic. For example, cotton production jumped 92 percent and 142 percent, respectively, between 1870 and 1880 in the parishes of Franklin and Richland.[19]

Cotton production was driven not only by the desire for a cash crop, but also by the fact that it was the only crop on which loans were extended. Many small farm owners had minimal cash reserves. Consequently, they were financially very vulnerable to crises created by war, floods, droughts, agricultural pests, and falling crop prices. As early as the 1840s, rural merchants in the backland parishes had begun accepting cotton as collateral for loans. But the need for credit and crop-lien financing soared to unprecedented levels in the aftermath of the Civil War.[20]

Not only did small farm owners need cash to rebuild their farms following the war, but they needed it to pay their escalating tax bills. The principal source of tax revenue in the lower southern states during the antebellum era had been the slave tax. This source of tax revenue had allowed land taxes to stay extremely low. After the abolition of slavery, southern legislators turned to the land tax to cover the loss of slave tax revenue. In Louisiana, the land tax rose 600 percent between 1860 and 1872—from 2.9 mills in 1860 to 20.5 mills in 1872. Even after a public outcry and the reduction of the tax to 14.5 mills in 1874, the land tax was still significantly higher than before the war. Plus, in addition to the mills levied on land for state taxes, there were parish taxes that had to be paid.[21]

Small farm owners in the backland parishes struggled to pay their tax bills and living expenses. They desperately tried to avoid crop-lien financing, aware that while it offered short-term economic assistance, it risked debt peonage. The farmer with a lien on his crop was under the control of the lien-holder until his account was paid in full. The lien-holder, whose concern was whether the farmer would eventually be able to pay off his debt, scrutinized his every purchase. He could buy only what the merchant agreed to sell him and had to pay whatever price the merchant chose to ask. Furthermore, he lost control over the marketing of his crop. Since the lien came due at harvest time, the crop could not be held off the market to wait for higher prices. Crop-lien financing would be the bane of the early cooperative, self-help efforts of the Populist movement.[22]

In addition to the increased dependence on crop-lien financing, another important change occurred in the backland parishes in the aftermath of the war: the growth of tenant farming, or sharecropping. Sharecropping had been rare in the South prior to the Civil War. Plantation owners cultivated their crops with slave labor, and the cheapness of land in the backland parishes enabled white farmers to purchase their land. In the aftermath of the war, however, sharecropping among whites grew as more prospective farmers did not have the cash with which to buy farmland and as a growing number of small farm owners lost their farms as a result of the economic woes that beset agriculture during the final two decades of the nineteenth century.

Fear of losing their farms served as a powerful emotional force among small farm owners, creating the conditions ripe for the rise of the southern Populist movement. In Louisiana, the Populist movement was in essence a revolt of small farm owners in the backland cotton parishes.[23] At the same time, the growth of tenancy created conditions that would undercut the strategies of the Populist movement, challenging its viability. Thus, the growth of tenancy was a double-edged sword that ironically both helped and hurt the movement.

The Sugar Fields

Sugar represented the second important cash crop in Louisiana. (See the map for the major sugar-producing parishes). An understanding of the structure of the sugar plantation is essential to understanding the mobilization difficulties that the Populist movement in Louisiana faced in the sugar parishes.

Sugar plantations required a much greater capital investment than did cotton plantations because of the expensive refining equipment needed. The cost of a moderate-sized sugar establishment has been estimated at about $200,000 at 1887 prices. The absence of an extensive rail system made it impossible to transport the bulky and perishable cane to central mills. Thus, sugar planters in areas not near river transportation could not engage in sugar production without also investing in refining machinery.[24]

The sugar industry was devastated by the war. Only about 10 percent of the 1,800 sugar estates in 1861 were producing sugar in 1865. The recovery of the sugar industry after the war was very slow, hampered by the fact that a significant portion of the crop had to be saved for use as seed cane for the next season. Many sugar plantations lay fallow during the war and had no seed cane. Also, about 40 percent of the sugar machinery was destroyed during the war. The slow recovery of the sugar industry is evident in the low levels of sugar production even 15 years after the end of the war: only 171,706 hogsheads of sugar were produced in 1880, less than one-third of the sugar production in 1860.[25]

Given the capital-intensive nature of sugar production, the expense of rebuilding was beyond the means of many sugar planters. Ownership of most sugar estates changed hands, but typically as intact plantations sold to northern investors who had the capital to restore them and who were lured by the potential profits created by sugar shortages in the postwar years. These investors successfully lobbied the federal government to levy a $0.02 per pound duty on imported sugar to protect them from stiff foreign competition. The protection given the sugar planters was a major source of irritation to the cotton farmers as they struggled with declining crop prices without any government assistance.[26]

The majority of the population in the sugar-producing parishes of southern Louisiana was black. Very few whites toiled alongside blacks on the sugar plantations. The difference in work routine from that which had existed under slavery was slight. The workers lived in cabins on the plantation, typically antebellum slave cabins. The only major difference was that the workers now were paid wages, albeit wages that declined significantly during the 1870s when planters colluded to fix wages at $15 per month. To make matters worse, many workers were not paid in full each month. Instead, planters withheld half of each monthly paycheck until the end of the harvest to ensure that workers would not leave before the sugarcane was harvested. Furthermore, most workers were paid in scrip redeemable only at the plantation store, where prices were exorbitant. Complaints among sugar workers of high prices at the company store were similar to those voiced by cotton farmers who paid "time prices" on goods purchased on credit.[27]

The daily work routine of laborers on sugar plantations significantly differed from that of tenant cotton farmers. While tenant farmers worked relatively autonomously on their designated acreage, sugar plantation workers were closely supervised and worked gang-style. Another important difference was that sugar workers received a set monthly wage, whereas many cotton farmers relied on crop-lien financing to cover their expenses until harvest. The factor that most acutely affected laborers on the sugar plantations—low wages and payment in the form of scrip—was an irrelevant factor in the economic plight of tenant cotton farmers who suffered primarily from falling cotton prices and exorbitantly high crop-lien interest rates. But one thing they shared was economic discontent. As one black sugar worker complained, in a fashion indistinguishable from the complaint of tenant cotton farmers: "I begin de year wid nothin' and end wid nothin'."[28]

While neither tenant cotton farmers nor sugar workers owned the land on which they toiled, they shared a common grievance with small farm owners: they worked long hours in the hot sun, cultivating crops for minimal economic return. A major challenge facing any attempt to mobilize a widespread agrarian protest movement in Louisiana would be the need to span class and race differences and to stress the common grievances of those who earned a livelihood from agriculture, while also addressing the different problems facing those in the cotton versus sugar fields. An Achilles' heel of the Louisiana Populist movement would be its failure to meet this challenge.

The bifurcation of commercial agriculture in Louisiana, with both cotton and sugar as major commercial crops, is important to any explanation of the challenges facing the Louisiana Populist movement. Sugar was the major commercial crop in eleven parishes, about 20 percent of all parishes.[29] In these parishes, cotton production was insignificant. Therefore, when the Alliance movement emerged and heavily focused its early attention on the problems of cotton farmers, the sugar-producing parishes were largely untouched by the movement. Without a movement base in the sugar parishes, when the movement shifted its attention to politics it faced mobilization challenges that were much more significant than in states where cotton was the undisputed King.

THE GREAT DIVIDES: RACE AND CLASS IN AGRICULTURE

It is important to remember that there can be multiples structures of domination. Social class, based on one's position relative to the means of production, has been identified as one of the most important sources of domination. It was of utmost importance to the Populist movement, as will become apparent as the history of that movement unfolds in the present study. Of equal importance was the role of race. Nowhere was the importance of race in the dominance structures of nineteenth-century America greater than in the agricultural sector of the South, where the intersection of race and social class, the two kingpins of stratification, had significant consequences for the Populist movement.

Planters were at the top of the stratification hierarchy. A plantation economy continued to dominate commercial agriculture in postbellum Louisiana. The idea of confiscating the plantation lands of Confederates and redistributing those lands to ex-slaves and small farmers never received much support in Congress. Respect for private property rights was stronger than any retribution motive in regard to the planter elite or any compensatory justice motive on behalf of the freedmen.[30]

While planters experienced economic difficulties in the aftermath of the war, their difficulties were cushioned in ways not available to small farm owners, tenant farmers, or agricultural laborers. They had access to loans on reasonable terms because their loans could be collateralized by their extensive landholdings.[31] Cotton planters also profited from the fixed rents paid by their cash tenants and/or from the accumulation of crop shares they received from sharecroppers. Furthermore, they benefited financially by serving as furnishing merchants to their tenants and extending crop-lien loans. Similarly, many sugar planters reaped large profits by establishing plantation stores, and then paying their wage workers in scrip redeemable only at those stores. Since these stores did not face competitive market conditions, their prices were often exorbitantly high.[32]

In regard to small farmer owners, owning their land was a source of considerable pride and an important part of their identity. This source of identity would serve as an important base for mobilizing the Populist movement. As economic times worsened, an increasing number of small farmer owners became dependent on crop-lien financing and worried about losing their farms. Their anger at the high interest rates associated with crop-lien loans put them at odds with planters who profited from extending such loans to their tenant farmers.

Farm ownership among blacks was almost nonexistent in the alluvial plantation parishes, but there were opportunities for black ownership in the backland parishes. About 14 percent of blacks in these parishes owned the land on which they farmed, although the valuation of their property was significantly less than that of property held by white farmers. These black small farmer owners would form the basis of the Colored Farmers' Alliance (CFA) when it emerged in Louisiana in the late 1880s.[33]

In regard to tenant farmers, black tenant farmers were the norm in the alluvial cotton parishes. Their life was a hard one. Their discontent became a major issue during what became known as the Exodus of 1879. More than ten thousand blacks left the state that year, most of them from the cotton plantation parishes. Historians have estimated that as many as five times that number tried unsuccessfully to leave.[34]

Attitudes toward blacks in the backland parishes were usually inhospitable, regardless of whether blacks were tenant farmers or small farm owners. The white population in the backlands did not depend significantly on blacks for labor. Consequently, their racial attitudes were not tempered by an economic dependence on blacks. Some of the worst racial conflicts in Louisiana in the postbellum years took place in parishes with sizeable backland areas where white small farm owners were the norm, but with enough alluvial plantation lands to result in a significant black population.[35]

White tenant farmers primarily lived in the backland parishes. Lacking the financial ability to own the farmland on which they toiled, they were either cash tenants who had to grow enough cotton to pay rent or share tenants who had to forfeit 50 percent of their cotton crop to the land owner. Most of them struggled to make ends meet and often were dependent on crop-lien financing. However, as a result of the rigid racial caste system at that time, their status was enhanced by their race, despite the fact that their financial situation was often remarkably similar to that of black tenant farmers.

Life among black agricultural wage laborers, who primarily toiled on the sugar plantations, was also harsh. Their wages were poor, and they were often paid in scrip that was redeemable only at the plantation store where goods were priced excessively high.[36]

The race/class divisions among farmers and agricultural laborers in rural Louisiana were reinforced by a population distribution pattern that had typified rural Louisiana in its antebellum period and persisted in the postbellum era: a black belt in the cotton and sugar plantation parishes, with the majority of rural whites living in the backland parishes. The population distribution by race reflected the fact that few whites farmed in the alluvial, plantation parishes. In the antebellum era, plantation owners had no need for white agricultural laborers and no interest in renting land to tenant farmers. Neither could most whites afford to buy alluvial land. Usually when plantations in alluvial areas were sold, they were purchased as intact property by wealthy buyers, not in more affordable small units. In contrast, farmland in the backland parishes was affordable. Although these lands produced only about one-half the farm product value per acre of the alluvial lands, they provided men of modest means an opportunity to own their own farmland. Land was also available for rent, should farmers not yet have the necessary funds to buy their own land.[37]

Since plantations survived the war and its aftermath largely intact, the only economically realistic farming opportunity in the plantation parishes for modest-income whites was that of a tenant farmer. Despite the greater fertility of the rich alluvial soils, few backland farmers could be enticed to move to the predominantly black-populated, plantation parishes to toil as tenant farmers. Consequently, in the plantation parishes with significant amounts of alluvial lands (which surrounded the Mississippi River and its major tributaries such as the Red River and Ouachita River), blacks continued to far outnumber whites.[38]

In sharp contrast to the alluvial parishes, the backlands remained populated primarily by small farm owners. The percent of farm ownership in parishes with sizeable backland areas reached as high as 94 percent.[39] Most of these farm owners were white. It was very difficult for freedmen to find land to homestead, and a homestead claim was useless unless the farmer had adequate tools and plow to farm. Homesteaders typically needed about $650 to establish a farm and raise the first crop. Since it was rare for a black tenant farmer to clear more than $20 per year, such an expense was a formidable obstacle to homesteading.[40]

In sum, the racial distribution pattern in Louisiana reflected and reinforced an important social class distinction: Most blacks lived in alluvial areas and worked either as cotton tenant farmers or wage laborers on sugar plantations. Most white farmers toiled on non-alluvial lands that they owned in backland parishes. This population distribution and land ownership pattern directly affected politics, as will be discussed in detail in later chapters. It also presented a serious mobilization challenge to the Populist movement. The success of the movement depended on the ability of leaders to form a broad-based movement that addressed the varied interests of tenant farmers, agricultural wage laborers, and small farm owners. The movement also faced the Herculean task of spanning the racial divide in its recruitment efforts, a task made all the more difficult by the geographical separation of black tenant farmers from white tenant farmers and small farm owners.

RECONSTRUCTION POLITICS

Small farm owners were disenchanted by the economic hardships that they experienced. Their struggles to rebuild their farms were exacerbated by the fall in crop prices during the 1870s, by the high interests on crop-lien loans, and by increased taxation. But the political opportunity for mobilizing a widespread protest movement among small farm owners in Louisiana was limited. Politically, the 1870s were dominated by an intense fear of Africanization and by a white supremacy movement that tolerated no dissension that threatened the unity of the white community.

The strong and unified resistance of whites to black political influence in Louisiana was apparent at a constitutional convention called by federal authorities in 1864 in the part of Louisiana that was Union-occupied. The primary objective of this convention was officially to abolish slavery, but other important issues were discussed as well. Chief among these issues was the determination of the voting qualifications to incorporate into a new state constitution. There was unanimous agreement on one point: the freedmen should not be given voting rights.[41]

When the war had ended, President Andrew Johnson declared that the only things the southern states needed to do to gain reentry into the Union were repudiate the Confederate debt, invalidate their acts of secession, and ratify the Thirteenth Amendment that abolished slavery. Many Republicans worried that Johnson's stance threatened to make the South more powerful than ever. Congressional representation was based on total population count, not electorate size. Whereas in the antebellum period three-fifths of the slave population had counted for the purposes of representation, now the entire black population would be counted. Consequently, the South's congressional representation would significantly increase.[42]

The fears of Republicans were well founded. Given Johnson's conciliatory stance, Louisiana and other southern states immediately granted voting rights to ex-Confederates and placed few restrictions on their ability to hold elected office. No voting privileges were given to blacks. The machinery of the state government in Louisiana and most other southern states quickly passed into the hands of Confederate sympathizers and, once in control, they elected a large number of ex-Confederate officers to Congress.[43]

After the Democratic Party's electoral successes on the heels of the war, more Republicans became agreeable to the notion of black suffrage. It was clear that the Republican Party would never have a chance to hold the reins of power in the southern states, and its control of national politics was in jeopardy, unless blacks were given the right to vote. Republicans in Louisiana attempted to reconvene the constitutional convention of 1864, which had authorized its reconvening should it be deemed necessary, with hopes of amending the state constitution to grant black men voting rights. Democrats lashed out in what became known as the New Orleans riot of 1866. Thirty-four blacks were killed and more than two hundred were wounded.[44]

Prompted by the Democratic victories throughout the South and the headline-grabbing violence of the New Orleans riot, the moderate and radical wings of the national Republican Party formed a coalition that successfully pushed through Congress the Fourteenth and Fifteenth constitutional amendments, in 1868 and 1870, respectively. These amendments granted citizenship and suffrage rights to the freedmen. Congress also passed a series of acts that provided for black voter registration and authorized voter registration drives before the 1868 elections.[45]

Politically, Louisiana was a powder keg at this point. Among ex-slaveholders, there was tremendous anger over the amount of wealth lost in the abolition of slavery. Johnson's moderate stance had mollified this anger to some degree by convincing many southerners that they would be able to minimize the degree of change in the racial status quo in the postbellum era. The conviction was destroyed by the congressional voting rights initiatives on behalf of the freedmen.[46]

In Louisiana, concern about the racial caste system was intensified due to the fact that it was one of only three southern states where the black population was in the majority: In 1870, there were 364,000 blacks and 362,000 whites. Blacks also constituted a numerical majority in more than half of the state's parishes. Furthermore, the pool of educated blacks to serve as political leaders was greater than in other southern states since New Orleans had been home to one of the largest communities of free people of color in the antebellum period. Thus, the granting of voting rights to freedmen created intense fears about the Africanization of the power structure within the state.[47]

Louisiana had already witnessed some early signs of black political activism. In January 1865, a group of blacks had organized a state convention of the Equal Rights League, which drew primarily from Orleans Parish but included delegates from other parishes as well. This organization, led by blacks such as the ex-slave Oscar Dunn, Dr. Joseph Roudanez (one of the publishers of the *New Orleans Tribune*), and P. B. S. Pinchback, soon merged with the political organization of the radical faction of the Republican Party. This faction had adopted an explicit and supportive stance on black voting rights. It had also attempted to enhance the mobilization of blacks by forming Union Leagues throughout the South for the purpose of advancing the political and economic status of the newly freed slaves.[48]

By 1867, there were more than 120 local organizations of the Union League in Louisiana alone. Their formation was facilitated by the indigenous structure of black communities, particularly black churches, which experienced an explosive growth during Reconstruction. Whites viewed the growth of black churches with concern, but were unsuccessful in their efforts to keep blacks within white-dominated churches. Blacks departed from white churches in droves and were primarily attracted to denominations such as the Baptists, which were less hierarchically organized and gave large amounts of control to local congregations.[49]

When another constitutional convention convened in Louisiana in 1868, the white power structure appeared to be in serious danger. Blacks had participated eagerly in the selection of convention delegates, and there were approximately equal numbers of white and black delegates. The *New Orleans*

Tribune, a black-owned newspaper, had urged black voters to use their newly granted suffrage rights to advance their race: "We compose a majority in the State, and with the help of our Radical white friends, we compose a majority in the Convention. . . . The colored masses are the masters of the field. Everything depends upon the colored vote."[50]

The Constitution of 1868 that resulted from this convention gave blacks many advantages, at least nominally. Not only did it grant voting rights to black males, but it also allowed blacks to hold political office. All public places were declared opened to everyone, regardless of race or nationality. Also, seats in both houses of the legislature were allotted according to total population, thus significantly increasing the number of seats in those parishes with large proportions of blacks and giving those parishes a significantly enhanced political voice.[51]

At the convention of the Louisiana Republican Party in 1868, a similar increase in the political influence of blacks occurred. A black candidate for the gubernatorial nomination, F. E. Dumas, narrowly lost by a forty-five to forty-three vote. Oscar Dunn, a prominent black leader, won the nomination for lieutenant governor. Also noteworthy was the passage of a party resolution calling for "equal rights for all men, irrespective of race, color or previous condition."[52]

White supremacy, a leading principle of the South, was under attack. By the federal election campaigns in the fall of 1868, however, a counterattack was fully underway. This election would prove to be a major battleground in the struggle over civil rights issues and political power in Louisiana. Emerson Bentley, the editor of the *St. Landry Progress*—a Republican paper supportive of the civil rights of blacks, was assaulted, and his printing press destroyed. When a large multiracial group convened to protest on Bentley's behalf, it was attacked. Approximately two hundred Bentley supporters were wounded, some of them fatally. Less than a month later, five white supremacists in the town of Franklin murdered two local leaders in the Republican Party who had taken a public stand supportive of the political rights of blacks. New Orleans also saw its share of violence: Sixteen Republicans were killed there in the week prior to Election Day. Klan notices were posted all over the city warning blacks not to vote.[53]

While the campaign of terror begun during 1868 was widespread throughout the South, nowhere was white violence greater than in Louisiana. The response to the pervasive violence was summed up well by the conservative *Planters Banner:* "Most of the negroes now show a disposition to vote the democratic ticket and live on friendly terms with the white people of the parish."[54]

The power of violence to subvert the election process is evident in the election statistics. Only 276 votes were cast for the Republican Party in the entire city of New Orleans, despite the fact that 21,000 voters in that city had registered as Republicans. In the countryside, violence also prevailed. In a sworn statement submitted to Congress, between 120 and 165 blacks were said to have been murdered in Bossier Parish during the election campaign. White conservatives in Caddo Parish were also noted in congressional testimony for their intimidation and violence against black Republicans. They had publicly declared that blacks who did not abide by their demand to not vote for the Republican ticket should be shot. More than forty blacks were killed in the months leading up to Election Day. The violence had the desired effect: Only one vote was cast in Caddo Parish for the Republican ticket, and the black who cast that vote was shot to death before the sun rose the day after he cast his vote. Electoral intimidation was equally effective in De Soto and St. Landry parishes. In De Soto, which had about two thousand registered black voters, not a single vote was cast for the Republican Party. St. Landry Parish, which gave the Republican nominees for the state constitutional convention 2,200 votes in April 1868, did not give the Republican ticket a single vote in the presidential election in November.[55]

Despite the apparent landslide victory of the Democratic Party, Republicans were able to remain in power. They controlled the election returning board, which was authorized to discard the votes in any election precinct in which there was evidence of fraud or voter intimidation. When the electoral returns from precincts with documented violence and intimidation were discarded, Republicans carried the election. Democrats angrily declared that Republicans had stolen the election.[56]

White violence peaked again during the 1872 election campaign and its aftermath. Anyone who did not clearly take a stand supportive of white supremacy was subject to intimidation. The Republican Party fielded a party ticket with William Kellogg as its gubernatorial nominee. Democrats nominated John McEnery as their gubernatorial candidate. McEnery was from Ouachita Parish, which had a reputation as one of the most violently oppressive parishes in the state in regard to black civil rights. The McEnery ticket was supported not only by loyal Democrats, but by conservative and disgruntled Republicans as well. After the election, there was a split in the returning board. An electoral crisis was precipitated when rival returning boards convened, with one declaring Kellogg and the Republican slate of candidates victorious and the other declaring McEnery and his slate of candidates as victors. Finally, a federal judge declared Kellogg and most of the Republican slate of candidates as the rightful winners of political office.[57]

McEnery supporters, however, continued to assert that their ticket won. In congressional testimony, they stressed that election *week* had passed smoothly without violence and, therefore, the government had no legitimate authority in overturning the election results. The conflict over the 1872 election results spilled into the rural parishes, as many local offices were also contested. In April 1873, one of the most violent episodes in Reconstruction history occurred in Colfax, the county seat of Grant Parish. Kellogg and McEnery had commissioned rival appointments for the sheriff and judge of the parish. Kellogg's appointees, supported by a large group of freedmen who were concerned that Democrats would repress their civil rights if allowed to take office, occupied the parish courthouse. On Easter Sunday, angry Democrats gathered in Colfax, armed with rifles and a small cannon, and ordered the Kellogg faction to leave the courthouse. Those who surrendered were put under armed guard. The courthouse was set on fire, and fifty to seventy more blacks surrendered under a flag of truce. All those who surrendered were eventually killed. Those who refused to surrender either died in the courthouse fire or were shot as they tried to escape.[58]

A governmental report on the Colfax killings estimated that 105 blacks and 3 whites were murdered. The U.S. attorney general in New Orleans, James Beckwith, argued that the massacre was uniquely "revolting and horrible in the details of its perpetration" and by its sheer level of "atrocity and barbarity."[59] The trial of those indicted for the massacre eventually would reach the U. S. Supreme Court, with a ruling that emboldened those who sought to gain and hold political power through terror and violence.[60]

"The Colfax system" of violence made it very hard to get Republicans to run for office in future elections. The Republican Party's advocacy of black political rights had made it a target for violent suppression. Leading Democrats expressed their determination "to force the white leaders of the Republican party in with us, run them out of the country, or kill them; the negroes will give us no trouble without their white leaders."[61] By May 1874, Louisiana newspapers were carrying a call to action addressed to all whites who wanted to redeem the state from the "Africanizing tendency" that beset it. Whites were asked to help with the formation of a White League committed to white supremacy. The White League was based on the premise that blacks were not the equals of whites and that all political offices should be filled by intelligent, tax-paying whites. Violence was advised "only when it is forced upon us as it was at Colfax."[62]

The White League was soon a major force with which the black electorate and its white Republican allies had to contend. A White League mob forced the resignation of local Republican officials in Natchitoches Parish in July 1874; one month later, the Republican sheriff of adjacent Red River Parish worried because the local White League was "red hot and on the war path." He informed key federal officials that while blacks were more than willing to put up an armed fight against the White League, it was useless without ample ammunition and the promise that the federal government would send backup troops when necessary. Otherwise, they were simply courting another Colfax Massacre.[63]

Black voters who cast their ballots for the Republican Party also faced economic threats. Many planters entered agreements to only hire laborers or tenants who voted for the Democratic Party. If violent tactics and economic threats were unsuccessful in intimidating Republican candidates and their supporters, another tactic reigned supreme: electoral fraud. There were a number of parishes that had a significantly larger number of votes cast than was legally possible, given their census count of eligible voters.[64]

The electoral violence and the accompanying electoral fraud in Louisiana played a major role in creating a crisis during the presidential election of 1876. The country stood on the brink of a legitimacy crisis as both Democrats and Republicans declared an electoral victory in the presidential race. The race hinged on the Electoral College votes of Louisiana and Florida. In both states, evidence of electoral violence and fraud undermined the legitimacy of the election returns. Eventually, the legitimacy crisis was resolved via the famous Compromise of 1877, wherein Republicans were appeased by the presidency being conferred on Rutherford B. Hayes, the Republican presidential candidate, and the Democrats were appeased by the official declaration of the end of Reconstruction. Thus, the perpetrators of the electoral violence and fraud in Louisiana had achieved their ultimate goal: the dismantling of Reconstruction.

During the Redemption era that followed, power was transferred to Democrats who credited themselves with redeeming the South from Republican rule. The issue of civil and political rights for blacks was, to a large extent, denationalized, with blacks left to the mercy of southern whites who were wedded to the principle of white supremacy.[65] Redeemer Democrats stressed party solidarity as essential to preventing a return to Republican rule and to undercutting the threat of the Africanization of politics. Whatever their differences on the major political issues of the day, most rank-and-file Democrats could be counted upon to stand united behind the party—that is, until the height of dissent among small farmers in the 1880s that culminated in the Populist revolt. The promise of the Populist movement, however, would ultimately be undercut by the strong white supremacy culture in Louisiana, as well as the tendency of its politicians to engage in electoral violence and fraud.

AN INTRICATE RELATIONSHIP BETWEEN THE POLITICAL OPPORTUNITY STRUCTURE AND FRAMING

In regard to political opportunity, social movement scholars have typically regarded schisms among the elite as optimizing factors in the formation and development of protest movements. Such a generalization, however, ignores an important contextual issue: the extent to which an aggrieved population identifies with an existing elite faction. If identification with the ideology or goals of an elite political faction is strong, members of the aggrieved population may choose to frame their grievances in a manner that does not threaten the interests of that elite faction.

Applying this logic, most white farmers in the South, and Louisiana specifically, were ardent Democrats with a strong antipathy to the Republican Party. This antipathy was a product of bloody-shirt politics and an entrenched culture of white supremacy that fiercely resisted the enfranchisement of black males. The antipathy was intensified by the significant increase in state and local taxes for small farmers under Republican rule. The tax increase was in large part a consequence of using a higher land tax to offset the tax revenues lost with the abandonment of the slave tax, a major source of tax revenue in the antebellum period. Louisiana's land tax rose approximately 600 percent—from a mere 2.9 mills in 1860 to 20.5 mills in 1872. While the rate was lowered beginning in 1874, taxes continued to be a significant burden for small farmers.[66]

One can argue in hindsight that the taxes were reasonable, especially since they were levied on land assessed at a small fraction of its market value. But such an argument misses a crucial point: For the first time, the burden of taxes had become an issue for the small farmer who operated on the edge of a cash economy. The tax issue became even more sensitive when cotton prices began to fall. Since cotton was the major source of cash income for small farmers, the decline in cotton prices was devastating: In the years immediately following the war's end, cotton had fetched as much as $0.86 per pound. But by 1872, it was selling for slightly less than $0.19 cents per pound and in 1875 only $0.11 per pound. Meeting their tax liability became a problem for small farmers.[67]

The anti-tax sentiment of small farmers, often coupled with white supremacist attitudes, resulted in a strong affinity for the Democratic Party. The two dominant political themes of Democrats in Louisiana from 1865 to 1880 were a more efficient and non-corrupt government that would allow for a major reduction in taxes and a united white vote to assure white political supremacy. Most small farmers saw no need to mobilize a separate, independent farmers' movement because they believed that the Democratic Party adequately defended their interests.[68]

The only organization among smallholders to arise in Louisiana during the 1870s was the Patrons of Husbandry, better known as the Grange. The Grange was initially organized as a fraternal club to combat the isolation of farmers and better educate them on scientific farming techniques. It expanded its purposes, however, to include economic cooperation—self-help strategies as a means to address the worsening economic conditions in agriculture. By the 1870s it was spreading to the South, including Louisiana.[69]

Interestingly, the Louisiana Grange gave minimal attention in its framing efforts to the root causes of the decline in crop prices that was hurting the economic viability of farmers. The drop in cotton prices was particularly important to small farmers in Louisiana since cotton was their primary cash crop. By 1875, cotton was selling for only $0.11, with about $0.05 to $0.08 per pound needed to cover the cost of production—the cost varying according to soil quality.[70] Since most small farm owners toiled on land that was considerably less fertile than the alluvial land that characterized the plantation parishes, their production costs were on the higher end. Therefore, many of them did not make enough to provide for their needs until the next year's harvest and became dependent at least to some degree on crop-lien financing.

The Louisiana Grange framed the economic travails of farmers as the result of excessive taxation. It focused on protecting the sparse profits of farmers from the burden of state and local taxation. The New Orleans Grange, for example, unanimously adopted a petition to be sent to the state legislature that demanded the exemption of all agricultural land from state taxation. The petition further demanded that parish taxes on agricultural land should not "exceed two mills on the dollar on any assessment of one-third of the cash valuation of the land thereof."[71] The Executive Committee of the Louisiana Grange complained that "taxes are eating up what little prosperity the late unhappy and fratricidal war left us."[72]

The Grange neglected to frame the problem of declining crop prices, which certainly affected the balance sheet of farmers every bit as much as tax bills. While this may initially seem odd, it makes sense in context of the political opportunity structure at that time. The struggle for power between Democrats and Republicans was fierce and all-consuming. There was no tolerance for any action or rhetoric that distracted attention or drained resources from that struggle. The Democratic Party had successfully framed the Republican Party as the demonic source from which all economic problems flowed. By choosing an excessive taxation frame, the Grange could concentrate its opposition on the same enemy identified by the Democratic Party—the Republican Party, both the enemy of white supremacy and the perpetrator of excessive taxation. This framing decision allowed the Grange to exist within a political climate that would have destroyed any organization that threatened to divide whites politically. Had it adopted a different frame—one, for example, that blamed furnishing merchants for price gouging or criticized powerful cotton brokers of the New Orleans Cotton Exchange for exploiting small farmers—it would likely have quickly found itself a victim of a harsh, unfavorable political opportunity structure.

Working in concert with Democratic Party leaders, the Executive Committee of the Louisiana Grange issued a formal appeal to Grange organizations in the northern states to aid efforts to end Reconstruction and restore the South to the rule of "the people." In declaring black male suffrage "a great evil," Louisiana Grange leaders went on record publicly as supporters of white supremacy in politics.[73] Grange members were reportedly allied with the White League movement. In St. Landry Parish, it was understood that the White League was "the political offshoot . . . of the Grangers."[74]

The Louisiana Grange experienced a rapid decline after 1875 and was defunct by 1878. Its decline is noteworthy, given that the decade of the 1870s had the most favorable recruitment pool from which to mobilize a small farmers' movement. The percent of farms in Louisiana operated by owners fell between 1880 and 1900, from a high of 64.8 percent in 1880 to only 38.6 percent in 1900. Furthermore, while cotton prices were not good during the 1870s, they had not yet fallen below the cost of production.[75] So the resources available to farmers to organize a movement were substantially better than in subsequent decades.

The reason for the Grange's rapid decline in Louisiana lies primarily in its framing choices. As argued earlier, its decision to adopt an anti-tax frame was conducive to its emergence. Given the high priority that both leaders and rank-and-file Democrats assigned to redeeming the state from the Republican Party, any organization or movement threatening this goal would have been resoundingly condemned and repressed. This political environment made it very risky to develop an alternative frame for the grievances of small farmers to compete with the tax relief frame espoused by the Democratic Party. The Grange's framing choice, however, was ultimately harmful to its growth. It chose to echo the rhetoric of the Democratic Party in its explanations of the ills facing small farmers. However, if the major problems facing farmers were the Republican Party's tax policies, then why should farmers spend their hard-earned money on dues to the Grange? After all, the Democratic Party was already fighting the Republican Party and aggressively assailing its tax policies. A Democratic victory seemed feasible, and farmers had been promised that tax relief would quickly follow that victory. Mobilizing Granges in parishes throughout the state, therefore, hardly seemed worth the effort.[76]

The intricate relationship between framing and the political environment of the times illustrates well the importance of a synthesis approach to understanding social movements. Without examining the political climate of the 1870s, it is hard to explain the framing choices of the Louisiana Grange and its failure to "frame" one of the root causes of the growing impoverishment of small farmers: the significant decline in crop prices, especially cotton. Only upon probing the political context of the times do the framing decisions of the Grange make sense. A more compelling frame for the woes of small farmers would have to await the end of Reconstruction.

3

The Rise of a Small Farmers' Movement

THE END OF RECONSTRUCTION in 1877 ushered in the Redemption era, so-named by Democrats who proudly proclaimed the redemption of the South from Republican rule. While the tax-relief actions of Redeemer Democrats reduced some of the economic pressures on small farmers, crop prices continued to decline. So in 1881, small farmers in Louisiana began a grassroots movement to explore possible remedies for their economic problems. This fledgling organization would form the basis for the Louisiana Farmers' Union.

In this chapter, the challenges of mobilizing small farmers are explored. The most important initial challenge was to effectively frame the farm crisis. This was a dual challenge. The first challenge involved developing a diagnostic frame that identified the major problems facing small farmers and the root causes of those problems. The second challenge entailed strategic framing—the development of strategies that held out promise for providing farmers with much needed financial relief.

One of the key tasks facing the leaders of the small farmers' movement was to develop a persuasive diagnostic frame that would effectively counter the explanation of falling crop prices popularized in the mainstream media: the overproduction explanation. The leaders devised an anti-monopoly diagnostic frame that traced the economic travails of small farmers to the rapacious greed of monopolists who reaped enormous profits at the expense of small farmers.[1] The strategic frame that emerged was a self-help approach that called for the development of trade agreements and farmer-owned cooperative stores, as well as cooperative marketing strategies such as cotton bulking. The self-help approach expanded in the late 1880s to include an organized boycott of the jute trust. The promise and limitations of each of these strategies will be explored in this chapter, with close attention being given to the impact of class divisions within the agricultural economy on the effectiveness of these strategies. Attention will also be given to geospatial variation in the structure of agriculture and the effect of that variation on the strength of the small farmers' movement in Louisiana.

Both the diagnostic and strategic frames of the small farmers' movement were crucial to the initial mobilization of the movement. Any effort to discuss the mobilization experiences of the movement would be seriously compromised without a careful examination of the diagnostic and strategic framing challenges facing the movement. The strategic frame would eventually prove to be insufficiently effective in addressing the plight of small farmers. This chapter carefully probes the reasons for its ineffectiveness, which had serious consequences for the mobilization of a large-scale agrarian movement.

IMPERFECT REDEMPTION AND THE RISE OF A FARMERS' MOVEMENT

The actions of Redeemer Democrats, at least initially, allayed some of the economic concerns of small farmers. State government expenditures were slashed, allowing tax rates to be significantly reduced. State property taxes were reduced to 6 mills on the dollar, down from about 20 mills in 1872. In 1879 the 6-mill rate was written into the state constitution as the maximum rate allowed. Another law established an upper limit of 10 mills on parish and local taxes unless a majority of property holders voted in approval of higher taxes.[2]

In general, political leaders from the rural parishes were supportive of efforts to reduce tax rates to the lowest possible level. The rural press extolled the Democrats for providing tax relief and rarely missed the chance to condemn Republicans for the high taxes during Reconstruction. The Republicans were said to have "heaped upon the people an enormous debt, grinding money out of them by a taxation that amounted almost to confiscation."[3] Small farm owners, struggling with declining crop prices, worried about tax obligations and possible foreclosure due to unpaid debts. Their fears were likely accentuated by the overdue tax notices that frequented the columns of rural newspapers.[4]

While there is no doubt that farmers appreciated the tax relief provided by the Democrats, it did not solve the farm crisis. Farmers became increasingly desperate as cotton prices continued their downward tumble. According to the Louisiana Cotton Growers Association, cotton had to have a market price above $.010 per pound to be produced profitably.[5] When cotton prices fell below this level in 1878 and remained there for years to come, cotton farmers were in serious financial trouble (see Table 1).

TABLE 1
Average Farm Prices per Pound of Cotton, 1870–1900

1870	$0.121	1881	$0.100	1892	$0.084
1871	0.179	1882	0.099	1893	0.070
1872	0.165	1883	0.090	1894	0.046
1873	0.141	1884	0.092	1895	0.076
1874	0.130	1885	0.085	1896	0.066
1875	0.111	1886	0.081	1897	0.066
1876	0.099	1887	0.085	1898	0.057
1877	0.105	1888	0.085	1899	0.070
1878	0.082	1889	0.083	1900	0.086
1879	0.102	1890	0.086		
1880	0.098	1891	0.073		

Source: USDA, *Yearbook of Agriculture,* 754.

The drop in cotton prices was devastating to a growing portion of small farmers. Prior to 1880, market access had remained a major obstacle to cotton production in many backland parishes. The Ouachita River, a principal water route for parts of north Louisiana, often receded to the dimensions of a creek, which prevented steamboats from approaching major market towns along the river. Roads were scarce. The roads that had been built were poorly maintained, making it very difficult to transport cotton any distance. Neither was rail transportation a viable option. In proportion to its population and wealth, Louisiana had built fewer miles of railways before 1860 than any other southern state, and railroad development continued to languish after the war. But the construction of the New Orleans Pacific Railroad during the 1880s opened up these backland areas to the market and prompted a marked rise in cotton production. As a result, more and more farmers in the backland parishes were strongly affected by the downward trend in cotton prices. Their plight was exacerbated by the fact that the less fertile soils in the backlands produced about half as many cotton bales per acre as produced in the alluvial parishes.[6]

Despite the fact that crop-lien financing destroyed a farmer's economic leverage in the purchasing of goods and supplies and in the marketing of his crop, small farm owners were increasingly forced to rely on crop liens as cotton prices fell. Those farmers avoiding crop-lien financing bitterly complained about declining crop prices and worried about how much longer they could stay true to their "pay-as-you-go" philosophy. Furthermore, sharecropping was becoming more common in the predominantly white backland parishes. Increasingly, these white sharecroppers were heavily dependent on crop-lien financing.[7]

Despite the hard times, Democrats offered no promising programs to bolster cotton prices or address the plight of small farmers dependent on expensive crop-lien financing. Small farmers discussed among themselves what, if anything, they could do about their plight. In the spring of 1881, those discussions finally led to action when small farmers in northern Louisiana formed a farmers' club in Lincoln Parish, one of the backland parishes where cotton was grown as a cash crop by most small farmers.[8] In 1880 almost 23,000 acres in the parish were planted in cotton, with about 9,700 bales of cotton produced. With cotton prices below the $0.10 per pound necessary for profitability, small farmers struggled to survive. Among those grumbling about the hard times was John A. Tetts who, along with Samuel Skinner, is credited with forming the Lincoln Parish Farmers' Club.[9]

By the end of 1881 only about forty farmers had joined the nascent club. However, by the summer of 1882 it was inactive. Farmers suffered through three more years of low crop prices before another notable attempt was made to form a farmers' organization to address the farm crisis. In the autumn of 1885, Tetts tried to regenerate interest in an organization to represent the interest of small farmers. He called meetings throughout Lincoln Parish. During the summer of 1886, he wrote a number of letters to various rural newspapers and periodicals, describing the need for small farmers to organize and discussing the establishment of a statewide organization that he named the Louisiana Farmers' Union (LFU). A constitution was drawn up and printed for distribution to those expressing interest. A state convention was scheduled for October 1886. Only four parishes had established LFU affiliates by the time of the convention: Lincoln, Bienville, Webster, and Union parishes.[10]

Clearly, hard times do not automatically precipitate a strong protest movement. From the first stirrings in 1881 to the autumn of 1886, attempts to create an organization to represent the interests of small farmers in Louisiana were minimally successful. Why did the economically struggling small farmer not embrace more readily the early mobilization efforts of Tetts and Skinner, the founders of the LFU? The answer seems to lie in the diagnostic and strategic framing challenges that were not successfully met. Economic hardship, in and of itself, does not give rise to a protest ideology or the development of promising protest tactics. Individuals can personalize the reasons for the hardships that they face, or they can view those hardships as inevitable and insurmountable. The LFU's ability to grow was tied to its persuasiveness in convincing small farmers that there were significant benefits to be gained from spending their time and money (in the form of dues) on the LFU. Its anemic growth prior to 1887 was a consequence of its failure to meet this challenge.

The most important failure of the LFU in its early years was its ineffectiveness in countering the leading explanation for the farm crisis of that time—the overproduction argument. Politicians and economists repeatedly told farmers that their woes were the consequence of impersonal market forces. Crop prices were falling because supply outstripped demand for farm commodities. Politicians declared that there was little that they could reasonably be expected to do about crop overproduction. Their proposed solution to the fall in cotton prices was for farmers to diversify their crops, and in so doing produce less cotton.

From its inauspicious beginning, the LFU grew to become a notable force in Louisiana politics, at least for a brief period of time. The year 1887 was the turning point. John Tetts had sent a copy of the LFU's constitution to the leaders of a similar organization in Texas, the Farmers' Alliance, asking about the possibility of a merger. Leaders of the Alliance were interested in expanding nationally, and the adjacent state of Louisiana was a good starting point. They had already chartered a few local Alliance organizations in the northwest parishes of Louisiana that bordered Texas. The official merger took place in January 1887.[11]

It is no coincidence that significant growth of the LFU awaited its 1887 merger with the more vibrant Alliance organization in Texas. The merger gave a much-needed boost to the organizational vitality of the nascent LFU. The Alliance was much further along than the LFU in regard to the development of diagnostic and strategic frames, both essential components to successful mobilization. It had already learned an important lesson in regard to mobilizing small farmers: leaders had to diagnostically frame the farm crisis in a way that would motivate farmers to organize, and then link that diagnostic frame to strategies that promised economic relief to beleaguered small farmers. The prevailing overproduction explanation and diversification solution to the farm crisis had to be attacked, an alternative diagnostic frame proposed, and specific strategies developed.[12]

The Alliance organization in Texas had struggled after its founding in 1880, much like the LFU. But its growth after 1883 was considerable. While only 30 delegates had attended its state convention in 1883, by 1884 there were 180 delegates in attendance. In 1885, 600 delegates attended. The Alliance's faltering start had been successfully addressed by the creation in January 1884 of a full-time, salaried post: that of a traveling lecturer whose job was to organize new local alliances throughout the state and to appoint lecturers where needed. The lecturers were seen as vital to the expansion of the Alliance. They were charged with disseminating the Alliance's diagnostic frame in regard to the economic problems plaguing agriculture. They also were responsible for giving direction to local Alliances as to what strategies would best address the plight of farmers. The interjection of specific strategy proposals into framing discussions of the farm crisis was the key to generating interest in the establishment of local Alliance organizations.[13]

DIAGNOSTIC FRAMING OF THE FARM CRISIS

One of the first actions of the LFU after its official merger with the Alliance was to appoint lecturers. The state was divided into four districts, each with its own appointed lecturer. These lecturers were responsible for framing the farm crisis both in terms of diagnostic framing—the process of developing a consensus within the organization as to a proper diagnosis of the root causes of the farm crisis, and in terms of strategic framing—the process wherein movement activists developed a consensus about the specific tactics that would best address the grievances experienced by movement participants. One member wrote that in his parish farmers interested in the LFU had been "laboring in the dark" for almost two years since no one had ever been sent to provide information on the organization. He was enthusiastic upon hearing that the LFU had appointed four lecturers.[14]

The LFU gathered momentum by following the lessons learned from its new merger partner in regard to the powerful link between framing and mobilization. During 1887 and 1888, it consolidated its strength in many of the cotton-producing parishes of Louisiana. Its growing vitality was apparent by the time of its 1888 state convention. Thirty two parishes were represented, with 71 delegates in attendance. It had come a long way since 1886, when only four parishes were represented at its state convention. A report on the status of the LFU put its state membership by the end of 1888 at 20,000, with local unions organized in 35 parishes.[15]

LFU lecturers typically delivered talks at social events organized by local LFU units. One of the most common social events was the picnic. The picnics and other social events were crucial to the creation of a movement culture.

They provided the opportunity for farmers to gather together to listen to lecturers frame the farm crisis and defend that frame against criticisms. In this fashion, a movement culture was created and maintained.[16]

In their influential work on reality construction and maintenance, Peter Berger and Thomas Luckman stress the importance of reality-affirming plausibility structures—that is, the social base and social processes through which a particular view of reality is created and maintained. While there are different techniques of reality maintenance, the most powerful technique is face-to-face conversations.[17] Mixing the language of Berger and Luckman with the language of social movement analysts, the LFU created a plausibility structure for its particular frame concerning the agrarian crisis. This was done through sponsoring social events for LFU members and potential recruits. Farmers could hear lecturers speak at these social events about the roots of the farming crisis and how best to address the crisis. Farmers could then mingle to discuss their plight and the message of the lecturers. In doing so, the frame disseminated by the lecturers was repeated and usually affirmed in each retelling, thereby creating a potent movement culture that could withstand criticism from outsiders.

In its diagnostic framing of the farm crisis, the LFU had to counter the most common explanation for the fall in cotton prices: overproduction. The overproduction explanation stressed that crop prices were regulated solely by the principles of supply and demand, and that crop prices were declining because there had been a significant expansion of commercial agricultural production in the aftermath of the Civil War. The overproduction argument was plausible in the context of Louisiana agriculture. Between 1870 and 1890, overall cotton production in the state almost doubled—from about 350,800 bales to almost 660,000 bales. Some of the most dramatic increases in production occurred in predominantly backland parishes where farmers prior to the Civil War had engaged primarily in subsistence agriculture. In Franklin Parish, for example, production increased 142 percent between 1880 and 1890. In Union and Richland parishes, the number of bales rose by 75 and 92 percent, respectively, during the 1880s.[18] Transportation improvements had provided better market access for farmers in the backland parishes, and small farmers in these parishes were increasingly pulled into commercial agriculture by their need for cash to pay rising tax bills. As cotton prices fell and farmers became more economically desperate, cotton cultivation paradoxically became even more essential: it was the only agricultural commodity on which crop-lien loans would be granted.

The significant increase in cotton production was not limited to Louisiana. The acreage devoted to the production of cotton in the United States increased from 6.3 million in 1866 to almost 15.5 million by 1880, an increase of more than 145 percent. The number of cotton bales marketed increased even more, by more than 200 percent, because of higher yields resulting from the use of fertilizers.[19]

Those touting the overproduction explanation for the farm crisis argued that the only effective remedy lay in crop diversification. Southern farmers were exhorted to plant less cotton. Cotton monoculture was said to be the root cause of overproduction, and farmers were told that they only had themselves to blame for the farm crisis.[20]

In framing the farm crisis, the LFU strongly criticized the calls for crop diversification. Its leaders argued that there was little point in diversifying by producing other commercial crops that were also falling in price and for which the southern soil was not as well suited. Wheat-belt farmers were able to produce an average sixteen bushels of wheat per acre, and corn-belt farmers produced an average of slightly more than thirty-two bushels of corn per acre. Southern farmers, in contrast, produced on average only seven bushels of wheat and thirteen bushels of corn per acre. Consequently, Southern farmers were in no position to compete in the corn and wheat markets.[21]

The task facing the LFU was to frame the farm crisis in a manner conducive to recruiting members. The grow-less-cotton solution was not well suited for this purpose. Many farmers had little or no choice about the percentage of their acreage they planted in cotton. Since cotton was the major cash crop of the South, they had to cultivate enough cotton to produce the cash that they needed to pay their taxes. Also, if they needed crop-lien loans to help cover living expenses, lien merchants demanded cotton as collateral. Telling farmers to grow less cotton ignored the fact that, for many of them, crop liens were their lifeline. In testimony before Congress, two Louisiana farmers stated that 70 to 80 percent of the farmers in their parishes—Lincoln and West Feliciana parishes, respectively—were in debt.[22]

The challenge to leaders of the farmers' movement was to find an alternative diagnostic frame for the farm crisis. Initially, this frame consisted of an "excessive-profiteering" ideology that excoriated capitalists for impoverishing the masses while raking in exorbitant profits. Newspapers affiliated with the farm movement stressed that agricultural production had become unprofitable on account of the pauperized condition of the people. The problem was not an oversupply of farm products, but rather the anemic demand for farm products by an impoverished population. The overproduction argument amounted to saying that "the reason why so many men are hungry is too much meat and bread in the world."[23]

In a similar vein, leaders of the farmers' movement posed the following questions: "Is it overproduction of cotton that causes the producers of the raw material [that] clothes are made [from] to go half clad through the summer's heat and winter's cold? Is it overproduction that causes thousands of children of the 'common herd' to stay out of public schools on account of not having clothes fit to appear in public? Is it overproduction that causes millions of this 'common herd' to go hungry half the time, and not have enough to eat the other half?"[24] The president of the LFU echoed this reasoning when, in his address at the state convention of the LFU in 1890, he argued: "There can never be overproduction as long as there is a hungry child or a half-clad shivering woman in all this beauteous, bounteous land."[25]

In economic jargon, "effective demand" was sluggish because of the impoverishment of much of the American population. Not only farmers were struggling, but also many urban laborers who toiled for inadequate wages while the capitalists grew rich. Movement leaders spoke of the "shameful abuses that the industrial classes are now suffering at the hands of arrogant capitalists and powerful corporations."[26] An appeal for members by the LFU chastised "the rich Shylocks of the great cities" and the "horde of pillagers and swindlers which . . . infest our land."[27]

Leaders also warned farmers that "the capitalists have bought and are controlling through the principal avenues of intelligence, the perceptions of trade, commerce, and finance in this country." By controlling the channels of information, "the capitalist holds your confidence in one hand, while with the other he rifles your pocket."[28] In his weekly LFU column, Tetts railed against "millionaire bankers and bondholders, the land monopolists, and railroad magnates."[29] The rapacious capitalist frame worked well with the economic strategies that the LFU proposed during the pre-1890 era. It is to these strategies that we now turn our attention.

EARLY STRATEGIC FRAMING

The pre-1890 strategies of the LFU, and the Alliance movement in general, were of two types: those focusing on the purchasing system, which stressed the excessive prices farmers had to pay for needed supplies; and those focusing on the marketing system, which stressed the low price of cotton. Let us turn to a discussion of these strategies that delineates their promise, as well as their limitations.

Trade Agreements and Co-ops

The difficulties that local merchants faced in making a profit were reflected in their high bankruptcy rates during the late 1800s. While it was true that they usually charged high interest rates on lien loans, many farmers defaulted on these loans due to the hard times. Furthermore, the merchants usually had to borrow money in order to buy the goods and supplies that they advanced to farmers. Therefore, they had to price their goods sufficiently high to cover those interest charges, as well as to cover the losses endured when farmers defaulted on their loans.[30]

Nevertheless, many farmers were understandably angry that while crop prices were tumbling, they paid more than ever for the supplies, goods, and services they purchased. The LFU proposed to address this problem through the use of trade agreements. The parish LFU would appoint a committee to confer with various merchants to see who would furnish the lowest markup on goods and supplies in return for getting the business of the entire parish LFU membership. The incentive for a merchant to enter into one of these agreements was the possibility of a significant increase in the volume of his store's business: The hope was that a decrease in profit per sale would be offset by an increase in sales volume. To not bid on the LFU business meant risking a serious decline in sales if former LFU customers shifted their business elsewhere. The same bargaining principle was used to seek better prices on services needed by farmers. For example, the LFU in Bossier Parish appointed a committee of three to confer with Shreveport cotton compress owners about their excess charges compared to the rates in other towns such as Monroe and Minden.[31]

Cooperative trade agreements also held out hope of undermining particular merchants who were exceptionally exploitative toward farmers. The ruthlessness of some merchants was noted in the rural press. Simon Witowski, for example, was a powerful merchant in West Carroll Parish. He was said to have schemed to fleece poor farmers to whom he had advanced supplies at "ruinous high rates." His ruthlessness in handling lien accounts was criticized at a mass meeting in the parish, with farmers charging that his wagons carried away all goods and property on unpaid liens immediately after the due date passed. Even food crops were confiscated, leaving the family with no sustenance. Some of these farmers were eventually "goaded to desperation by his oppression." They burned his house to the ground and killed his bookkeeper.[32]

Given the complaints from farmers concerning the retail prices of merchants, most parish LFU organizations tried the trade agreement strategy. At least initially, the reports were generally favorable. One member enthusiastically declared that in his parish, supplies could be purchased "on much more reasonable terms than before" because of trade agreements. The Grant Parish LFU reported that it received four bids from local merchants, and it was able to finalize a trade agreement calling for only a 7 percent markup on cash purchases and an 18 percent markup on credit purchases.[33]

However, the trade agreement strategy had drawbacks. First, and foremost, while trade agreements stipulated a certain charge above wholesale cost, farmers were in general uninformed about the wholesale costs of products. Disputes over pricing were inevitable, and LFU members struggled with a way to assure compliance with the terms of the trade agreements. The LFU in Grant Parish authorized its Trade Committee to negotiate putting "a union man" in the store of the local merchant with whom it had a trade agreement. It also established a special committee to examine the books of the merchant, checking bills and invoices to ensure compliance with the terms of the trade agreement.[34]

Another major problem with the trade agreement strategy concerned its long-term viability. In areas where the LFU was strong, a trade agreement with one merchant could mean a serious loss of cash customers to other merchants in that town. Since most country merchants were in debt to wholesalers, the latter had a stake in retail profits; an unprofitable store jeopardized debt repayment. Thus, wholesalers often pressured merchants cooperating with the LFU to not renew their trade agreements. Recalcitrant merchants faced the possibility of having wholesalers revoke their credit line or significantly constrict it.[35]

Another economic strategy proposed by the LFU in parishes with sufficient members and assets was the establishment of cooperatives. Cooperatives had two potential advantages over trade agreements. First, the problem of assuring compliance with the trade agreement was eliminated since the farmers themselves owned the cooperatives and set prices on goods, supplies, and services. Second, the cooperatives could either be run as nonprofit stores with prices being marked up from wholesale just enough to cover operating costs or they could be established as for-profit, joint stock corporations with farmers receiving dividends on their stock. Either way, cooperative stores promised to leave more money in farmers' pockets.[36]

Rural newspapers carried numerous references to the establishment of local cooperatives after 1888. Farmers were reportedly enthusiastic in their support of these enterprises. The co-ops were said to be busy and flourishing financially. While many of the cooperative enterprises were stores, the LFU in some parishes also constructed cooperative mills and cotton gins in order to process their members' crops at reduced prices.[37]

In September 1888 a statewide farmers' cooperative store, the Farmers' Commercial Association of Louisiana, was established in New Orleans. Its purpose was to act as a wholesale agent for the purchase and sale of farm supplies and products, with stock being purchased by local LFU organizations rather than individuals. At least initially, this store was declared a major success by its purchasing agent, T. A. Clayton, who claimed that it was saving farmers from 15 to 40 percent on supplies and goods.[38]

Illustrating the importance of tactics to mobilization, the cooperative store strategy played an important role in mobilizing support for the LFU. The early reports of the success of the co-ops in reducing prices on goods, supplies, and services were presented as evidence that small farmers were not completely helpless and, if united, could do something about their plight.[39] Furthermore, since membership in the LFU was a requirement for making purchases at the cooperative stores, the reduced co-op prices played an important role in enticing farmers to join the Alliance movement.

However, there were limitations to the cooperative enterprise strategy. These limitations are critical to understanding the shift away from self-help economic, cooperative strategies beginning in 1890. One limitation was the inability of cash-starved farming communities to raise the capital sufficient to establish local co-ops. A certain level of capitalization was necessary to allow for the pre-purchasing of goods to stock the store prior to its opening. In regard to cooperative mills and gins, funds had to be raised to purchase the necessary machinery. Furthermore, a high level of capitalization was required to establish a credit relationship with major wholesalers, a level of capitalization that relatively few cooperative stores achieved. In his account of the Alliance movement, historian Lawrence Goodwyn heavily stressed the hostility of wholesalers and bankers to the Alliance cooperatives.[40] He neglected situating this hostility, however, in a structural context. It was simply not good business for wholesalers to extend credit to undercapitalized cooperatives that struggled to survive in the depressed economy.[41]

Another major limitation to the cooperative enterprise strategy was the inability of many farmers to benefit from established co-ops. Most of the coop stores did not have sufficient financial backing to allow farmers to buy on credit. Therefore, farmers who were unable to pay cash for their purchases could not trade with the co-ops. They were forced to give their trade exclusively to merchants who could extend crop-lien loans.[42]

The inability of crop lien-dependent farmers to participate in the cooperative strategies was a serious limitation that threatened the survival of the cooperative effort. As hard times worsened, the ranks of tenant farmers grew, with many of these tenant farmers dependent on crop-lien financing. The volume of trade at the cooperatives fell as fewer small farmers had the cash necessary to conduct their business there. Tetts was well aware of this problem, reporting in 1890 that the vast majority of farmers in Louisiana were in debt and in need of loans to meet their needs. By 1891, reports of co-ops failing had become common.[43]

The seriousness of the limitations of the self-help strategies may well have varied since there were significant differences among the major cotton-producing states in terms of the percent of farmers who were tenant farmers.[44] As shown in Table 2, the tenancy rate ranged from a low of about 26 percent

TABLE 2
Percent of Farms Operated by Tenant Farmers in the Ten Major Cotton-producing States, 1900

STATES	% OF FARMS OPERATED BY TENANTS
Alabama	57.7
Arkansas	45.4
Florida	26.5
Georgia	59.9
Louisiana	**57.9**
Mississippi	62.4
North Carolina	41.4
South Carolina	61.0
Tennessee	40.5
Texas	49.7
AVERAGE	50.2

Source: USBC, *Twelfth Census of Agriculture,* vol. 5, 48.

to more than 62 percent. With a tenancy rate of almost 58 percent, Louisiana had the fourth highest rate among the ten major cotton-producing states. Its tenancy rate was significantly higher than in the adjacent state of Texas, where its merger partner, the Texas Alliance, was mobilizing. These important variations in farm tenancy need to be considered when pondering the challenges facing the small farmers' movement. Unfortunately, they have often been overlooked. For example, Goodwyn attributed the weakness of the movement in Louisiana to weak leadership. Completely absent in his explanation was any discussion of the variation in the structure of agriculture in Louisiana.[45]

A final limitation of the cooperative purchasing strategy was that it did nothing to address directly the decline in cotton prices. Even when farmers could cut their purchase costs by buying through a cooperative, their economic hardships persisted. Prices on the goods they purchased represented only one part of their budget woes. Equally, if not more important, was the market price on their main cash crop—cotton. Their economic situation would not significantly improve if cotton prices continued to hover close to or below the cost of production.

Given that tactical success, or at least the perception that tactics will eventually succeed, is critical to successful mobilization, Alliance leaders had to implement strategies directly addressing the poor market price for cotton. The two strategies that they developed were cotton bulking and cotton withholding.

Cotton-bulking and Cotton-withholding Strategies

Cotton sold in the United States was marketed through one of the twenty or so cotton exchanges. One of the largest exchanges was the New Orleans Exchange through which the bulk of the Louisiana cotton crop was marketed. Cotton brokers conducted the business of these exchanges, buying and selling large lots of cotton for a flat commission rate per bale, usually about $1. Small farmers could not sell their cotton directly to exchange brokers because only very large bale allotments were handled by the cotton exchanges and because brokers mandated certain levels of capitalization to back the sales contract. Consequently, small farmers had two marketing options: to sell to a country merchant or to sell to a traveling cotton agent. Country merchants bulked the cotton they purchased from local producers or received as payment on crop-lien loans. If the number of bales was sufficiently large, they sold the cotton through an exchange broker; otherwise, they sold their bulked cotton to a traveling cotton agent. The cotton agent made money by purchasing cotton from numerous individuals and, after amassing large quantities, reselling the cotton at a higher price to the exchange broker.[46]

Small farmers had little leverage in the cotton market and were largely at the mercy of country merchants or traveling cotton agents. A leading LFU member stressed that farmers had to become skillful in the sale of their products, not simply in production.[47] To increase the small farmers' leverage, and thereby increase the price that farmers received for their cotton, the LFU embraced the marketing strategies of cotton withholding and cotton bulking. The idea behind cotton withholding was simple: withhold enough cotton from the market to affect the cotton supply, which would in turn bolster cotton prices.[48] The strategy of cotton bulking differed in that it entailed LFU farmers aggregating their cotton and attempting to sell it at a price higher than they could get individually. The hope was that the bulked cotton would attract a number of cotton factors, and thereby improve the prices farmers got for their cotton by introducing competitive bidding. While some parish LFUs bulked cotton at the local level, others shipped their cotton to LFU State Agent T. A. Clayton for bulking.[49]

A number of problems, however, developed with the cotton-withholding and cotton-bulking efforts. The biggest problem with the cotton-withholding strategy was that a large, and growing, percentage of farmers grew cotton under crop-lien arrangements.[50] Consequently, they no longer controlled the marketing of the share of their crop that had been used as loan collateral. At harvest this cotton had to be turned over immediately to the lien-holder so that accounts could be settled. With so many farmers using their cotton crop for collateral, too little cotton could be withheld from the market to affect cotton prices.

Cotton-bulking efforts encountered a similar problem. In a growing number of localities, so many farmers grew cotton under crop-lien arrangements that there was little cotton free from encumbrance and available for bulking. Even when a large number of bales could be collected for a bulk sale, it did not ensure success. When cotton factors had access to an ample supply of cheaper, non-bulked cotton, they had little interest in paying a premium price for bulked cotton. They made their best profit by buying cotton at the lowest possible price and then bulking the cotton to sell to a broker at a major cotton exchange. Another problem occurred when individual members participating in a bulk sale gave up and withdrew their bales when a premium price was not garnered in a timely fashion. This effectively undermined the strategy; cotton buyers realized that if they waited long enough, the bulking or withholding attempt would collapse.[51]

In Louisiana, cotton-withholding and cotton-bulking tactics were particularly problematic given that the alluvial rural parishes—where black sharecropping and crop liens were the norm—produced a disproportionately large share of the cotton crop. For example, the cotton crop of Concordia and East Carroll—about 33,000 and 38,000 bales, respectively—dwarfed the 3,000 bales of Winn Parish and the 5,000 bales of Grant Parish, both LFU strongholds.[52] Almost all of the cotton produced in the alluvial parishes flooded onto the market immediately following harvest. This large influx made the cotton-bulking and cotton-withholding efforts of the LFU seem similar to the effect of a raindrop on the volume of water in the ocean.

In sum, the strategies of the LFU and the Alliance movement in general to improve cotton prices were largely ineffective. Cotton prices remained below $0.10 per pound, a price at which many small farmers could not make a profit.[53] New strategies had to come to the forefront, or the movement risked demobilization. No movement can survive long once the promise of its strategies has been exhausted.

A Strategic Frame Innovation: The Texas Alliance Exchange

No discussion of the cooperative strategies of the Alliance movement would be complete without a look at the boldest cooperative strategy of all—the creation of the Texas Alliance Exchange, which served as a test case of a plan to create a statewide purchasing and marketing system, and most important, to free farmers from the hated crop-lien system of financing. If successful in Texas, the Alliance planned to expand the business model of the Texas Alliance Exchange to other states that had been mobilized by the Alliance.

In regard to the purchasing system, the Texas Alliance Exchange planned to bypass both wholesale and retail merchants. The Alliance planned to raise sufficient funds to capitalize the Exchange at a level that would allow it to trade directly with manufacturers. The result would be significant savings, which would be passed along to Alliance members. Alliance leaders claimed, for example, that about 25 percent of the $25 million spent annually in Texas on farm implements and machinery, or $6.25 million, would be saved by buying directly from the manufacturers.[54]

The Texas Alliance Exchange also proposed to short-circuit the existing cotton marketing system for small farmers. Rarely did the local bulking efforts of the Alliance garner enough cotton to sell directly to cotton brokers, and even when they did, local and county Alliances lacked the required capitalization to underwrite a sales contract with brokers. Given insufficient capitalization, they could not simply send grade and quantity information to the broker. The bulked cotton had to be shipped to the broker to be examined firsthand and then reshipped to the final buyer. This was expensive, and the shipping costs often consumed any improved profits. The Texas Alliance Exchange planned to correct that deficiency by raising the necessary capital to underwrite sales contracts and by implementing an elaborate marketing plan. That plan called for county Alliance business agents, working through local Alliance cotton yards, to gather samples of each bale in separate packets and to ticket each packet with information on cotton yard number, weight, and grade. After accumulating packets from twenty-five or more bales, the agents were to forward the packets to the Texas Alliance Exchange in Dallas to be displayed in a sample room where buyers could examine them. In this fashion, cotton farmers could bypass the middlemen and sell directly to the textile industry and other cotton buyers—all for a mere $0.25 per bale service fee.[55]

The boldest and most important aspect of the Texas Alliance Exchange, however, was its joint-note plan. Under this plan, local Alliance members who depended on crop-lien financing were to collectively estimate their supply needs for the year. They were then to make a joint note for the cost of those needs, pledging cotton worth at least three times the amount of credit requested. Each signer of the joint note, and typically there were from eight to forty signers, had to specify the number of acres cultivated in cotton and grain and the value of their livestock. The joint note was then sent to the county Alliance business agent along with the supply order. The county agent scrutinized the note and, if acceptable, forwarded it to Alliance headquarters in Dallas. There the note was again examined by an Acceptance Committee and, upon approval, forwarded it to the business manager of the Exchange who was authorized to conduct business on the basis on the joint notes. There would be no "time prices," and this fact alone meant significant savings to indebted farmers. The only charge would be 1 percent per month from the date of shipment of the supplies until the date of payment.[56]

The cooperative, joint-note plan was an ambitious, bold plan that held promise of breaking the grip that crop-lien financing had on small farmers. One Alliance member commented that it had brought forth "the highest pitch of excitement in contemplation of abolishing the awful credit system which is a veritable millstone about the neck of the improvident farmer." He added that there was "the most hopeful and enthusiastic spirit possible to imagine, amounting to almost a universal conviction that financial salvation was come."[57]

If successful, the Alliance Exchange held the potential for not only the financial salvation of small farmers, but also a dramatic expansion of the Alliance movement. Up to this point, the Alliance movement had recruited primarily small farm owners. It had not been nearly as successful in recruiting tenant farmers, primarily because the early Alliance cooperative strategies often required a financial standing or financial autonomy that tenant farmers did not have. A successful cooperative, joint-note program held tremendous potential to expanding the Alliance movement beyond the class confines of small farm owners.

The success of the Texas Alliance Exchange was predicated on sufficient capitalization to underwrite purchasing and marketing contracts. Total capitalization of the Exchange was set at $500,000. To raise this sum, each Alliance member was assessed $2. The assessments had barely begun to trickle in when the Exchange opened its doors for business in September 1887. Originally, it had been hoped that the capital of the Exchange would be sufficient to purchase the required supplies, allowing the joint notes to remain in the office of the Exchange. But it soon became apparent that this would not be possible. The Acceptance Committee had approved joint notes worth $200,975 by April 1888, yet only slightly more than $20,000 had been collected in assessment fees.[58]

Faced with this critical situation, the Exchange Board of Directors authorized the use of the joint notes as collateral with which to seek bank loans. Bank loans were considered the most desirable source of funding. It was cheaper to borrow money at reasonable interest rates to purchase supplies directly from the manufacturers than to purchase goods on credit. Credit prices, even for goods bought in bulk, were much higher than cash prices.[59]

With loan negotiations beginning, the business agent of the Texas Alliance Exchange began ordering goods to fill the numerous local supply orders that had been forwarded to the Exchange. More than $100,000 worth of supplies was ordered. Unfortunately, the search for bank loans was largely unsuccessful. When the bill came due on the ordered supplies, a crisis was precipitated.[60]

Alliance members were called upon to save the Exchange: "faltering now means unconditional surrender. It means a perpetuation of the invidious discriminations which do now and have in the past deprived us of the just share of the proceeds of our labor." Alliancemen were not only called upon to pay the original $2 assessment fee, but an additional $2 fee. The entirety of the latter fee was to be pro-rated among the various creditors of the Exchange for the purpose of decreasing the Exchange's indebtedness.[61]

Insufficient additional funds, however, were forthcoming. By September 1888 the joint-note program was formally discontinued, and a cash-only purchasing program was once again the only option for Alliance farmers. The beleaguered Exchange survived for only about one more year before creditors foreclosed in late 1889, and the Exchange building was sold at auction.[62]

In assessing blame for the Exchange crisis, Alliance leaders placed it wholly at the feet of hostile capitalists. Banks were deemed the villain, with their loan officers refusing to extend loans to the Exchange allegedly in order to protect their established relationships with wholesalers and retail merchants who would be hurt if the Exchange were successful.[63] In his influential account of the Alliance movement, Goodwyn also made the banks the villain in the collapse of the Exchange.[64] While the refusal of banks to extend loans to the Exchange was certainly a major factor precipitating the crisis, no account of the fall of the Exchange should blame the crisis exclusively, or even primarily, on the hostility of the banks or established wholesale and retail businesses in general. A major factor in the fall of the Exchange was its inadequate capitalization. No account that slights this factor is complete. Even the state organ of the Texas Alliance, the *Southern Mercury,* recognized that "a safe business cannot be done without capital commensurate with the magnitude of the undertaking." It conceded that a minimum of $500,000 in capital was essential to the prudent financial management of the Exchange. Yet the Exchange never received even one-sixth of that amount.[65] Consequently, it was a very risky business proposition. That fact alone justified the banks' reluctance to extend loans to the Exchange.

While the Exchange had joint notes backed by significant assets, such notes did not help the capitalization status of the Exchange. City banks had never loaned money on agricultural joint notes: the signers of these notes lived too far away for the banks to decide whether the crop or commodity loan was a good risk, and the distance made the procedures for collecting on bad loans complicated and burdensome. Thus, in refusing to loan the Exchange money with only joint notes as collateral, city banks were implementing a long-standing loan policy.[66]

The Texas Alliance Exchange was an ambitious attempt to create an alternative purchasing and marketing structure to assist farmers in garnering greater economic returns for their hard labor. It was a bold effort to break the farmer free from the exorbitant costs of crop-lien financing. Had it succeeded, the consequences would have been substantial. It could have transformed small farming agriculture into a cooperative marketing and purchasing powerhouse that replaced, or at the very least, competed with existing marketing and purchasing systems. Such strategic success would have also likely meant a significant expansion of the Alliance movement, as its appeal to the growing number of crop-lien dependent farmers would have dramatically increased.

The Jute Boycott

The demise of the Texas Alliance Exchange and the continued collapse of numerous local cooperatives may well have doomed the Alliance movement had there not been another important development: the price of jute soared as a result of the collusion of the major jute-bagging corporations. Jute bagging was an integral part of readying cotton for market. Cotton bales were bound together with approximately 6.5 yards of this bagging. In August 1888, with cotton prices barely rising about $.08 per pound, the price of jute bagging jumped more than 60 percent—from $0.07 to about $0.11 to $0.12 per yard. The already hard-pressed farmers were furious about the increase and the ability of manufacturers to increase their prices while farm product prices remained depressed. In their minds, it was just one of many examples of how the American economy was increasingly controlled by large corporations that had sufficient power to manipulate the market.[67]

A government investigation of the jute price increase came to a conclusion that resonated with that reached by farmers. It blamed the increase in jute prices on the organization in 1888 of a consortium composed of eight American jute-bagging corporations. The companies in the consortium had agreed to cooperate in setting the price of jute and were bound by the price agreement unless a majority of the eight corporations revoked it. The agreement significantly increased their corporate profits since the cost of manufacturing jute bagging was said to be only $0.033 per yard.[68]

Alliance leaders were determined to undermine the jute trust. Talk of a jute boycott spread through the organization. The harvest was approaching, and for a boycott to be successful a substitute for jute bagging had to be available. Arrangements were made with Lane Cotton Mills in New Orleans to manufacture a bagging substitute made of cotton.[69] This was declared a major victory that "speaks in thunder tones of the importance of organization among the tillers of the soil. A few years ago such a fight against the money power would have been hopeless. . . . In union, there is strength."[70]

Cotton bagging had a number of important advantages over jute bagging. First, the production of bagging from cotton would increase the demand for cotton and, thereby, hopefully increase its market value. About 125,000 bales of cotton would be needed to manufacture sufficient bagging to wrap the nation's annual cotton crop. Second, the production of cotton bagging would create a market for low-grade cotton. Third, cotton bagging would be manufactured in the South, thus creating new jobs at a time when the southern economy desperately needed the boost. Finally, cotton bagging had several important qualities that were lacking in jute bagging. It was less flammable, and therefore baled cotton would be cheaper to insure. It was more impervious to moisture, dirt, and sand. It was also lighter, so freight costs would be lowered.[71]

But the arrangements with Lane Mills were not formalized until October 1888. The company, therefore, could not supply a sufficient volume of the new bagging to meet the needs of the farmers who wanted to participate in the boycott during that year's harvest. Consequently, many of the farmers begrudgingly had to wrap their cotton in jute.[72]

The advantages of cotton bagging, coupled with the anger directed at the jute trust, led farmers to intensify their efforts to make the jute boycott a success. Two major problems had to be tackled by the next cotton harvest: procurement of an adequate supply of cotton bagging and the adjustment of the tare on bales wrapped with cotton bagging instead of jute bagging.[73]

In regard to the first problem, obtaining an adequate supply of cotton bagging, T. A. Clayton, head of the LFU Commercial Association of Louisiana, issued an early warning call. He stressed that approximately fifty million yards of cotton bagging were needed to cover the nation's cotton crop. Lane Mills was unable to meet this demand. Even if it ran its factory day and night and dedicated production solely to cotton bagging, it would not be able to produce the quantity of cotton bagging needed. Other manufacturing sources were vital to the success of the jute boycott. The problem was that most American mills had looms that were incapable of producing cotton bagging, and mill owners were reluctant to take the investment risk that buying new looms entailed.[74]

Some LFU leaders argued that if the farmers wanted a sufficient supply of cotton bagging, they would have to establish a cooperative cotton-bagging factory. At an LFU meeting in Alexandria in May 1889, delegates from twenty-one parishes met to discuss the prospects for such a factory. The delegates decided to appoint a committee of three from each parish to solicit stock subscriptions for a factory. The town council of Alexandria offered free land on which to build the factory, as well as $2,000 annually for the first five years of its operation. While interest in a cooperative bagging factory was strong, in the end nothing was done because "the present conditions of union finances did not warrant the investment."[75] Consequently, at harvest time there was again a shortage of cotton bagging. LFU officials predicted that only about one-quarter of the cotton crop would be able to be wrapped in cotton bagging.[76]

The tare issue compounded the problem with the cotton-bagging supply. The cotton bagging used to wrap a bale weighed about eight pounds less than the equivalent amount of jute bagging. This created a problem because the established practice of the cotton exchanges was to weigh a bale, bagging and all. Then to determine the weight of the cotton alone, a standard 6 percent was deducted from the total weight. This reduction, known as a "tare," was based on the fact that the jute bagging weighed about twenty-four pounds, or about 6 percent of the weight of a standard four hundred-pound bale. Without a tare adjustment, farmers who wrapped their bales with cotton bagging would lose about $0.065 per bale.[77]

While farmers lost money because the lack of a tare adjustment in 1888, by the next season T. A. Clayton, the state agent for the LFU Commercial Agency, announced that he had successfully negotiated a tare adjustment with certain New Orleans cotton buyers. All cotton shipped through him would benefit from this adjustment. Farmers trading with the Shreveport Exchange, however, were not able to obtain a tare adjustment.[78]

However, cotton exchanges that were initially receptive to tare adjustment began to rethink their position. The Liverpool exchange, the largest single export market for U.S. cotton, announced that it would not adjust its tare formula. As a result, if American cotton exchanges made a tare adjustment on cotton-wrapped bales, they would lose money if that cotton were subsequently sold to Liverpool or to any other exchange adopting Liverpool's stance on the tare issue. The $0.65 loss per bale would result in significant monetary losses for the large exchanges.[79]

Farmers interpreted the decision of the Liverpool cotton exchange in a manner consistent with their ideology of rapacious capitalists. Jute was a major product of the British Empire. The replacement of jute bagging by cotton bagging threatened the economic interests of major jute producers.[80] For some farmers, a principle was involved in the jute boycott that was more important than money, and they willingly suffered a monetary loss on their cotton-wrapped bales in support of the boycott. For example, when one farmer complained that honoring the boycott meant losing money because of the lack of a tare adjustment, another farmer rebuked him: "Well, is money worth more than principle? . . . this is not a fight for dollars and cents, but upon principles of justice to the producer of King Cotton, and in keeping with the spirit of our ancestors when they threw the tea overboard."[81]

Supply problems, coupled with strong demand, led to increased prices for cotton bagging. It sold for $0.125 per yard in the fall of 1889 which, ironically, was the same as the jute price that had precipitated the boycott. Despite its high price and losses due to lack of tare adjustments, the campaign to replace jute with cotton bagging may have succeeded had it not been for the capitulation of the jute trust. Fearing for their economic survival should cotton bagging become a viable substitute, the members of the jute-bagging consortium reduced jute to $0.09 per yard. Farmers who continued the boycott would lose money on the price of bagging, as well as losses due to the lack of a tare adjustment on cotton-wrapped bales. Consequently, despite the desire of some farmers to continue the jute boycott, the boycott faltered.[82]

Although the boycott had failed to realize its larger goal—the establishment of cotton bagging as a permanent alternative to jute—it had been a major success in that it was responsible for the collapse in the price-fixing effort of the jute trust and for that success farmers were jubilant. The link between strategy success and the growth of the Alliance movement was recognized by an Alliance leader who boasted: "It seems to me that the Alliance is about to swallow up Everything. *Our* bagging *Spark* seems to have set fire to the whole farming community."[83]

The jute boycott had a significant impact on Alliance mobilization. Given its importance, it is surprising that it received very little attention in Goodwyn's influential study of the Alliance movement in contrast to his extensive discussion of the cooperatives.[84] The impact of the boycott was partly the result of its success in undermining the price-fixing effort of the jute trust. A victory, even a partial one, is always relished. But its impact was also a consequence of another important factor: it had deflected attention, at least momentarily, from the increasingly obvious limitations of the early cooperative strategies of the Alliance. The importance of such deflection should not be underestimated. Mobilization is sensitive to strategy outcome. Strategy failure, or major strategy limitations, can set into motion a process of demobilization as movement participants reassess their involvement and begin to question the benefits of participation.

COOPERATIVE STRATEGIES: AN ASSESSMENT

In his influential work on the Alliance movement, Michael Schwartz argues that the jute boycott faltered because of the "rapidly crystallizing interests of the Alliance leadership," which he claims had become more interested in courting external support for the Alliance movement than in building the internal organizational structure necessary to sustain the boycott. He contends that Alliance leadership worried about the adverse effects of the continuing boycott on the development of good relations with external allies.[85] This line of argument, however, is faulty. Nothing makes this more apparent than the fact that, as will be discussed in detail in the following chapter, once the Alliance turned its attention away from the jute boycott its leaders turned in a direction almost guaranteed to threaten and alienate exactly those external allies that Schwartz alleges Alliance leaders were trying hard to appease. The leaders turned to the political sphere and began touting a bold and highly controversial proposal to address the fundamental problems plaguing agriculture, a proposal that became known as the subtreasury plan.

Further undermining Schwartz's argument is the fact that the jute boycott was limited in its beneficial economic impact on three major counts. First, it did nothing to address the problem of low cotton prices. Second, after the Cotton Exchanges refused to make a tare adjustment on bales wrapped in cotton bagging, farmers who chose to use the alternative bagging lost money. Third, the long-term success of the boycott was hampered by the lack of a sufficient supply of alternative bagging. Most major cotton mills were leery about the capital investment necessary for the manufacture of alternative bagging.

A hefty capital investment in the different looms needed to manufacture the alternative bagging would result in huge financial losses if the boycott faltered and farmers returned to jute bagging. Without an adequate supply of alternative bagging, the jute boycott's long-term success was doomed. Cotton bales could not be sent to market without bagging; no matter what their bagging preference, if alternative bagging were not available farmers would have to use jute bagging.

Schwartz also errs in arguing that the Alliance "began the year 1890 in a good position to attack many elements in the system of cotton supply and sales. For the first time since the tenant farming system had begun to develop, farmers were in a position to mold and reshape its structure."[86] This bold claim is at odds with the facts. With the faltering of the jute boycott, the Alliance movement was at a critical juncture. It confronted a major dilemma: no significant improvement in the economic lives of small farmers in the South would occur without a rise in the price of cotton—the main cash crop of the South. Yet the only Alliance strategies that had been proposed to help farmers garner more money for their cotton—cotton withholding and cotton bulking—had been of limited benefit.

The failure of the Alliance's early marketing strategies to address the falling price of cotton lies in the fact that most tenant farmers, who typically grew their cotton under crop-lien arrangements, could not participate in these strategies. At harvest, their cotton had to be turned over to the lien-holder to settle their loan accounts. Since almost half of all farms in the South were operated by tenant farmers, this meant that a sizeable amount of cotton flowed onto the market immediately after harvesting, thereby undermining the cotton-withholding and cotton-bulking strategies of the Alliance. In fact, since many tenant farmers toiled on highly fertile alluvial land, they produced a disproportionate share, almost 60 percent, of the cotton crop.[87] The only way to make Alliance strategies work more effectively would be to mobilize the cotton belt so thoroughly that the Alliance controlled the cotton supply. Yet such control was impossible, given the dependency of many cotton farmers on crop-lien financing, which gave control of the cotton crop to the lien-holder immediately upon harvest.

The limitations of the early Alliance strategies in addressing the needs of farmers who depended on crop-lien financing are reflected in its relatively poor recruitment success among tenant farmers. Historians have reported that the Alliance was primarily a movement of small farm owners.[88] To assess the degree to which this held true for the LFU, the names of all LFU members

TABLE 3
Race of Sharecroppers in the Ten Southern States, 1900

STATES	SHARECROPPERS % WHITE	SHARECROPPERS % BLACK
Alabama	56.6	43.4
Arkansas	64.5	35.5
Florida	52.8	47.2
Georgia	51.8	48.2
Louisiana	**28.2**	**71.8**
Mississippi	24.9	75.1
North Carolina	63.2	36.8
South Carolina	37.1	62.9
Tennessee	78.5	21.5
Texas	75.3	24.7
AVERAGE	53.3	46.7

Source: USBC, *Twelfth Census of Agriculture,* vol. 5, 54.
Note: Southern states, as designated by the U.S. Bureau of Census.

in Grant Parish reported between 1888 and 1890 in that parish's newspaper, the *Colfax Chronicle,* were collected. This parish was selected for two major reasons: it had one of the most active LFU chapters, and it had one of the best rural newspapers. There was the added advantage that the editor of this newspaper, H. G. Goodwyn, was an active member of the parish LFU during its early years and gave extensive coverage to its activities. After gathering the names of LFU members, manuscript schedules of the 1880 census of agriculture were examined to determine whether these members were farm owners or tenant farmers.[89] Of those members whose manuscript schedules were found (N = 45), 84 percent were farm owners.

The status of the LFU as a class-based organization of mostly small farm owners warrants closer attention. Its class basis was, to a certain degree, derivative of the fact that small farm owners had more economic autonomy and were, therefore, easier to mobilize. It was also likely a consequence of the intermingling of race-class influences. Louisiana was unique in that more than 70 percent of sharecroppers in the state were black. As Table 3 indicates, in most southern states the majority of sharecroppers were white. Given the predominance of black sharecroppers in Louisiana, any attempt to develop strategies to more effectively mobilize that aspect of the farming community entailed reaching out to blacks. This would have required a transformative shift in identity framing, wherein the importance of race differences was minimized and the importance of shared economic grievances heavily emphasized. Given the white supremacy culture of the times, any major effort to broaden the race and class appeal of the movement in Louisiana may well have faced insurmountable challenges.

In sum, the strategy choices of the early Alliance movement were inextricably linked to its status as a class-based organization of primarily small farm owners. The strategies were not well suited to the needs of tenant farmers, and consequently recruitment success among tenant farmers was modest. The fact that most tenant farmers in Louisiana were black played a significant role in the failure to mobilize a broad-based agrarian movement. The limited mobilization compromised the Alliance, eventually undermining the effectiveness of its early strategies. Contrary to Schwartz's claim, the Alliance was not in a good position to mold and reshape the system of cotton supply and sales. Its attempt to bolster the price of cotton through cotton-bulking and cotton-withholding schemes was about as effective as holding back flood waters with a bucket. While the strategies represented a sincere effort to abate the economic crisis, they were simply not up to the challenge of remedying the monumental problems facing the cash-starved, lien-dependent farmers.

POLITICAL REACTION TO THE SMALL-FARMER MOVEMENT

As noted previously, initial efforts by Tetts and Skinner to mobilize Louisiana's small farmers met with minimal success. The lack of success, however, was not due to a hostile or unfavorable political climate. Mobilization efforts had met with such little success that they did not even register on the state's political barometer. An extensive search of the newspapers from 1881 through 1886 demonstrated that the nascent LFU was given almost no attention by the media and political establishment. Not a single negative statement about the LFU could be found.

The growth of the LFU following its merger with the Alliance was dramatic. As it grew, newspapers started to pay attention to it and were generally accepting of its ideology and strategies. Even the conservative editor of the *Shreveport Daily Times* stated that from what he knew of the Alliance and LFU "great good should result to the farming class from their establishment." The editor then added that the general public should benefit as well since "a depressed agricultural interest means depressed business everywhere."[90] The president of the planter-dominated Louisiana State Agricultural Society also declared the LFU to be a "beneficent organization."[91]

The tolerant political climate was, in large part, due to the fact that the LFU was not a major threat to the interests of the political elite of the state at this time. Given its focus on self-help economic strategies, rather than political solutions to agricultural problems, the loyalty of its members to the Democratic Party was not at risk. Most LFU members maintained their close ties to the Democratic Party. For example, H. G. Goodwyn served at various times as a lecturer, secretary, and chair of the Executive Committee of the Grant Parish LFU, as well as a frequent delegate to state conventions of the LFU. He was also prominent in the parish Democratic Party, serving as chair of the Parish Democratic Executive Committee. Another sign of ties between the LFU and the Democratic Party was that top officials in the Democratic Party were often invited to address LFU audiences at various social and political functions.[92]

The economic threat that the LFU posed to planters was also minimal. As an organization of primarily small farm owners, it was cautious on matters relating to wage labor in agriculture. For example, the LFU paid little attention to the economic problems of the sugar workers or to the violent repression of a sugar strike organized by the Knights of Labor in 1887.[93] Its inattentiveness was, in part, due to the fact that the strike as a tactic was alien to the work experiences of small farmers. Strikes were not a strategy option for small farmers who owned their farmland. Another reason for its inattentiveness was the class conflict between agricultural laborers and farm owners. Farm owners economically benefited from the low pay for agricultural wage laborers. This was true whether the farm owner was a large planter hiring large numbers of wage laborers to help with harvest or a small farm owner hiring relatively few wage laborers.

The economic threat of the LFU to the politically powerful sugar and cotton planters was also minimized by the fact that it explicitly adopted a whites-only membership policy, as did all state organizations affiliated with the Alliance movement.[94] Consequently, the LFU was virtually absent from the alluvial plantation parishes that were home to the planter elite. The whites-only membership policy appears to have been strongly supported by Alliance members. For example, alarm was expressed when the whites-only clause was left out of one of the admissions policy debated at the 1889 national Alliance convention in St. Louis: "What about the St. Louis convention leaving out the word 'white' in the qualifications for membership? Was it an oversight or was it done to let Sambo in?"[95]

In 1889, however, a potentially threatening development occurred. The Colored Farmers' Alliance (CFA) began organizing in Louisiana. Race concerns had kept struggling white small farmers loyal to the Democratic Party, despite the fact that their economic interests were unlikely to be adequately addressed in the planter-dominated Democratic Party. Should a strong LFU-CFA coalition emerge, the Democratic Party would be vulnerable. But, as the following chapter demonstrates, mobilizing such a coalition would be a major challenge.

4

The Colored Farmers' Alliance

R. M. HUMPHREY, A WHITE MINISTER dedicated to the economic improvement of black farmers and farm workers, established the Colored Farmers' Alliance (CFA) in 1886. From its origins in Houston County, Texas, it spread throughout most of the southern states.[1] While the archival records relating to the CFA are much more scant than those relating to the whites-only Alliance, the records are sufficient to reconstruct in broad outline its framing and mobilization challenges, as well as the political climate it confronted.

This chapter explores several key aspects of the CFA, which was established as a parallel organization of the whites-only Alliance. The idea was that biracial economic cooperation was important and that it could be best fostered by a parallel, albeit segregated, organization of blacks who earned their livelihood through farming. First, we will explore the diagnostic and strategic frames of the CFA. In terms of its diagnostic frame, it borrowed the anti-monopoly frame of the Alliance that blamed greedy monopolists for the economic problems of struggling farmers. But its dissemination of that frame was complicated by the high rates of illiteracy among black farmers. It also adopted the self-help, cooperative strategic frame of the whites-only Alliance. Unfortunately, this strategic frame significantly hampered its ability to mobilize within the black agricultural community in Louisiana because the pre-1890 strategies of the Alliance were poorly suited to the needs of crop-lien dependent black sharecroppers or black laborers in the sugar fields. It would be difficult to overstate the importance of its strategic frame in undercutting its mobilization success.

Second, this chapter explores the impact of the CFA on the Alliance movement, an impact that varied among the major cotton-producing states in proportion to the relative size of the black population. In southern states where blacks were the majority of the population—Louisiana, Mississippi, and South Carolina—the failure to mobilize black farmers had a much more serious effect than in states where blacks represented a smaller percent of the population. This important geospatial effect has, surprisingly, been neglected in accounts of the Alliance movement. For example, in explaining the relative weakness of the Alliance movement in Louisiana, Lawrence Goodwyn focused on an alleged weakness of leadership and never mentioned as a potential factor the racial composition of Louisiana's rural population.[2]

Third, this chapter examines the role that racial attitudes played in the mobilization of the Alliance movement in Louisiana. Any attempt to understand the role of agency and the choices made by LFU leaders in the absence of attention to racial attitudes is doomed. Both the statements and behavior of LFU activists are explored in an effort to better understand the extent to which the LFU worked to disseminate a transformative identity frame that transcended the racist culture of the times.

Finally, this chapter explores the tensions between the CFA and the whites-only Alliance. The economic and political interests of blacks who earned a living from farming and the white, small farm owner constituency of the Alliance diverged on some critical issues, thereby creating tensions that undercut effective cooperation between the two organizations. For example, major tension occurred over the call for a strike by the Cotton-Pickers League (CPL), which represented blacks who earned their livelihood as itinerant farm laborers. There was also a major clash of opinion in regard to the Lodge election bill, which was a federal bill aimed at reducing electoral fraud. Furthermore, chronic tension existed as the result of the white supremacy culture, which the LFU never effectively challenged.

FRAMING THE PROBLEMS OF BLACK FARMERS

As an organization developed to assist black farmers, the CFA could have represented a major threat to the interests of the planter elite. There were a number of different ways to diagnostically frame the economic problems facing black farmers. Since most blacks in the cotton parishes worked the land as tenant farmers, the CFA could have adopted a diagnostic frame that vilified planters for exploiting their tenant farmers. It could also have targeted planters with strategies designed to change the common fifty-fifty crop split to, say, a forty-sixty split favoring the tenant farmer. Or it could have developed political strategies aimed at getting the state or federal government to regulate the credit rate charged on crop-lien loans. Any of these strategies would have directly challenged the economic interests of the planter elite.

The CFA, however, followed a more conservative path. It opted to establish itself as a parallel organization of the whites-only Alliance and adopted the anti-monopoly diagnostic frame and self-help, cooperative strategic frame of that organization. Humphrey, aided by activists within the various state CFA organizations, worked to establish cooperative business agencies to serve black farmers. While at times these endeavors were independent of the whites-only Alliance cooperatives, they were more commonly contractual agreements with cooperatives already established by the Alliance.[3]

By 1889, Humphrey had organized black farmers into CFA affiliates in sixteen states. Membership was reported at five hundred thousand, although some outsiders regarded the membership numbers with suspicion. Humphrey scheduled the 1889 national meeting of the CFA at the same time and place as the whites-only Alliance—in early December in St. Louis, Missouri—to facilitate communication and cooperation between the two organizations. Approximately fifty delegates attended the CFA national convention. These delegates represented eleven of the sixteen states that had been organized: Alabama, Arkansas, Florida, Georgia, Louisiana, Mississippi, North Carolina, South Carolina, Tennessee, Texas, and Virginia.[4]

Given the growth of the CFA, the Alliance formed a Committee on Cooperation at its 1889 St. Louis convention to reflect on the type of relationship it wanted with the CFA. The committee concluded: "Whereas, a large percent of the products of this country are produced by the colored farmers and laborers, and a large proportion of supplies are purchased by them; therefore, Be it resolved, That it is detrimental to both white and colored to allow conditions to exist that force our colored farmers to sell their products for less and pay more for supplies than the market justifies; therefore we recommend cooperation."[5] This recommendation of cooperation was in harmony with the attitude of most state and local Alliance organizations at that time. According to a well-known Alliance activist, Harry Tracy, white Alliance organizations manifested a "unanimous desire to cooperate with them [CFA members] on financial matters."[6]

Importantly, however, the Committee on Cooperation also took the stance that the "white organizations shall positively prohibit the admission of colored men to membership into their organizations."[7] The recommendation was clear: cooperation, but not integration. Despite the explicit recognition of common economic interests between white and black farmers, the Alliance movement could not rise above the segregationist culture of the times. Mobilization would continue to proceed along racial lines.

The CFA was first mentioned in Louisiana newspapers in the spring of 1889.[8] Its first annual state convention was held at Alexandria in Rapides Parish on July 4, 1889, with about thirty delegates in attendance. The delegates were described as "colored men who own or control farms." L. D. Laurent, a black farmer from Rapides Parish, was elected superintendent, which was the highest state office within the CFA. He held this position until 1891. He was succeeded at that time by Isaac Keys from Catahoula Parish, who also served as one of the three trustees of the national CFA organization.[9]

The Louisiana CFA was modeled after the LFU with which it sought to cooperate. To address the black farmers' need for cheaper prices on goods, it successfully negotiated a trade contract with the LFU's Commercial Agency in New Orleans in an attempt to obtain lower prices without the expense of a separate agency.[10]

The CFA benefited in a number of ways from establishing itself as a parallel organization to the rapidly growing national Alliance. First, it minimized the threat that it posed with its image as an organization that mimicked the whites-only Alliance. In the words of the editor of the *Opelousas Courier:* "the colored race is, in large degree, purely imitative . . . white men have formed alliances for declared purposes, and in imitation, colored men are doing the same thing."[11] Second, it benefited from a ready-made diagnostic frame of the agrarian crisis and from a developed repertoire of self-help strategies. Third, the relatively non-threatening nature of those strategies protected it to a large extent from repression by politically influential planters. As long as it focused on self-help, cooperative tactics, it was not deemed a major economic threat. Its threat was further minimized when the national CFA officially declared that it would steer clear of political activities. This decision was incorporated into its formal constitution, which declared that its members should "withdraw their attention from political partisanship."[12]

MOBILIZATION CHALLENGES FACING THE CFA IN LOUISIANA

Despite the benefits reaped by establishing itself as a parallel organization of the white Alliance, the CFA faced significant mobilization challenges.

One of its most significant challenges was the high rate of black illiteracy. The illiteracy rate among blacks in Louisiana was 72 percent, the highest in the country.[13] Given the serious literacy problem, the CFA in Louisiana had an insufficient readership base to support its own newspaper or newsletter. While several LFU parish organizations had local newspapers and the state LFU organization had column space in the *Shreveport Weekly Caucasian,* the CFA local organizations struggled to a great extent as isolated, independent units without the benefit of a written communication network.[14]

As a result of the high illiteracy rates of blacks, the CFA's framing of the farm problem had to be disseminated orally. This necessitated sending traveling lecturers to black farming communities throughout the state. The CFA, however, did not have the capital to pay for lecturers. Most black cotton farmers were tenant farmers with minimal cash resources. Even among the approximately 15 percent of Louisiana black cotton farmers who owned the land on which they toiled, hard economic times hampered their ability to fund a lecturing circuit. The lack of funds to pay for lecturers was not offset by economic contributions from the LFU. The latter chose to spend its limited funds exclusively on mobilization efforts within the white farming community.

Another serious mobilization challenge flowed from the establishment of the CFA as a parallel organization with strategies similar to those of the whites-only Alliance. These strategies were not geared to the needs of sharecroppers who were often enmeshed in the crop-lien financing system. This was a serious problem since almost 85 percent of black farmers in Louisiana, versus 32 percent of white farmers, were sharecroppers.[15] By emulating the strategies of the whites-only Alliance, the CFA dramatically limited its ability to recruit black farmers.

Grievances alone, no matter how intense, do not recruit the aggrieved to social movements. The strategies proposed by a movement must fit the needs of those it is seeking to recruit. A mismatch of strategies and needs can seriously undercut mobilization efforts. The class structure was very different for blacks and whites who earned their living through farming in the late nineteenth century. In the cotton parishes of Louisiana, most white farmers were small farmers who owned the land that they tilled; in contrast, most blacks in those parishes were landless tenant farmers with very little, if any, cash reserves. These differences in class structure had important ramifications for mobilization. Tactics developed by and implemented on behalf of small farm owners were ill-suited to black communities, where indebted tenant farmers were the norm. Thus, by emulating the tactics of the whites-only Alliance, the CFA significantly compromised its mobilization potential.

Not only was the CFA of little help to black sharecroppers in the cotton parishes, it was also irrelevant to the black wage laborers who worked on the sugar plantations. Cotton bulking, cotton withholding, and the jute boycott were for obvious reasons of no relevance to sugar workers. Neither did other early Alliance strategies, such as trade agreements and cooperative stores, address the needs of wage laborers on the sugar plantations. These laborers were usually paid in scrip and did not have the freedom to shop where they chose. The absence of the CFA in the sugar parishes was, therefore, a direct consequence of the mismatch between its strategies and the needs of black sugar workers.

The CFA's failure to promote strategies that addressed the needs of most black farmers and farm workers constrained its ability to extend the reach of the small farmers' movement into the black community. Basically, the CFA was employing strategies most suitable to the needs of small farmers with at least modest cash reserves. Yet it was promoting those strategies in communities dominated by tenant farmers who were cash-starved and dependent on crop-lien loans. Without question, there was a poor match between CFA strategies and the position of most black farmers within the class structure of agriculture. Consequently, the mobilization success of the Louisiana CFA was modest.

Interestingly, in his attempt to explain the "incomplete Alliance organizing effort" in Louisiana, Goodwyn made no mention of race or class structure.[16] This was a major oversight, since blacks accounted for a majority of the state's population, as well as a majority of those in the state who earned a living through agriculture. As Table 4 indicates, the relative proportion of black to white population significantly differed among the ten major cotton-producing states. It varied from a low of 27,960 blacks per 100,000 whites in Texas to a high of 149,117 blacks per 100,000 whites in South Carolina. If the Alliance failed to mobilize effectively black farmers in Texas, the impact would be very different from such a failure in states like Louisiana, where blacks were the majority of the population.

TABLE 4
Relative Proportion of Black to White Population in the Ten Major Cotton-producing States, 1890

STATES	# BLACKS TO 100,000 WHITES
Alabama	81,381
Arkansas	37,755
Florida	73,875
Georgia	87,781
Louisiana	**100,143**
Mississippi	136,287
North Carolina	53,158
South Carolina	149,117
Tennessee	32,221
Texas	27,960
AVERAGE	77,968

Source: USBC, *Twelfth Census of Population,* ciii.

Without successful mobilization of black farmers, the efforts of the LFU to improve the economic situation of small white farmers were hopeless. No significant improvement could occur unless the market price of cotton increased. Yet the cotton-bulking and cotton-withholding strategies of the Alliance were doomed without the participation of the black tenant farmers of the alluvial parishes who produced a disproportionate share of Louisiana's cotton crop. Therefore, the weakness of the CFA in Louisiana cannot be ignored by those studying the experiences of the LFU. The two organizations were intricately linked: the weakness of the CFA undercut the strategies of the white Alliance, thereby weakening the latter as well.

The constraints that the Alliance movement experienced in mobilizing blacks are highlighted by the conflict surrounding the organization of the CPL. The president of the CFA, R. M. Humphrey, was interested in assisting the cotton pickers who labored long hours during harvest season on cotton farms for very low wages. Rather than mobilizing cotton pickers under the banner of the CFA, he established a separate, independent organization—the CPL. The CPL argued that planters had colluded to pay cotton pickers only $0.40 per 100 pounds of cotton. It claimed that laborers typically picked about 100 pounds of cotton per day, so at current wages they only made $12 per month for a 7-day workweek. Little if any money was left once board was deducted from their wages.[17]

To address the plight of cotton pickers, the CPL demanded that wages be increased to $1 per 100 pounds of cotton, plus board. If this demand were not met, the CPL would strike.[18] The official CPL proclamation read: "Whereas, the planters and speculators are firm in their demand that you pick at starvation wages, and leave your families to suffer the fearful consequences . . . . I, R. M. Humphrey, by virtue of the authority in me vested, do issue this, my solemn proclamation, and fixing the TWELFTH DAY OF SEPTEMBER, 1891 . . . as the day upon which our people shall cease from . . . picking cotton."[19]

Humphrey's creation of the CPL as an organization separate from the CFA was based on his realization that small farmers and agricultural wage laborers had different and competing economic interests. The Alliance movement was primarily composed of small farm owners whom Humphrey feared would oppose the CPL. His fear was well founded. Linn Tanner, an activist in the LFU and treasurer of the national Alliance organization, argued that the strike was unwarranted. He claimed that at current pay, black cotton pickers earned better wages than from any other employment opportunity. He also expressed serious concern about the economic viability of small farmers who were already hard-pressed, given the low market price of cotton.[20] Leonidas Livingston, president of the Georgia Alliance and prominent in the national Alliance organization as well, called the demands of the CPL absurd and criticized the incendiary public comments of Humphrey such as his statement that he had "kindled a fire in the south that shall burn every chain from colored limbs."[21] The president of the national Alliance, L. L. Polk, charged that the CPL strike was an attempt to better one portion of farmers at the expense of another and therefore reprehensible.[22] Apparently Polk was blind to the realization that keeping the wages of cotton pickers low also bettered one portion of farmers at the expense of another. He had reacted to the strike threat with an acute sensitivity to the economic problems of small farmers and social class blinders that hindered his sensitivity to the economic struggles of agricultural wage laborers.

In additional to class tensions, the creation of a biracial coalition was hampered by a difference of opinion on one of the most controversial political issues of the time: election reform, particularly in the form mandated by the Lodge election bill. Senator Henry Cabot Lodge of Massachusetts submitted the Lodge election bill to Congress in 1889. The intent of the bill was to allow federal intervention in congressional and presidential elections to ensure that they were conducted in a fair and honest manner. The bill was a response to complaints that election fraud was rampant, particularly in the South. Hearings on contested elections had become commonplace in Congress.[23]

Most black politicians supported the Lodge election bill because of their awareness that the exercise of their voting rights and a fair count of their votes were unlikely without federal involvement.[24] That belief was well founded. In Louisiana, state officials had demonstrated their unwillingness to protect the voting rights of blacks. As noted by Louisiana historian William Hair, "Every major Louisiana election between the Civil War and the twentieth century drew a measure of human blood."[25] The disinterest of state officials in honest elections was demonstrated early in the post-Reconstruction era. In the elections of 1878, huge Democratic majorities had been reported in many of the black-belt parishes. These parishes, which had been Republican strongholds during Reconstruction, returned such large majorities for the Democratic Party that the *New Orleans Democrat* was moved to comment that the "immense majorities . . . are confusing—almost incomprehensible."[26] The reasons for the immense majorities, however, were clear in testimony before Congress: there existed a pervasive pattern of intimidation, violence, and fraud.[27]

While the Republican Party and black politicians argued that the bill was essential to protect the voting rights of blacks, southern Democrats were extremely hostile to the bill. They argued that it granted too much power to the federal government to intervene in southern politics and referred to it as the "force bill." The *Shreveport Daily Caucasian* spoke of the outrage of the federal government interfering in state elections. It argued that the election bill was unconstitutional and, if passed, would replace state autonomy with "centralized despotism."[28] It reprinted approvingly the remarks of a southern politician who had declared: "You may pass force bills, but they will not prevail. . . . Never, Sir, will a single state of this Union, North or South, be delivered again to the control of an ignorant inferior race."[29] The *New Orleans Daily Picayune* remarked that the South "can afford to take no chances on any bill aiming at control of elections in the South or elsewhere."[30] The *New Orleans Daily States* went even further by declaring that if the force bill became law, the southern states should use all means possible to compel blacks "to vote with whites." It suggested such tactics as making the funding of black schools or the loaning of money to blacks conditional on blacks voting for the Democratic ticket.[31]

The Lodge election bill became a major partisan issue, with Democrats universally opposing it and most Republicans supporting it. The bill was hotly debated within the LFU. Despite awareness of the serious problems that undermined fair elections in the state, the LFU opposed the bill.[32] The national Alliance organization also publicly condemned the bill. At the annual session of its Supreme Council in 1890, the following resolution was adopted and forwarded to all U.S. senators: "Whereas the President of the United States . . . recommends and urges the immediate passage of a measure known as the Lodge election bill; and whereas, the said bill involves a radical revolution in the elective machinery of this union, both State and National, and its passage will be fatal to the autonomy of the States. . . . Therefore, be it Resolved by the National Farmers Alliance and Industrial Union, in national convention assembled, That we most solemnly protest against the passage of said election bill."[33]

It is telling that nowhere in the above resolution or in recorded discussion of the resolution is there any mention of the problem of voter intimidation and fraud in U.S. elections. It has been estimated that as many as twenty congressional seats might have changed hands if southern blacks had been allowed to vote as desired and their vote counted honestly.[34] The Alliance seemed more concerned with avoiding a radical change in the election machinery and in defeating a bill that threatened the autonomy of the states than with fair elections and voting rights. This stance would ultimately prove fatal. The small farmers' movement would eventually be the victim of voting rights violations that the Lodge election bill might have effectively addressed.

In stark contrast to the Alliance's opposition to the Lodge bill, the CFA took an overtly supportive stand. Its leaders cogently argued that the object of the bill was to protect the ballot box from fraud. They stressed that the reforms that farmers were seeking would not be possible if electoral reforms were not forthcoming.[35] After the CFA voted to support the Lodge election bill at its annual convention in December 1890, the LFU in St. Landry Parish lashed out. Earlier, it had formed a committee to consider the advisability of helping to organize black farmers into separate sub-unions. But after the CFA's "unexpected and improper" adoption of a resolution supporting the Lodge election bill, it quickly declared: "We do not believe it politic to take any steps looking to their organization at present."[36]

RACIAL ATTITUDES AND THE SMALL FARMERS' MOVEMENT

An important factor undercutting the prospects for a strong biracial agrarian coalition was the racism of Louisiana whites. Making definitive claims about the racial attitudes of whites in Louisiana is difficult because of the absence of reliable survey data. However, it seems reasonable to depict the racial views expressed in leading newspapers of the times as a rough proxy for the views of the white population. This argument is premised on the contention that newspapers that routinely offended their readership with their editorializing on racial issues risked losing readership.

In discussing the prevailing race culture in Louisiana, I rely heavily on the *Shreveport Daily Caucasian*, and its weekly version that was aptly named the *Weekly Caucasian*. This decision was based on several considerations. First, it was the newspaper with the largest circulation in the state outside of New Orleans during the time that the Louisiana Populist movement was seeking to mobilize. Second, it was the largest newspaper published in the Fourth Congressional District of Louisiana, where the Populist movement drew much of its support. Third, it was the newspaper in which the LFU published a weekly column beginning in 1889.

The *Caucasian* was published in Caddo Parish, where a racist and white supremacy culture often manifested itself in white-against-black violence in an effort to maintain white control in a parish that was more than 70 percent black.[37] Pronouncements of the importance of white supremacy were almost daily fare in the paper. It proclaimed: "The feeling in the South is kindly to the Negro, but it is kindly only so long as there is no attempt at black domination and social equality. The Caucasian . . . must and shall be supreme, and there's the end of it." Any suggestion of social equality between the races was condemned. The paper declared that "what God has not made equal, man can not."[38]

The paper did not limit its protest to social equality issues. It also railed against political equality, especially the Fifteenth Amendment to the U.S. Constitution, which had given voting rights to black males. It claimed that the amendment was a "mortal and degrading affront" to southern whites, an "unspeakable humiliation."[39] It argued that southerners "hold the negro to be utterly, hopelessly, and permanently unfit for citizenship." Consequently, "they regard it as their right and duty to stand firmly together in opposition to the effective exercise of the franchise by the negro."[40] It insisted: "The inexorable law of race superiority will prevail, and efforts to bolster up the cause of the Ethiopian by legislative enactments must always and forever fail. The Caucasian, in the very nature of things, must and shall rule when brought into contact with inferior races." It added: "There can be no satisfactory adjustment, no permanent peace between the two races in the South, until the negro abandons politics."[41]

To justify the call for white supremacy, the *Caucasian* typically referred to blacks in disparaging terms. For example, an editorial discussed "the low instincts, the viciousness and treachery of the negro character" and commented that "his [the black male] brutality is proverbial, his animal propensities beyond question; his thieving habits cannot be denied."[42] The paper went so far as to condone lynching, claiming that the courts could not be relied upon to dispense justice.[43] It declared that "Judge Lynch will doubtless pass sentence on the fiends," adding that the verdicts of Judge Lynch "are rarely unjust and always faithfully executed."[44]

The *Caucasian* criticized all attempts to aid the southern black, with especially harsh words to those who saw merit in the education of blacks. The latter was alleged to create serious problems: "The more a negro learns from books, the more averse he is to manual labor to earn an honest living."[45] The paper elaborated: "A little learning is a dangerous thing. . . . It unfits him [blacks] for his vocation in life, warps his mind into the conviction that if he can read a little he is fitted for something higher in life than the tillage of the soil."[46] The concern about educated blacks was echoed by the New Orleans newspaper, the *Daily States,* which argued that "the very worst nigger for a voter is an educated nigger."[47]

The editor of the *Daily Caucasian* also expressed the concern that enhancing the education of blacks would lead them to demand social equality, a demand that few southerners were willing to concede.[48] Furthermore, the paper depicted a zero-sum game whereby any educational gains by blacks were losses to whites: "What sense is there in frittering away the pittance [of financial funding] by dividing it with the negroes?"[49] The *Weekly Caucasian* added: "Every dollar spent for that purpose is misdirected, as it ought to go for the education of our own race. . . . Our own children need, and sadly need, every dollar that can be raised to save them from lapsing into ignorance and losing the prestige of their race."[50]

Another popular topic of discussion in the *Daily Caucasian* was the advisability of exporting blacks out of the South. The paper declared: "The race problem in the South can never be satisfactorily settled with the present ratio of blacks to whites in our population. When the Negro is clearly in a numerical minority, . . . the race issue will disappear. But not till then."[51] The paper printed articles supportive of efforts to encourage the migration of blacks to the North to serve as cheap house servants and to the sparsely populated western territories. But the paper's favorite colonization schemes entailed exporting blacks to colonies created in foreign lands such as Mexico, Cuba, and Haiti. It claimed that "some of the leading minds of the country believe colonization is both desirable and practical as a solution to the race problem."[52]

Consistent with its goal of changing the racial demographics of the state, the *Caucasian* harshly decried the sponsored immigration of blacks to Louisiana by some planters "who are determined to Africanize the State, if necessary, to make more cotton with nigger labor. It is nigger and cotton, regardless of future consequences."[53] The harsh language is noteworthy because the paper is generally viewed as being closely affiliated with the planter wing of the Democratic Party. But the close affiliation clearly did not prevent it from criticizing planters whose behavior threatened the goal of shifting the demographic balance of the state to the advantage of whites.

Encouraging the export of blacks was only one strategy promoted by the paper in its efforts to shift the racial demographics of the state. It also stressed the importance of enhancing economic opportunities for whites in hope that more whites would migrate to the state, thereby offsetting Louisiana's black majority. It applauded efforts to reserve jobs, especially the better-paying jobs, for whites. Its proposal that blacks be excluded from the better jobs, better in either pay or working conditions, became known as the Shreveport Plan.[54]

In conclusion, if one accepts the argument that ideas routinely voiced in the leading newspaper of an area are at least a rough proxy for the beliefs of its readership, then one must conclude that there was widespread racism among the literate white population of northern Louisiana, the readership base of the *Caucasian.* The prevailing racist culture posed a formidable challenge to any attempt by the LFU to forge a strong biracial coalition with the CFA.

There is the possibility that racial attitudes within the ranks of the small farmers' movement were less racist than in the white population in general. Discerning those attitudes, however, is difficult. Expressions of racism by members can certainly be cited. One farmer wrote a letter in anger at the possibility of the word "white" being omitted from the qualifications for membership in the Alliance.[55] The editor of the *Colfax Chronicle,* H. G. Goodwyn, who was a prominent member of the Grant Parish LFU and its lecturer in 1889,[56] volunteered his view on race: "The fact of the subaltern position of the negro still remains, and he will ever remain, a hewer of wood and drawer of water as the God of nature made him."[57] LFU founder J. A. Tetts also made a statement alluding to race as it related to politics in Louisiana: "In the South we cannot help but be Democrats for nature has drawn the line that we cannot safely ignore."[58] On a similar note, a speaker at one of the annual state conventions of the LFU called upon members "to rise as one man and determine that . . . none but the 'sons of liberty' be elected to control the destinies of the state."[59]

In assessing racial attitudes within the LFU, attention needs to be given not only to racial commentary, but also to key decisions by the LFU that reflect underlying racial attitudes. An assessment based on these decisions suggests that the racial attitudes within the LFU did not markedly differ from those held by the general white population of Louisiana. Racial bigotry is implicit in the fact that the LFU and all other state Alliance organizations were exclusively white organizations, as dictated by their formal membership policy. While black farmers were eventually targeted for mobilization, they were targeted by activists outside of the local and state organizations of the whites-only Alliance. Furthermore, an effective coalition between the whites-only Alliance and the CFA would have necessitated close communication and interaction between leaders of the two organizations. Yet there is no historical evidence that leaders of the LFU interacted or communicated with CFA leaders in any systematic way. While at the national level the Alliance and CFA called their annual conventions at the same time and place to facilitate at least some exchange, no such coordination occurred at the state level between the LFU and the Louisiana CFA.

Another key decision suggestive of racism was the decision by the LFU in January 1890 to adopt the *Shreveport Weekly Caucasian* as its official newspaper.[60] The name of the paper in and of itself spoke volumes about its stance on racial matters. If its name left any doubt about where it stood, a cursory examination of the paper would have been sufficient to discover its white supremacist leanings. A bold caption on the front of every issue declared the devotion of the paper to the rule of "intelligence and white supremacy in every department of the State and National Government."

Selecting the *Caucasian* as the official state organ demonstrated a racial insensitivity that cannot be denied. Despite the white supremacy stance of the paper, LFU leaders stated that it was "a paper that is worthy of our warmest support."[61] Not a single objection by LFU members to the adoption of the *Caucasian* as the official LFU organ could be found in the historical record. Nor were there any recorded objections by LFU members when the *Caucasian* dismissed rumors about a possible coalition between the biracial Knights of

Labor and the Alliance by saying that the latter was a white man's organization that did not wish "to be drawn into affiliation with any society that has negroes."[62] It can be surmised, albeit without definitive proof, that the absence of recorded objections was because most members of the LFU had assimilated the racist culture of the time.

Racial attitudes within the LFU can also be examined at the parish level. One of the strongest LFU parish organizations was in Grant Parish. The variation in racial attitudes among its members is noteworthy. Some members, such as Benjamin Brian, were well known advocates of forming interracial alliances between white farmers and blacks in the parish's alluvial areas. Benjamin Brian's son, Hardy Brian, would become one of the most important leaders of the Populist movement in Louisiana. Initially, he pushed for a biracial political coalition. In 1891 he and other parish LFU activists would surprise some political observations by inviting black voters to participate in the first primary election of the Grant Parish People's Party.[63]

Other members of the Grant Parish LFU, such as Thomas Hickman and W. D. Irwin, had different views. Both Hickman and Irwin had been among the nine leaders of the Colfax Massacre of 1873, discussed at length in chapter 2. While Hickman's participation in the LFU was fairly marginal, Irwin held a number of prominent positions: He was treasurer of the parish LFU in 1887 and served as its president in 1890. He also served as a delegate to the state LFU convention in 1888. Testimony at the Colfax Massacre trial indicated that he was involved in setting the Colfax courthouse on fire. He was also identified as one of the guards of the blacks who were executed after surrendering. In addition, witnesses testifying at the trial identified him as being among the small group of men that killed Jessie McKinney, a black tenant farmer who was shot in the head while tending to his fields in the days preceding the Colfax Massacre.[64]

In a further link to the Colfax Massacre, the parish LFU negotiated a trade agreement with local merchant C. C. Nash, who had been among the nine leaders of the massacre prosecuted by the federal government. Although all of those prosecuted were eventually exonerated on a technicality regarding the inappropriateness of trying the case in federal courts, their role in the massacre was never in doubt. While several other merchants bid on the LFU business, with at least one other merchant bidding competitively with Nash and offering a viable alternative, the parish LFU finalized a trade agreement with Nash.[65]

The presence of men such as Hickman, Irwin, and Nash—either within the ranks of the LFU or partnered with it—likely compromised the mobilization of a parallel CFA organization within the parish. Blacks may have, understandably, been reluctant to ally themselves with an organization that had members who had once led a brutal massacre of more than a hundred blacks. Such reluctance is reflected in the statements of blacks within the Fourth Congressional District who publicly declared that they had refused to join the CFA because the LFU, after which the CFA was patterned, had within its ranks "anti-negro regulators."[66]

In probing racial attitudes within the LFU, the Bloch appointment controversy warrants special attention. The controversy was well documented, but surprisingly it has received no attention in the historical literature. The nature of the controversy speaks directly to the issue of the racial attitudes of LFU leaders and rank-and-file members. It is one of the few debates on which a vote was recorded that makes clear the racial sentiments of LFU members.

The Bloch controversy unfolded in a LFU stronghold, the Sixth Congressional District parish of St. Landry. Evidence suggests that many members of the St. Landry Parish LFU worried about the role of blacks in Louisiana politics. One member wrote: "The suppression of the negro vote in many parts of the South—a thing otherwise indefensible becomes right if white supremacy alone can preserve our civilization."[67] Tellingly, the editor of the official journal of the parish LFU, the *St. Landry Clarion,* approvingly published the written comment. No objections by readers were recorded in subsequent issues of the paper.

In March 1891, citizens of St. Landry Parish learned that a black man, Henry Bloch, had been appointed postmaster of Opelousas by the federal government. A mass meeting was convened to protest the appointment. The call for the meeting read: "The people of the town of Opelousas who believe that White Men should rule this country and hold its offices respectfully invite their fellow citizens . . . who entertain the same opinion, to assemble in Mass Meeting."[68]

The LFU was at the forefront of the protest over Bloch's appointment. Major M. R. Wilson, a prominent LFU member, called the mass protest meeting to order. He declared himself a friend of the black man and respectful of his rights "so far as they did not conflict with the principle of white supremacy." He firmly declared that all positions of trust and responsibility should be filled exclusively by white males. He added: "The thanks of our people are due to the farming element of this parish for having taken the initiative in this movement [against Bloch's appointment]."[69]

The editor of the parish LFU newspaper, the *St. Landry Clarion,* agreed wholeheartedly with Wilson. He commented upon "the danger of the drift of politics to the days of radical supremacy" and called upon "all white men to nip the flower in the bud." He reported that a resolution condemning Bloch's appointment had been unanimously passed at the mass meeting, with a pledge to withhold support from anyone advocating Bloch's appointment.[70]

The *Opelousas Courier* quoted in full detail the resolutions passed at the meeting, which became known collectively as the Wilson resolution:

> Resolved, That we, the white people, unhesitantly condemn and denounce the aforesaid appointment and solemnly protest against this humiliation. Be it further Resolved, That we will not have our mails scrutinized by colored postmasters, far less do we propose to have our wives and sisters and daughters subjected to the official familiarity of colored men. . . . Be it further Resolved, That we denounce any white man or set of white men who will aid, encourage, or countenance said appointment. . . . Be it further Resolved, That the thanks of our people are due to the farming element of this parish for having taken the initiative in this movement. . . . Be it further Resolved, That we respectfully demand the revocation of the appointment and consequent humiliation.[71]

A Committee of Five was appointed to share these resolutions with Bloch and ask him his intentions. The committee members reported back that Bloch had informed them that he would be soon assuming the duties of postmaster.[72]

Newspapers commenting on the Bloch appointment often noted the leading role of the LFU in the ensuing protest. The *Acadia Sentinel* commented that the LFU had met and denounced "everything connected with the negro and his appointment."[73] The *Baton Rouge Advocate* noted that the Bloch appointment had resulted in "numerous protests by the Farmers Union."[74] The *Opelousas Courier* reported that the parish LFU had met at Bellevue and condemned Bloch's appointment. It also noted that most of those present at the mass meeting protesting Bloch's appointment were LFU members. It reported that when a local judge addressed the mass meeting and declared that anyone who tried to intimidate Bloch would be arrested and that the parish would not be ruled by "regulators," someone in the audience retorted that neither would it be ruled by Negroes.[75]

The St. Landry Parish LFU formally adopted the anti-Bloch, Wilson resolution. When a few members pushed to rescind the adoption of that resolution at the next parish LFU meeting, their efforts were decisively defeated. The Wilson resolution was sustained upon a vote of eighty-nine to five, with all local sub-alliances represented. Furthermore, Wilson was supported in his bid for re-election as an officer of the parish LFU and was elected parish LFU lecturer in 1892.[76]

The role of the LFU in the Bloch controversy suggests that many LFU members were steeped in the culture of white supremacy that begrudged blacks a political voice. Certainly, racially tolerant comments on the part of LFU leaders can be found. LFU founder J. A. Tetts proudly pronounced that "the horns of the Ku Klux were knocked off" by the small farmers' movement.[77] T. J. Guice, a state lecturer for the LFU, and Benjamin Brian, as well as his son Hardy Brian, called for biracial cooperation and unity. The national organ of the Alliance movement, the *National Economist,* boldly declared: "the great question to be solved by the American people is not the negro problem but the money question. . . . Slavery is slavery, be it white or black."[78] But a few selected statements by Alliance or LFU leaders do not qualify as a concerted assault on the dominant white supremacy beliefs of the time. Those beliefs were so pervasive that they only could have been significantly weakened by an all-out attack, not the occasional remark about the common interests of black and white farmers and the need for biracial cooperation. If such an attack on racism had been made, it would be impossible to miss in the historical record. The historical record is clear: while occasional calls for racial cooperation were made, there was no concerted attack by LFU leaders on the racist culture of the times. Racist attitudes remained a major impediment to sporadic efforts to mobilize a biracial coalition to push for reforms to address the farm crisis.

In defense of the LFU, however, challenging the prevailing culture of racism would have been very difficult. It may well have failed even if it had been attempted. It would have entailed challenging a number of beliefs that went to the very core of southern culture.[79] Had the LFU—and the Alliance in general—aggressively and persistently attacked racist attitudes, it would have clearly been an attempt at transforming the prevailing "us" versus "them" racial identity frame. Transformative identity frames almost always face very strong cultural resistance.[80]

Challenging the racist culture and creating a new biracial identity frame based on common economic grievances would have been a monumental task given the passion that still infused discussions in the South about race. The small farmers' movement faced a no-win situation: its failure to attack the culture of racism made the mobilization of a biracial reform coalition improbable; yet any concerted attack on racism would have likely cost it dearly among its white constituency. The loss of white support may well have exceeded the gain in black support. For reasons discussed earlier, the CFA had not been very successful in mobilizing black farmers. The mobilization success of the LFU dwarfed that of the state CFA. Therefore, challenging white supremacy—which risked alienating members of the LFU—in hopes that a strong coalition would be forged with the CFA would have been a very risky gamble.

5

The Shift to Politics

THE POLITICIZATION OF THE SMALL farmers' movement was a touchy process. While the anti-monopoly diagnostic frame remained in place, a contentious strategic framing shift occurred that thrust the movement into one of the most hotly debated monetary issues of the post–Civil War era. The shift significantly increased the political threat of the movement and, consequently, changed the attitudes of the political elite toward the movement—initially to a stance of anxious caution, and eventually to outright hostility and determination to destroy the farmers' movement.

Given that the strategic framing shift represented such a crucial turning point in the farmers' movement, it merits close attention. This chapter probes the reason for the shift away from the self-help strategies of the early Alliance movement. It also discusses in detail the subtreasury plan. No account of the southern Populist movement is complete without careful attention to the subtreasury plan. It was a vital part of the strategic shift that took place in the early 1890s, and the hostility of the Democratic Party to the plan played a major role in moving the Populist movement from a pressure-politics strategy to third-party advocacy.

This chapter also strives to evaluate the shift to politics within the Alliance movement. The evaluation is complicated because there were strong reasons justifying the shift, but equally valid reasons for resisting the shift. The most important factors supporting the shift were the serious deficiencies of the self-help strategies of the early movement and the inherently political nature of addressing the monetary contraction believed to be responsible for the deepening agricultural depression. The major reasons for resisting the politicization of the movement were the inhospitable shifts in political opportunity that it occasioned. The political opportunity for achieving success via pressure-politics within the Democratic Party was severely undercut by the control that the planter elite exercised over nominating conventions. Planters were apportioned a grossly inflated number of seats at the nominating conventions as a result of their manipulation of the black vote in the alluvial parishes. Their overrepresentation allowed them to control the candidate selection process, as well as the content of the official party platform. The only alternative to pressure-politics was third-party politics. However, the latter challenged what had become a core tenet of the prevailing white political culture in Louisiana—that white polity unity under the banner of the Democratic Party was essential to avoid the "Africanization" of state politics and that white supremacy in politics was more important than any other pressing political or economic issue.

This chapter seeks to highlight the inextricable relationship between the Alliance's strategic frame, its mobilization experiences, and the political opportunity structure that it faced. Its initial self-help frame, which the political elite regarded as non-threatening, had produced a tolerant political climate. However, once the limits of the self-help cooperative frame became clear, demobilization would have occurred if new strategies had not been developed. A bold new strategy was imperative. To this end, Alliance leaders developed the subtreasury plan and demanded that politicians either support it or risk losing political support. While the strategic framing shift solved some problems, it created others. Most important, it precipitated an extremely unfavorable shift in the political reaction of elites to the Alliance movement.

A SHIFT IN STRATEGIC FRAMING

Beginning in 1889, a struggle was waged between those who insisted that the Louisiana Farmers' Union (LFU) remain a "strictly business" organization and those who advocated a shift to politics. Representative of the former group was the secretary of the Grant Parish LFU, H. G. Goodwyn, who was upset with the political tone of the LFU annual meeting in August 1889: "We look on the farmers' union as being organized strictly for business purposes, and it is eminently improper to incite political discussions and hamper the order with debates and divisions over abstruse questions of political economy." His views were echoed by an observer who commented that "plunging headlong into politics will bring eventual disintegration to their order, and defeat the primal object of their co-operative system."[1] Another observer similarly declared: "The greatest drawback to their [LFU members] advance is their side issues. If the Farmers Union is anything it is a business organization."[2] Others who advocated avoiding politics seemed primarily motivated by a concern that independent political candidates might seek support from a politicized LFU, and a divided white vote invoked the dreaded prospect of Republican victories at the polls.

Many Alliance leaders, however, criticized the stay-clear-of-politics view. They were convinced that a continued focus on economic self-help, cooperative strategies was not viable. At the national convention of the Alliance in December 1889, one of the Alliance's chief strategists, C. W. Macune, discussed the deepening agricultural depression and the available strategy options for obtaining economic relief. In his speech, he explicitly addressed the "business cooperation in buying and selling" strategy approach versus the political, corrective legislation approach. He stressed the limitations of the cooperative, self-help strategies. After all, for the past five years the Alliance had extensively employed these strategies, yet farmers continued to suffer economically as crop prices stayed dismally low. It was time to consider different tactics.[3]

Macune insisted that any shift in tactics needed to be guided by a deeper understanding of the root causes of the farm crisis. In discussing those causes, he singled out for primary consideration the federal government's monetary policy. He stressed "a generally known and universally acknowledged maxim of political economists: that a general rise in prices always attends an increase in the volume of the circulating medium of the country, and a general fall in prices always attends a general decline in its volume." Applying this maxim, he declared that low crop prices and the ailing economy were due primarily to the contraction of the money supply following the Civil War. To address effectively the root cause of the agricultural depression, farmers needed to use their political power to change the federal government's monetary policy.[4]

This was not a new idea—it had been part of Alliance ideology as early as 1886, when the Texas Alliance adopted the so-called Cleburne Demands. These demands incorporated the notion that significant economic relief necessitated an expansion of the currency supply. To address the immediate problem of an insufficient currency supply, a purposefully inflationary measure was proposed: the "rapid extinguishment of the public debt of the United States, by operating the mints to their fullest capacity in the coining of silver and gold." The Cleburne Demands also called for a revamping of the monetary system, advocating a federally administered banking system that would ensure an adequate supply of currency by issuing legal tender treasury notes based on a predetermined per capita circulation. This federally administered treasury-note plan would replace the existing gold-standard, national banking system.[5]

The controversy of the monetary reform demands stemmed from the fact that they thrust the Alliance movement into an ongoing and contentious monetary debate concerning the country's banking system. During the war, the nation had deviated from the time-honored gold standard to meet the financial demands placed on the treasury by the war. The Treasury Department regarded the abandonment of the gold standard as a temporary, emergency measure that would be corrected as soon as possible after the war ended. In 1865, however, there was a bitter debate concerning the desirability of returning to a gold standard. Hard-money advocates believed that a sound currency system had to be based on precious metals. Among these advocates were two distinct groups. Monometallists insisted that the use of both gold and silver was infeasible; in choosing between the two metals, gold was preferable since its value had been more stable over time. Bimetallists wanted both gold and silver as legal tender to allow for the expansion of the volume of circulating currency. In opposition to hard-money advocates, the fiatists, or Greenbackers, argued that the amount of money in circulation should be determined by the business needs of the country and the country's population size, rather than by the unpredictable supply of precious metals.[6]

In 1875 the monometallists secured a victory with the passage of the Specie Resumption Act, which called for a return to the gold standard and the retirement of greenbacks from circulation. By the summer of 1875, the nation's currency had contracted by $13 million. An economic recession accompanied the currency contraction, fueling the debate concerning the type of monetary system necessary for a healthy economy.[7]

While the Alliance movement addressed monetary reform issue in its early ideology, its monetary reform demands remained secondary throughout the 1880s to its cooperative, self-help vision of reform. Only after self-help strategies had been tried and found wanting did leaders of the Alliance movement move the monetary issue to front and center stage. At the annual convention of the national Alliance in 1889, which was held in St. Louis, Alliance leaders turned their attention to a monetary reform plan that would both expand the circulating currency and directly address the problem of low crop prices. They argued that what was needed was a flexible currency that could readily be expanded or contracted to meet the fluctuating business needs of the country. They were concerned about the heavy demands placed on the currency supply when the bulk of crops was marketed in the fall and winter months. This heavy demand, in their view, overtaxed the existing monetary supply, thereby driving down farm commodity prices. While a larger supply of currency was needed, a larger per capita supply was not the appropriate remedy. If the supply of currency was unresponsive to the need for it, for one-half the year (spring and summer) there would be too much money and for the other-half (fall and winter) too little.[8]

The Alliance proposal for how to achieve a sufficient and flexible currency was called the subtreasury plan. It had both a land-loan and a commodity-loan component. The basic purpose of the land-loan feature was to provide a sufficient currency volume. Land loans were to be made until the volume of money in circulation reached the level of $50 per capita. Loan applicants were to receive up to an 80 percent loan on the value of their farmland, with a maximum loan value of $3,000. The proposed ceiling on the interest rate for these loans was a mere 2 percent per annum.[9] If implemented, this component of the subtreasury plan would tremendously benefit cash-strapped small farmers who depended on crop-lien loans that charged 20 percent or more in interest.

Under the commodity-loan feature of the subtreasury plan, federal warehouses were to be established in every county where at least $500,000 in agricultural products was marketed annually. Farmers could store their nonperishable crops in these warehouses, or "subtreasuries," and borrow up to 80 percent of the local market price on their crops at the time they were deposited. The proposed annual interest rate for these loans was also 2 percent, with nominal additional charges for handling, storage, and insurance. If implemented, the commodity loans would provide an inexpensive alternative to crop-lien financing for farmers who were cash-renters of their farm land or sharecroppers and, therefore, would not be able to participate in the land-loan program. In most states, this was a significant percent of all farmers. In Louisiana, for example, about 45 percent of all farms in 1890 were cultivated by non-owners.[10]

Alliance leaders stressed that the commodity-loan feature of the subtreasury plan was also crucial to creating a more flexible currency system. Approximately $300 million worth of cotton was sold annually at the marketplace, much of it in the months of September and October. Given that the Treasury Department placed the gross volume of currency in circulation at $1.8 billion, to move the cotton crop alone demanded the use of one-sixth of the total U.S. currency in circulation. This put tremendous strain on the money supply, causing a serious deflation in crop prices. The commodity-loan feature of the subtreasury plan, by providing inexpensive storage facilities and loans at an affordable interest rate, would allow for strategies such as cotton withholding when market prices were low. It would also increase the volume of money in circulation, as farmers deposited their crops in subtreasuries and took advantage of the inexpensive loan option. The increased currency supply, in turn, would bolster crop prices. When the commodity loan was terminated by the withdrawal of the stored crop, the loan money would return to the government and could be withdrawn from circulation. Thus, the supply of money could be readily expanded or contracted as needed.[11]

Most Alliance members enthusiastically embraced the subtreasury proposal. In Louisiana, LFU founder J. A. Tetts began to echo the farm crisis explanation being touted by national leaders such as Macune. In his weekly LFU column, he stressed that the financial problems that beset farmers were largely the result of bad financial legislation that had contracted the nation's circulating currency. He pointed out that while there was $50 per capita in circulation in 1866, by 1890 only $5 to $8 per capita was in circulation. He blamed this monetary contraction for the severe depression in crop prices and the high interest rates on crop-lien loans. He referred to the financiers who benefited from the contracted currency supply as "legalized robbers" and insisted that the farmer's economic salvation lay in implementing the subtreasury plan to bypass the "extortion."[12]

Cooperative, self-help strategies by their very nature did nothing to address the contraction of the nation's money supply. So when the money-contraction explanation of the farm crisis became a central part of the official diagnostic frame of the Alliance movement, farmers who remained in the movement had little choice but to shift their attention from cooperative, self-help strategies to the political arena, where the goal was to push Congress to approve the subtreasury plan. In his weekly LFU column, Tetts began touting the subtreasury plan. He claimed that it would effectively address the root causes of the agricultural crisis and do more to help farmers economically "than ten successive good crops."[13]

At the request of President T. S. Adams, parish unions were asked to inform their members about the details of the subtreasury plan, pass resolutions endorsing it, and forward those resolutions to their congressional representatives. Responses to this request were frequently reported in the LFU column of the *Shreveport Weekly Caucasian.* For example, the Lincoln Parish LFU reported that it had asked Congressman Boatner to use all of his influence to secure passage of national legislation consistent with the subtreasury plan. Likewise, East Baton Rouge Parish LFU reported that it had unanimously adopted a resolution supporting the subtreasury plan and requested that Congressman S. M. Robertson work hard to pass legislation consistent with that plan. It also noted that the meeting at which the subtreasury was discussed was "one of the most enthusiastic" since the founding of the LFU in that parish.[14]

However, there is no question that the subtreasury plan was viewed as too radical by many outside of the farmers' movement. The scale of reform, and extent of governmental intervention in the economy that it entailed, was unprecedented. Leaders of the Democratic Party anxiously monitored the political activity of the LFU and the CFA, wondering about the consequences of a politicized small farmers' movement. Would farmers stay loyal to the Democratic Party?

THE ROLE OF RACE IN POLITICS

When the LFU turned its attention to politics in 1890, the Louisiana Colored Farmers' Alliance (CFA) did likewise. The CFA of St. Landry Parish, for example, declared that its key purpose was "to educate ourselves that we may more intelligently vote on questions of vital importance to our people."[15] One issue that the CFA clearly deemed important was the subtreasury plan, which its members were discussing with great interest. This interest is not surprising since so many black farmers were deeply in debt. The inexpensive loans incorporated into the subtreasury plan were undoubtedly appealing.[16]

A biracial political coalition pushing for the subtreasury plan seemed highly advantageous. There were 119,815 black males and only 106,079 white males of voting age in Louisiana in 1890. Voter registration figures also showed the potential for considerable political influence by blacks. Official voter registration rolls in 1886 recorded 110,445 black voters and 111,791 white voters, close to a 50-50 racial split.[17]

But the shift to politics within the Alliance movement created significant challenges. Most whites in Louisiana were uneasy at best, and violently intolerant at worst, with the notion of black influence in politics. Furthermore, to obtain desired reforms many LFU activists initially insisted upon the use of pressure-politics within the Democratic Party. But blacks tended to support the Republican Party and often held very negative views of the Democratic

Party. The racial division in political party loyalty was a major obstacle to seeking reform within the existing party system and, as such, merits close attention.

In addressing delegates to the annual convention of the LFU in 1890, President T.S. Adams insisted that the focus should be on reforming the Democratic Party from within. Other LFU activists expressed similar stances. The editor of the *Colfax Chronicle*, who was active in the LFU and had served as the secretary of the Grant Parish LFU since its inception, insisted that all the evils complained of by LFU members could be remedied through the Democratic Party.[18] The editor of the *St. Landry Clarion*, an LFU paper, stressed that while LFU members were displeased with certain aspects of both the Republican and Democratic parties, they were comfortable with many of the stated ideals of the Democratic Party, such as its anti-tariff stance and its active opposition to the Lodge election bill. For this reason, the LFU had "plainly shown a disposition to trust the Democratic Party." The *Shreveport Weekly Caucasian*, in which the LFU regularly published a news column, declared that the political outlook would be "bright" if the Democratic Party, with the backing of the Alliance, gained control of Congress.[19]

Most whites were hostile to the Republican Party, which they held responsible for Reconstruction. Their view of Reconstruction was filtered through a white supremacy lens that depicted the era as one where blacks had dominated politics: "The spectacle of a superior race governed by an inferior was never seen in the history of the world, except for a brief period in the southern states where the inferior race was backed by Federal bayonets."[20] The strong political influence of "inferior" blacks during Reconstruction was bitterly resented by whites who had been heavily inculcated with the white supremacist culture that had underlain the institution of slavery.

The raw emotion engendered by discussions of the Civil War and Reconstruction politics was palpable in newspaper editorials and articles. An "us" versus "them" mindset typified race relations in Louisiana. Any transformative identity frame that called for a reconfiguration of collective identity along class lines, rather than by race, faced the Herculean challenge of surmounting a centuries-old southern culture holding the white race superior and calling for white control of the economy and polity. The antipathy of most whites in Louisiana toward the Reconstruction era, when the federal government had attempted to rebuild the South in accordance with more equitable political and economic principles, remained intense. In 1889 donations were solicited for a monument in New Orleans to commemorate the "glorious Fourteenth of September, 1874," the date of the White League uprising against the Republican administration of that city.[21] In a similar vein, when Jefferson Davis died in December 1889, he was referred to as "the chieftain of a cause whose glorious memories are so dear to the Southern people." The South was said to be mourning the loss "as a mother weeping for her first born."[22]

The attitudes of most blacks in Louisiana toward the existing political parties were the reverse of those of whites. They tended to support the Republican Party and regarded the Democratic Party with antipathy. This attitude was reflected in the largest black-owned newspaper in the state, the *Weekly Pelican*. It declared that the Democratic Party did not and never would protect the constitutional rights of blacks guaranteed by the Thirteenth, Fourteenth, and Fifteenth amendments. In reporting the frequent refusal of voter registration offices to register blacks, the editor insisted that the only way to protect the voting rights of blacks was to wrest the state from Democratic misrule. The fiercely anti–Democratic Party stance of the paper was also evident in its comment that the Democratic Party had a "wretchedly weak" platform.[23] Furthermore, the editor noted the stark contrast between the "loud-mouth protestations of honesty" of Democrats when they took over at the end of Reconstruction and the large sums stolen from the state treasury under Democratic administrations of the 1880s. In the presidential race of 1888, the paper expressed delight in the defeat of the Democratic incumbent, President Grover Cleveland. When Republicans gained control of the White House in 1888, the paper called upon President-elect Benjamin Harrison to exclusively appoint Republicans when he made his various presidential appointments.[24]

In state politics, the political hostility of most blacks toward the Democratic Party was fueled by the complicity of Democrats in atrocities against blacks during Reconstruction. The leaders who had organized the Colfax and Coushatta massacres in 1873 were now all active in the Democratic Party. The White League, which perpetuated much of the violence against blacks in the mid- to late 1870s, was widely considered an appendage of the Democratic Party. To make matters worse, Democrats still boasted proudly of their role in redeeming the state from Africanization and continued to nominate candidates for office that had played major roles in the violent repression of blacks during Reconstruction.[25]

The political attitude of blacks toward the Democratic Party was also soured by the pervasive intimidation and fraud that persistently characterized

Louisiana elections. Prior to the state elections of 1888, the *Weekly Pelican* called upon Republicans to do all in their power to defeat Francis Nicholls, who was predicted to be the Democratic Party nominee for governor. It ridiculed the notion of Nicholls as a reform Democrat, a notion popular among LFU activists. It claimed that the label merely referred to a Democrat who was out of office and without money. It reminded its readers that Nicholls was "the central figure in the Democratic Party at the time when their right of suffrage was most trampled upon, when ballot box stuffing and mob violence was at its height in this state, and that he rode into power upon the wings of corruption, impurity, and treachery."[26] As for Nicholls's likely competitor for the Democratic nomination, incumbent governor Samuel McEnery, the paper expressed disgust. McEnery had served as governor since 1881 and, therefore, was closely associated with the electoral intimidation and fraud that typified Louisiana elections during the 1880s. To make matters worse, he had publicly boasted about the electoral frauds, granting them cultural legitimacy because of the reputed need for white supremacy. The paper concluded: "If any black man, any Negro with one spark of manhood in his composition, advocates, either by act or word, the re-election of McEnery, he is unworthy of being a free man, and should be scorned and treated as if he were a viper."[27]

Given the strong antipathy of most blacks to the Democratic Party, CFA leaders faced a major dilemma. If they cooperated with the Alliance effort to achieve reforms such as the subtreasury plan through the Democratic Party, they faced the formidable challenge of getting their members to support a party that had played a major role in their victimization. On the other hand, if they did not cooperate with the reform-through-the-Democratic Party plan, they divided the reform backers of the subtreasury plan and undermined the chances for reform.

One solution to this political dilemma was the creation of independent political tickets. While it was an uphill battle to get blacks to vote for the Democratic ticket, the CFA had shown its willingness to endorse independent tickets. The CFA in Catahoula Parish, for example, ignored the Republican congressional candidate in 1890 and officially endorsed the LFU-independent candidate.[28] Another possible solution was the creation of a new third party. But many LFU members, and members of the Alliance throughout the southern states, were wary of this option. The debate over pressure-politics within the Democratic Party versus the creation of a third party loomed large, and prospects for a strong biracial political coalition hinged in large part on how the debate was resolved. No other strategic framing debate was of greater importance to the future of the Alliance movement.

At this point, it is worthwhile to explore further the white supremacy culture of Louisiana. The broad concept of white supremacy can be broken into four distinctive beliefs: first, the belief that whites were the superior race; second, the belief that only whites should hold major political offices; third, the belief that only whites should have voting rights; and finally, the belief that white political unity was paramount and no issue should be allowed to divide the white vote.

Without question, there was variation with the LFU, and later within the People's Party, in regard to these various beliefs. To combine these different beliefs amorphously under the white supremacy label risks clouding important distinctions. While the historical record suggests that there was widespread agreement within the white population, including those who were members of the LFU, that whites were a superior race, there was less agreement in regard to beliefs about black voting rights and political office-holding. Selectively reporting the commentary of various movement participants has resulted in confusion, with conflicting images being portrayed of the racial attitudes within the movement. However, such conflicting images reflect the fact that various members of the LFU drew the line differently in regard to where they parted ways with the prevailing notion of white supremacy.

Of all the beliefs entailed in the broad notion of white supremacy, the belief on which the growth of the Populist movement came to depend most was the degree of importance attached to a unified white vote. Unless LFU members were willing to break with the Democratic Party, their demands for reform could be ignored. A voter whose support can always be counted upon regardless of party decisions is a voter without political influence. After the strategic shift of the Alliance movement into politics, appeals by the Democratic Party for white political unity took on an increasingly shrill tone.

The editor of the *Colfax Chronicle*, a former LFU activist who broke with the organization after the shift to politics, stressed party loyalty. He emphatically declared that the Democratic Party could remedy all the evils that farmers endured.[29] The *Shreveport Daily Caucasian* also urged farmers to fight for reform within the Democratic Party: "It is not new parties that are needed, but it is better parties."[30]

Tetts, one of the founders of the LFU, issued more cautious reform-through-the-Democratic Party advice. In his weekly column in the *Weekly*

Caucasian, he stated that the LFU preferred to pursue reform through the Democratic Party because of the color line in politics and concerns about the consequences of dividing the white vote: "In the South we cannot help but be Democrats for nature has drawn the line that we cannot safely ignore." But he also expressed reservations about achieving reform via the Democratic Party. As early as 1888, he had emphatically declared that "neither of the two old parties are the friend of any class of labor."[31]

Tetts urged LFU members not to be deflected from their reform demands. In effect, he was directly challenging the fourth belief component of the broad notion of white supremacy—the belief that white political unity was paramount and no issue, political or economic, should divide the white vote. He was arguing that Alliance reform principles should be given a higher priority than white political unity. He warned: "We may remain Democrats or Republicans still, but we propose to make those terms mean more than party harness in which to pull men into office who will sell out the wealth producers to a set of money kings."[32] He later added that while most LFU members expected to vote as Democrats, "we will send men to Congress who . . . guarantee to us that they will do all they can to relieve us from . . . the unlawful combinations that oppress us, and from opportunities granted the money power to rob the producer of wealth." He warned: "If wanting these laws will cause a rupture in party lines then let it come, for we had better have no party lines than so much poverty."[33]

It was precisely this type of threat that worried Louisiana politicians. Their anxiety level grew as activists in various parish LFU organizations declared their enthusiastic support for the subtreasury plan, with one activist declaring that LFU members "will work for it, talk for it, write for it, and last but not least, we will vote for it."[34]

THE LOUISIANA CONGRESSIONAL ELECTIONS OF 1890: A TALE OF TWO DISTRICTS

During the congressional election campaigns of 1890, Democrats paid close attention to the elections in the Fourth and Fifth Congressional districts in northern Louisiana. The Fourth Congressional District, which comprised the parishes in the northwestern portion of the state, was a hotbed of LFU activism. Many Democratic leaders in the district were alarmed, and with good reason. The Democratic Executive Committee of at least one parish in the district—Grant Parish—was under the firm control of the LFU.[35] In a number of other parishes, LFU members vied for control of the Democratic Executive Committees. In recognition of the power of the LFU, Fourth District Democrats added a carefully worded plank to their platform that advocated legislation, within the scope of the Constitution, to implement the principles laid out in the subtreasury plan. The editor of the *Colfax Chronicle* labeled it "insincere buncombe" that was the result of Democrats "pandering to popular clamor."[36] The plank was likely the result of a compromise within the Committee on Platform and Resolutions that included two prominent LFU men, Hardy Brian of Winn Parish and M. E. Swafford of Grant Parish.[37]

The Democrats, however, were willing to go only so far in courting LFU support. When it came to nominating a candidate for Congress, the district Democratic Party convention supported incumbent Newton C. Blanchard. The convention was dominated by delegates from the plantation parishes who ignored the strong opposition of the LFU to Blanchard. The LFU had criticized Blanchard for refusing "to put himself in line" with the reforms advocated by the LFU.[38] It did not help that he was a wealthy lawyer who, as a member of Congress for almost a decade, had done little to address the farm crisis. He was also disliked by many farmers because of his support of the "Backbone Railroad" land grant, initially given by Congress in the 1870s on the condition that the specified railroad (between New Orleans and Shreveport and then over to Texas) was completed by 1876. When no railroad tracks were laid prior to this deadline, homesteaders moved onto the lands. Ignoring the interests of these homesteaders, Blanchard (and the rest of the Louisiana members of Congress) extended the time frame of the grant. In 1881, the beneficiaries of the original grant sold the rights to the grant for $1 to a combine of railroad magnates who eventually laid claim to almost 700,000 acres of land. Hundreds of small farmers lost their homesteads in what one paper called a "fraud of the first magnitude."[39]

To many LFU members, the renomination of Blanchard reflected the lack of concern in the Democratic Party for the interests of small farmers. It also demonstrated a weak commitment to LFU reform principles. While district Democrats had incorporated a subtreasury plank into their party platform, their nomination of Blanchard who had taken a public stand in opposition to the subtreasury was indicative of their lack of genuine support for that plank.

Consequently, some LFU activists were interested in naming one of their own to run for Congress as an independent. Winn Parish LFU sent out a call to parish LFU organizations in the district to elect delegates to a convention to be held in Natchitoches on the first of October for the purpose of discussing the desirability of nominating an independent candidate. At this convention, delegates from Grant, Rapides, Sabine, Vernon, and Winn parishes strongly advocated fielding an LFU-independent candidate for Congress. LFU members in these parishes had given their delegates a clear mandate to support such an idea. For example, at the Grant Parish LFU meeting held to elect a delegate to the Natchitoches convention, all but four of the eighty LFU members in attendance supported the nomination of an independent LFU candidate.[40]

Opposing the notion of an independent ticket were delegates from De Soto and Natchitoches parishes. They left the convention after it became clear that their protests against an independent campaign represented a minority voice.[41] It is important also to note that the LFU in five other parishes in the district—Bienville, Bossier, Caddo, Red River, and Webster—did not send delegates. It is unclear how to interpret their absence from the convention. Perhaps it was due to distance since, with the exception of Red River Parish, these parishes did not share borders with the parish of Natchitoches where the convention was held. Or it might have been the result of ambivalence in regard to the proper political stance in the upcoming election. But whatever their reason, their inaction threw the balance of influence at the convention to the five parishes that were strong advocates of fielding an LFU-independent ticket.

The president of the LFU, T. S. Adams, was well aware of the purpose of the Natchitoches convention and was very upset by it. Soon after the convention was called to order, the delegates received a strongly worded telegram from him: "Do not, under any circumstances, nominate an independent candidate for Congress. Your honor and that of the order is pledged to the support of the Democratic nominee. . . . Go forth like men and rally your entire forces to the flag of the Democracy . . . . bide your time with patience."[42]

Despite President Adam's sharply worded telegram, the delegates proceeded to nominate an independent candidate for Congress. They chose T. J. Guice, who had been the LFU's state lecturer for several years. He was well known in LFU circles as a very effective orator. He had also been active in the national organization of the Alliance, having served on its Cotton Bagging and Tare Committee in 1889.[43]

Democrats lost no time in lambasting the dissenters. The *Colfax Chronicle* remarked that the decision to field an independent candidate was ill-advised and would meet with "deserved rebuke by a large majority of the farmers of this district." It also invoked the mantra of party loyalty and labeled the fielding of an independent ticket as "political treachery."[44] Other papers responded by invoking white supremacy rhetoric: "the men who would cause dissension in the party ranks today or bring about a split or division, are allies of the Republicans. . . . Let them be known for what they really are—enemies of white supremacy and civilization."[45]

Harsh, vituperative criticism was also personally aimed at Guice, who tried to deflect the white supremacy rhetoric by promising that he would not court the black Republican vote. Such assurances did little to silence his critics. Importantly, criticism was not leveled solely by those outside of the LFU. The editor of the *Colfax Chronicle*, a former LFU member and a steadfast Democrat, called Guice a "designing demagogue." The editor claimed that the prevailing sentiment in the state was that Guice had always been "afflicted with a diarrhoea [sic] of words and a constipation of ideas."[46]

LFU President Adams, unable to stop the nomination of Guice, turned his energy toward getting Guice to decline the nomination. He stressed that only a minority of parishes in the Fourth Congressional District had voted in support of an independent ticket, given that only five of the twelve parishes in the district had sent delegates to the Natchitoches convention. Furthermore, one of the parishes that had been part of the convention had rescinded its support for an LFU-independent campaign. Guice finally relented, declining the nomination "after advice from prominent union men, and especially that of our most worthy brother and State president, T. S. Adams. . . . It is the opinion of President Adams that the fight must be made within the party."[47]

On Election Day, Guice still received 277 write-in protest votes. At some precincts, such as Union precinct in Grant Parish, he polled more votes than Blanchard. But a more important sign of trouble brewing was the low voter turnout in the district "owing to the Alliance bolters refusing to take part."[48] Blanchard received only 8,307 votes, compared to the 16,302 votes he had received in 1888. The results from Winn Parish, a hotbed of LFU activism, were especially foreboding: almost the entire electorate refrained from going to the polls after being encouraged to boycott the election by Hardy Brian, a leading LFU activist in that parish. Only seventy-six votes were cast in the entire parish, a marked contrast to the approximately one thousand votes cast in past congressional elections.[49]

The congressional elections of 1890 were equally contentious in the Fifth Congressional District, which comprised the parishes in the northeastern portion of the state. Incumbent Charles Boatner was the Democratic Party candidate. He was a planter and a lawyer, known for his conservative political stances. He had publicly criticized the LFU, especially its subtreasury plan. Most LFU members had strongly objected to his nomination. Dissenters had convened in October in the town of Monroe, but they failed to nominate an independent candidate. This did not stop some parish LFUs in the district from organizing electoral protests. The president of the Lincoln Parish LFU, for example, urged farmers to boycott the election. His suggestion was heeded by many, and Boatner's level of support in the parish plummeted compared to his support in 1888.[50]

Another Fifth Congressional District parish in which the LFU was strong, Catahoula Parish, chose a different way to protest. Rather than urging farmers to boycott the election, parish LFU leaders promoted a write-in candidate, T. E. Pritchard. In a similar act of political rebellion, the CFA affiliate in Catahoula Parish urged its members to ignore the Republican congressional candidate and support the LFU-independent ticket instead. Pritchard ended up carrying the parish.[51]

These forms of electoral protest on the part of small farmers represented the beginnings of what would become a major challenge to the Democratic Party in the Fourth and Fifth Congressional districts in northern Louisiana. Although the Democrats won in both districts, the number of votes cast for the party was half of what it had been two years earlier in the elections of 1888. There was concern among Democrats about retaining their political dominance should growing numbers of small farmers break ranks and support independent or third-party candidates. The biggest threat looming on the horizon was the LFU's persistent advocacy of the subtreasury plan, which most Democratic leaders strongly opposed.

A FRAMING CONTEST: THE SUBTREASURY DEBATE

The Democratic press repeatedly declared that LFU demands and Democratic Party principles were in accord except for the subtreasury proposal.[52] Such declarations were then typically followed by an attack on the subtreasury plan. The *New Orleans Times-Democrat* claimed that the extreme nature of the plan "has antagonized a large number of men who were very well disposed toward them [LFU]."[53] The editor of the *Colfax Chronicle*, who had once been active in the Grant Parish LFU, declared that the subtreasury plan had been "hatched from a diseased brain." Its provisions were labeled as "wholly impracticable," "one of the most absurd ideas ever advanced," and "fallacious and unfeasible, if not unconstitutional and undemocratic."[54] Critics also argued that the subtreasury plan was intentionally devised to undermine the support of farmers for the Democratic Party because Alliance leaders were surely aware "that the Democrats of this section of the country would never support such a stupid proposition."[55]

The hope was that farmers would reconsider their support for the subtreasury proposal if it was vehemently assailed. The specific arguments against the plan revolved around four points: it would be too expensive and result in increased taxes; it represented class legislation; it would promote the centralization of power in the federal government; and it was unconstitutional. In regard to the first criticism—that the subtreasury plan would necessitate increased taxes—opponents stressed that the plan would be very expensive to implement. The commodity-loan and land-loan aspects of the subtreasury plan would be costly, as would be the construction of the subtreasury warehouses and their subsequent staffing. The critics insisted that expenses would lead to higher taxes, and farmers were reminded of their frequent complaints about high taxes.[56]

Then there was the issue of class legislation. For years, farmers had complained about legislation that benefited certain classes at a cost to other, often less privileged, classes. In fact, an early motto of the Alliance movement had been: equal justice for all, special favors to none. That motto was deemed by critics to be inconsistent with the subtreasury proposal. Critics argued that many groups in economic need, such as agricultural laborers and urban wage laborers, would not benefit from the subtreasury plan. In fact, these groups would likely suffer economically if the plan were implemented because farmers could store their products in subtreasury warehouses and hold them off the market "until the rest of the world is willing to pay them enormous prices." The critics charged that this was class legislation at its worst.[57]

Finally, opponents of the subtreasury argued that it would result in greater centralization of power in the federal government by dramatically increasing its patronage powers. Thousands of warehouse workers and managers would need to be hired. The editor of the *Opelousas Courier* expressed deep concern that it advocated a principle of centralization that was anathema to southern political culture. Similarly, the *New Orleans Picayune* reported that northerners were pleasantly surprised that farmers in the South were now crying for federal intervention to solve their problems, in vivid contrast to their wartime cry of states' rights and decentralized governmental authority.[58]

This latter criticism was powerful, given that states' rights had been as stridently defended in Louisiana during the Civil War and Reconstruction era as it had been in other southern states. How could southern farmers support a plan that would give the federal government such extensive patronage powers? Democrats predicted that the federal government would fill the subtreasury warehouse positions with Republican federal officeholders much like it did with positions linked to the New Orleans Custom House. The latter positions had made federal patronage in Louisiana greater in proportion to its population than in any other state.[59]

The generation and maintenance of commitment to a specific reform proposal, when most of the mainstream media is harshly criticizing that proposal, is a major framing challenge for any social movement. Meeting this challenge necessitates an extensive education campaign to deliver a viewpoint to counterbalance the views advanced in the mainstream media. The leaders of the LFU, as well as leaders in Alliance-affiliated organizations throughout the South, fully realized that they were engaged in a framing contest. They understood the importance of educating farmers on the details of the subtreasury plan and providing them with counterarguments to the growing criticism. They realized that the harsh criticisms of the subtreasury plan, if left unaddressed, would undermine support for that plan among farmers.[60]

In his presidential address at the 1890 Ocala convention, Alliance President L. L. Polk stated: "If asked what is the greatest and most essential need of our order as contributing most to its ultimate and triumphant success, I should unhesitantly answer and in one word—Education." Elaborating on this point, he discussed the importance of the reform press and the expansion of the Alliance lecturer system. In keeping with this sentiment, the Supreme Council of the national Alliance organization recommended that at least one-fourth of annual revenues in its national treasury be expended on the lecture department.[61]

One of the main sources for the educational campaign on behalf of the subtreasury proposal was the *National Economist*, the national mouthpiece of the Alliance movement that had been established in the summer of 1889 under the editorship of C. W. Macune. Its weekly circulation was reportedly more than 100,000.[62] Its influence, however, was even greater than this circulation suggests. Commentary from its columns frequently found its way into the numerous reform papers that existed in many rural counties and parishes. Also, it was the economic "bible" for many Alliance lecturers who subscribed to it and frequently quoted from it.

One tactic of the *National Economist* was to counterbalance the cries of heresy leveled at subtreasury supporters by reference to religion and to political history. For example, Alliance principles and the subtreasury plan were said to be in line with Christian principles. Referring to political history, the *National Economist* declared: "It requires just as much patriotism to be loyal to the principles of the Farmers Alliance and fight its enemies as it did for our forefathers to wrest control from the British crown. . . . The same principles are involved and every member of the Farmers Alliance who now deserts his organization is as much a traitor to his country and the freedom of his children as was Benedict Arnold."[63]

The attempt to legitimate the Alliance frame by linking it to culturally sanctioned principles occurred simultaneously with an educational campaign that addressed criticisms of the subtreasury proposal. One of the first criticisms addressed was the charge that the subtreasury was class legislation that would benefit farmers while hurting other groups. Many farmers supported the subtreasury plan because they believed that its warehousing provisions were crucial to obtaining better prices for their crops. But they were sensitive to the charge that they, like bankers and industrial capitalists, were just out for their own economic interests and totally oblivious that other groups, such as consumers, would economically lose if the subtreasury plan were implemented.

To counter this charge, the reform press associated with the Alliance movement stressed that the subtreasury plan was meant to be an alternative to the present monetary system. One of its primary purposes was to ensure a sufficient and flexible currency. If it achieved this purpose, the entire country would benefit. Since money was the lubricant of the economy, its inadequate supply was the primary cause of the economic ills of the country that negatively affected the lives of most Americans. If the monetary supply was increased as a result of the subtreasury proposal, the economy would be healthier and the general population would benefit.[64]

Alliance leaders conceded that the warehousing features of the subtreasury plan would benefit farmers in a very direct way, but they insisted that those benefits would not be reaped at the expense of consumers. The warehousing provisions would simply allow farmers to receive the profits that previously had been gone to speculators in agricultural commodities. It was argued, for example, that while corn sold for about $0.70 per bushel, farmers received only $0.20 of this amount; speculators reaped the $0.50 differential by buying corn when supply outstripped demand and selling it at a later date. With the warehousing and low-cost loan provisions of the subtreasury plan, farmers would be able to hold their crops for better prices and reap the profit that had formerly gone to speculators.[65]

In responding to the charge that the subtreasury plan was too expensive, defenders of the plan stressed that the operating costs of the subtreasury warehouses would be borne by farmers depositing their commodities there. LFU activist A. J. Dunn remarked: "No expense is too great, as long as profits exceed them, especially so when that expense is derived from those whom the plan is intended to benefit."[66]

The reform press also labeled as unfounded the charges that the subtreasury plan would require a significant tax hike. This charge was said to be a clear sign that subtreasury opponents did not understand the plan that they so vehemently opposed. After all, a chief purpose of the subtreasury plan was to increase the volume of money in circulation. To take money from taxpayers and loan it to farmers would defeat this purpose. The plan required the government to use its constitutional right to coin or print the money that would be loaned to farmers with the intent of obtaining a per capita circulating currency of $50.[67]

Advocates of the subtreasury plan also addressed the charge by opponents that the plan was unconstitutional. One LFU activist retorted: "We will not be put aside by assertions of unconstitutionality. We see the homes of farmers passing into the hands of the few. We see everything managed in the interests of the speculators."[68] Another LFU activist argued: "If the subtreasury plan is not a [constitutional] remedy, then let its critics butt heads and formulate a remedy. The farmers want relief, not ridicule."[69] In commenting on the alleged unconstitutionality of the subtreasury plan, the editor of the *St. Landry Clarion,* an LFU paper, quipped that if legislators could take a "bad thing" such as the land grabs of the railroad and land syndicates and make those constitutional, "why cannot a good thing [the subtreasury] be made so?"[70]

Finally, the reform press addressed the charge that the subtreasury plan would enhance the patronage powers of the federal government, thereby increasing the number of federal officeholders in the South. The logic of this charge was attacked: the postal system was federally run, with postmasters being federally appointed. Should it be abolished simply because it increased the number of federally appointed officials? It was argued that the critics of the subtreasury would not likely respond affirmatively to this question, and therefore were inconsistent in their expressed concerns about federal patronage. Furthermore, legislation implementing the subtreasury plan could mandate the local or state election of the personnel necessary to run the subtreasury warehouses.[71]

The subtreasury proposal was not, however, without its critics within the Alliance movement. In most state Alliance organizations, there were at least some outspoken anti-subtreasuryites. Their opposition seemed to stem largely from their fears about the political consequences of persistent loyalty to the subtreasury proposal in the face of the unflinching opposition to the proposal by most Democratic Party leaders. It was feared that the ideological conflict would undermine the loyalty that white, small farm owners in the South traditionally had toward the Democratic Party.[72]

However, largely as a result of the educational campaign on behalf of the subtreasury, the Alliance as an organization stood firmly behind the subtreasury reform proposal throughout 1890 and 1891. Delegates to the LFU's annual convention in summer 1891 unanimously declared themselves in support of the proposal. At the national level, the delegates to the Alliance conventions in 1890 and 1891 also declared themselves in favor of the proposal.[73]

Thus, despite heavy criticism by the Democratic Party, the Alliance movement had officially stood by its subtreasury reform proposal. As a result, the acceptance that had been extended to the farmers' movement in the pre-1890 era was rescinded. The farmers' movement was now deemed a serious threat to white political unity. The Alliance's insistence on the adoption of the subtreasury plan, despite the opposition of Democratic Party leaders, was viewed as an ominous indicator of an uncontrollable, rebellious spirit among small farmers that could ultimately undermine their traditional loyalty to the Democratic Party.[74]

BETWEEN SCYLLA AND CHARYBDIS: EVALUATING THE SHIFT TO POLITICS

Evaluating the shift to politics is difficult because there were some strong reasons justifying the shift and equally strong reasons against the shift. The two most important factors supporting the shift were the serious limitations of the self-help strategies and the unavoidably political nature of addressing the monetary contraction that was believed to be the major factor underlying the ailing farm economy. The most serious arguments against the shift to politics were the divisiveness of the shift, the inhospitable political opportunity structure, and the uphill struggle of establishing a viable third party should the two major parties be unwilling to meet the Alliance major demands.

In terms of the logic of politicization, tactical escalation was essential to the survival of the Alliance movement. Its early focus on self-help, cooperative strategies had failed to address directly the dramatic downward spiral of crop prices. By 1890 southern farmers had endured more than a decade of low prices on their major cash crop, cotton. The low price of cotton had caused more and more small farmers to become dependent on crop-lien financing. They simply did not make enough to pay cash for all their needs until the next harvest. Unfortunately, the early tactics of the Alliance had done nothing to forestall the plummeting market price of cotton. Neither had they addressed the economic desperation of farmers caught in the vise of the crop-lien system of financing. Such financing had become a necessary evil: essential for economic survival, yet an economic albatross once utilized. Given the rising levels of crop-lien dependent farmers, a continued focus on economic self-help tactics courted disaster. Indebted farmers did not have the economic autonomy to participate in tactics such as cotton withholding or cotton bulking. Nor did they have cash to contribute to the necessary capitalization of cooperative stores or to trade at those stores. What was desperately needed was a tactic to help farmers avoid the exorbitantly high-interest loans associated with crop-lien financing or even better, a tactic that would effectively raise the market price of cotton so that it could be profitably farmed.

The subtreasury proposal addressed the farming crisis in a way that early self-help, cooperative tactics did not. Its land-loan and commodity-loan components would provide farmers with low-interest loans, only 2 percent annually versus the 20 percent or higher rates associated with current crop-lien loans. Furthermore, its warehousing feature held promise as a remedy to the depression of cotton prices caused by the massive supply of cotton flooding the market in the months of September and October. Farmers would be able to afford withholding their cotton from the market until its price improved.

In his analysis of the Alliance movement, Michael Schwartz is critical of the shift away from its early economic, self-help tactics. He argued that the

Alliance was in a good position to redress the problems of small farmers through its cooperative marketing and purchasing tactics. In his view, the tactical shift to politics in 1890 was the result of oligarchization within the Alliance and the political aspirations of its leaders.[75] Although Schwartz's work is excellent on many counts, on this particular issue his argument is faulty. Contrary to his contention, the Alliance was *not* in a good position to attack and reshape the cotton marketing system. As argued previously, cotton withholding and cotton bulking were ineffective tactics since many farmers could not participate because of their dependency on crop-lien financing. Even the Alliance's most successful cotton-marketing tactic, the jute boycott, had been limited in its positive economic impact.

Schwartz's planter-oligarchy argument is weak on yet another ground. Contrary to his claim that a shift to politics was advocated by a planter oligarchy that had gained control of the Alliance, the shift to politics was feared by most planters. They tended to have strong ties to the Democratic Party and worried that the subtreasury debate could lead to a possible split in the party. They were concerned about the prospect of LFU-endorsed candidates running as independents. These worries were certainly present in Louisiana, where planters firmly controlled the reins of power in the Democratic Party and were critical about any political shift that threatened white unity. This attitude held true for the president of the LFU in 1890, T. S. Adams, who was a planter from East Feliciana Parish.[76] As a Democratic loyalist, he steadfastly opposed any spirit of political rebellion within the LFU. He had opposed the nomination of an independent candidate for Congress by the farmers in the Fourth Congressional District and had sent a very strongly worded telegram warning them to stay loyal to the Democratic Party.

In sum, given the limitations of the early self-help, cooperative strategies of the farmers' movement, the shift away from those tactics was essential to the survival and vitality of the Alliance movement. Without this tactical shift, the movement would have been highly vulnerable to demobilization. Why should farmers continue to participate in a movement whose tactics had failed to redress their grievances? Indeed, the economic plight of most farmers had worsened.

While the shift from self-help, cooperative strategies was essential to the survival of the farmers' movement, the shift was fraught with challenges. The subordination of political demands during the early years of the farmers' movement had been a response to concerns about the negative consequences of a political focus. The political insurgency of the Cleburne Demands had caused a serious split in the Texas Alliance in 1886, with a minority faction condemning the political demands and threatening to set up a rival farmers' organization. The fear was that in an organization as young as the Alliance, a premature shift to politics could be fatal.

Nowhere was the shift to politics more risky than in Louisiana. A united white vote for the Democratic Party was viewed as essential for maintaining white supremacy. Louisiana was one of only three southern states with a black-majority population, and the threat of the black vote was a pervasive theme in political writings of the time.

White political unity under the banner of the Democratic Party was of paramount importance to many who had lived through the turmoil of Reconstruction. The political memories of the Reconstruction era were very strong among many white Louisianans. While Reconstruction had ended over a decade earlier, references to the alleged abuses of carpetbaggers and their black political allies during this era were still common.[77] Prominent southern Democrats were frequently extolled for their political actions during this era. Democrat John McEnery, for instance, was praised for his "heroic fight for Democracy and white supremacy during reconstruction"[78] and for "the prominence of his actions in the great struggle for white supremacy during the dark days of reconstruction."[79] Congressman H. W. Ogden was commended for being "true to his people's cause" during Reconstruction. He was described as "one of the fearless of the boldest leaders in the days of reconstruction, and it is to the efforts of such men that Louisiana was redeemed from shame and spoliation."[80] In a similar tone, the *New Orleans Times-Democrat* talked reverentially of the harmonious spirit that existed within the Democratic Party during the "glorious days of 1876," when the Republicans and their "horde of negroes" were thrown out of power.[81]

Given the white supremacy culture of Louisiana and the fear of the consequences of a divided white vote, any call for desertion of the Democratic Party would precipitate a strong backlash. Whenever a united white vote was threatened, Democrats increased their emphasis on the importance of white political solidarity and their retelling of emotional horror stories of the Reconstruction era to shore up party loyalty. Thus, emotion played a major role in the framing contest between the Democratic Party and the political rebels within the LFU. The question was whether the spirit of political rebellion building within the LFU would survive the emotional manipulation by leaders of the Democratic Party.

The president of the LFU, T. S. Adams, flatly declared that a third-party revolt would be suicidal.[82] The editor of the *Shreveport Daily Caucasian* concurred: "the white people . . . are not ready, as yet, to divide themselves and let their old enemies get possession of the reins of government again."[83] The "us" versus "them" white supremacy rhetoric served the Democratic Party well. Even those with serious complaints often pushed for reform within Democratic ranks.

While fighting for major reform outside of the Democratic Party was anathema to many white Louisianans, fighting for such reform *within* the Democratic Party was a daunting challenge. The political opportunity for successful advocacy of major reform proposals within the party was minimal. In no other post-Reconstruction state did planters so effectively dominate the political process. Their power derived primarily from their control of district and state nominating conventions of the Democratic Party and from the extraordinary appointive powers granted to the governor of Louisiana.[84]

The control the planter elite exercised in regard to the nominating conventions resulted from the landslide electoral victories it was able to orchestrate in the black-belt areas of the state. The number of Democratic votes cast in the previous election determined seat apportionment at the nominating conventions. The larger the Democratic vote, the greater the number of seats allotted to the parish. The ballots of black voters in the black-belt parishes, manipulated or falsified and counted for the Democratic Party, gave planters control over nominating conventions and allowed them to defeat reform nominees or reform planks in the party platform that threatened their economic interests.[85]

Complaints frequently surfaced about the illegitimate basis of planter control over district and state nominating conventions. The *Shreveport Daily Times,* for example, railed against the egregious ballot box stuffing in Tensas Parish. It claimed that "unblushing fraud" converted the black votes in that parish into "bogus Democratic ones" and resulted in the parish garnering an unfairly inflated number of seats in nominating conventions.[86] Planters in Tensas Parish were certainly not alone in their manipulation of the election process. After the 1886 state elections, the *Shreveport Daily Times* declared: "Madison Parish, having learned the political multiplication table, comes to the front as a rival of Tensas."[87] The *Louisiana Journal,* published in Claiborne Parish, concurred: "Tensas has a rival at last."[88] Concordia, another large black belt Parish in the Fifth District, racked up an impressive Democratic victory in the elections as well. Tensas, Madison, and Concordia together delivered a total of 7,558 votes for the Democratic Party in the 1886 elections, despite having only about 1,700 registered white voters.[89]

The overrepresentation of alluvial, plantation parishes in nominating conventions caused one newspaper editor to fume that after rising up to crush the Republican Party and end Reconstruction, whites now found themselves political victims of those who "bulldoze . . . the nigger vote in the river parishes to . . . dictate to their betters" at Democratic nominating conventions.[90]

Louisiana historian William Hair argued that the evidence clearly demonstrated that blacks were generally hostile to the Democratic Party and if allowed to vote without interference would cast their votes for anything besides the Democratic ticket. He stressed that many black voters endured serious hardships, even death, in voting against the Democratic Party. Thus, he supported the view that landslide victories for the Democratic ticket in black-belt areas were the result of fraud.[91]

Interestingly, Democratic leaders were at times quite open about the fraud. One outspoken Democrat, the editor of the *Natchitoches People's Vindicator,* told fellow Democrats during the 1878 election campaigns to "pile on your majority."[92] The manipulated black vote became such an important basis of power that Democrats, who were adamant about the need for white supremacy, ironically added thousands of black voters to the voter registration rolls in the decade following the end of Reconstruction. In 1880 there had been 88,024 black registered voters, 2,573 more than whites. By 1888, the number of blacks registered to vote had increased to 128,150, an astonishing 45 percent. The number of whites added to the voter registration rolls was much more modest, so that black voters outnumbered white voters by 3,743. The doctoring of the registration rolls in the black-belt parishes was reflected in the fact that white registration in the state was reasonably close to the census count of the actual number of white males over the age of twenty-one. In contrast, 8,335 more blacks in that age group were on the rolls in 1888 than were counted in the census two years later.[93]

The power of the planter elite over the nominating conventions of the Democratic Party is particularly significant in light of the fact that the general elections in Louisiana usually played a minor role in the political process. After the end of Reconstruction, Republican chances for success in statewide elections were virtually nonexistent. It was at the Democratic nominating conventions that the real selection of officeholders occurred. As the *Morehouse*

Clarion, a rural newspaper in the Fifth Congressional District, succinctly declared: "The fight is only for the nomination, which means election."[94] The only exception in races for major state offices was when a split occurred in the Democratic Party and two tickets were fielded, but such splits were rare. While Democrats fought over party nominations, once the nomination process was completed they typically "close up their ranks and present a solid, unbroken front."[95]

Whenever that united front was jeopardized, white solidarity-anti Republican rhetoric was employed in an attempt to shore up Democratic loyalty. In 1884, for example, there was a bitter fight for the Democratic Party gubernatorial nomination. Nicholls, who was favored by the majority of small farmers, vied for the nomination against McEnery, who was favored by the large planters and urban political elite. Predictably, given the large delegation apportionments of the plantation parishes at the nominating convention, McEnery won the nomination. Some Nicholls-backers were so angry that on Election Day they scratched McEnery's name off the ballot and recorded no vote for governor. The Democratic press railed against the rule-or-ruin sentiment that resulted in such political behavior: "These immaculate Reformers may indulge in the poor boast that they never voted for a Republican, but not many of any intelligence can draw a distinction between voting for a Republican and the failure to vote for a Democrat when the two tickets are in the field."[96]

Planter control over the gubernatorial selection process was significant because the governor of Louisiana had extraordinary appointive powers. Not only were a large number of state-level political positions appointed by the governor, but many parish-level positions were appointed as well, such as registrar of voters, parish tax assessors, and police jurors. While the extensive appointive powers ensured white political control in black-belt parishes, those powers undercut democracy by eliminating the ability of voters to choose who served in a large number of state- and parish-level political positions. The *St. Landry Democrat* complained: "We appreciate the circumstances which induced the Legislature to take the elections of them [parish officials] from the people, but we have been long since disembarrassed of all impediment to white supremacy."[97]

In sum, there was an inextricable relationship between the Alliance's frame, its mobilization experiences, and the political opportunity structure that it faced. Its initial self-help strategic frame, which the political elite regarded as a relatively non-threatening attempt by farmers to improve the profitability of farming, had produced a tolerant political climate. By 1890, however, the limits of the self-help strategic frame had become clear. If different strategies had not been forthcoming, demobilization would have occurred as a result of the continued downward spiraling of crop prices.

With about 70 percent of the backland farmers in debt,[98] a bold new strategy aimed at low crop prices and debt relief was imperative. To this end, Alliance leaders developed the subtreasury plan and demanded that politicians support that plan or risk political retaliation. With its shift to politics, the political environment in which the Alliance functioned became hostile. Politicians from the old parties regarded the Alliance's strategic framing shift with alarm. They initiated a gloves-off, negative campaign aimed at the subtreasury plan, with hopes of undermining support for the plan.

Herein lay the dilemma of the shift of the Alliance movement to politics: The shift from self-help strategies was essential to the movement's survival. The shift to politics, however, required that the Alliance operate within an extremely hostile political environment that posed survival risks as well. The strategic framing shift thrust the Alliance into the quagmire of southern politics. Achieving major reform, such as entailed in the subtreasury plan, through the Democratic Party was unlikely due to the fact that large planters exerted disproportionate control over the nominating conventions of that party. But mobilizing support for a movement that challenged the hegemony of the Democratic Party was equally daunting. White voters who deserted the Democratic Party were harshly criticized as traitors to the white race. To many white southerners, abandoning white political unity under the banner of the Democratic Party was unthinkable. If efforts to achieve desired reforms through the Democratic Party proved futile, the success of the small farmers' movement would hinge on making the unthinkable happen.

6

The Rise of the Third-party Revolt

DURING THE EARLY 1890S, the LFU struggled with an increasingly bitter strategic framing dispute between activists who insisted that reform could be achieved through the Democratic Party and those who insisted that genuine reform required a third-party revolt. The dispute escalated when a reform faction within the state Democratic Party initiated a campaign against the notorious Louisiana Lottery Company. The goal of the campaign was to prevent the rechartering of the powerful lottery company that for twenty-five years had held a highly profitable monopolistic charter on lottery business within the state.

Some LFU members believed the anti-lottery campaign resonated sufficiently well with the anti-monopoly diagnostic frame of the Alliance movement as to merit cooperating with the anti-lottery wing of the Democratic Party. Other LFU members argued that the anti-lottery campaign was a diversion. Genuine reform, they insisted, would occur only if the Democratic Party supported the major reform proposals of the LFU, especially its subtreasury proposal. In the absence of such support, they argued that LFU members needed to abandon the Democratic Party and support a third-party movement. The sentiments of this faction took on new meaning after the national organizational structure for a third party, the People's Party, was created in May 1891.

As the southern Populist movement began its strategic shift from a reform-through-the Democratic-Party approach to a third-party revolt, mobilization challenges loomed. To be viable, the third party in Louisiana would have to garner support not only from parishes where it could mobilize using the organizational base of the LFU, but from parishes where the LFU had never effectively recruited, such as the black-belt alluvial parishes. To this end, in a move that would stun some Louisianans, initially the third party courted the black vote. Unfortunately, it was an uphill battle because of the absence of social networks that could be used for effective recruitment, the scarcity of funds for organizing and campaigning, and the unfavorable political opportunity structure created by the known proclivity of the planter elite to manipulate the black vote.

THE BIRTH OF THE PEOPLE'S PARTY

Three hundred to four hundred delegates from at least seven different reform organizations answered a call to meet in Cincinnati in May 1891 to discuss the prospects for establishing a third party. More than 1,400 people were in attendance. This convention made headlines across the nation when the majority of delegates voted in favor of organizing a third party, to be called the People's Party, to push for economic reforms.[1]

Importantly, there were no official delegates representing the national Alliance organization at the Cincinnati convention, for reasons that will be discussed shortly. The convention call was, however, answered by the CFA and such diverse reform groups as the Union Labor Party, organizations of former Union and Confederate soldiers, the Farmers Mutual Benefit Association, women suffragists, prohibitionists, and the Knights of Labor.[2]

The eclectic composition of the convention delegation is important to understanding subsequent developments within the People's Party. While historians have rightfully argued that to understand Populism one must understand the Alliance movement,[3] it is not true that understanding the Alliance movement suffices to understand Populism. The People's Party was composed of many different politically dissident groups. Furthermore, the absence of delegates from the national Alliance organization at the founding convention of the People's Party had repercussions for the makeup of the party's national committee. The composition of that committee was of vital importance because it would be called upon to make crucial political decisions, such as what issues to highlight during political campaigns and when to schedule nominating conventions. While historian Lawrence Goodwyn has argued that the makeup of the national committee was "unusual,"[4] to the contrary it was the predictable outcome of the composition of the delegations to the Cincinnati convention of 1891.

Since the absence of official delegates at the Cincinnati convention from the national Alliance organization had important consequences, close attention needs to be given to the major reason for that absence: the victory of advocates of pressure-politics in a framing contest with third-party advocates at the Ocala convention of the Alliance in 1890.

A FRAMING CONTEST: PRESSURE-POLITICS OR THIRD-PARTY POLITICS

The advisability of a third-party move was hotly debated at the Ocala national convention of the Alliance in December 1890. Charles Macune, a prominent Alliance leader and editor of the *National Economist*, recommended a cautious stance. He strongly believed that the Alliance should, at least in the near future, press for the subtreasury and other reforms through existing party structures. He feared that an alignment with the third-party movement could be fatal. He fully understood that any organization or movement that threatened the unity of southern white voters under the Democratic Party banner would be harshly attacked. In his view, many white southerners were not yet ready to abandon the Democratic Party because they remained convinced that they could win enough support within that party to obtain needed reforms. Therefore, Macune reasoned that third-party advocacy should only be a last resort, a stance taken only after all efforts to win reform through existing party structures had clearly been exhausted.[5]

Many LFU leaders in Louisiana agreed with Macune's cautious stance toward the notion of a third party. Tetts, for example, insisted that the Democratic Party had not been "fully and fairly tried" and argued that the LFU should "make itself felt" within that party. Expressing a similar sentiment, another farmer quipped: "When the horses are hitched to the Democratic wagon, we clod-hoppers mount it and crack our whip and if the other fellows . . . don't like it [they] can just lump it."[6]

On the other hand, third-party advocates within the Alliance were cynical about the chances of significant reform through existing party structures. They noted that the root causes of the economic problems plaguing agriculture and the nation in general required reform at the federal level. With farmers north of the Mason-Dixon Line, as well as black southern farmers, remaining loyal to the Republican Party and white southern farmers remaining loyal to the Democratic Party, reform was improbable. Furthermore, third-party advocates believed southern farmers were naïve about their ability to control the party machinery of the Democratic Party. Planters controlled the nominating conventions of the Democratic Party in most southern states, they argued. The manipulation of the vote in the plantation parishes resulted in the overrepresentation of those parishes at political party nominating conventions. Consequently, planters could usually defeat reform proposals or reform candidates not to their liking. Since the planter elite had steadfastly opposed the subtreasury proposal, what was to be gained by staying loyal to the old parties? As one third-party advocate within the Alliance stated, "it seems to me a man would be a fit subject for an asylum when he continues to stay in a path that takes him in a circle and he never gets anywhere."[7]

Despite pushing hard to get the Alliance to commit to the third-party movement and to send representatives to the Cincinnati convention, third-party advocates were unsuccessful. Instead, delegates to the national Alliance convention in Ocala in 1890 adopted a compromise proposed by Macune: Consideration of the third-party movement would be delayed until the presidential election year of 1892, at which time the Alliance would host a reform convention of its own to consider the issue of third-party advocacy. The delay would give the Alliance more time to assess the viability of reform through the existing parties and to assess grassroots sentiments in regard to a third-party revolt.[8]

While the Alliance voted against participating in the Cincinnati convention, a decision with which the LFU's delegation concurred, the CFA was not so hesitant. Delegates to its national convention approved sending representatives to the Cincinnati convention. The signatures of three prominent black CFA activists in Louisiana were affixed to the convention call: J. B. Lafargue, state secretary of the CFA in Louisiana; L. D. Laurent, general superintendent of the Louisiana CFA; and I. Miller.[9]

The cautious position of the Alliance in regard to third-party advocacy had a powerfully debilitating effect on the appeal of the third-party movement in the South. There were only thirty-six delegates from the entire South at the Cincinnati convention—and some of these had come to argue against a third party.[10] Only two delegates from the state LFU organization were present at the convention. However, several parish-level LFU organizations sent representatives. The LFU organization in Calcasieu Parish sent I. J. Mills of Lake Charles. The LFU organization in Winn Parish sent Hardy Brian with a letter authorizing him as its representative. The authorization letter bore the signatures of 1,200 adult males, only 131 short of the total adult male population of the parish. Brian claimed that he also was the beneficiary of "the advice, consent, and help" of the LFU organizations in Catahoula, Grant, and Vernon parishes.[11] Also attending the Cincinnati convention was L. D. Laurent, an activist in the

Louisiana CFA. His name would also appear on the call for a People's Party nominating convention in Omaha in July 1892.[12]

To increase the southern appeal of the third-party movement, officials at the Cincinnati convention successfully pushed for the adoption of a platform almost identical to that adopted the previous summer at the Ocala convention of the Alliance.[13] This was clearly an attempt to curry favor with the Alliance, which was rightfully viewed as the key to garnering southern support.

But many Alliance leaders, including Macune, remained firm in their refusal to rush onto the third-party bandwagon. They chastised members who had endorsed the Cincinnati convention, insisting that the resolution adopted at the Ocala convention to postpone the decision about a third-party movement was a wise one. Time was needed to test fairly the ability to achieve needed reforms through the existing political parties. Macune warned that the Alliance was "in the outer edge of the coming storm . . . before six months has rolled by, it will be in the very midst of the warring element." He urged leaders to use the time wisely to educate the masses on the principles of the Alliance and to test fairly the feasibility of achieving needed reforms through the existing political party structure. Undue haste, he argued, had been the bane of all previous reform efforts.[14]

In the aftermath of the Cincinnati convention, LFU co-founder Tetts echoed his earlier warning about the third-party movement: "As to the matter of going into the third party, that is all in the future." He stated that he would not endorse the third party until the "proper authority" said that it was the will of the majority to go into the third party to get their demands.[15]

The Macune compromise adopted at the Ocala convention, and endorsed by the LFU delegation to that convention, held little appeal to some LFU activists. For example, at a LFU meeting in Grant Parish soon after the Cincinnati convention, all but three of those present supported the Cincinnati convention and its decision to form a third party.[16] A resolution passed by the Montgomery subunion in Grant Parish reflects the exasperation of these third-party advocates: "Whereas the people have received only sarcasm, abuse and ridicule from both political parties in answer to their pleadings for relief, Therefore be it resolved . . . That we endorse the platform framed by the National Farmers' Alliance at Ocala, Florida and adopted by the National Conference at Cincinnati, Ohio and Be it further resolved, That we stand in readiness and heartily pledge our entire support to the People's Party in its effort to relieve the people of their oppressive burden." Another noteworthy resolution passed by the Ada and Dison subunion in Grant Parish not only declared in favor of the shift to third-party politics, but boldly declared itself in favor of uniting with black voters: "Resolved, That we the citizens of Ada and Dison communities in mass meeting assembled . . . heartily endorse the People's Party movement. That we invite the colored people of the parish to cooperate with us in our effort to free the country from plutocratic usurpation and tyranny."[17]

Over the next couple of months, the LFU parish organizations in Calcasieu, Catahoula, Franklin, and Vermillion parishes followed suit with resolutions renouncing ties to the Democratic Party and endorsing the third-party movement. Growing support for the People's Party among LFU activists was reported in Natchitoches, Rapides, Sabine, and Vernon parishes.[18]

State LFU leaders were well aware of the growing third-party sentiment in some parishes and the strategic framing crisis that was brewing over the appropriate course of action. The president of the LFU, T. S. Adams, tried to forestall the growth of third-party advocacy by taking a very public stand against the third party. A. D. Lafargue, a LFU lecturer, declared that a third-party movement would be "the extreme of folly."[19] The editor of the *Opelousas Courier*, the official paper of the LFU in St. Landry Parish, called upon third-party supporters in the LFU to "cease this nonsense and rally to its [the Democratic Party] support and save the party from possible ruin."[20] He warned that third-party advocates were risking another Republican Congress, which would likely pass the Lodge election bill, or "force bill." He hysterically declared: "Are you willing to have . . . a squad of U.S. soldiers around every poll and a bayonet behind every ballot? . . . White Leagues and Ku-Klux will again rear their heads. Riot, bloodshed, arson, rape, murder, frenzy, anarchy, and worse than Reconstruction days will be ours then. Better, far better, that the Alliance be sunk ten thousand fathoms deep than that we again pass through the horrors of 1868."[21]

Whether the third-party movement was supreme folly or the right move continued to be a hot topic of debate. State leaders were not able to extinguish the passionate framing contest that was taking place at the grassroots level of the farmers' movement, a framing contest that was intricately tied to beliefs about the possibility of achieving reform via pressure-politics within the Democratic Party and beliefs about the political viability of a viable third-party movement.

THE DIVERSION OF THE ANTI-LOTTERY CAMPAIGN

Leaders of the Democratic Party in Louisiana were relieved that the national Alliance had refused to send official delegates to the Cincinnati convention.

They praised the political loyalty of the Alliance to the Democratic Party.[22] They were, however, deservedly wary. The ideological link between the People's Party and the Alliance movement was uncomfortably close. Despite there being no official delegates from the national Alliance at the Cincinnati convention, some local groups had responded to the decision by the organizers of the Cincinnati convention to accept delegates representing state or parish/county Alliance organizations.

Southern Democrats were acutely aware that the tie of a growing number of Alliance members to the Democratic Party was tenuous. They urgently searched for moderate reform issues that might divert the attention of farmers from radical demands such as the subtreasury plan. In Louisiana, the diversion took the form of an anti-lottery campaign that had considerable success in diverting support for the nascent third-party movement.

Beginning in the summer of 1890, Louisiana Democrats initiated a campaign against the Louisiana Lottery Company. Reform-minded Democrats had long complained about the Louisiana Lottery Company. In 1868, the Republican administration of Governor Warmoth had granted this company a monopolistic twenty-five-year charter. When the Republicans began to lose their grip on power in the late 1870s, the company quickly transferred its allegiance to the Democratic Party. It subsequently built a statewide political machine that, in the words of Louisiana historian William Hair, "could shake every corner of the state."[23] Its power in large part derived from the fact that the company had become one of the most lucrative business endeavors in the country. It reportedly sold up to $30 million in lottery tickets every year, much of that coming from sales outside of Louisiana. Despite its tremendous profitability, the company's charter required it to pay only $40,000 per year to the state's coffers. With only about half of its profits going to prizes, its annual payment to the state represented less than 0.5 percent of its profits.[24]

The LFU had taken an overt stand against the renewal of the lottery charter at its 1889 and 1890 state conventions. It depicted the Lottery Company as an evil monopoly that embodied much of the ills of American capitalism. It claimed that the company controlled most of the press in the state, using money to buy influence. J. A. Tetts, in his LFU column in the *Shreveport Weekly Caucasian,* commented that the influence of the Lottery Company was enhanced by the fact that its lobbyists were smart enough "to make the average man believe that green persimmons can be used for sweetening coffee."[25] So strong were the feelings of many LFU activists in regard to the lottery that when the LFU was searching for a newspaper that it could adopt as an official state organ in 1890, it made as one of the key conditions the dropping of all advertisements for the lottery. Since such ads were lucrative, many papers were unwilling to meet that condition.[26]

Reform Democrats concurred with the anti-lottery stance of the LFU. The twenty-five-year charter of the Louisiana Lottery Company was up for renewal in 1893, and they were determined to defeat its bid for renewal. They recognized the difficulty of their goal. The company had already begun a campaign to get its charter renewed. It had offered to increase significantly its annual payment to the state, from the present $40,000 to $500,000, or $12.5 million for a twenty-five-year charter. In paid advertisements in newspapers throughout the state, it stressed how that money could be used to reduce the state debt; to lower state taxes, or at least keep them from rising; to improve educational funding within the state; and to construct and maintain the levee system that protected below-sea level lands in the state from flooding.[27]

Anti-lotteryites were well aware of the attractiveness to state politicians and voters of the offer of a half-million-dollar annual payment to the state coffers. They were even more alarmed when the Lottery Company increased its offer to $1.25 million annually, or more than $31 million during the course of the next twenty-five-year charter. Newspapers touted the benefits of this offer, especially in regard to the desperate need for educational funds to address the state's high illiteracy rate. The editor of the *Opelousas Courier* went so far as to say that the money would be "a godsend."[28]

Alarmed by the Lottery Company's rechartering campaign, leading anti-lottery advocates met in Baton Rouge in August 1890 to organize an Anti-Lottery League to fight against the Lottery Company's bid for constitutional recharter.[29] They also began their efforts to get the leaders and rank-and-file of the LFU to join forces with them. A reform Democrat, LFU anti-lottery coalition would have two major political advantages. First, it would significantly strengthen the anti-lottery campaign. Second, and of equal importance, it would avert the LFU's attention away from more radical demands such as the subtreasury plan.

Leaders of the LFU, such as President T. S. Adams and J. A. Tetts, were attracted to the idea of a coalition with anti-lottery Democrats. They worried that the Lottery Company would use its money and political influence to get a pro-lottery plank in the state Democratic Party platform, which would jeopardize the loyalty of farmers to the Democratic ticket. The fear was that the

Democratic vote would be significantly diminished, thereby giving the Republicans a better chance to regain control of the state government.[30] It is hard to say which was perceived as the greater danger: a Republican victory at the polls or a victory for the Louisiana Lottery Company. Either way, the reasoning of Adams and Tetts reflected their persistently strong ties to the Democratic Party. They were not yet willing to sever those ties, despite the urgent call by some LFU activists for a third-party movement to push for the full slate of Alliance reforms.

Hair depicted the coalition between the Anti-Lottery League and the LFU as a successful attempt by Anti-Lottery League Democrats to capture the LFU. But it is important to recognize that the idea of a coalition was as attractive to many LFU leaders and activists as it was to the leaders of the Anti-Lottery League. In fact, pro-coalition LFU activists depicted the coalition as an effort by the LFU to capture the Democratic Party. They believed that such a political alliance would allow them to capture a majority of the delegates to the Democratic Party nominating convention. With this control, they could be sure the party platform included an anti-lottery plank and candidates for state office were committed to reform.[31]

When the LFU convened in Lafayette on August 4, 1891 for its annual convention, members of the Executive Committee of the Anti-Lottery League were present to meet with LFU officials. A coalition agreement was soon reached. It stipulated that the coalition would work together to elect a sufficient number of anti-lottery delegates to the nominating convention of the Democratic Party to gain control of the convention. If successful in controlling the convention, the agreement stated that the LFU delegates would choose the candidates for governor, treasurer, and superintendent of education, and the Anti-Lottery League delegates would name the lieutenant governor, auditor, attorney general, and secretary of state.[32]

In his speech to the delegates at the LFU convention, T. S. Adams insisted that farmers remain loyal to the Democratic Party. He stressed the importance of a coalition with the anti-lottery faction of that party in order to defeat the Louisiana Lottery Company. In regard to the third-party movement, he argued: "if we did not have the power to hew our way to success within the ranks of the dominant party, much less would we have the strength to win success by committing our bark to untried seas, and do not, I pray, press the demand for a third party before the emergency for it arises, if, indeed, it ever does." He added: "I beseech you to . . . hold in abeyance all other questions until the burning question of the hour—the Louisiana lottery—is settled. Otherwise the anti-lottery bloc in the Democratic Party will be seriously weakened."[33]

When a vote was finally taken on whether to form a coalition with the Anti-Lottery League, about three-quarters of the LFU delegates voted in support. The seventy-three yes, twenty-two no vote for what would soon become known as the Lafayette Compact or Combine was a pivotal point in the history of the LFU. In the months immediately following the convention, numerous parish unions and subunions passed resolutions declaring their support for the compact. The Lafayette Compact, however, would become increasingly contentious in the months ahead.[34]

It is telling that in his address to the convention, President Adams spoke of the lottery as the burning issue of the hour. His displacement of the subtreasury proposal and other Alliance demands to the back burner angered some delegates. What did the lottery have to do with low cotton prices or with excessively high crop-lien interest rates? It was as if the diagnostic framing efforts of the past year in regard to educating LFU members on such key Alliance reform demands as the subtreasury proposal were forgotten.

That a leader such as Adams could convince a large majority of LFU delegates to put aside major Alliance demands demonstrates the incredibly difficult task of retaining commitment to major reform in social movements. Selective endorsement of relatively minor reform demands or deflection of attention to other issues is an ever-present threat to movements once they are perceived as a viable force for reform.

The twenty-two delegates who voted against the Lafayette Compact, about one-fourth of the total delegation at the annual LFU convention, would be later referred to as "the famous twenty-two who fought the dicker in which the Alliance was sold for offices." They were angry that the LFU had bargained away Alliance principles "for the promise and uncertainty of Tom Adams receiving the governorship of Louisiana." As for Adams himself, they speculated that his loyalty to the Democratic Party had been cemented a year earlier when Governor Nicholls had appointed him state secretary of agriculture. In their view, he had betrayed the true interests of the small farmer in return for political spoils.[35]

The "famous twenty-two" demanded nothing less than total commitment to the entire slate of Alliance reform principles. They represented the LFU in ten parishes, including some of the parishes where the LFU was strongest. They included three well-known "at large" delegates to the state LFU convention—T. A. Clayton, R. L. Tannehill, and T. J. Guice.[36]

S. W. Lacroix, a member of the LFU in Grant Parish, minced no words in explaining his support for the twenty-two delegates who had refused to embrace the Lafayette Compact: "There is no question but what both parties of the present age are so corrupt that they have become a stench in God's nostrils." He also was skeptical, and deservedly so as coalition advocates were soon to discover, about the ability of the LFU to secure its preferred candidate, T. S. Adams, for governor as the coalition agreement promised.[37] Equally suspicious of the intentions underlying the compact was L. A. Traylor, the editor of a new paper *The Ocala Demand.* While opposing the Louisiana Lottery Company and all other monopolies in the country, the paper proclaimed the Lafayette Compact "a nefarious effort to destroy the policy and power of the Farmers Alliance in the State of Louisiana."[38]

National Alliance leaders and the national news organ of the Alliance, the *National Economist,* were also critical of the Lafayette Compact. While the *National Economist* had praised the LFU in 1890 for its courage in arraying itself against the powerful monopoly held by the Louisiana Lottery Company,[39] it now concurred with the current president of the national Alliance, L. L. Polk, who warned that the compact was "subversive to principles of the Order." According to Polk, the compact meant "the utter abandonment of every important principle of our Order, as it requires us to surrender . . . every one of our demands in order that we may secure the cooperation of men to suppress an evil, which should have the unqualified condemnation of every good citizen of whatever class or party."[40]

The *National Economist* also reprinted a circular letter written by Hardy Brian, an LFU activist in Winn Parish who was critical of the Lafayette Compact. The letter complained that the compact "studiously ignores" Alliance reform demands. Most important, the letter communicated Brian's call to action. He was not content to stand by quietly while, in his view, the Democratic Party co-opted the LFU. He called upon all LFU activists disgruntled by the Lafayette Compact, who preferred principle over party and who had the courage to stand firm on Alliance reform principles, to unite behind efforts to develop the fledgling state People's Party organization. His comments were a direct attack on a central tenet of white supremacy, the belief that white political unity was of paramount importance and took precedence over principles of reform.[41]

A bitter dispute emerged between those claiming that the LFU had betrayed Alliance principles and, therefore, did not merit their continued support and those remaining loyal to the LFU. Defectors to the People's Party defended themselves as courageous reformers who were willing to support Alliance principles "in spite of the party lash." They accused LFU loyalists of being traitors to the principles of the Alliance movement. LFU loyalists reversed that accusation, labeling those who defected to the People's Party as traitors. They argued that the LFU had to stand united in order to succeed. In their view, those opposing the Lafayette Compact had presented their arguments at the LFU convention and lost fair and square when a vote was called. At this point, they should have accepted the wishes of the majority and cooperated with the anti-lottery Democrats to ensure the death of the lottery.[42]

LFU loyalists, such as Tetts, defended themselves against the charge that they had abandoned Alliance principles. They argued that the Lafayette Compact bound them to the Democratic Party only in regard to state executive offices—that is, the governor, lieutenant governor, treasurer, secretary of state, and superintendent of education. They were free to lay aside the "Democratic harness" in legislative races and vote for candidates who supported the reforms in the Alliance Ocala Platform. This was, they argued, an acceptable compromise. They reasoned that since most of the Alliance reforms could only be achieved through national legislation, combining with the Democrats on races for state executive offices was not too great of a sacrifice. This reasoning is reflected in the following resolution adopted by the Morehouse Parish LFU: "Whereas the Ocala platform embraces national questions only, therefore be it resolved, that while we favor the Lafayette agreement as regards State politics, we are in favor of the Ocala platform in all national and legislative issues."[43]

LFU defectors, however, argued that the leaders of the anti-lottery faction in the Democratic Party would close ranks after the state election and recombine with the lottery faction. The reunified Democratic Party would then work to defeat any candidate campaigning in the national elections in 1892 on a platform endorsing the Ocala Demands.[44]

There is no question that in securing the Lafayette Compact, reform Democrats had scored a major victory. Not only had they successfully brokered an alliance with the LFU to help them in their fight against the powerful Louisiana Lottery Company, but they had provoked a schism within the LFU that ensured that it would not officially endorse the new third party in the state election campaign of 1892.

The election campaign took an interesting turn as the Democratic Party's nominating convention set for mid-December 1891 neared. When the Central Executive Committee of the Democratic Party convened in New Orleans in mid-October, it discovered that its members were closely divided on the lottery issue. Thirty-nine members were pro-lottery advocates, and thirty-eight members opposed the lottery. Unfortunately for lottery opponents, the chair of the committee supported the lottery and was upset by the deal that the anti-lottery faction had struck with the LFU.[45]

The prediction was that delegates to the upcoming Democratic Party nominating convention would be deeply divided as well. A negative campaign was already underway, with the pro-lottery faction charging lottery opponents with violating the time-honored tradition of party loyalty. The tradition allowed heated competition for the party's nominations, but once those nominations were made all Democrats were expected to lend their support to the ticket. It was deemed disloyal and politically unacceptable to threaten, as the anti-lotteryites had done, to bolt the nominating convention if an anti-lottery plank were not included in the party platform and if a lottery opponent did not head the ticket. Splitting the Democratic Party ticket risked a victory for "Republicans and negro rule."[46]

Members of the anti-lottery faction countercharged that a pro-lottery stance was immoral and tainted from the political and economic bribery of the monopolistic Louisiana Lottery Company. Under no circumstances would they betray their values and support the lottery. They also attacked the favored gubernatorial candidate of lottery supporters, Samuel McEnery, who had governed the state from October 1881 until May 1888 and who, in reference to his apparent servility to the powerful influence of the Louisiana Lottery Company, had been dubbed by his foes as "McLottery." They stressed that rampant fraud and corruption had plagued McEnery's terms as governor. Under his watch, the state treasurer of Louisiana, Edward A. Burke, had been responsible for irregularities in the state treasury reaching almost $1.3 million. Burke was living in self-imposed exile in Honduras to avoid prosecution.[47]

When the state Democratic convention met in December, there was a bitter contest over certification of delegates. Some parishes had two different delegations, one opposing and the other supporting the lottery, with each claiming to be the rightful delegation. An additional source of complaint was the apportionment of delegates to the convention. This was not a minor issue. Since a nomination on the Democratic Party ticket in Louisiana had since the end of

Reconstruction virtually assured the candidate's victory on Election Day, the real political power was exercised at the nominating conventions.

The backland parishes of the Fourth and Fifth Congressional districts had long complained about the overrepresentation of the alluvial parishes in Democratic Party nominating conventions. Representation was determined by a formula based on the parish Democratic vote in the last state election prior to the convention. Since the electorate of alluvial cotton-belt parishes was primarily black, one would expect that these parishes would not fare well in delegate apportionment. The preference of blacks for the Republican Party was well known. However, Democrats had a reputation for "bulldozing" the black vote in the river parishes. They greatly inflated the number of votes cast for Democratic candidates through several tactics: by intimidating blacks to vote for the Democratic ticket (there was not a secret ballot at this time); by keeping blacks away from the polls and then casting their votes *in absentia* for the Democratic ticket; by allowing and even encouraging the practice of "repeating" among Democratic voters; and by casting Democratic votes for no-shows who were kept on the registrar books despite having moved or died. The landslide victories of the Democrats in the alluvial cotton parishes resulted in hefty delegate apportionment to nominating conventions, which ensured that the white planter elite had a strong influence in selecting party nominees and in shaping party platforms.[48]

This apportionment system was in large part responsible for the control that the pro-lottery faction was able to exercise at the 1892 Democratic Party nominating convention. For example, Tensas Parish, an alluvial cotton parish whose voting-age male population was 90 percent black, was allotted twenty-three delegates to the nominating convention. Similarly high delegate allotments were given to Concordia and Madison—twenty-one and eighteen delegates, respectively. These three alluvial parishes alone controlled sixty-two votes at the convention, earned largely by virtue of a manipulated black vote. All of these votes were expected to be cast for McEnery, the pro-lottery gubernatorial candidate.[49]

In anger, the anti-lottery faction bolted to hold its own nominating convention. In a press release critical of the bolters, the pro-lottery faction declared: "The democracy of Louisiana regard fealty to the party and faithful adherence to its organization as above all considerations, and the only means of sustaining and perpetuating white supremacy and good government in Louisiana." In a similar vein, the *New Orleans Daily States* railed against lottery opponents for creating a split in the Democratic Party, claiming it risked "nigger domination" of the state.[50]

The pro-lottery conventioneers nominated McEnery, as anticipated. The gubernatorial nomination process at the anti-lottery convention did not go as smoothly. The leaders of the anti-lottery faction recognized that they would need a well-known, strong candidate if they were to win with a split Democratic ticket in the field. LFU President Adams did not fulfill this requirement. Anti-lottery Democrats worried about "Ocala Adams and his Alliance backers" who supported "the subtreasury bill and other dangerous and cranky theories and semi-socialistic legislation."[51] Therefore, they worked behind the scenes to convince Adams that his candidacy was not viable.

When members of the LFU nominated Adams at the anti-lottery convention, they were "utterly ignorant of the fact that the pliable Adams had yielded to the appeals of his anti-lottery friends, and had consented to be the sacrifice upon their altar, and were shocked beyond the measure of words, when . . . [Adams] arose before them and declined their nomination."[52] Adams's refusal to accept the nomination was met with disbelief and anger by the LFU delegates at the convention. The protest was to no avail. Murphy Foster was nominated and confirmed as the anti-lottery faction's candidate for governor. Adams received, and accepted, the nomination of secretary of state. The editor of the *Opelousas Courier* declared it "a trade pure and simple . . . Farmers deserved better."[53]

Some political observers had astutely predicted the unraveling of the Lafayette Compact when it had become clear in October how close the split was on the Democratic Party's Central Executive Committee between the anti-lottery and pro-lottery factions. At best, lottery opponents would have to compromise with the pro-lottery faction in regard to the gubernatorial nominee. If such a compromise was not forthcoming, members of the anti-lottery faction would have to bolt, and it was highly unlikely that they would be willing to field a gubernatorial candidate connected to such controversial proposals as the subtreasury. They would also need a nominee who was well-connected to individuals with the funds necessary to organize an effective campaign. The editor of the *Opelousas Courier* had declared: "They will never accept Adams. Just watch."[54]

The betrayal of the Lafayette Compact represented the beginning of Adams's demise as a major figure within the LFU. Many farmers were angry with him for making no public statement prior to the convention of his intention to decline the nomination. In their view, the unraveling of the Lafayette Compact had intentionally been kept secret until sufficient time had passed to prevent the LFU from organizing a separate campaign.[55] To some LFU activists, the betrayal represented one more reason to question the possibility of reform through the Democratic Party and was the final nudge needed to prompt their defection to the People's Party.

MOBILIZATION OF A THIRD PARTY IN LOUISIANA

The lottery issue had strengthened the ties between the LFU and the Democratic Party (the anti-lottery faction of the Democratic Party, more specifically) and in doing so had driven from the LFU those activists who were strongly commitment to a full slate of reforms. The defectors chastised those who had joined forces with the Democrats for the upcoming election. They warned that Democratic politicians were only dramatizing "the hideous figure of lottery rule, to intimidate you and prevent you from grasping the hand held out to help you escape from your political dungeon. Must a man be bound hand and foot in Democratic fetters before he can be trusted to vote against the lottery?"[56]

The defectors from the LFU issued a call for a convention on October 3 in Alexandria to establish a state-level organization of the People's Party. The call was signed by nineteen former LFU activists from nine different parishes. The Alexandria convention opened with seventy-eight delegates from seventeen parishes. Almost half of the delegates were from Orleans Parish where T. A. Clayton, the manager of the LFU Commercial Association of Louisiana, had provided funds to spread the word about the newly founded third party. The endorsement of the People's Party by the New Orleans *Issue,* a labor paper, also helped. Of the delegates outside of the Orleans contingent, most came from the parishes in the Fourth Congressional District, the hotbed of LFU activity.[57]

The primary accomplishments of the convention were the establishment of a state People's Party organization and the election of key officers. Former LFU activists were elected to most of the major offices. T. A. Clayton became chair of the state Executive Committee, and Hardy Brian became secretary of the party.[58]

The new officers of the party lost no time in getting out their message. A press release from the convention made clear their intent to appeal to lottery opponents who might be dissuaded from their support of the Democratic and

Republican parties. In their comments directed to Republicans, they stressed that the Republican Party had degenerated into a machine controlled by the money kings: "Concentration of political power, concentration of corporate power, concentration of money power is the creed of Republicanism." To Democrats, they challenged: "Have you not the experience of uninterrupted Democratic rule in this State? What has it done for you? Are your children growing up better equipped in the battle of life than you were?"[59]

While all who had attended the morning session of the convention were white, in the afternoon Superintendent Isaac Keys of the state CFA was admitted to the speaker's platform. Keys' presence lent credibility to the sentiment expressed at the convention about appealing to black voters for support. In their "Address to the People of the State of Louisiana . . . Irrespective of Class, Color, or Past Affiliation," third-party activists had appealed for support from black Republicans:

> You colored men, who in your natural exuberant gratitude to the party that claimed the exclusive merit of freeing your race from the bonds of slavery, furnished the votes that have kept the Republicans in power so many years, and whose continued allegiance they claim on account of what they have done for you, you must feel that you have fully repaid all you owe them by your long . . . political servitude. You must now realize that there is no hope of any further material benefit to you in the Republican party, and that if you remain in it you will be hewers of wood and drawers of water in the future as you have been in the past.[60]

Just as Alliance-affiliated organizations such as the LFU would serve in the South as a bridge between the Democratic Party and the new People's Party, the CFA had the potential to serve as a bridge in the black community between the Republican Party and the People's Party. The national CFA had taken a keen and early interest in the prospects for a new third party. It had sent J. J. Rogers, one of its key officials, to the Cincinnati convention at which the People's Party was founded in 1891. In Louisiana, leaders of the CFA also took an early interest in the third-party movement. In fact, the only Louisiana signatures on the call for the Cincinnati convention in 1891 were blacks who were members of the CFA: J. B. Lafargue, state secretary of the CFA in Louisiana; L. D. Laurent, general superintendent of the Louisiana CFA; and I. Miller, an activist in the Louisiana CFA.[61]

In their efforts to court black voters, Louisiana Populist leaders did not likely encounter significant resistance based on black support for the anti-lottery campaign. Generally speaking, the black community was accepting of the lottery. All four black senators in the state legislature supported the lottery, as did the entire black delegation in the House.[62] The daunting challenge they faced in courting the black vote came from a different source: While CFA leaders were friendly to the idea of a third-party movement, the CFA as an organization had not been very successful in mobilizing blacks throughout the state. Therefore, it would not serve as an adequate base from which to mobilize black voters and gain their political loyalty. State Populist leaders would be, to a large extent, starting from scratch in their efforts to create networks through which to gain the political support of blacks.

Populist leaders warned those white voters who were wary of efforts to court the black vote that the "spectre of negro supremacy has been used to keep you in the toils of the scheming machine politicians."[63] The appeal of third-party leaders to both black and white voters, and their attack on the white supremacy rhetoric of the Democratic Party, caused the editor of the *Daily Picayune* to declare: "IT MAY BE RIDICULOUS, BUT IT IS REVOLUTION."[64] Intensifying the concern of many Democrats were the actions accompanying the rhetoric of third-party activists. For example, both blacks and whites were invited to a huge barbecue hosted by third-party leaders in Grant Parish. Approximately 750 people attended, about one-third of whom were black.[65]

The third party movement got a boost from the national Alliance reform convention that finally convened in St. Louis in February 1892. Alliance leaders had organized this convention as an alternative to the Cincinnati reform convention of May 1891, which they regarded as premature in that it did not allow sufficient time to test reform efforts through the Democratic Party. Eight different organizations were included in the St. Louis convention call, with the Alliance and CFA the largest of those organizations. Together these two organizations were originally allotted almost one-half of the convention delegates. However, many more organizations sent delegates to the convention than had been included in the original call. Eventually about eight hundred delegates, representing twenty-two different reform organizations, were granted official seats by the Credentials Committee.[66]

L. L. Polk, Alliance president and a third-party supporter, was elected as chair of the St. Louis convention. Third-party advocates appeared to be in a majority at the convention, as suggested by the fact that convention delegates voted to grant the official seats of the Georgia Alliance to its third-party faction rather than its anti-third party faction. There was a significant and vocal contingent, however, opposed to an explicit third-party declaration. To avoid divisiveness, convention leaders waived a formal vote on a third-party resolution. But by prearrangement, when the convention formally adjourned, third-party supporters remained in their seats and proceeded to elect a committee of fifteen to confer with the Executive Committee of the People's Party in regard to calling a nominating convention for the upcoming 1892 presidential campaign.[67]

The state nominating convention of the People's Party in Louisiana met in Alexandria on the heels of the St. Louis convention. The party again made a strong appeal to black voters. Its adopted platform stated: "We declare emphatically that the interests of the white and colored races of the South are identical. . . . Equal justice and fairness must be accorded to each."[68] It is also noteworthy that about 15 percent of the delegates present—24 of the 171 delegates—were black. Two of the black delegates, L. D. Laurent and Charles Roxborough, became members of the state Executive Committee of the People's Party. Laurent was a leader in the CFA, while Roxborough had recently resigned from the Republican Party in frustration over the racism of its leaders.[69]

Given that the culture of rural whites in the South, and certainly in Louisiana, insisted on rigid racial segregation, the declaration about biracial economic interests, the presence of black delegates at the nominating convention, and the appointment of blacks to the party's state Executive Committee are rather remarkable. Louisiana Populism, at least in its early years, was making a serious effort to break down racial barriers in hopes of creating a powerful biracial voting bloc. It was willing to go beyond the efforts of the Alliance movement, which had periodically declared the common economic interests of white and black farmers while insisting that black farmers remain segregated within the parallel CFA organization.

LOUISIANA POPULISTS AND THE STATE ELECTION OF 1892

For its gubernatorial candidate, the Louisiana People's Party chose Robert Tannehill. He was a resident of Winn Parish and had presided over the LFU in that parish, which was one of the strongest and most vocal in the state. Not only was it one of only two parish LFU organizations to send a delegate to the

Cincinnati convention in 1891, it was one of the first to give its allegiance to the third party. Tannehill had also been very active in the state LFU organization, serving as its treasurer in 1889. In 1891 he had been one of the "famous twenty-two" dissenters that had refused to approve the Lafayette Compact.[70]

Tannehill, however, was almost completely unknown outside LFU circles. His obscurity made his chances for victory remote, particularly given the lack of adequate campaign funding. Hope for a decent electoral showing rested primarily on the bitter splits that had occurred between the pro-lottery and anti-lottery factions of both the Republican and Democratic parties during the election campaign. These splits had resulted in two Democratic tickets and two Republican tickets, with nasty barbs exchanged between supporters of these different tickets. For example, the editor of the *New Orleans Daily States,* a McEnery supporter, fretted that anti-lottery Democrats would use their control over the election machinery to "count out" McEnery. He warned that "to count out a 'nigger majority' in defence (sic) of the civilization of the State, and to attempt to count out a majority of the white voters and Democrats in the interest of a gang of political pap-seekers, are two entirely different things."[71]

Ironically, given all the uproar over the lottery issue, this issue was removed in the final month of the election campaign. The federal government passed a law banning the use of the U.S Postal Service to transact lottery-related business. Without mail service, the company could not profitably function. Much of its profits came from out-of-state sales of lottery tickets that were transacted via the postal system. The U.S. Supreme Court upheld the constitutionality of the ban in February 1892. In response, the Louisiana Lottery Company retracted its offer of $1.25 million annually to the state's coffers and withdrew its bid for recharter.[72]

Now that the lottery issue was moot, the Executive Committees of the two Democratic factions met to resolve the split in the state Democratic Party ticket. Since the end of Reconstruction, Democrats had always fielded a united ticket out of fear that a split ticket could lead to a Republican victory. A decision was made to conduct a whites-only Democratic primary on March 22 to determine the relative strength of the McEnery and Foster factions. Whoever won the majority of votes in the primary would be the nominee of the party. The Executive Committees also stipulated that, if agreed upon by a majority of voters in the white primary, the basis of representation at future nominating conventions up to and including the next state nominating convention would be the total vote cast for both Democratic nominees in the primary.[73] This stipulation, had it been implemented, would have represented a major victory for the population of the backland parishes. Planters had always dominated nominating conventions of the Democratic Party by virtue of the large Democratic vote they were able to orchestrate through the manipulated black vote in the black-belt parishes. Delegate allotment based on votes cast in a white primary promised to tilt the balance of power significantly.

Events, however, did not unfold as planned. Returns of the primary were so close, there was a five-day delay in reporting the final count. McEnery had a slim majority after the initial count, having polled well in Orleans Parish and in the alluvial parishes. But Foster and his supporters contested the results, especially in some of the wards of Orleans Parish. To resolve the electoral dispute, a Committee of Seven was created. It was composed of three members from each faction, and a neutral member elected by those six. This committee declared Foster the victor by 549 votes. Supporters of McEnery cried foul and refused to abide by the decision. Importantly, they also refused to accept the decision to base delegate apportionment to nominating conventions on the total vote cast in white primaries rather than in the general election.[74]

On Election Day for the first time since Reconstruction, there were two Democratic tickets in the field. The schism in the Democratic Party improved the political opportunity for the nascent third-party movement in the state. With the state Democratic Party vote split into two rival factions, the Populists faced a divided foe. However, their gubernatorial candidate, Robert Tannehill, still came in last in the five-man race, receiving 9,792 votes, or 6 percent of the total vote. The editor of the *Colfax Chronicle,* a loyal Democrat, declared that it was "just exactly what every body expected who had a mind two inches long and was not blinded by prejudice, and did not have a little private hatchet to grind."[75]

Tannehill ran ahead of his Democratic and Republican opponents in only four parishes, predictably strong LFU parishes: Catahoula, Grant, Vernon, and Winn. In those parishes, the majority of smallholding white farmers deserted the Democratic Party and formed the bedrock of Populist support. For example, in Grant Parish, Tannehill received 81 percent of the vote cast in the hill precincts where small white farm owners resided.[76]

In regard to the other candidates for governor, the two Republican candidates polled about 42,000 votes combined. The Democratic Party's combined vote of 126,425 dwarfed that of its opponents. As to the electoral performance of its two candidates, Foster received 79,388 votes to McEnery's 47,037. McEnery only won in twelve parishes.[77] McEnery supporters angrily declared that Foster and his supporters had stolen the election: "No one who glances over the figures of some of the parishes can doubt for a second that the boxes were stuffed and stuffed recklessly and monstrously." The editor of a major urban newspaper declared: "Let us hope, for the credit of the State, that no more votes have been counted in the boxes than there are actual voters in their respective parishes."[78]

As for the state legislative elections, the Populists were successful in electing only four candidates to the state legislature. All but one of these candidates had come into the People's Party via the LFU. Benjamin F. Brian, an LFU leader in Grant Parish, was elected to the state Senate by a large margin and would hold his office until his death in 1896. His son, Hardy Brian, who had represented the Winn Parish LFU at the Cincinnati convention and edited a third-party paper, the Winn Parish *Comrade*, was elected to the House. The other two candidates elected to the House on the third-party ticket were John Franklin, an LFU activist in Vernon Parish, and Albert Shelby of Grant Parish who had recently left the Republican Party.[79]

The third-party legislators quickly formed an agrarian coalition with LFU Democrats in the state legislature. But the agrarian coalition was seriously hampered in its attempts to obtain reforms by its small size. It consisted of only four senators out of thirty-six in the state Senate, and twenty-two of the one hundred members in the House.[80] The coalition was also hampered by the fact that most Democrats were hostile to the major reforms advocated by the LFU and the People's Party.

One might argue that Tannehill's poor showing was primarily the result of his having to compete against a reform Democratic ticket. That is, voters may have simply decided to vote for the lesser evil among the candidates most likely to win. Viewing a Populist victory as extremely unlikely, reform-minded voters may well have viewed Foster as the lesser evil among the remaining candidates and may have feared that a vote for Tannehill risked the victory of McEnery.

While there is likely some truth to this argument, it is certainly not the only explanation. This is made clear by contrasting Tannehill's electoral performance with that of the third-party candidate for governor in the neighboring state of Texas, Thomas Nugent. Nugent garnered almost 25 percent of the vote, despite the fact that—like Louisiana Democrats—Texas Democrats had fielded a split ticket. Incumbent Governor James Hogg headed the reform ticket, while G. Clarke was the candidate of the conservative faction. In his first administration, Hogg had fulfilled a campaign promise and established a railroad commission to regulate intrastate freight charges. While the Alliance had not been pleased with the appointive feature of the commission, having campaigned for elected commission members, the commission still represented a significant reform. Since its establishment, it had reduced freight charges by more than $1 million. Clark had opposed the commission and labored hard to defeat the bill establishing it. There was concern that if Clarke were elected, he might dismantle the commission or undermine its effectiveness. The Hogg faction of the Democratic Party had played upon this concern, arguing that a vote for Nugent would split the reform vote and risk a victory for Clarke. Despite this looming threat, Nugent managed to attract the support of one out of four voters.[81]

Tannehill's poor performance in the gubernatorial election, therefore, demands further explication. One additional factor that played a role in his poor showing was the dearth of support in Orleans Parish, where he received only 71 of the almost 38,000 votes cast.[82] Many of the early advocates of the third party within the state had been small farmers who had been active in the LFU. The LFU had offered little in its platform, rhetoric, or strategies that appealed to the urban population. Its heavy focus on the decline in cotton prices did not appeal to the personal economic interests of urban residents who might have perceived themselves as beneficiaries of low cotton prices in the form of cheaper textiles and clothing. Therefore, the LFU was not an effective base from which to mobilize third-party support in the urban setting of Orleans Parish.

Another factor that played a major role in undercutting the third-party movement in Louisiana was its lack of success in appealing to black voters in the backland parishes. This held true even in parishes where the CFA had a significant presence, such as in Grant and St. Landry parishes. In Grant Parish, Tannehill received only 6 percent of the vote in the three black majority voting precincts. He did not receive a single vote in the Fairmount precinct of Ward One, which was regarded as the "negro stronghold" in the parish. Most blacks in the parish had stayed loyal to the Republican Party.[83] In St. Landry Parish, where blacks represented 53 percent of the voters, he received only 183 votes in contrast to the 3641 votes garnered by the Republican gubernatorial candidates. After the election, local papers gleefully commented on the poor showing of the third party in the black precincts of the parish. Thus, despite its call for biracial political cooperation, the Louisiana People's Party had minimal success in appealing to black voters for their support.[84]

Another significant factor undermining the third-party movement in Louisiana was the pivotal role of race in influencing the voting behavior of whites in Louisiana. Louisiana was one of only three states in the country where blacks were in the majority. This posed a political dilemma: a divided white vote risked giving political control to blacks and their leaders. This fear was frequently voiced in the leading newspapers of the state. Election returns suggest that this fear had a notable effect on voting behavior. Even in parishes where the LFU was well established, the Populists did poorly if blacks were a majority of the parish population. For example, despite the LFU and CFA being firmly established in St. Landry Parish, Tannehill polled only 282 votes out of the almost 2,500 votes cast in that parish.[85] The third party had not been able to overcome the fear of the consequences of a divided white vote in parishes with a sizeable black population. This bode poorly for the prospects of the third party being able to surmount the white supremacy frame passionately advanced by the Democratic Party.

A final factor in the poor showing of the third party was the dismal performance of Tannehill in the plantation parishes, as indicated in Table 5. He received less than 5 percent of the vote in all but one of the cotton plantation parishes. He polled only ninety total votes in the four parishes of Concordia, East Carroll, Madison, and Tensas. He fared equally poorly in the major sugar-producing black-belt parishes. In four major sugar parishes, he garnered less than 1 percent of the total vote. In the other eight major sugar plantation parishes—Ascension, Assumption, Iberville, LaFourche, St. John the Baptist, St. Mary, Terrebonne, and West Baton Rouge—he did not get a single vote.[86]

Tannehill's poor showing in the plantation parishes reflected the fact that the third-party movement in Louisiana was, to a large extent, an extension of the LFU and CFA.[87] While the strong presence of the LFU and CFA did not guarantee the Populists a following, the complete absence or weakness of the LFU or CFA was strongly associated with a failed mobilization effort on the part of the third-party movement. Unfortunately, the LFU and CFA had never successfully mobilized in the plantation parishes. The lack of an organizational base upon which to build in these parishes created a serious hurdle for the third-party movement in Louisiana and is worthy of close attention.

TABLE 5

Election Results in the Major Sugar and Cotton Plantation Parishes of Louisiana, 1892 Gubernatorial Race

SUGAR-PRODUCING PARISHES*	% DEMOCRAT	% REPUBLICAN	% POPULIST
Ascension	73	27	0.15
Assumption	53	47	—
Baton Rouge, W.	43	56	1
Iberia	82	18	—
Iberville	64	36	0.25
Lafourche	71	29	—
Plaquemines	54	46	—
St. Charles	23	77	—
St. James	46	54	—
St. John the Baptist	41	59	—
St. Mary	87	13	.09
Terrebonne	86	14	—

MAJOR BLACK-BELT, COTTON PLANTATION PARISHES**	%DEMOCRAT	% REPUBLICAN	% POPULIST
Bossier	95	5	0.2
Caddo	90	7	3
Concordia	83	14	4
East Carroll	22	78	—
East Feliciana	95	0.2	4
Madison	92	7	0.2
Morehouse	96	3	0.1
Ouachita	98	0.7	0.7
Rapides	62	27	11.5
Point Coupee	40	60	0.2
Tensas	21	79	—
West Feliciana	93	7	0.1

Source: Report of the Secretary of State, 562.

*Defined as parishes with at least five thousand acres planted in sugarcane.

**Defined by three characteristics: slave population in 1860 was > 60% total population; > 60 percent black population in 1890; > 20,000 bales of cotton produced in 1890.

The large landowners in the black-belt, cotton parishes were not typically attracted to the LFU. They profited from the crop-lien loans that they extended to their tenants. The attacks by the LFU on the crop-lien financing system and its later advocacy of the subtreasury proposal, largely an effort to supplant that system, threatened their economic interests.

As for the CFA, it had limited appeal to the black tenant farmers who were prevalent in the alluvial cotton parishes. Participation in the early Alliance strategies, which focused heavily on cooperative stores and cotton withholding and bulking, required an economic autonomy that these black tenant farmers did not have. Consequently, the strategies proposed by the CFA were irrelevant to their economic lives. Furthermore, the lack of economic autonomy on the part of black tenant cotton farmers often translated into reduced political autonomy. Cotton planters, the vast majority of whom were Democrats, were very uneasy with the notion of black political influence. They were steeped in the white supremacy culture that dictated that whites alone should make all the important political decisions. They were particularly vigilant about black political influence in parishes where blacks comprised the vast majority of eligible voters. Importantly, the planters had the power to distort the electoral process so that they could remain politically dominant. They could demand that their black tenants stay home on Election Day. Or, given the absence of the secret ballot, they could demand that their black tenants vote for the Democratic Party. Among the economic consequences that they could impose should their tenants not abide by their demands were a refusal to provide future crop-lien financing and employment blacklists.[88] So even if black tenant cotton farmers had been attracted to the third-party movement, the powerful white planter elite would have likely exercised its economic clout to prevent a strong third-party showing.

Neither had the LFU or CFA had much success in recruiting members in the black-belt sugar parishes. The framing of the farm crisis by these organizations held little attraction to sugar plantation owners. The cooperative store strategy was largely irrelevant to them, if not threatening since they profited from the high pricing practices in plantation stores that serviced their laborers. Neither were they attracted by a discussion of alternatives to crop-lien financing. They already had access to credit lines with reasonable interest rates, collateralized by their extensive land and sugar-processing equipment. Furthermore, the anti-tariff stance of the LFU was a threat. The Louisiana sugar industry was profitable only because of federal government subsidies provided by tariff legislation. The fall in the price of sugar from $0.06 per pound in 1889 to $0.03 by 1894 was cushioned by a $0.02 per pound bounty provided by existing tariff law. Any revision of those laws threatened their subsidies.[89]

As for laborers on the sugar plantations, their economic interests lay primarily in their demand for higher wages, paid in cash rather than scrip to be used solely at plantation stores. The leaders of the LFU and CFA had paid little attention to these issues. Furthermore, a competing social movement organization, the Knights of Labor, had mobilized workers on the sugar plantations and was more attuned to their economic needs.

Also problematic was the natural antagonism or conflict of interest between agricultural laborers and the small farmer constituency of the Alliance. The LFU focused on the economic needs of small farmers who were struggling for economic survival amid the steady deterioration in crop prices. The last thing small farmers needed were demands for higher pay by farm laborers whose help might be needed at harvest time. The conflict of interest between agricultural laborers and farm owners was reflected in the silence of the LFU when a strike by Louisiana sugar workers in 1887, organized by the Knights of Labor, was violently suppressed.[90]

As for politics, the situation in the sugar parishes was complex. Black political power in these parishes, exercised primarily through the Republican Party, had continued to be important after the end of Reconstruction. The sugar plantation's centralized production process afforded black sugar workers an opportunity to mobilize collectively to protect their political rights. In regard to sugar and politics in Louisiana during and after Reconstruction, John Rodrigue argues that blacks who abandoned the Republican Party faced ostracism within the black community. He also contends that the precarious nature of sugar production protected black workers to a certain extent from political intimidation by sugar planters. Planters worried that intimidation of their workers might jeopardize keeping them, and competition for laborers was intense. They also fretted about work stoppages or slowdowns in retaliation for political intimidation. A few days' neglect could devastate a sugar crop if it occurred at the right moment, such as during rolling season.[91] Therefore, throughout the 1880s and early 1890s, blacks exercised their voting rights more freely in the sugar plantation parishes than in the cotton plantation parishes. Unfortunately, this did little to help the third-party movement. The absence of the CFA in the sugar parishes meant that there was no pre-existing organizational structure on which to build a third-party movement. An organizational base would need to be built anew, a daunting task given the paltry funds in the third party's treasury.

In sum, leaders of the third party had a lot of work to do if their party were to become a more important political player. They were sensitive to the argument that no one "except cranks, office-seekers and disgruntled politicians would dare sever their political relations with their old parties."[92] With the lottery issue resolved and state elections behind them, they resolved to build a stronger third-party movement. However, they faced an almost insurmountable challenge. There was no strong foundation on which to build in populous Orleans Parish or in the plantation parishes. Since 60 percent of the state's population resided in these parishes,[93] the political viability of a third party hinged on garnering more support in these parishes. Unfortunately, prospects for garnering this support were bleak.

7

Third-party Framing Shifts, 1892–1894

WITH THE STATE ELECTION CAMPAIGNS of 1892 behind them and the congressional and presidential election campaigns of 1892 approaching, LFU leaders were pressured to take a clear political stand, as were leaders of the national Alliance movement. Their response was to avoid the quagmire of partisan politics by insisting that while devotion to Alliance reform principles was of paramount importance, the Alliance would leave to the individual conscience of its members the decision as to how best to achieve those demands. This approach avoided the difficult decision of whether to officially endorse the People's Party and risk the full wrath of the Democratic Party.

However, after the Democratic Party adopted conservative party platforms and fielded conservative candidates in the national elections of 1892, the individual-conscience approach became highly problematic. It was one thing to support a candidate posing as a reform Democrat. It was quite a different matter to support candidates whose political positions were blatantly conservative and in clear opposition to Alliance reform demands. This chapter focuses on the tensions between Democratic loyalists and third-party advocates within the LFU and Alliance movement in general, which played a major role in the demobilization of the Alliance as a social movement organization.

After the Democratic Party had shown that it would not bow to the pressures of reform advocates, the leaders of the third-party movement in Louisiana hoped to garner more support. But in order to do so, they had to weaken the powerful white supremacy frame of the Democratic Party, especially its insistence on white political unity. They had to convince white voters that unity under the banner of the Democratic Party would perpetuate not only the political status quo, but the economic status quo as well. This chapter focuses on their efforts to weaken loyalty to the Democratic Party by emphasizing that the agricultural depression had worsened under the financial principles advanced by both of the old parties.

Populist leaders, however, had underestimated the tenacity with which most white Louisianans would cling to the Democratic Party. White political disunity was effectively portrayed by Democratic politicians as a serious threat to the existing benefits that flowed from whites monopolizing office-holding and decision-making positions of power. Pragmatic politics finally won out. One month before Election Day in November 1892, they brokered a fusion arrangement with the state Republican Party. This chapter explores the logic of pragmatic politics, as well as the reasons why it did not result in greater electoral success.

The poor showing of the People's Party in the national elections of 1892 elicited a major strategic framing shift. In a stark turnabout from its earlier efforts to court the black vote, and motivated by the cold logic of politics, Louisiana Populist leaders such as Hardy Brian began to embrace some of the key tenets of white supremacy in a desperate attempt to garner more support from white voters. The only component of the white supremacy frame that they persistently attacked was the one concerning white political unity. The other belief components—that whites were the superior race, that major political offices should be filled exclusively by whites, and that only whites should have voting rights—were at times embraced, at other times avoided as topics of conversation, but rarely publicly criticized. It was a pragmatic "if you can't beat them, join them" response that the leaders hoped would lead to greater success at the polls.

Let us now turn to a more detailed discussion of these important developments within the Populist movement.

REFORM PRINCIPLES AND THE BIRMINGHAM CONVENTION

As the national election campaigns of 1892 neared, the Executive Committee of the national Alliance sent out a circular calling for the presidents of each state Alliance organization to meet in Birmingham on May 3. The circular warned that the Alliance was facing a critical period in its history: "Never has there been such a universal and loud cry from the order to the officers for directions in how to conduct the local fight. Never has there been so little concert of action among the officers of different states and sections. This, if allowed to continue, must be fatal."[1]

The majority of attendees at the Birmingham conference reportedly favored the third-party movement. The chair of the national Executive Committee of the Alliance, C. W. Macune, however, once again successfully suppressed any decisive statement in favor of that movement. Instead, a call for harmony was released to the press: "Let none condemn a brother who stands squarely by the principles of the order, or speak in any way despairingly of him because they may differ as to the best methods of enforcing our principles . . . and let those who value their partisan affiliation more than their Alliance obligations be informed that the order demands strict and full devotion to its principles and leaves each to his own choice as to methods."[2]

Therefore, as the nominating conventions for the presidential election campaign of 1892 approached, the Alliance as an organization remained politically neutral. Each Alliance member was left to decide for himself the best method of securing Alliance principles.

Southern Democrats were relieved about the indecision at the Birmingham Alliance conference. They were well aware, however, that Grover Cleveland, who was favored to receive the Democratic presidential nomination, was unpopular with most farmers. He had run, and lost, the presidential election of 1888 after campaigning largely on a single issue: tariff reform. Many farmers worried that if he won the Democratic Party nomination, he would again focus on the tariff issue. Farmers had tired of the tariff debate, which in their view deflected attention from the ills responsible for declining crop prices.[3] The editor of the *St. Landry Clarion,* an LFU paper, spoke disparagingly of "the herculean efforts of the two old parties" to make the tariff the central issue of the 1892 presidential campaign. In his LFU column, J. A. Tetts declared that the farmers did not wish to send more politicians to Washington to discuss endlessly the issue of tariff reform. They wanted legislation that would "relieve us from the . . . unlawful combinations that oppress us, and from opportunities granted money to rob the producer of wealth."[4]

Members of the LFU were also upset with Cleveland's "sound money," conservative stand in regard to the nation's monetary system. He was aligned with the gold-standard Democrats who insisted that the stability of the nation's economy depended on the continued reliance on a gold standard. In contrast, the Alliance and the People's Party vehemently opposed the gold standard. They pushed for monetary reforms based on both the notions of bimetallism and fiatism.[5]

Bimetallism called for a national monetary supply based on both gold and silver. Free silver had been included among the Alliance reform demands since 1886 and had been incorporated as one of the major planks of the People's

Party platform. Basing the monetary supply on both gold and silver reserves, it was believed, would ease the contracted money supply and help address the ills created by the insufficient currency in circulation. Fiatism entailed the principle that the amount of money in circulation should not be dictated by the availability of precious metals, but rather should be based on the business needs of the country. Paper currency should circulate in quantities sufficient for a healthy economy. A contracted money supply, due to the inadequacy of gold and/or silver reserves, drove credit rates up and strangled the debtor class.

The espousal of both free silver and fiatism emanated from the desire of the Alliance to appeal to any and all dissenters who were demanding an increase in the nation's currency supply. A bigger contingent of people demanding change would have a better chance of success. Alliance leaders such as Macune, however, argued that significant economic relief demanded a more dramatic expansion of the currency in circulation than would be possible under bimetallism. Therefore, a shift to a fiat money supply such as that entailed in the subtreasury proposal would ultimately be required.[6]

Since its Ocala convention in December 1890, the Alliance had waged an educational campaign on the necessity of reforming the monetary system. Alliance leaders who remained loyal to the Democratic Party now warned that if the Democrats nominated a fiscal conservative, gold standard advocate such as Cleveland for the presidency, the People's Party would be the beneficiary of that decision. The president of the national Alliance organization in 1892, L. Polk, echoed this warning: "Don't be mistaken the alliancemen will fall into line simply because they are democrats."[7]

NOMINATING CONVENTIONS AND CAMPAIGN STRATEGIES, 1892

Despite the threat of losing the support of Alliance members, delegates to the national Democratic Party nominating convention chose Cleveland as the party's presidential candidate. Predictably, his acceptance speech focused on the need for tariff reform and "sound money." To appeal to southerners, he also stressed his opposition to federal control over the election process.[8]

At their nominating convention, the Republicans selected incumbent President Benjamin Harrison as their candidate. They also endorsed the gold standard in their platform. In opposition to the Democrats, however, they supported the notion of federal control over national elections to ensure the integrity of those elections.[9]

Political observers followed with interest the actions of delegates to the first national nominating convention of the People's Party, which opened in Omaha on July 2. The platform that had been adopted at the party's founding convention in Cincinnati—one identical to past platforms of the Alliance—was formally presented to the delegates for a vote. The platform included both a free-silver plank and a fiatist demand for an expanded, flexible currency through the subtreasury or similar plan. It received unanimous support. For their presidential candidate, the delegates chose James Weaver, who had served as a general in the Union Army and had long advocated the need for monetary reform. In an effort to balance the ticket, the vice president nomination went to James Field, who had been a Confederate general in the Civil War.[10]

The conservative national platforms and nominees of the Democratic and Republican parties amplified the significance of decisions at the People's Party convention. The conservative factions of the old parties had controlled their respective conventions, with the result that the choice was clear. A vote for the Democratic or Republican presidential candidate was a vote for the economic status quo. Farmers could not hope for major financial reforms under either Cleveland or Harrison. The 1892 presidential election would serve as a test of the degree of commitment among small farmers to the financial reform demands of the Alliance movement.

Equally conservative were the outcomes in district nominating conventions of the Louisiana Democratic Party. For example, at the Fourth Congressional District Democratic Party nominating convention, Blanchard was selected as the congressional candidate for a fifth consecutive term. This decision represented a clear disregard of the farming element of the party in an area of the state where the small farmers' revolt was strongest. Blanchard's nomination in the 1890 congressional elections had precipitated a revolt because of his strong opposition to the subtreasury. Many farmers had shown their strong disapproval of the nomination by staying away from the polls. Despite the unpopularity of Blanchard with small farmers, Fourth District Democrats had again nominated him to represent the district in Congress.[11]

Fourth District Populists chose T. J Guice to run against Blanchard in the 1892 congressional election. Guice had led the efforts of third-party advocates to take control of the state LFU at its annual convention in August 1892 with considerable success: third-party advocates won four of the six elected state positions.[12]

In sum, the Democratic and Republican parties refused to bow to the pressures from the small farmers' movement. In Louisiana, politicians from the old parties refused to endorse Alliance reform demands and nominated candidates for office who were known to be unpopular with most LFU members. The question loomed: How would southern farmers sympathetic to Alliance reform demands respond to the intransigence of the old parties? What strategies would the Democratic Party use in the South to deflect the call for financial reform?

In the election campaigns, the primary tactics used by Louisiana Democrats to undermine support for the third party were appeals to party loyalty and sectionalism, criticisms of the third-party platform, and character assassination of third-party candidates. The major newspapers in the state, which strongly favored the Democratic Party, used all of these tactics. Nowhere were the attacks more frequent than in the Fourth Congressional District, where the LFU and the third party received their strongest support. The editor of the *Colfax Chronicle,* a major weekly newspaper in the district, declared that the principles entailed in the third party's platform were similar to those of the Democratic Party, except for those that were "impractical." He also appealed to sectionalism and the antipathy of most white voters to the Republican Party by warning that votes for the Populist ticket would divide the white vote and risk losing Louisiana's Electoral College votes to the Republican Party. He recognized that farmers wanted change, but argued that "change from thirty years of Republican corruption, force, and misrule to Democratic economy and tariff revision" was more than sufficient. He defended Cleveland's previous administration, 1884–1888, by claiming that it had been hampered by a Republican-dominated Congress. It was also unreasonable, he argued, to expect Cleveland to correct in one term all the evils that had resulted from a generation of misrule by Republicans.[13]

In regard to the Fourth District congressional nominees of the People's Party, the editor of the *Colfax Chronicle* repeatedly referred to T. J. Guice with negative epithets, the most common being "Greasy" Guice. He also declared that the "demagogues who seek to rise to the top as leaders in the People's Party are as veritable scum as the political pot ever bubbled to the surface."[14] His disparaging remarks are all the more important because he had been very active in the LFU during the years in which it had focused on cooperative, self-help strategies. His virulent criticisms serve as a reminder that not all LFU activists had been persuaded of the wisdom of the shift to third-party politics.

The editors of other newspapers in the state also filled their political columns with criticisms of Populist candidates and doctrine, often resorting to bloody-shirt rhetoric. The editor of the *St. Landry Clarion*, for example, vilified the third-party presidential candidate, James Weaver, who in his view was appropriately assaulted with rotten eggs while campaigning in Georgia. He argued that Weaver, a Union general in the Civil War, had no business in the South. When Weaver visited Louisiana during the campaign, the *Baton Rouge Advocate* remarked that he should "thank his stars" that he was allowed to leave Louisiana in one piece.[15]

Populist leaders understood that the viability of the People's Party depended on their convincing white voters that a united white vote under the Democratic banner doomed the cause of reform. If white voters sympathetic to Populist reform demands persisted in their attempts to seek reform from within the Democratic Party, the Populist movement was doomed. Without a viable threat of large-scale defection to the People's Party, politicians in the mainstream parties had little incentive to implement reform.

Consequently, Populist leaders made a concerted effort in their campaign to convince voters that bloody-shirt politics would perpetuate the economic status quo. They argued that loyalty to the old parties had allowed the financial ills besetting farmers to persist: "The South and West must come together politically. . . . There must be some common ground on which . . . Democrats and Republicans can gather and dictate terms to the arrogant East. This can never be done so long as people cling to old party names." As for those intent on seeking reform inside old party lines, Populist leaders countered that it was "as void of sense and sound politics as the talk of one army trying to achieve victory over another by dictating to the generals of the opposing forces when and where the lines of battle must be drawn."[16]

The strategic frame of third-party leaders in Louisiana was clear: if farmers wanted major economic reform, they had to shift their political loyalties away from the old parties. As to the leaders of the old parties, Populist leaders argued that it made no difference whether those leaders were "incapable of perceiving and applying the proper remedies; or whether they have entered into combinations with the plutocracy—for a share of the spoils—to enslave the people."[17] The important fact was that neither of the old parties had adequately addressed the agricultural crisis that was jeopardizing the economic viability of a growing number of small farmers.

Commenting on the Democratic Party specifically, the Populists charged that it had of late been "making 'platforms' for the proletariat to grow poor on, and laws for the plutocrats to live and grow rich upon." As for die-hard Democrats, the third-party leader attempted to persuade them that the "truly grand, old historic, Heaven commissioned party" could only be purified by working outside its ranks.[18] As long as farmers stayed loyal to the Democratic Party on Election Day regardless of its platforms and voting record on financial reform, calls for reform would be ignored.

The Populist movement, however, needed more than supportive articles in Populist newspapers. To a large extent, this was the equivalent of "preaching to the choir." Furthermore, there were relatively few Populist newspapers in Louisiana to help disseminate the third-party message. The limited circulation of Populist newspapers was dwarfed by the circulation of the major daily and weekly mainstream newspapers, most of which were strongly supportive of the Democratic Party and harshly critical of the third party movement. The *Baton Rouge Daily Advocate,* for example, appealed "to the patriots of Louisiana to shun this monstrous political gangrene as they would a leper at the gates." In a similar vein, the *New Orleans Daily States* labeled the third party as the "miserable excrescence of the Democratic and Republican parties."[19]

Any social movement that is harshly and almost universally criticized by the mainstream media faces an uphill battle in recruiting supporters and maintaining their support. This was certainly true of the Louisiana Populist movement. Building a third-party movement necessitated an extensive grassroots campaign that stressed the importance of Populist reform demands and the problems created by continued loyalty to the Democratic Party. Grossly inadequate funding, however, prohibited such a campaign. Officials at the state headquarters of the People's Party in New Orleans frequently were unable to mail out literature because they could not afford postage. This lack of funding also created other organizational challenges for the third party. In congressional districts where the party was struggling to establish itself, nominating conventions were occasionally cancelled due to insufficient funds. The expenses of traveling, which neither the party nor its leaders could easily afford, also hampered efforts to coordinate a statewide campaign. The chair of the party's state Executive Committee, first T. A. Clayton and later Andrew Booth, lived in New Orleans whereas the state secretary of the party, Hardy Brian, lived in Grant Parish. The cost of traveling kept their strategy planning meetings to a bare minimum.[20]

Given inadequate campaign funds, Populists struggled to reach voters with their message. Their battle for the political loyalty of voters was complicated by the intense concern among southern whites of the political consequences of a divided white vote. A core tenet of the white supremacy frame of the Democratic Party, that white political unity was essential to preventing the Africanization of the state, had amazingly powerful resonance with white voters. It is hard to overstate the emotion associated with the passionate pleas of Democrats for white political unity. White political disunity was perceived by many whites as a serious threat to the southern way of life and to the monopoly that whites held, and wanted to preserve, in regard to political office-holding and decision making in a black-majority state.

Having underestimated the tenacity with which whites would cling to the Democratic Party and its white political unity frame, and given their limited success in weaning black voters from the Republican Party, Populist leaders in Louisiana struggled to determine the best course of action. It was a strategic framing dilemma on which the viability of the third-party movement hinged. Realism finally won out over idealism. Recognizing the stark reality of the unfavorable political opportunity that the third party faced, Populist leaders negotiated a deal with leaders of the state Republican Party. One month before the November election, they finalized arrangements whereby the Populists would field candidates in the Fourth, Fifth, and Sixth Congressional districts, and the Republican Party would help campaign for those candidates. Republicans would field candidates in the Second and Third Congressional districts, and Populists would lend their support to these candidates. In the First District, an independent candidate agreeable to both Populists and Republicans would be fielded. In regard to the presidential ticket, there would be a fused Weaver-Harrison ticket. If the fusion ticket were successful, the electoral vote of Louisiana would be split evenly between Weaver and Harrison.[21]

The fusion deal drew strong criticism from the rural press. The editor of the *Colfax Chronicle* reminded readers that Guice, one of the Populist leaders who had helped arrange the fusion deal with Republicans, had been among those who had strongly opposed the Lafayette Compact in 1892. While unwilling to ally himself with the Democratic Party, as the Lafayette Compact required, he had now negotiated fusion with the Republican Party. The editor declared that it was a transparent ploy that placed office-seeking above principle. The *St. Landry Clarion,* which had served as the official journal of the St. Landry LFU and had previously reported fairly neutrally on the People's Party, also expressed disgust.

The editor claimed that third-party leaders were at last showing their "true colors" and were apparently willing to combine with anyone, "even negroes," to win office. He further argued that money from Republican plutocrats would now flow into third-party coffers, making a sham of its reform principles.[22]

It is difficult to determine exactly what most rank-and-file Populists thought about the fusion deal. There are few surviving records of their publicly expressed opinions. One of those expressed opinions, however, reflected reluctant acceptance. Hardy Brian, the state secretary of the People's Party and current editor of the third-party newspaper *Winnfield Comrade,* wrote that he accepted the political necessity of the fusion arrangement. Nevertheless, he was bothered by the decision to share Weaver electoral votes with a "plutocrat" like President Harrison, who clearly did not support the platforms of the LFU and People's Party.[23]

CONGRESSIONAL AND PRESIDENTIAL ELECTION RESULTS, 1892

Louisiana Populists must surely have been disheartened when the votes from the congressional races were released. None of the Populist congressional candidates had even come close to unseating the Democratic incumbents. As Table 6 shows, all of the Democratic congressional candidates won by large margins.

TABLE 6
Democratic and Fusion Ticket Returns by District, Congressional Election in Louisiana, 1892

	DEMOCRATIC TICKET	FUSION TICKET	% DP VOTE
First Congressional District	10,878	4,787	69
Second Congressional District	12,588	6,102	67
Third Congressional District	14,033	3,123	82
Fourth Congressional District	16,442	5,167	76
Fifth Congressional District	19,571	4,301*	73
Sixth Congressional District	12,258	2,043	86

Source: *Report of the Secretary of State,* 575–576.
* The editor of the Monroe *Bulletin,* A. A. Gunby, also ran as an Independent with Populist leanings; he garnered 3108 votes.

Neither the Republicans nor the Populists appeared to have benefited much from their fusion deal. In fact, support for the Republican Party fell in the parishes of the First, Second, and Third Congressional districts. The election returns suggest that many Republicans stayed away from the polls. As Table 7 indicates, the total vote count in the major sugar-producing parishes of these congressional districts was significantly lower than it had been in the state elections held earlier in the year. The number of votes plummeted from about 35,000 to 20,298—a whopping 40 percent decline. Furthermore, fewer of those who voted cast their ballot for the Republican Party, with the party falling in its share of the total vote in seven of the eleven sugar-producing parishes.

TABLE 7
Election Returns in the Major Sugar-producing Parishes of the First, Second, and Third Congressional Districts, 1892

	TOTAL VOTE IN ELECTION		% REPUBLICAN VOTE	
PARISH	STATE	CONGRESSIONAL	STATE	CONGRESSIONAL
Ascension	4,491	2,319	27	8
Assumption	3,637	2,002	47	35
Iberia	2,345	616	18	5
Iberville	3,947	2,241	36	27
LaFourche	3,950	3,160	29	3
Plaquemines	2,991	2,125	46	56
St. Charles	1,347	1,048	77	67
St. James	2,926	2,005	54	41
St. J. Baptist	2,197	1,617	59	67
St. Mary	4,061	1,588	13	16
Terrebonne	2,088	1,577	14	22
TOTAL	33,980	20,298		

Source: *Report of the Secretary of State*, 575–576.

Neither did the Populists' chances for winning in the Fourth, Fifth, and Sixth Congressional districts improve as a result of the fusion deal. Landslide Democratic victories of 95 percent or greater occurred in nine parishes in these districts: Avoyelles, Bossier, Concordia, East Carroll, Madison, Point Coupee, Tensas, West Feliciana, and West Baton Rouge. These congressional districts remained Democratic strongholds despite the fact that voting-age black males represented the majority of voters in seven of the twelve parishes of the Fourth District, in ten of the fifteen parishes of the Fifth District, and in eight of the thirteen parishes of the Sixth District (see Table 8). Democrats had inordinate influence over the election process in the black-belt plantation parishes of these districts, which ensured strong Democratic electoral majorities.[24]

TABLE 8

Percent of Voting-age Males in Louisiana Who Were Black, by Congressional District and Parish, 1890

FOURTH DISTRICT	%	FIFTH DISTRICT	%	SIXTH DISTRICT	%
Bienville	39	Caldwell	49	Acadia	11
Bossier	77	Catahoula	39	Avoyelles	50
Caddo	69	Claiborne	53	E. Baton Rouge	63
De Soto	62	Concordia	83	East Feliciana	66
Grant	39	East Carroll	90	Livingston	16
Natchitoches	57	Franklin	52	Point Coupee	74
Rapides	55	**Jackson**	31	St. Helena	50
Red River	67	**Lincoln**	38	St. Landry	53
Sabine	19	Madison	90	St. Tammany	35
Vernon	7	Morehouse	76	Tangiopahoa	32
Webster	53	Ouachita	64	Washington	26
Winn	11	Richland	66	W. Baton Rouge	69
		Tensas	90	West Feliciana	80
		Union	38		
		West Carroll	60		
TOTAL	46	TOTAL	61	TOTAL	48

Source: USBC, *The Compendium of the Eleventh Census*, 782–783.

Note: Parishes carried by the Populist congressional candidates are noted by **boldfaced** print.

The black-belt challenge that faced the third party in Louisiana is also apparent when reflecting on the seven parishes that the Populist congressional candidates successfully carried in the election: Grant, Jackson, Lincoln, Sabine, Union, Vernon, and Winn. These parishes shared a common characteristic: their population primarily consisted of small white farmers. As indicated in Table 8, black males represented less than 40 percent of the voting-age male population in these parishes. Unfortunately for the future prospects of the third party, this population profile was true of only a small minority of Louisiana parishes.

There was other evidence that the Populist-Republican fusion had not helped much in securing the black vote. Even in the seven parishes that Populist congressional candidates carried, the fusion ticket fared poorly in the alluvial areas where blacks tilled lands that had once been part of plantations. For example, the fusion ticket lost in ward one of Grant Parish—the only ward in that parish where blacks were the majority of the electorate. The fusion ticket garnered only 51 percent of the Republican vote cast in that ward in the 1892 gubernatorial elections held six months earlier. Furthermore, the poor voter turnout in that ward did not characterize other parish precincts, which had similar or higher voter turnout compared to that in the recent gubernatorial election.[25]

The challenge facing the third-party movement in Louisiana was a serious one: securing the black vote was vital to its success. But getting that vote—both in terms of winning the political loyalty of black voters and in getting their votes honestly counted—was a formidable challenge. Getting the black vote without alienating its white voter base was an equally daunting challenge. Therein lay the dilemma that would prove to be the Achilles' heel of the Louisiana Populist movement.

In the presidential race, Cleveland carried Louisiana by a very large margin. He polled 87,992 votes, or 77 percent of the total vote cast, against 26,563 for the fusion Harrison-Weaver ticket. The fusion ticket carried only six parishes: three strong LFU parishes—Grant, Lincoln, and Winn parishes—and three sugar-producing plantation parishes that usually went Republican in national elections—Plaquemines, St. Charles, and St. James parishes.[26]

The presidential election results are significant because Cleveland by no stretch of the imagination could be seen as a reform candidate. Small farmers had declared their anti-Cleveland sentiments well in advance of the Democratic Party nominating convention, but had been ignored. Those who still chose to vote for Cleveland had indicated their willingness to vote the Democratic ticket regardless of who received the presidential nomination. Despite the hopes of third party leaders, party loyalty and bloody-shirt politics still reigned supreme.

Unfortunately, commitment to reform is not an automatic response to hardship. In fact, generating commitment to a third-party reform movement is a formidable task in America's winner-takes-all political system. A third party faces two very difficult challenges: it must convince a majority of voters of the uniqueness and importance of its platform, and it must convince voters of the viability of the third-party challenge. Both of these challenges must be met. If the first—but not the second—challenge is successfully addressed, many voters in agreement with the third-party reform demands may nevertheless vote for the least objectionable of the old-party delegates.

THE LFU AND THE PEOPLE'S PARTY

Historian Lawrence Goodwyn has stressed the importance of the Alliance as a bridge to the People's Party in the South.[27] To a considerable extent, his point is well taken. Any attempt to mobilize support is immensely aided by the ability to mobilize through already existing organizations. By 1890 the Alliance had well more than a million members by conservative estimates and perhaps as many as three million.[28] Therefore, it was potentially of tremendous value to the newly formed People's Party. Recognition of this value may well have been one of the major reasons behind the delegates to the People's Party founding convention adopting a platform identical to that of the Alliance.

The bridge from the LFU to the People's Party is clearly evident when discussing leadership. Most of the early leaders of the third party in Louisiana were from the LFU. However, in terms of delivering the masses of supporters needed to win elections, the LFU served as an unreliable, rickety bridge to the People's Party. Leaders of the third party worked hard to get the political endorsements of parish LFU organizations. But most of these organizations followed the lead of the national Alliance organization and state LFU. They avoided an explicitly third-party stance, opting instead to pass resolutions that simply declared it was the duty of members to support candidates and political parties that endorsed the demands of the LFU.[29] Since the People's Party was the only party to adopt the full slate of Alliance demands, one could argue that such resolutions were implicitly third-party endorsements. But the fact that the endorsements were, at best, implicit ones points to the sensitive nature of partisan politics in the LFU. Clearly, many LFU members were still struggling over the clash between their desire for reform and their desire to stay loyal to the Democratic Party.

Even if the LFU had officially endorsed the third party movement, it would still have had serious limitations in terms of its ability to deliver votes for the People's Party. The distribution of LFU membership was heavily skewed toward the Fourth Congressional District and the parishes in the western part of the Fifth Congressional District—only two of the six congressional districts in Louisiana. An election cannot be won with such a limited political base, as was vividly apparent after the 1892 election returns were tallied.

By the end of 1892, the Alliance movement in most states was experiencing significant demobilization. Louisiana was no exception. While the betrayal of the Lafayette Compact played a role in the decline of the Alliance-affiliated LFU, it was by no means the sole factor. Parish LFU organizations were torn asunder by bitter accusations traded between those who remained loyal to the Democratic Party and those who strongly believed that reform was only possible via a new political party that transcended sectional hostilities. The strategic framing contest centered on the appropriate response to the following questions: What was the best means for achieving desired economic and political reforms? Was reform through a third-party movement a fool's dream, as loyal Democrats in the Alliance movement argued? Or was continued loyalty to an unresponsive, corrupt Democratic Party a sell-out of Alliance principles, as third-party advocates claimed?

In those parish LFU organizations that came to be dominated by third-party supporters, members who refused to break their ties with the Democratic Party felt unwelcome and often resigned. Conversely, in parish LFU organizations where Democratic loyalists prevailed, third-party advocates became frustrated and often resigned. They reasoned that there was no sense remaining loyal to an organization that put party loyalty before principle.[30]

Soon the LFU was in serious disarray. Its problems were mirrored nationally. At the Alliance's national convention in Memphis in 1892, held shortly after the national elections, a bitter conflict erupted between the Democratic loyalist and third-party factions. One of the central questions debated at the convention was: Could an Allianceman in good faith vote against the People's Party, the only party to support all of the Alliance demands in its platform? The majority response at the convention was "no." This sentiment was reflected in the election of a new Alliance president. Charles Macune, a driving force in the Alliance and editor of the *National Economist*—the Alliance's national organ—had been considered for the presidency. But he had taken an ambivalent stance, erratically swinging between arguing for pressure-politics within the Democratic Party and support for the third-party movement. His ambivalence cost him the presidency. For the first time in the history of the Alliance, a non-southerner was chosen as president—Henry Loucks of South Dakota, an avid Populist who had argued that no true Allianceman could support any political party but the People's Party. The convention delegates proceeded to elect exclusively third-party supporters as the other national officers of the Alliance.[31] The Populist movement was clearly transitioning into its phase as an exclusively third-party movement.

FRAMING CHALLENGES AND POLITICAL OPPORTUNITY

The third-party movement faced two major challenges in the aftermath of the 1892 elections. First, it had to persuade more voters of the accuracy of its diagnostic framing of the economic problems facing the country. Then it had to convince them of the wisdom of its strategic frame: that a third party was the best way to achieve reform.

In regard to its diagnostic frame, the Populists hoped to benefit from an unexpected economic development. In 1893, the country experienced the beginnings of a general economic depression that not only intensified agrarian suffering, but also created serious economic problems for a large cross-section of Americans. The decade of the 1880s had been characterized by business expansion financed largely through credit. In 1893, credit dried up. As the economy worsened, many businesses could not honor their debts. There were about 500 bank failures and nearly 1,600 business bankruptcies in 1893 alone. Unemployment soared as large numbers of workers were laid off.[32]

In his presidential campaign, Cleveland had claimed that if the nation stood firmly on sound-money policies that required continued allegiance to the gold standard, the economy would improve. Under his sound-money policy, however, the economy of the country had worsened. Concerns about the economy prompted more and more people to present paper currency for redemption in gold. Cleveland, who subscribed to the prevailing view that a gold reserve of $100 million was essential to preserve the gold standard, viewed the swift outflow of the Treasury's gold reserve with alarm. To maintain the reserve, he sold more government bonds for gold. No sooner was the gold reserve replenished, than a new wave of redemptions depleted it again. Cleveland was forced into numerous bond issues, with one bond issue following another with disconcerting rapidity. Interest on the bonds reached into the millions. The financial crisis is generally known as the Panic of 1893.[33]

Amid the financial panic, Cleveland requested the repeal of the Sherman Silver Act. He reasoned that demands for redemption would fall if the financial community was assured of the continuation of the gold standard. His request inflamed the passions of those who believed that the financial woes of the country were the result of a severely contract currency supply.[34]

Caustic criticism of Cleveland and his insistence on the gold standard became common across the South, and Louisiana was no exception. Some Democratic leaders were advising voters to repudiate Cleveland and apply a "silver test" to all Democratic candidates for office. The editor of the *Shreveport Daily Caucasian* echoed this sentiment. He declared that the gold standard meant currency contraction and economic stagnation. He argued that the Cleveland administration was a disaster and to avoid defeat in the upcoming elections, the party had to repudiate Cleveland.[35] The ideological schism within the Democratic Party provided the third-party movement with the political opportunity to bolster its support.

The debate over monetary policy inflamed passions because the worsening economy greatly impacted the lives of many citizens. In regard to the plight of small farmers, the bulk of the population of Louisiana, cotton prices were below the $0.08 per pound needed for most farmers to make a profit. In congressional hearings on the farm crisis, farmers from the backland parishes of Louisiana reported that 70 to 80 percent of farmers within their parishes were in debt to crop-lien holders. A growing number of farmers were losing their farms.[36]

The leaders of the third-party movement hoped to benefit from the growing discontent with Cleveland. They promoted their diagnostic frame that blamed the economic depression on an inadequate circulating currency, focusing heavily on the role that silver demonetization and the imposition of a gold standard had played in the contraction of the nation's money supply.[37] Louisiana Populists blasted both Republicans and the Cleveland administration for their insistence on a gold standard. Both were said to be too cozy with financial capitalists who benefited from the tight money supply. The *Louisiana Populist* declared that the leaders of the old parties were more concerned with the profitability of capitalists than with the growing poverty among the common folk: "We have monopolies of every conceivable kind, all demanding and getting their tribute from our people. These are the fruits of Republican and Democratic rule."[38] It later exclaimed: "How merchants do display and advertise cut prices on goods, trying to sell them to people who need them bad enough, but have no money and can get none. If they would only expend half their energy in trying to find out why the people who buy of them have less money than in former years, and the bankers and such who do not buy of them have all the stuff. . . . They are about as wise as the diamond merchant who cultivated the patronage of beggars."[39]

Louisiana Populists were unquestionably successful on one score: they shifted the talk of reform in the mainstream media from its customary focus on the tariff to a discussion of the nation's monetary policy. Many Louisiana newspapers were now espousing free silver, a topic to which they had given little attention prior to 1892. The *Shreveport Daily Caucasian* emphatically declared: "Silver is the issue in this country."[40]

While Louisiana Populists had succeeded in promoting their monetary reform frame—or at least the anti-gold standard, free-silver component of their reform frame—they struggled with the challenge of convincing voters that such reform was possible only through the People's Party. A large number of free-silver advocates remained loyal to the Democratic Party, and they used the mainstream press to advocate pushing for reform through the Democratic Party.[41] They pointed with optimism to the growing number of state and national Democratic leaders who were publicly declaring for free silver. They also stressed the growing support of free silver among rank-and-file Democrats. For example, when the white Democrats of the Fourth District were polled on the free silver issue, they declared themselves in favor of free silver by a vote of 3,270 to 226.[42]

With support for free silver growing strong, Democratic loyalists reasoned that it was within their powers to achieve reform from within the Democratic Party. The *Shreveport Progress* appealed to farmers to remain loyal to the party: "No paper believes more strongly in the sound doctrine of the Alliance demands than we do, but we think it useless waste of energy and good time to seek them through any but the Democratic party, at this time." The St. Landry *Clarion*, once the official paper of the LFU of that parish, agreed. It argued that seeking reform through the third party was futile and dubbed the third party "the one-third party" because of its performance at the polls.[43]

In response, the *Louisiana Populist* emphasized the worsening economic depression and pleaded: "Can you contemplate the sad reality and at the same time not rise beyond and above that old party sentiment? You have been trying that for years and have continued to grow worse."[44] It also argued that the Democratic Party could not be trusted because the gold-standard faction controlled the party and had ensured the selection of Cleveland as the party's presidential candidate against vehement protest by farmers. Furthermore, at the state level, Governor Murphy Foster and most of the state

Executive Committee of the Democratic Party supported Cleveland and his gold-standard position. As the only party united in its demand for free silver, the People's Party merited the support of all those truly interested in financial reform.[45]

Louisiana Populists also pointed out that free silver was only one of the many reforms needed. They reiterated their support of the entire slate of Alliance reform demands, which included the regulation of the banking and transportation industries, as well as the fiatist principles embodied in the subtreasury plan: that the volume of circulating currency needed to be sufficient for the transaction of business, and that it should be based on the needs of the economy rather than on the availability of gold and/or silver. While free silver or bimetallism would allow for some expansion of the nation's circulating currency, and therefore was worthy of support, Populists warned that it would be insufficient to pull the economy out of the current serious recession.[46]

But the Populist message of fiatism was hard to disseminate. The scarcity of funds limited the printing and distribution of third-party campaign literature. Other avenues for educating voters on fiatism were restricted. Both the Republican and Democratic parties refused to allow Populists to participate in public debates on the major political issues of the campaign.[47] The mainstream press generally ignored the issue of fiatism. Without question, free silver dominated financial reform discourse throughout the nation. When fiatism was given attention, it was typically ridiculed. The editor of the *Colfax Chronicle,* for example, talked of the "rag-baby" of fiat money.[48]

Free silver was a much easier "sell," and discussion of fiatism among Louisiana Populists became much less common than discussion of free silver. The tilting of monetary reform talk to free silver was very apparent in the columns of the *Louisiana Populist,* where advocacy of free silver began to far outweigh discussion of fiatism.

Some Populists recognized the significant limitations of free silver as a reform and believed that free-silver advocates attached an importance to that reform that grossly exaggerated its benefits. But the People's Party was a political party composed of factions of varying sizes. Fiatist Populists represented one faction. Free-silver advocates represented a different faction, one increasingly motivated by the logic of politics in a winner-takes-all electoral system. It was a faction that by 1894 was gathering considerable strength.[49]

Given the shift of focus in discussions of monetary reform within the Louisiana Populist movement, a political fight loomed large between free-silver

Democrats and Populists for the loyalty of free-silver supporters. In the summer of 1894, free-silver Democrats won a major victory. State legislators who had been elected to the legislature on the Alliance platform crafted a resolution requesting that third-party supporters join with the Alliance legislators to make a fight in the upcoming congressional elections within the Democratic Party. Importantly, the resolution was condemned by only two of the Alliance legislators, Representative Hardy Brian of Winn Parish and his father Senator Benjamin Brian from Grant Parish.[50]

The debate between Democratic loyalists and Populists spilled over into the 1894 annual LFU state convention. Twenty-four parishes sent delegates to the convention. The majority of the delegates were from parishes in the Fourth and Fifth Congressional districts, which remained the hotbed of the farmers' revolt. The Populists were able to rally enough support to defeat a resolution calling for reform through the Democratic Party. They failed, however, to get a pro-third party resolution passed.[51] This failure is notable given that the majority of delegates were from parishes that were among the most supportive of the third-party movement. Thus, contrary to the claim of historian William Hair, the LFU had not by the summer of 1894 become an "adjunct of the People's Party."[52] It was still determined to remain nonpartisan and leave to the personal conscience of its members the decision as to whether to fight within the Democratic Party or join the People's Party.

Thus, while Populists had succeeded in shifting political talk from the tariff to monetary reform, they struggled in their effort to convince voters that monetary reform was possible only through the People's Party. In their desperation to wean more white voters away from the Democratic Party, some Louisiana Populist leaders began to openly embrace some of the basic beliefs encapsulated in the white supremacy frame of the Democratic Party. As the 1894 election campaign heated up, some Populist leaders openly declared themselves in favor of some of the basic tenets of white supremacy, such as the belief that major political offices should be held exclusively by whites. The *Louisiana Populist* boldly declared that Populists believed "in a white man's government."[53] It later elaborated: "the intelligent white man has become determined to act for himself and finding that the Democratic party is either unwilling or unable to carry into law any of its pledges, they have decided to form their forces with the People's party. . . . Why not act now, and help to build up and carry to success a party composed of the intelligent white element of the country? If you want white supremacy, join the Populists."[54]

Further illustrating the racist rhetoric and strategy of Louisiana Populists is the preamble written by the People's Party Executive Committee in the Fourth Congressional District to accompany its proposal for a white primary. By proposing to restrict voting rights in the primary to whites, the committee was bowing to another basic tenet of the white supremacy frame—that the voting rights of whites were of supreme importance. The preamble is important enough to the longstanding debate over the extent of racism within the Populist movement that it is reprinted here in full:

> Whereas, all other political issues have for many years been overshadowed in the South by the question of white supremacy, which question has held the white people together often against needed reforms, and Whereas, the only plausible argument made by the Democratic party against the People's party is the claim that the organization of such a party in the South will and does endanger white supremacy, dear to the heart of every white man in the South, and Whereas, we believe that many honest Democrats are deluded with that fear, and kept out of the People's party against their convictions of reform, and Whereas, the People's party in this State is a white man's party, as evidenced by its vote in every election since its organization, and by the utterances of its platforms, press and speakers in this State, Therefore, be it resolved, that the People's party Executive Committee of this district, make the following proposition to the Democratic party in the 4th Congressional District, to-wit: . . . That after the Democratic Party has held its Congressional convention, made its platform and placed its candidate thereon, said candidate and the candidate of the People's party on their respective platforms, be submitted to a white primary in which every white legal voter in the district shall be allowed to vote.[55]

The third party's proposal of a white primary catered to the belief that whites should reign supreme in political matters. The proposal declared that whichever candidate won the primary would then be declared the white man's candidate, with the losing candidate withdrawing from the race.

This preamble, written by the People's Party Executive Committee in the Fourth Congressional District to accompany its proposal for a white primary, starkly lays to rest any image of Louisiana Populism as a movement persistent in its call for a biracial, class-based reform movement. The notion of a biracial coalition that had characterized its beginnings had disappeared by the summer of 1894. The stance of Louisiana Populists at this time clearly was at odds with the description of Populists popularized by noted historian C. Vann Woodward, who declared that "the most remarkable aspect of the whole Populist movement was the resistance its leaders in the south put up against racism and racist propaganda and the determined effort they made against incredible odds to win back political rights for the Negroes."[56] While historian Robert McMath has recently argued that "there is still much to commend Woodward's nuanced claim about Populist leaders' efforts to resist racism [and] defend the political rights of African Americans,"[57] Woodward's image of a racially progressive movement clearly did not accurately characterize the Louisiana Populist movement by the summer of 1894.

The Executive Committee of the Fourth District Democratic Party declined the Populists' white primary proposition. Populist leaders lost no time pointing out the inconsistency between the white supremacy rhetoric of the Democratic Party and its refusal to endorse white primaries. To Populists, this suggested that the Democrats intended to continue reaping the electoral benefits of a manipulated black vote. The editor of the *Louisiana Populist* responded: "we deem it as settled as to which of the two parties wants white supremacy under a fair count."[58]

The Democratic Party persisted in its use of the specter of "negro domination" in its efforts to retain the loyalty of white voters. The *Louisiana Populist* retorted that it was "an insult to any white man to tell him that the time will ever come when the negro will dominate the caucasian race." On the eve of Election Day, it expressed exasperation with reformers who stayed loyal to the Democratic Party out of fear of dividing the white vote: "As the dog returns to his vomit and the sow to her wallow, so will old party slaves . . . nominate the servants of the plutocracy."[59]

In explaining the racist rhetoric of Louisiana Populist leaders in 1894, which starkly contrasted with the racially conciliatory approach Populist leaders had adopted during earlier election campaigns, three major factors are paramount. First, efforts to attract the black vote were costly in terms of courting the white vote. Many, if not most, of southern whites had been reared in the culture of white supremacy and were uncomfortable with, if not overtly hostile to, the notion of a black-white political alliance. Second, Populist leaders in Louisiana had largely given up on efforts to win the black vote. They did not have the resources to campaign effectively in black-belt parishes. Importantly, there were no pre-existing organizations in these parishes through which they could recruit. The CFA had never been successful in these parishes, and the Knights of Labor organization had been crushed during the sugar strike in 1887. While the Republican Party was formally organized down to the precinct level, fusion arrangements between the People's Party and the Republican Party in the 1892 elections had done little to improve black support for the third-party movement. Third, Populist leaders in Louisiana had come to realized that a political alliance between black and white farmers was doomed by the fact that Democrats controlled the electoral process in the black-belt parishes and could manipulate the black vote, through intimation and fraud, to secure their victory on Election Day.[60] No matter how much effort Populist leaders expended in appealing to black voters and no matter how successful they might become at winning the electoral allegiance of black voters, on Election Day the black vote would not likely be counted for the third party.

Thus, political pragmatism was likely responsible for the shift in racial rhetoric of leaders of the Louisiana Populist movement. By seeking the support of disgruntled white Democrats, they were essentially doing the unpardonable: they were attempting to divert white voter support from the Democratic Party, which in a black-majority state such as Louisiana risked bringing the Republican Party back into power along with its black allies. Such a risk was anathema to many white southerners. Therefore, southern Populist leaders were butting up against the widespread and tenacious culture of white supremacy. Fully cognizant of the power of this culture, and recognizing that strong appeals to black voters in 1892 had proved futile, Populist leaders began to embrace some of the major tenets of white supremacy in an effort to use it to their own advantage. Their brief experiment with the notion of a powerful biracial political coalition for reform was over.

RESULTS OF THE 1894 CONGRESSIONAL RACES

Louisiana Populists fielded congressional candidates in four of the six congressional districts. In the Fourth District, they nominated B. W. Bailey, who had been one of the earliest converts to the People's Party and was current owner and editor of Winn Parish's third-party newspaper, the Winnfield *Comrade*. He was widely known as a powerful stump speaker. On Election Day, he carried six of the twelve parishes in the Fourth District: Bienville, Grant, Natchitoches, Sabine, Vernon, and Winn. In two other parishes, Bienville and Webster, he lost by less than forty votes. But his chances for victory were ruined by the landslide victory of the Democratic candidate and incumbent congressman, Henry Ogden, in the remaining four parishes, including the three most populous parishes in the district. District-wide, Bailey received 5,932 votes against 12,257 for Ogden.[61]

Populists charged that the election had been stolen for Ogden. They complained that "whether the negroes are dead or alive, they voted the Democratic Party ticket solidly." Blacks in De Soto Parish were allegedly warned that if they did not vote for the Democratic Party, they would get a "midnight visit." In Rapides Parish, nearly a third of Ogden's vote came from a single black precinct, which the *Louisiana Populist* complained gave Ogden 1,200 votes, even though it had less than 700 registered voters.[62]

In the parishes that Ogden carried by wide margins, no opposition-party commissioners had been allowed at the polls. Ogden's margin of victory in these parishes was very suspicious. In Bossier Parish, the Democratic Party received 98 percent of the vote despite the fact that black voters outnumbered white voters three to one. In Caddo Parish, Bailey received only sixty-six votes—a significant decline from the Populist vote in that parish in the 1892 congressional elections.[63] When a Democratic official was asked to comment on the number of votes that would likely be cast at a certain precinct, the official tellingly commented: "Just as many . . . as we need."[64]

The Fifth District congressional races pitted Alexis Benoit, a liberal legislator and a recent Populist convert, against incumbent Congressman Boatner, a conservative Democrat and gold-standard advocate. Benoit received 4,549 votes to 14,755 for Boatner. He carried only three parishes in the district: Jackson, Lincoln, and Union parishes. Populists alleged massive electoral fraud. In about half of the parishes in the district, the third party had been denied representation at the polls. In Concordia and East Carroll parishes, predominantly black parishes, Benoit had polled only 26 votes to Boatner's 4,119 votes. In the parish of Tensas, where the vast majority of the population was black, Benoit did not garner a single vote. In Ouachita Parish, employers were alleged to have cast the votes of their black employees. In Madison Parish the Democratic officials had gotten carried away and played their hand a bit too obviously: Boatner's vote exceeded the number of registered voters in the parish by almost a thousand. The evidence of fraud was compelling enough that the U.S. House of Representatives ruled the election invalid. A new election was held, which Boatner won. Benoit contested again, but the congressional investigative committee merely cut the victory margin from more than 6,000 to 802 votes and declared Boatner the legitimate congressional representative of the district.[65]

The People's Party candidate fared no better in the Third District congressional race. The most significant challenge to the incumbent Democratic congressman, Andrew Price, was Republican Party candidate Taylor Beattie. The latter garnered 8,620 votes, while incumbent Congressman Price received 14,383 votes. The Populist candidate, J. Lightner, did not carry a single parish in the district. He garnered only 3 percent of the district-wide vote, or a mere 741 votes.[66]

The performance of Republican Beattie in the Third District congressional race is noteworthy. One interpretation of his much stronger performance relative to the Populist candidate is that it reflected the preference of many black voters in the district for the Republican Party and their disinterest in the third-party movement. If this interpretation is accurate, it is all the more striking because Beattie had played a major role in violently suppressing the strike by black sugar workers in 1887. At least thirty blacks had been killed and hundreds wounded in the violent suppression.[67] An alternative explanation is that the sugar planters in the district pressured black sugar plantation workers to cast their vote for the Republican Party in congressional elections because of that party's steady support of sugar subsidies. Either interpretation meant that Populists struggled for votes in the sugar plantation parishes.

In the Sixth District, M. R. Wilson ran on the third-party ticket. He had come into the party via the LFU. He had played a major role in the Bloch controversy of St. Landry Parish and had been very outspoken about the inappropriateness of blacks holding political office. He only carried two of the thirteen parishes in the district, Livingston and Washington parishes. He lost a third parish, St. Helena, by only six votes. He did reasonably well in Acadia, East Feliciana, St. Landry, and Tangipahoa parishes, receiving from 20 to 40 percent of the vote. His Democratic opponent, however, won landslide victories in the remaining parishes of the district. In St. Tammany Parish, Wilson received only eight votes. Worse yet, he did not get a single vote in the parishes of Avoyelles, Pointe Coupee, and West Baton Rouge—all of which had a majority-black electorate.[68]

Louisiana was certainly not the only state where third-party candidates did poorly. An examination of the results of the congressional elections nationwide shows that of the 350 congressional races across the nation, the third party won in only 8. Six of those eight victories were achieved via fusion with either the Democratic or Republican Parties. Furthermore, in only about 10 percent of the congressional races did the third party poll more than 40 percent of the vote.[69]

To make prospects even more bleak, in a number of key states heavily represented in the Electoral College (such as Illinois, Ohio, New York, and Pennsylvania), few Populist candidates were even fielded, and those few performed poorly. The electoral performance of the third party was not likely to change in these states since there were weak networks through which to build a strong following for the Populist movement. For example, the president of the influential American Federation of Labor, Samuel Gompers, was hostile to the idea of trade union leaders becoming involved in partisan politics. While the leaders of the Knights of Labor had expressed sympathy for the Populist movement and had been present at the founding convention of the People's Party, the Knights of Labor was struggling for survival as an organization. So its support was not very helpful. Thus, the avenues for disseminating and defending Populist reform principles among wage laborers in major urban areas were limited.[70]

Populists struggled to depict a good slant to the election results by focusing on the fact that the People's Party had received nearly two million votes nationwide, almost double its number of votes in the presidential elections of 1892.[71] Nevertheless, the poor performance of the third party at the polls was a major blow. The major demands of the third party—such as financial reform of the nation's monetary system—could only be implemented through congressional legislation at the national level. Yet the third party had performed dismally in the congressional elections. The tension between these two realities hung over the Populist movement. It would be difficult to overstate its importance in producing the pragmatic-politics response of Louisiana Populists, and Populists in general, in the post-1894 years.

8

Framing Challenges in the Mid-1890s

LOUISIANA POPULISTS FACED SEVERAL major framing challenges in the mid-1890s. One strategic framing issue concerned electoral fraud, particularly in the black-belt parishes. Populists were fully cognizant of the fact that political opportunities for reform were severely compromised by electoral irregularities in these parishes. The problem was clear: no electoral reform, no economic reform. In strategically framing how best to reduce the level of fraud, they proposed a secret ballot. This chapter probes the flaws of this proposed remedy and the reason why Populists refused to promote other more promising solutions.

Discussion of election reform took center stage when the state Democratic Party pushed to address the problem of fraud through a suffrage amendment to the state constitution. Populists worried that suffrage restrictions might deprive poor rural whites, whom they saw as their major constituency, of their voting rights. Their campaign in opposition to the suffrage amendment bill is explored in this chapter.

A second challenge concerned how to balance the demand for free silver and the demand for an irredeemable currency supply, the latter of which entailed a much more radical change. Ever since the inception of the People's Party, Populists had focused on the need to expand the volume of circulating currency in order to address the agricultural depression. For this purpose, they had initially stressed their preference for an irredeemable currency system. But as long as the nation had a redeemable currency system, they favored bimetallism over the monometallic, gold standard. As free-silver advocacy soared as the election campaigns of 1896 neared, Populists faced a major framing decision: Should they emphasize the inadequacy of free silver as a reform and stress the importance of an irredeemable currency system? The factors influencing their decision, as well as the consequences of their decision, are major topics of this chapter.

A third strategic framing issue surfaced as the state campaign of 1896 approached. An opening in political opportunity was created by a fissure among the state's planter elite. Sugar planters broke from the Democratic Party in anger over the Cleveland administration's repeal of a sugar subsidy that had previously funneled millions of dollars to sugar planters. Populist leaders had to decide whether to take advantage of the split and fuse with the sugar-planter wing of the Republican Party. Fusion could redress several major problems. First, it would alleviate the dire financial straits of the state People's Party that constrained its ability to effectively campaign. Second, it made sense in terms of electoral arithmetic: the strength of the Republican Party in the First, Second, and Third Congressional districts complemented the strength of the People's Party in the Fourth, Fifth, and Sixth Congressional districts. Third, fusion with Republican sugar planters could reduce the extent to which the black vote in the sugar parishes was manipulated for the benefit of the state Democratic Party.

The benefits of fusion, however, had to be weighed against the risks that it entailed. Populist leaders were well aware that fusion with the Republican Party would be an affront to some white voters who had supported the third party in past elections. It was one thing to defect from the Democratic Party in order to support the People's Party. It was a very different matter to fuse with Republicans. Populist leaders faced the difficult task of predicting whether the strategic benefits of fusion outweighed its risks.

STRATEGICALLY FRAMING THE ELECTORAL FRAUD PROBLEM

Populists were well aware of the problem created by electoral fraud. Any success in winning the hearts and minds of voters to the third-party movement was for naught if votes could not be freely cast without intimidation and then honestly counted. Their tactics for addressing election fraud, however, were ineffective. Their demands that voters be allowed to cast their ballots without intimidation and that votes be honestly counted were ignored by the leaders of the Democratic Party. So was their demand that all political parties have representatives present during the counting of the votes. The strategy of contesting elections was expensive and, therefore, impractical when election fraud was pervasive. It was also not very effective: Alexis Benoit, the Populist candidate in the Fifth Congressional District, had successfully contested the district's congressional election in 1894 on the grounds of election fraud. But rather than grant the seat to the Populist candidate, Congress merely declared the seat vacant pending another election.[1]

When powerful leaders of a dominant political party willfully and repeatedly compromise the integrity of the democratic process, more powerful remedies are in order. But Louisiana Populists refused to advocate the most powerful and effective remedy—removing the authority of those who committed the fraud and replacing them with federal election supervisors. Neither the LFU nor the Louisiana People's Party was willing to endorse the federal supervision of elections in districts plagued by election fraud. The Lodge election bill, introduced in Congress in 1891, had proposed such supervision. But the LFU, as well as the national Alliance organization, had fiercely opposed it. Later, the People's Party adopted an identical oppositional stance.

The opposition of the Alliance and People's Party to federal intervention in the electoral process is perplexing. In the case of the Alliance, it mounted an elaborate campaign to promote the subtreasury plan, which called for massive federal intervention in the agricultural economy with the establishment of subtreasury warehouses in every major agricultural parish and county in the country. One of the central reform tenets of the People's Party was its demand that the federal government assume a much larger role in managing the monetary system. Therefore, the resistance to federal involvement in election monitoring does not derive from a general resistance on the part of Populists to the federal government taking on a more activist role. Rather, the Populists pushed for a greater federal government role in the economy (a precursor to the sentiments that would later result in the New Deal programs), but were opposed to the involvement of the federal government in southern political matters. The most likely source of this resistance was the strong emotion still engendered in the South by the political intervention of the federal government during the era of Reconstruction. Emotion in this particular instance derailed a calm, dispassionate strategic framing of the problem of electoral fraud. The refusal to advocate for more federal supervision to address voter intimidation and to ensure an honest count would be one of the most serious failings of the Populist movement.

In responding to the electoral fraud that persistently marred the election process in Louisiana, state Democratic legislators adopted a classic "blame the victim" frame. They ignored the illegal and corrupt behavior of political leaders who manipulated the electoral process, instead faulting the ignorance of voters who were unable to prevent their ballots from being falsely cast or counted. Such ignorance, in their view, warranted some type of suffrage restriction.

Calls for suffrage restriction were nothing new to political discourse in Louisiana.[2] Such calls, however, had been hampered by two concerns. First, interest in suffrage restriction had been undercut by the challenge of disfranchising black voters without also restricting the voting rights of many poor whites. Any attempt to restrict suffrage on the explicit basis of race violated the Fifteenth Amendment. Suffrage restriction based on either education or property ownership, however, would deny many whites their voting rights. Second, suffrage restriction threatened the interests of the planter elite. As the editor of the black newspaper the *Weekly Pelican* had astutely observed: "What influence or power would Madison, Tensas, Ouachita or Carroll Parishes have? Could they then, as they can now, with the aid of two or three more parishes name the Governor at nominating conventions?"[3]

Despite such concerns, talk of suffrage restriction gathered momentum in the mid-1890s. Passage of suffrage restrictions in other southern states had emboldened Louisiana lawmakers. Equally important, the threat of the third-party movement, which was gaining strength in the predominantly white-populated backland parishes, lowered the resistance of Democratic legislators to the idea of disfranchising poor whites.

Populists could have responded to the suffrage restriction campaign in a number of different ways. They could have run a counter-campaign that pushed for stronger penalties on those committing electoral fraud, with the federal courts as the venue for prosecutions of electoral fraud. They could have called for neutral federal officials to oversee and certify the electoral process. In the language of social movement theorists, Louisiana Populist leaders exercised agency and decided to eschew both of these approaches. Instead, they proposed the secret ballot as a solution to electoral fraud. They argued that a secret ballot would eliminate the harassment of those who voted against the wishes of the political powers-that-be. It would also address the problem of votes being bought since the payer would never really know whether the vote was cast as promised.[4]

The secret-ballot solution, however, was deeply flawed. It did nothing to ensure that votes would be counted as cast. Populists had to have been well aware that their strategic approach to electoral fraud was fatally flawed. They had heatedly complained about ballot-box stuffing in the plantation parishes. The secret ballot would be irrelevant as a reform measure if the vote count was manipulated once the polls closed.

Why would Louisiana Populists propose such an ineffective solution? The answer to this important question lies in the challenge facing the leaders of the Populist movement in Louisiana: the historical record clearly indicates that the political culture of Louisiana in the late nineteenth century was racist. Any attempt in the political arena to surmount racism faced almost insurmountable challenges. Consequently, when Populist leaders engaged in the framing process, any major departure from the prevailing culture made their mobilization efforts more difficult. Political pragmatism dictated that Populists avoid a campaign explicitly focused on protecting black voting rights. As a result, in strategically framing the problem of electoral fraud, Populists chose a piecemeal approach to reform that avoided any reference to race. If adopted, a secret ballot would have at least been a step in the right direction. It would have increased the odds that a vote could be cast without fear of personal retribution or harassment.

THE SUFFRAGE AMENDMENT BILL

Convening shortly after the elections of 1894, state legislators followed the advice of Governor Foster and proposed a bill that would place a constitutional amendment restricting suffrage on the ballot in 1896. The amendment proposed restricting voting rights to adult males who could read the state constitution in their native language or who owned property assessed at $200 or more. An amazing proviso was attached to the amendment. It declared that state legislators were empowered to rewrite the amendment, if approved by voters, with the rewritten amendment becoming part of the constitution without resubmission to the people.[5]

The bill proposing a suffrage amendment to the state constitution was brought to the floor of the state legislature in the summer of 1894. State legislators overwhelmingly supported the bill. The final vote in the House was seventy-four in support of the bill, nine against. Of the three Populists in the House, two voted against the bill and the third was not present at the time of the vote. The Senate approved the bill unanimously. The only Populist in the state senate, Benjamin Brian, had taken a public stand against the bill. But he was absent when the vote was taken.[6] It is curious that on such an important bill, two of the four Populist state legislators were not present to cast a vote.

Populist opposition to the suffrage amendment bill seems to have been primarily rooted in concern about the impact the amendment would have on the voting rights of poor whites. An important indication of their limited concern for the voting rights of blacks was their strong support for reforming the electoral process by adopting a secret ballot. Under the secret-ballot bill proposed by Populist state legislator Alexis Benoit, voters did not have to be taxpayers or property owners. They only had to be able to read and write sufficiently well to read the ballot and make their choices in the privacy of a voting booth. Suffrage restriction under this proposal would have disfranchised far fewer whites than a suffrage amendment with property or educational requirements. The percent of white voters who "made their marks" instead of writing their name was relatively low in the parishes where most small cotton farmers resided—and these were the parishes where the LFU was strongest and where the third party had its best chances for success. Benoit's bill, however, would have eliminated a majority of black voters. In almost every parish except Orleans, few black voters signed their names to their ballot.[7]

Another indication of the minimal concern of Louisiana Populists for protecting black voting rights was their endorsement of white primaries that excluded blacks from the important process of selecting political candidates.[8] Populist concern about the political rights of blacks can also be questioned in light of the declarations of the major Populist newspaper in the state, the *Louisiana Populist.* The paper lambasted Democratic Party leaders for their manipulation of the black vote and referred to the Democratic Party as the "negro party" because of its dependence upon black votes for electoral success. It criticized the Democratic Party for its hypocrisy in proclaiming the importance of white supremacy, and then riding into office on the basis of landslide victories in the black-belt parishes. It declared: "Verily, the Democratic party is no longer a party of white supremacy. . . . How foolish the misguided people who follow that party thinking that it stands as it once stood for white supremacy."[9] The editor of the *Louisiana Populist,* Hardy Brian, asked: "You Democrats, white men of pure blood, who have devoted your money, your life work, and in many cases, risked your lives in battle, for the principle of white supremacy, how do you regard this betrayal of your interests by the Democratic party?"[10]

Not only did the *Louisiana Populist* criticize the Democratic Party for its failure to uphold white supremacy in politics, it went one step further and declared that the Populist Party was the only party truly committed to the principle of white supremacy in politics. It declared "negro domination . . . objectionable"; "We are for a white man's government and a white man's party."[11] It challenged white voters to stay true to the cause of white supremacy by shifting their loyalty to the People's Party.

In sum, the historical record suggests that the opposition of Louisiana Populists to the suffrage amendment bill of 1894 lay primarily in the effect that the bill would have on poor whites, many of whom would likely be disfranchised by its education and property ownership stipulations. During the debate over electoral reform that occurred from 1894 through 1896, not a single public expression of concern by Populists about black voting rights could be found. The framing debate centered on the effect of suffrage restriction on the voting rights of poor whites, with Populist leaders being particularly concerned about the voting rights of rural whites who were the bulk of their constituency.

Concern about the disfranchisement of poor whites under the proposed suffrage amendment was not limited to Populists. The *New Orleans Times-Democrat* declared: "We wish to get the negro out of politics in Louisiana, as our brethren in Mississippi have done, so that the white people of the State can settle their political differences among themselves by fair and honest elections and without risk of negro supremacy. The amendment does not solve this problem. It does . . . place it within the power of election officers to disfranchise colored votes, but the officers can disfranchise whites as well."[12]

Another major criticism of the suffrage amendment bill concerned its proviso that the amendment could be rewritten by the legislature without resubmission to the people for approval. The proviso became the lightning rod for criticism. The fear was that the legislature would increase the property value assessment needed to qualify for voting rights, and thereby disfranchise more whites. The editor of the *Louisiana Populist* railed against the proviso, predicting that the legislature would later raise the property qualification significantly higher than the $200 stipulated in the bill. He argued that the amendment was a "stepping stone to perpetually place this government in the hands of the rich, depriving the poor of any rights except to eke out their lives in hovels."[13] Thus, the campaign against the suffrage amendment bill focused attention on social class and the specter of plutocracy.

At its 1895 annual state convention, the LFU passed a resolution declaring that fair elections "temporarily outrank" all other issues. It condemned the proposed suffrage amendment largely on the grounds of the authority it granted to the state legislature to alter the amendment without resubmitting it to the people. The Central Committee of the People's Party, meeting in late August, also took a firm stance against the amendment.[14]

An intense framing contest developed between those who supported and those who opposed the suffrage restriction amendment. Supporters of the amendment argued that its passage was essential if the state was "to lift itself out of the political cesspool into which it has drifted."[15] The editor of the *Colfax Chronicle* chastised those fighting against the amendment. He argued that amendment opponents wanted "everything with two legs, outside of the penitentiary" to be able to vote. He remarked that the educational qualification stipulated by the amendment was reasonable and essential in order to rid ignorant blacks and whites from the electoral process. He also argued that the property qualification was minimal and that any man making a sincere effort could meet the $200 property value requirement in a few years. He declared: "If a man is both ignorant and incapable of the accumulation of property, he is not a worthy American citizen. He should not have a voice in the making of laws that control the rights and property [of others]." The purpose of the amendment, in his view, was laudable: to eliminate the "ignoramuses and shiftless human beings from the polls." Such elimination was essential if citizens wanted to be governed by "intelligent white men without the necessity of miscounting ballots and without bulldozing."[16]

The conservative editor of the *New Orleans Daily States* also decried universal suffrage, claiming that it gave the same power to the ignorant as it did to intelligent citizens. He argued that the granting of voting rights to blacks and to the ignorant had compelled the leading citizens of the state to protest "first by revolution and, finally, wearying of turmoil, by the far more ignoble but quieter methods which now almost completely dominate our politics."[17] In discussing electoral fraud, he stated: "it would be humiliating, to recall the history of election methods in this state and in the South during the last twenty years. We all know they have been bad, so bad that they are indefensible."[18] In his view, the only way to halt electoral fraud was to restrict voting rights so that the votes of the ignorant could not be manipulated or would not have to be overruled through a manipulation of the ballot count. Since the proposed suffrage amendment would accomplish this, he deemed it worthy of support.

The *Shreveport Daily Caucasian* echoed the call for an educational qualification for voting rights. It approvingly noted the ballot-box practice in Caddo Parish during Reconstruction. Any ballots put in the wrong box, such as a ballot with a Republican vote that was placed in the third box rather than the official Republican Party box, was not counted. The intent of this practice had been to lessen the political influence of voters "lacking the qualifications necessary to exercise the right of suffrage intelligently."[19] The paper declared that it stood "unqualifiedly for the rule of intelligence and white supremacy, which can be maintained by limiting the privilege of the franchise to those having sufficient qualification to use it intelligently."[20] As the framing debate raged in regard to how to best reform the electoral process, it was unclear which arguments were having the most sway with voters. All sides claimed to be winning the battle for the hearts and minds of voters.

STRATEGICALLY FRAMING FINANCIAL REFORM IN THE STATE CAMPAIGN, 1896

While the suffrage restriction issue was an important one in the 1896 state campaign, it was not the only issue to which attention was given. There was a lively debate concerning the role of free silver in the state campaign. In a meeting of the Bimetallic League, Senator Blanchard opposed interjecting the silver issue into the state election campaign. He argued that free silver was a national issue since there was little the state could do in regard to national financial policy. C. D. Hicks, who had run for Congress on an independent ticket in the Fourth District in 1892, and V. Grosjean, editor of the *Shreveport Daily Caucasian,* led the opposing camp. They argued that free silver needed to be a central issue in the upcoming state election because it was important to maximize the number of free-silver advocates elected to the state legislature. The legislature selected Louisiana's two U.S. senators, and free-silver legislation would be impossible without the approval of the Senate.[21]

The Blanchard faction, however, succeeded in persuading the state Bimetallic League to pass a resolution asking that the upcoming state election campaign set aside the free-silver issue, relegating it to the realm of national politics: "Resolved, . . . the money question belongs to the realm of national politics, and that it is inexpedient and unwise to inject the same as an issue in the State campaign about to ensue. Resolved, further, that the paramount question in the State election is the continued supremacy of the Democratic Party in the counsels of the state, leaving the money question as the paramount issue in the national campaign of 1896."[22] When the state Democratic convention convened, it complied with the request of the state Bimetallic League, and its platform evaded the free-silver question.[23]

When the state People's Party platform was revised for the 1896 campaign, Populist leaders refused to heed the request that the financial issue be set aside.

A free-silver plank was included in its adopted platform. But in a major move, the free-silver plank was the only financial plank included in the party platform. There was no demand for an irredeemable currency nor was the subtreasury plan, which had played such an important role in the shift of the Alliance movement into politics, mentioned. In 1895, the *Louisiana Populist* had reprinted a lengthy speech by W. S. Morgan, secretary of the People's Party National Reform Press Association, in which he advocated abandoning the subtreasury plan. He stated that "our opponents think there is a better system, and I think so too." He claimed that there were misgivings concerning the specifics of the subtreasury proposal as early as 1892, when it was included in the Omaha platform of the People's Party. But he added: "We had made excellent strides in educating the people along the sub-treasury lines. It was thought best by our people not to drop it entirely at that time." But the time had now come, he concluded, to jettison the proposal since its "only utility . . . is to furnish democratic orators a theme to talk about . . . in order to give the people a rest on the tariff racket."[24]

The framing shift that had increasingly focused the attention of Populists on the financial demand for free silver had now become the official party line of the Louisiana People's Party. Every issue of the *Louisiana Populist* prior to the state election of 1896 reprinted the third-party platform, and there is no evidence of any objection from the readership to the paring down of financial demands in the platform.

By narrowing their campaign focus to free silver, Louisiana Populist leaders had once again exercised agency and had chosen pragmatic politics over idealism. It was a strategic framing decision born out of the realization that the political opportunity facing the third-party movement was extremely unfavorable. Given the party's sparse resources, paring its financial reform demands down to the demand for free silver improved its chances for electoral success. By 1896 free silver had clearly captured the limelight in the mainstream media. The *Louisiana Populist* claimed only 1,400 subscribers.[25] Much better funded and widely disseminated newspapers restricted monetary reform talk to the gold standard versus bimetallist debate, dismissing fiatism, or the idea of irredeemable currency, as financial heresy unworthy of serious discussion. Reaching sufficient numbers of voters and convincing them of the limitations of free silver and the greater value of fiatism would have been an uphill battle.

The emphasis on silver and bimetallism within the Populist movement represented a modification of its diagnostic frame. Prior to 1896, the diagnostic frame of the movement had harshly criticized the "money kings" as part of its overall anti-monopoly frame. It claimed that they manipulated the volume of currency to maximize their profits. The *Louisiana Populist* had seriously questioned the reform value of free silver in articles published as late as 1895. Hardy Brian, the editor of the *Louisiana Populist,* had declared: "There is much more in this movement than free silver. . . . It is only one phase of the financial question, [and] is equaled in importance by other planks in our platform."[26] He argued that free silver was not an adequate solution to the economic ills besetting the economy. Free-silver legislation, he acknowledged, would increase the per capita currency in circulation. But without any other changes in the economic system, "in two or three years at most it [silver] would all be in the hands of a few individuals and corporations, or enough of it to enable them to dictate the price of all products just as they do now." He stressed that "who is to control the volume of currency in this country is of greater importance to the people than the question of free silver."[27] He insisted that adequate control of the volume of circulating currency required fiatism, or full legal tender paper currency backed by the federal government.

At this point, it is important to address the work of historian Lawrence Goodwyn. In his classic work on the Populist movement, Goodwyn depicted the free-silver push within the movement as a shadow movement led by those who had "no understanding of the cooperative crusade of the Alliance or of the greenback doctrines that the cooperative struggle had raised to preeminence in the agrarian movement."[28] He argued that this shadow movement overpowered the true spirit of Populism. His argument, however, is a poor description of the free-silver stance within the Louisiana Populist movement, which was largely the result of decisions by leaders who had been both major participants in the LFU and key activists within the Louisiana People's Party from its birth in 1891. They did not come to the movement late, and they were not ignorant of the cooperative strategies of the early Alliance. The historical record is clear on this point: they were not participants in a shadow movement.[29]

A much more compelling explanation for the free-silver stance of the leaders of the Louisiana Populist movement invokes aspects of all three major social movement theories. In Louisiana, and in many other states as well, the Alliance movement did not lay adequate groundwork for a move into electoral politics. The strong mobilization of the LFU in the Fourth Congressional District and its notable, but more modest, mobilization in the Fifth and Sixth Congressional districts were insufficient for a viable third-party movement in the state. With six congressional districts, any reasonable hope for electoral victory meant that the state People's Party had to go significantly beyond the mobilization achievements of the LFU. To make matters more challenging, this mobilization would have to take place in the context of a movement starved for money and in a state that was characterized by a highly unfavorable political opportunity structure. It was within this context that Populist leaders grabbed at what they likely saw as a life-line—free silver. This did not make them shadow Populists. A much more apt descriptor is that they were pragmatic Populists.

Furthermore, labeling as true Populists only those who came to the third party via the Alliance movement is problematic. Confining the third-party movement in Louisiana to former members of the LFU—advice that seems to be implied by Lawrence Goodwyn's identification of true Populism with the Alliance movement—would have guaranteed failure. At the national level, had the People's Party remained exclusively an extension of the Alliance movement, it would never have garnered the level of support that made it one of the largest third-party revolts in American history. A viable third party has to garner support from a wide variety of sources. The Alliance was only one source of support for the People's Party, albeit an important one in southern states. It should also be remembered that the Alliance as an organization was slow to show its support for the third-party movement and, consequently, was poorly represented at the founding convention of the People's Party.

Historian Joel Sipress has argued that while the rise of Louisiana Populism fits well with Goodwyn's classic account, its struggles and fall do not. According to Sipress, there was a "narrowing of vision" among leaders of the Louisiana Populist movement, such as Hardy Brian, in which their focus shifted from cooperative strategies to electoral politics and an emphasis on free silver at the expense of the broader Populist agenda of structural change. But he argues that this narrowing of vision was not due to a shadow movement, but rather was presided over by Populists with deep roots in the Alliance movement.[30] On this point, his views are consistent with the findings of the present study.

In interpreting the shift in strategic decisions of the leaders of the Louisiana Populist movement, Sipress attributes the change to their "lost faith" in the power of their vision of a cooperative commonwealth to inspire a successful political revolt. Instead, they embraced the logic of electoral politics, "and upon that logic their vision foundered."[31] This interpretation of the shift in strategic framing leaves important questions of strategy unanswered. It is unclear how Sipress thinks the vision of Hardy Brian and other Louisiana

Populists would have been best pursued. If Brian had not embraced the logic of electoral politics, how else was his vision of structural change to be realized? Sipress concedes that "the South's system of agricultural finance could not be overturned through cooperative marketing and purchasing alone."[32] Thus, he understands the logic of the politicization of the Alliance movement. But he then argues that the failure of Louisiana Populism lies in its transformation from an insurgent grassroots movement into a conventional political party. After both old parties denigrated the reform demands of the grassroots Populist vision of change, however, it is unclear what realistic option other than a third-party movement existed. Present-day scholars are advantaged by hindsight. For Populist leaders making difficult framing decisions in the 1890s, pragmatic politics likely seemed a reasonable course of action for securing reform demands that were inherently and inextricably political demands. Also, the structure of the political party system at that time was likely perceived as significantly more mutable, given that the Whig Party had successfully formed in opposition to the Democratic Party in the 1830s and had elected several presidents before being destroyed by the debate over slavery in the territories in the 1850s.

POPULIST-REPUBLICAN FUSION IN LOUISIANA: A CONTENTIOUS STRATEGY

In the state election campaign of 1896, representatives from the state Republican Party met with members of the People's Party State Central Committee to negotiate a possible fusion ticket. Important changes promised to make Republican-Populist fusion in Louisiana more potent than it had been previously. Sugar planters had suffered from the sting of falling sugar prices, which had declined from about $0.06 per pound in 1889 to $0.03 in 1894. Initially, planter profitability had been cushioned by a $0.02 per pound subsidy provided by the McKinley-tariff legislation sponsored by Republicans. Between 1890 and 1894 sugar planters had received about $30 million in subsidies. But the Cleveland administration had repealed the subsidy. Even worse, Louisiana's two Democratic senators had supported the bill that rescinded the subsidies.

Sugar planters believed that rescinding the bounty violated a moral contract. The McKinley tariff legislation had called for granting the bounty for fifteen years. With confidence backed by this legislation, sugar planters had borrowed money to make expensive capital improvements. With the bounty eliminated, they were left with large debts and faced possible financial ruin.[33]

In anger, the sugar planters had formed the National Republican Party. The "national" in the party name signified their initial intent to vote Republican in national elections, while voting Democratic in state and local races and standing unified with whites on issues such as race and the appropriate place for blacks socially and politically. Members of the National Republican Party faction were, consequently, often referred to as Lily-White Republicans. However, after all of their congressional candidates were defeated in the 1894 elections, with electoral fraud playing a large role in their defeat, their plans changed. As the 1896 state election approached, they made plans for a much more active role in state election politics.[34]

In their meetings with the Central Committee of the People's Party, the representatives of both the Regular Republicans and the Lily-White Republicans promised that if Populists would campaign against the suffrage amendment and nominate candidates for state office that opposed the amendment, then Republicans would support the People's Party state ticket. Since the third party opposed the suffrage amendment and would retain control over the nomination process, its Executive Committee reasoned that fusion made political sense. Two other factors encouraged fusion: the third party lacked the funds to run an independent statewide campaign and their support was weak outside of the Fourth, Fifth, and Sixth districts. The fusion with Republicans addressed both factors. The sugar planters had an abundant treasury chest to fund the campaign. Also, the strength of the state Republican Party was in the First, Second, and Third Congressional districts—precisely where the Populists needed the most help.[35] Thus, in terms of strategic framing, the Central Committee of the People's Party decided that fusion with the Republicans represented the only chance for political victory, and without victory at the polls the Populist movement would be doomed.

The political reasoning of the Central Committee of the state People's Party, however, did not sit well with some Populists, who were angry at another fusion deal with Republicans. The editor of the *People's Demands,* a third-party paper, argued that the committee had sold out to the "Sugar Teat Aristocrats."[36] Many small farmers who supported the People's Party had always resented the fact that large sugar planters had received millions from the federal government in sugar subsidies to compensate for the fall in sugar prices, while cotton farmers had received nothing to help them with the economic trauma caused by extremely low cotton prices.

The Populist-Republican fusion was also criticized on ideological grounds. Nationally, the Republican Party took a very strident gold-standard stance, which the Populists had always opposed. Furthermore, while the Republican Party consistently supported the tariff, most southern farmers opposed tariffs. Given the fusion deal, the claim that the third party stood firmly on the principles enunciated in its platform was bogus. The editor of the *Colfax Chronicle* put it bluntly: "They are either howling idiots or take all the people for fools" when they say that they stand firmly on their principles.[37]

The Republican-Populist fusion was also attacked on racial grounds. The editor of the *Colfax Chronicle* ridiculed the third party for its on again-off again relationship with the black voter. His commentary on "the new found love for the negro just now pretended by the Populists"[38] was justifiably cynical in view of the racist rhetoric of the major Populist newspaper in the state, the *Louisiana Populist,* since the 1894 election campaign. Populist leaders had wearied of directly challenging the powerful white supremacy culture of the times. They had begun fighting racism with racism. They had declared their agreement with the Democratic Party's tenet that whites must remain politically dominant. They argued, however, that whites should gather under the People's Party banner, the true white party, instead of the Democratic Party, which held on to its power through the manipulation of the black vote.

The claim that the People's Party was the true white party was at odds with the decision of Populist leaders to form a fusion ticket with the Republican Party, which was supported in Louisiana primarily by black voters. The inconsistency between rhetoric and action represented a serious challenge to the state Populist movement. Furthermore, given the strong antipathy of most whites to the Republican Party, fusion was a political gamble.

To complicate matters, the Populist-Republican fusion arrangement soon developed serious problems. Six days before the People's Party state nominating convention was scheduled, the Lily-White faction of the Republican Party assembled in New Orleans and nominated E. N. Pugh, a conservative sugar planter, for governor. This violated the fusion deal, which had given Populists the authority to choose the candidates for state office. When the Populist nominating convention convened on January 8, there was both anger and confusion. Almost none of the delegates were willing to endorse Pugh. The problem, however, was in finding someone to nominate who was ideologically acceptable, had a statewide reputation that made his candidacy credible, and was willing to run. The gubernatorial nomination finally went to Andrew Booth, state chairman of the third party.[39]

Nominees were also selected for the other offices on the state ticket. In a clear rebuke to the sugar Republicans, not a single nominee was a sugar planter. Perhaps this is not surprising, given the poor representation of the sugar parishes at the nominating convention. Although each parish was guaranteed at least one delegate, additional delegates were apportioned for every two hundred votes, or fraction thereof, cast for the Populist ticket in the 1894 congressional elections. Since none of the major sugar-producing parishes received more than the guaranteed one delegate, they had only 11 delegates at the nominating convention out of the 148 delegates present. The Fourth and Fifth District parishes dominated the convention, with a total of eighty-four delegates, or almost 60 percent of the total delegates in attendance.[40]

In a frustrating repeat of the T. S. Adams fiasco that befell the LFU in 1891, shortly after his nomination Booth asked the Central Committee of the People's Party to help him prepare the convention for his resignation so that Pugh could head the ticket. Outraged, the committee asked Booth to resign as nominee and as state chairman of the party. He refused, saying that he would remain the party's nominee until Pugh replaced him. Before adjourning the convention, frustrated delegates adopted a resolution granting the Central Committee the right to fill any vacancies on the ticket created by resignations "or otherwise."[41]

Approximately two weeks after the Populist nominating convention adjourned, the Central Committee of the People's Party again met with Republican leaders. The new fusion deal specified that the Populists could select all the nominees, but the positions of governor, auditor, and attorney general had to be filled from the ranks of the sugar planters. The positions of lieutenant governor, secretary of state, and treasurer were to be filled from the ranks of the People's Party. The gubernatorial candidate chosen by the Populist committee for the new ticket was John N. Pharr. He was one of the largest sugar planters of St. Mary Parish, and one of Louisiana's wealthiest men with a total worth exceeding $1 million. Importantly, he was a strong supporter of bimetallism.[42]

While most Populists reportedly were supportive of the new ticket, there were some that openly protested.[43] R. P. Webb, who had been a Populist candidate for Congress in the Fifth District in 1892, repudiated the fusion ticket as an attempt to barter party principles for the spoils of office. Displaying the racist side of Louisiana Populism, he declared that he had too much faith in the integrity of Louisiana Populists to believe that they would surrender to "the men and political party who tried and who succeeded in Africanizing poor, oppressed Louisiana from 1865 to 1874." He asked:

> Is there outside of our central committee a white man who's ready to help Louisiana Republicans come to power again in our State? . . . in the interest of our party, both state and nationally, in behalf of our principles, in the protection of our wives and daughters, and in behalf of an abiding duty or obligation resting on us to the Caucasian race, . . . tear to pieces the damnable plot gotten up to dump the Populists of our State into the lap of gold bugs, high tariff, [anti]silver, sugar, and negro Republicans . . . Away with, and to Hades with all such dirty, foul, filthy, slimy, villainous, cowardly combines.[44]

There was also grumbling against the fusion ticket among the leaders of the Regular Republican Party faction who were angry that they had been left out of the final negotiations. Since they represented the majority of Republican voters in the state, they felt entitled to participate in any fusion negotiations. Some of them threatened that the black vote either would not be cast or would go to the Democrats. Officially, however, both the Regular Republicans and Lily-White Republicans endorsed the fusion ticket.[45] Their official endorsement is not surprising, given that the fusion deal increased their chances of defeating the proposed suffrage amendment. If the amendment passed, the Republican Party would cease to be a significant factor in Louisiana politics.

Hoping to reduce black support for the fusion ticket, Democrats attacked the fusionists' choice of Pharr for their gubernatorial candidate. They drew attention to his ejection of sugar workers from cabins on his plantation during the strike of 1887. They also stressed how he was a leader in his parish of efforts to keep down the wages paid to sugar workers.[46]

Pharr himself did his share to alienate the black voter. In a speech before a large group of several thousand blacks, he told them in classic white supremacy rhetoric: "The white man is your superior and you must be educated by him. We, the white men of the State, recognize your worth as laborers . . . but you can never hope to occupy the first positions and rule in this land."[47] Importantly, the *Louisiana Populist* published excerpts from his speech with no critical commentary.

In hopes of dissuading white voters from supporting the fusion ticket, Democrats highlighted the alleged evils of the Republican Party during Reconstruction: "It is perfectly evident that the same old leaders of reconstruction days have again forged to the front, and are seeking . . . to dupe and fool the people of this State that they may again assume the reign of power and the privileges of public plunder." They also played up the race factor by referring to Pharr as a "nigger lover" or as "John N(igger) Pharr." The editor of the *Colfax Chronicle* referred to the ticket as "the mongrel ticket" and claimed that "the honest Populist shrinks from it as a horrid monstrosity." He likened the fusion arrangement between the third party and the Republican Party to the 1892 fusion deal, "niggers and all."[48] The *Natchitoches Enterprise* exclaimed: "We are told that politics makes strange bedfellows, and we believe it; now we never expected to see the Populists lying down with the nigger."[49] Finally, in hopes of alienating poor cotton farmers who struggled for financial survival, Democrats noted that Pharr had received federal sugar subsidies of $196,000 from 1891 through 1894. In discussing his wealth, they claimed that he had made his money "grinding the poor."[50]

Not all attacks were directed to Pharr personally. Referring to the fact that the nominees on the fusion ticket were selected by the Populist Central Committee, Democrats argued that the ticket was not a "product of the people," but rather the choices of a "handful of men." They also railed against the fusion ticket as a "disgraceful scramble for spoils," "a shameful dicker," and a "disgraceful sell-out."[51]

Some critics were more muted and sympathetic in their comments. After assuring his readers that he was "no apologist of the Populists," the editor of the *Shreveport Daily Caucasian* argued that citizens should not forget "the service they [the Populists] rendered the State, when as Democrats, they contributed their power and influence to the emancipation of Louisiana from the rule of ignorance and venality." He added that the spread of Populism was due to Democratic Party leaders ignoring the ideological views of the rank-and-file. He asserted that the interest of Populists "in the perpetuation of the rule of intelligence and white supremacy is no less great than their Democratic neighbors and friends." He advised Democratic leaders to appeal to Populists by adopting reform principles and warned that third-party supporters would not be induced to return to the fold "through abuse nor by methods of the political machine."[52]

But such advice was not heeded. The barrage of criticism continued unabated. Populist leaders tried to counter its effects by establishing Populist clubs in as many wards throughout the state as possible. The intent of the clubs was to provide an environment supportive of the third-party movement. Populists also organized numerous barbecues and basket picnics at which candidates on the fusion ticket gave speeches.[53]

The third-party press was also crucial to efforts to defend the People's Party from harsh criticism. Interestingly, and likely the consequence of generous financing by Sugar Republicans, the third-party press significantly expanded in Louisiana in 1895 and 1896. Of the forty-seven papers in Louisiana that endorsed the People's Party in the 1896 election, thirty-one of them debuted in either 1895 or 1896.[54] Fusion had clearly resulted in a major infusion of funds necessary to expand the reach of the third-party press.

In defending the third party from racist criticism aimed at the Populist-Republican fusion ticket, Populist leaders often resorted to racism themselves. For example, the *Louisiana Populist* proclaimed that the leaders of the People's Party had "never negotiated or conferred with any negro individual, committee, or convention unlike the Democrats."[55] In addressing the white supremacy rhetoric of Democrats, it declared: "The colored voter has come to the conclusion long since that the white people must and will control the affairs. . . . The wild shrieks of . . . negro domination fall on deaf ears in the hills of North Louisiana; these brave people have no fear of the negro controlling them, and ever stand ready to enforce the will of the white people."[56]

While battling racism with racism made political sense within the prevailing culture of Louisiana, it certainly was not the way to forge a durable coalition with the bulk of Republican voters who were black. The racist rhetoric within the Louisiana Populist movement reflected its failure to develop and promote a movement culture that transcended the racist, white supremacy culture of the times.

REPUBLICAN-POPULIST FUSION AND POLITICAL OPPORTUNITY

On the eve of the state election of 1896, the Republican-Populist fusion ticket seemed to have the upper hand in the framing of substantive issues. Support for free silver was strong, and state Democrats had excluded the free-silver issue from their campaign. In contrast, Populists had persisted in their calls for reform of the monetary system and argued that the silence of Democrats on the financial issue spoke volumes about their degree of commitment to reform.

Furthermore, those advocating the fusion ticket were positioned to benefit from the increasingly bitter campaign issue of suffrage restriction. The Democrats were faced with the awkwardness of having sponsored the suffrage amendment bill, which was proving to be unpopular with many voters. Governor Foster, who was seeking reelection on the Democratic ticket, was a strong proponent of the bill and claimed that its passage was crucial so that politics in the state would be controlled by the intelligent. This did not sit well with many white, traditionally Democratic voters who disagreed with the disfranchisement of poor whites. It certainly did not resonate with poor whites or blacks.[57] An educational qualification for voting rights threatened to have a much more severe effect in Louisiana than in other states. The state's illiteracy rate was the highest of any state in 1890. Among whites it approached 20 percent, versus 7 percent for the U.S. population in general. For the black population, it exceeded 70 percent.[58] The state's high illiteracy rate was largely a consequence of its abysmally low educational funding. During the late 1880s, the state had spent only $0.52 per capita on public schools compared to the $18.74 per capita funding in Massachusetts. Even the editor of the *Colfax Chronicle*—always loyal to the Democratic Party and a Foster supporter—caustically commented that before disfranchising people based on their lack of education, the state should have at least provided adequate educational opportunities.[59]

The suffrage amendment debate created strong interest among blacks in the election. Since the candidates on the fusion ticket were the only ones who publicly opposed suffrage restriction, the fusion ticket was reportedly garnering strong support among blacks. Populist leaders hoped that blacks might become sufficiently agitated to resist voter intimidation efforts. There was evidence in some parishes to justify this hope. In East Carroll Parish, where 90 percent of the population was black, the parish newspaper commented on local blacks who were "brewing up trouble" by advocating the fusion ticket. Likewise in Morehouse Parish, a leading Democrat railed against "ignorant" blacks who were enthusiastically advocating the fusion ticket.[60]

The prospects for the fusion ticket also benefited from the significant expansion of resources as a result of the relatively fat purse strings of the National Republicans. In contrast to the sparse funding of past Populist election campaigns, Populists now experienced an influx in external funding that allowed the reform press to expand dramatically and reach a much wider audience. Pharr, the gubernatorial candidate of the fusion ticket, also had the funds to campaign aggressively throughout the state.[61]

Another major benefit to the fusion ticket was the expanding political opportunity resulting from a shift in the power alignment among the state's political and economic elite. The sugar planters had split with state Democrats because of the abolishment of sugar subsidies by the Cleveland Democratic administration. Never before had a component of the planter elite abandoned the Democratic Party in a state election. Although many sugar planters had voted Republican in national elections in order to protect their sugar subsidy, most had remained loyal Democrats in state elections. The *Iberville South* expressed the dismay of many Democratic leaders when it declared: "To think that any number of the Southern planters . . . should now go over . . . to the coons and to a small body of communists in the northern corner of the State, is more than astounding!" The *New Orleans Daily States* railed against the political combination of "hayseed and canejuice . . . and malodorous nigger wool."[62]

The strength of the sugar planter elite in the First, Second, and Third Congressional districts nicely complemented the strength of the Populists in the Fourth, Fifth, and Sixth Congressional districts. Consequently, an electoral victory for a fusionist Republican-Populist ticket seemed possible. Prospects for victory also seemed to be enhanced by the fact that reform Democrats in Orleans had split with the Democratic political ring run by the mayor of New Orleans and had formed the Citizens' League. Although the latter organization remained officially neutral in regard to the Foster and Pharr contest, it strong opposed the re-election of Mayor John Fitzpatrick who was a political ally of Foster. Supporters of the fusion ticket hoped that the strong anti-Fitzpatrick sentiment would undercut support for Foster. They also hoped that the Citizens' League reformers would be able to forestall much of the ballot-box tinkering that typically occurred in the precincts of Orleans Parish.[63]

Populists also hoped to benefit from the strong anti–Cleveland sentiment among many Democrats. Cleveland remained committed to the gold standard, despite the worsening economy. Crop prices had hit a fifty-year low for cotton, the mainstay of most small farmers in Louisiana. Tremendous resentment was building. Anti-Cleveland sentiment had grown so strong by 1895 that the *Shreveport Daily Caucasian*, traditionally a fiercely loyal Democratic paper, declared that the people would no longer respond to calls for party loyalty without regard to party principles. It argued that "it were better that the party be dead and buried" than that it be supported despite its denouncement of silver and its support of Cleveland.[64]

However, highlighting the importance of depicting the concept of political opportunity multi-dimensionally, the political opportunity for the electoral success of the fusion ticket remained very poor on one crucial dimension: the extent to which the political system was open to voter influence. If the integrity of the democratic process is significantly compromised by intimidation and fraud, as it was in Louisiana elections, then the political sentiments of voters are less important. If votes are not counted as cast, efforts to court voters are futile. Given voter intimidation and fraud in Louisiana elections, particularly in the alluvial cotton parishes, the fusionists were still struggling upstream. This was the Achilles' heel of the Populist movement, the fatal flaw in its strategic framing. Regardless of its success at convincing voters to cast their ballots for the fusion ticket, the Democrats held the upper hand as long as they had the ability to manipulate electoral results.

The Central Committee of the state People's Party was very aware of this obstacle to success and spoke with top officials in the Foster administration about election fraud. The committee informed these officials that the people would no longer peacefully submit to these frauds and warned them that "if the peace of the state is endangered it will be by those who are trying to rob the people of their sacred right of suffrage."[65] But the warning appears to have had little effect. Intimidation in the days leading up to Election Day was overt. Shreveport, the major town in Caddo Parish, was such a reactionary bastion that Pharr chose not to include it in his campaign speaking tour. The printing press of a Populist newspaper in the town of Minden in Webster Parish was destroyed. In East Baton Rouge Parish, a Populist candidate for office was shot and another had his barn burned. In regard to the intimidation of black voters, the *Lake Providence Banner-Democrat* warned blacks in East Carroll Parish to leave politics alone if they wanted to reside in the parish. Governor Foster had to send troops to quell political violence that erupted in St. Landry Parish when Democrats violently reacted to the efforts of fusionists to register more black voters.[66]

Although the most common form of intimidation was the threat of bodily harm, some blacks were killed in political conflicts during the campaign. As Louisiana historian William Hair observed, the "bitter passions unleashed by the campaign helped give the state another unenviable niche in the record books of violence."[67] In 1896 there were twenty-two people lynched in Louisiana, about one-fifth of the total number of lynchings in the United States for that year.[68] Although all of the lynchings cannot be conclusively linked to politics, the racial tensions surrounding the campaign at least indirectly contributed by fostering a climate in which violence against blacks was tolerated, if not encouraged.

As Election Day neared, it became clear that some Democrats were determined to win the election by whatever means necessary. A leading Democratic newspaper in Caddo Parish, the most populous parish in the Fourth Congressional District and where third-party sentiment was strong, declared: "It is the religious duty of Democrats to rob Populists and Republicans of their votes whenever and wherever the opportunity presents itself and any failure to do so will be a violation of true Louisiana Democratic teaching. The Populists and Republicans are our legitimate political prey. Rob them! You bet!"[69]

Shortly before Election Day, Hardy Brian declared that it would take a "gigantic piece of stealing" to count Pharr out.[70] Unfortunately, Democrats were up to the challenge.

ELECTORAL SHENANIGANS

The official returns gave Foster a victory over Pharr, 116,116 to 87,698. While Foster garnered about 57 percent of the total vote, he only carried seven of the thirty-two parishes in which whites represented a majority of the registered voters. His victory rested on his strength in the voting returns of the twenty-three parishes where registered black voters outnumbered whites. The seven largest black parishes—Bossier, Concordia, East Carroll, Madison, Morehouse, Tensas, and West Feliciana—gave 16,933 votes to Foster and only 467 to Pharr.[71] These were cotton parishes, where sugar planters did not have the political influence to forestall extensive electoral fraud.

Populists railed against the fact that Foster's victory rested on the vote count in the black parishes. The *Louisiana Populist* commented: "How senile and ludicrous the continued cry of 'Negro domination!' sounds in the face of the fact that nearly every white parish in the state gave the Pharr ticket a majority. . . . The real negro domination which afflicts us is the wholesale counting in of the negro votes for the Democratic candidates to counteract the ballots of the white citizens who voted the other way."[72]

Populists argued that voter registration figures in the alluvial cotton parishes were padded. Their complaint was legitimate, since there were more adult males registered to vote in these parishes in 1896 than were counted in the population census four years later. For example, in Tensas there were

5,877 adult males registered to vote, but only 4,814 males over the voting age of 21 recorded in the 1900 census. To make matters worse, the number of votes counted in many parishes on Election Day exceeded the embellished number of registered voters.[73]

Populists also alleged that Democrats had distributed large sums of money on Election Day to blacks to get them to vote for the Democratic ticket. Furthermore, they complained that they had been denied representation at the polls and suspected that the final vote count had been manipulated.[74] Their suspicions were understandable, given Foster's landslide victories in most of the alluvial cotton parishes. As Table 9 indicates, his victories in these parishes contrasted sharply with the returns in the alluvial sugar plantations. Had the vote distribution in the eight alluvial cotton parishes resembled that in the alluvial sugar parishes, the race would have narrowed dramatically.

TABLE 9
Election Results in Major Alluvial Parishes of Louisiana in the Gubernatorial Election, 1896

MAJOR COTTON PARISHES	FOSTER	PHARR
Bossier	3,464	58
Caddo	3,210	277
Concordia	3,013	80
East Carroll	2,635	—
Madison	1,803	—
Morehouse	1,032	385
Tensas	1,968	—
West Feliciana	3,093	1
MAJOR SUGAR PARISHES		
Ascension	1,946	1,909
Assumption	1,087	2,699
Iberia	1,045	1,284
Lafourche	1,817	1,934
Plaquemines	1,832	1,583
St. James	1,801	1,795
St. Mary	1,102	3,483
Terrebonne	1,286	2,203

Source: Report of the Secretary of State, 563.

Adding to suspicions of massive electoral fraud was the fact that election results in most of the alluvial cotton parishes sharply contrasted with those in East Baton Rouge Parish, a heavily black parish where factional fights among parish Democrats allowed black men the freedom to vote without the usual harassment and intimidation and to have their vote counted as cast. Pharr carried the parish 4,859 to 1,470. Returns from this parish suggest what the fusion ticket might have accomplished had there been free and fair elections in other majority-black parishes.[75]

The solid performance of the fusionist ticket in the black precincts of backland parishes is also noteworthy, given that elections in these parishes were relatively free of the manipulation that typified the alluvial cotton parishes. For example, in the Colfax precinct of Grant Parish where most voters were black, Pharr polled 219 votes to Foster's 43 votes.[76]

Few Democratic spokesmen bothered to deny that election fraud had occurred. In fact, some openly boasted of the fraud. It was justified, they argued, because the "opinion of property, intelligence and virtue must take precedence over the wishes of the corrupt mass."[77] They were willing, it appears, to turn a blind eye to the corruption of the political elite within their party.

Tensions mounted over the allegations of election fraud. The governor sent troops to Natchitoches, where hundreds of armed Populists threatened to attack the parish seat of government. They were furious over the refusal of Democratic election supervisors to count the ballots from black precincts where the fusion ticket was known to have been popular. Likewise, troops were sent to St. John Parish when black supporters of the fusionist ticket seized a ballot box they claimed had been stuffed by white Democratic election officials. In the conflict that followed, two white men were killed.[78]

Newspapers were predicting major bloodshed if the fusionists did not accept the official election results. But Populist leaders showed no inclination to capitulate. Hardy Brian, editor of the *Louisiana Populist* and chairman of the state People's Party, called upon the "white men of the state" to assemble in Baton Rouge to legally challenge the election results. If that failed, he advocated the use of violence to overthrow the Foster administration.[79]

It appeared, at least initially, as if the state might be on the brink of a civil insurrection. Nine thousand Populists were reportedly assembling for a march on the state capitol. Sugar Republicans were said to have a boat equipped with munitions of war anchored in the Mississippi River. Alarmed, Democratic leaders began rapidly mobilizing paramilitary units to defend the capitol.[80]

But reason prevailed. Most of the leaders of the fusionists realized that they did not have the organization or munitions sufficient for seizing the capitol and retaining control by force. Consequently, they placed their hope in a legislative investigation into the state election returns. There was at least a thread of hope that the legislature might overturn the election returns. Although Democrats had a legislative majority, thirty-five members of the newly convened General Assembly had actively campaigned against the Foster administration—four independents, thirteen Republicans, and eighteen Populists. Additionally, twenty-seven Citizens' League Democrats had been elected in Orleans Parish. The Citizen Leaguers' electoral success had been primarily rooted in an antipathy toward the mayor of New Orleans, who was closely tied to the Foster administration. The hope was that antipathy toward the mayor would taint Governor Foster as well and result in a voting alliance among the Citizen Leaguers, the Populists, and Republicans. But that hope was quickly extinguished. On May 14, a joint session of the legislature convened to consider the election returns. The state legislators refused, by a vote of eighty-six to forty-eight, to investigate the election returns. Most Citizen Leaguers sided with the Democrats.[81]

The supporters of the Populist-Republican state fusion ticket strongly believed that the election had been stolen from them, and an examination of the election returns lends credibility to that belief. Populists had once again learned a bitter political lesson: the political sentiments of voters are immaterial when the electoral process is corrupt.

On one important point, however, the fusionists had been victorious. Their campaign against the suffrage restriction amendment was successful. The amendment was defeated in almost every parish. Voters had refused to support the idea of a constitutional amendment curtailing the right to vote.[82] This success, however, would be short-lived. Democrats would soon find a way to bypass opposition to suffrage restriction, as will be discussed in detail in the following chapter.

Louisiana Populists anxiously looked to the upcoming national elections. Despite the unpopularity of the incumbent Cleveland administration, political opportunity for the third-party movement was bleak. With Democrats willing to use their control over the election machinery to ensure victory, prospects for a Populist victory in the state were poor to nonexistent. The *Louisiana Populist* clearly understood the challenge when it declared that in the November elections "every man who wants honest elections will have to go to the polls with his shotgun."[83]

9

The Collapse of the Populist Movement

AS THE NATIONAL ELECTION CAMPAIGNS of 1896 unfolded, political developments in Louisiana further undermined the state Populist movement. The strength of the Populist-Republican fusion ticket in the white-dominated parishes of Louisiana in the state election of 1896 had alarmed leading Democrats. Consequently, the Foster administration moved to mend the rift between the Foster and McEnery factions of the party by orchestrating the approval by the state legislature of McEnery as one of Louisiana's U.S. senators. It was a narrow victory, with a seventy to sixty-four final vote, but it accomplished the desired effect of bridging the chasm between the two major factions of the party.[1] The healing of the rift significantly reduced the chances for a split in the ranks of the state Democratic Party. A united Democratic Party, in control of the election machinery and with leaders who were not averse to stealing the election, was unbeatable.[2]

Another daunting obstacle threatened to derail the Populist movement. A contentious framing dispute erupted over the proper role of free silver in the upcoming national elections. This dispute had huge implications. The key demands of the Populist movement could only be implemented if the movement succeeded at the national level; a weak national movement unavoidably undercut the movement at the state level. While some Populists wanted to fuse with free-silver advocates, anticipating that such fusion would be under the People's Party banner, others insisted on a campaign devoted to the entire Populist slate of reforms. After the Democrats nominated a free-silver presidential candidate and included a free-silver plank in their national platform, a strategic framing crisis ensued as to whether Populists should endorse the Democratic ticket so as not to divide reform forces. This chapter explores that crisis, its outcome, and the growing factionalism within the third party that would play an important role in its demise.

Another challenge facing the Louisiana Populist movement was the contraction in political opportunity due to the success of suffrage restriction in

1898. This chapter explores the divided opinions among Populists about the disfranchisement campaign and the eventual effects of disfranchisement on the voting base of the third party. It also examines the political decisions made by a constitutional convention in 1898 concerning apportionment to state nominating conventions and seat apportionment in the state legislature. As a result of these political decisions, the structural obstacles to reform—whether through pressure-politics or a third-party movement—were insurmountable.

The coup de grace to the Populist movement came in the form of a credibility crisis for an important part of its diagnostic frame. Since the early 1890s, Populists had emphasized the role that a contracted currency played in the agricultural depression. They had insisted that without bimetallism, and eventually fiatism, an economic recovery was impossible. The partial economic recovery that began in 1898 under the gold-standard policies of the William McKinley administration challenged the credibility of that argument.

STRATEGIC FRAMING IN REGARD TO FREE SILVER

The growing tidal wave of support among voters for free silver was regarded as a momentous development by many leaders within the Populist movement, who believed that the People's Party would be the beneficiary of the popularity of free silver as a reform demand. They were confident that neither of the old parties would endorse free silver in their national platforms, leaving the People's Party to reap the benefits of being the sole party to support the popular reform demand. This reasoning found expression in the *Louisiana Populist:* "Two events are destined to occur at the same moment—the Democratic party will give the country the free coinage of silver when the sea gives up its dead."[3]

Free-silver Democrats were regarded with a great deal of suspicion by the *Louisiana Populist.* The paper had once labeled them as "goldbugs in disguise" and claimed that they were motivated solely by their interests in winning political office. Free-silver Democrats, such as R. P. Bland and William Jennings Bryan, were said to be demagogues who were no more honorable than the party they represented. Acutely aware of the dangers of issue co-optation by the Democratic Party, the *Louisiana Populist* warned its readers that free-silver advocates within the Democratic Party were desperately attempting to lure those interested in reform back into the party. Their free-silver campaign was labeled "one of the cheekiest political moves that has been fathered by any set of political nondescripts since the birth of the devil." As to the possibility of

Populists joining with Democrats under the banner of the Democratic Party should it officially endorse free silver at its national convention in 1896, Brian responded: "Well, hardly. We all remember the spider and fly episode. Come to us."[4]

But concern about the trustworthiness of free-silver Democrats was not shared by all Populists. Some prominent third-party leaders were much more willing to entertain the idea of cooperating with free-silver advocates in the upcoming presidential campaign. A full-fledged framing contest was underway within the Populist movement. The national chair of the People's Party, H. E. Taubeneck, declared in a letter to W. S. Morgan, chair of the National Reform Press Association: "The trouble, Mr. Morgan, is that you are dealing with theories and abstract ideas. . . . That is the difference between you and I. Mine is a cold-blooded, practical politics, and yours is a dreamland, living on theories and abstract ideas."[5]

Tension mounted within the People's Party between free-silver fusionists, who envisioned all those opposed to the gold standard uniting under the banner of the People's Party for the upcoming election, and those advocating a "middle-of-the-road," anti-fusion stance. The *Louisiana Populist* adopted the latter stance: "No fusion, no single plank, no sacrifice of principle. . . . Fusion is disintegration and destruction. Stay in the middle of the road and invite all good men [who desire reform] to join us."[6]

The middle-of-the-road faction, however, was disadvantaged by the fact that Taubeneck had enough support among members of the national Executive Committee of the People's Party to schedule the party's nominating convention to follow the Republican and Democratic nominating conventions. He and his supporters expected both old party conventions to declare for "sound money," leaving the People's Party as the sole bearer of the free-silver cause.[7]

Taubeneck's strategy to gather the free-silver forces under the People's Party banner looked promising after the national Republican Party's nominating convention in June 1896. The Republican Party crushed any hope of free silver through that party. The convention declared for the gold standard by a landslide vote of 818½ to 105½.[8]

The chairman of the Democratic Party predicted, as Taubeneck had, that gold-standard advocates would also dominate the Democratic nominating convention. The Cleveland administration, with the advantage of incumbency and control over patronage and other resources of the executive branch, was thought to have sufficient strength to block the endorsement of free silver at the convention. Less than a month before the Democratic convention, Cleveland expressed confidence that the party would not endorse free silver.[9]

Cleveland, however, had underestimated free-silver sentiment within the party. When the Democratic convention met three weeks after the close of the Republican convention, free-silver Democrats swept the convention. A free-silver Democrat, William Jennings Bryan, was elected as the party's presidential nominee after impressing the conventioneers with his Cross of Gold speech in which he argued that the gold standard had destroyed the economic well-being of rural America and that free silver was essential for economic recovery.[10]

It is important to note that the Democratic Party changed its stance on the need for monetary reform only after the electoral threat to the party was serious enough to threaten the viability of the party in national elections. Thus, the Populist movement should receive credit for success on at least one dimension—it had pushed a major political party to reverse itself on the money question and, in the process, had created an historical first. For the first time in American history, a political party had repudiated its party's incumbent president.[11]

The nomination of a vice president, however, did not go as well for reform Democrats. Arthur Sewall, a shipping and railroad magnate, managed on the fifth ballot to secure the nomination. Although he was one of the few major businessmen in the nation to support free silver, many reformers regarded his business interests and connections to the railroad industry with suspicion. He would be a major detriment to efforts to promote a national Democratic-Populist fusion ticket.[12]

The reform Democratic Party ticket produced a major framing challenge to the Populist movement: the Democratic Party had adopted the only Populist reform demand that had large following among voters—free silver. If the People's Party insisted on a "middle of the road" course and refused to endorse the Democratic Party ticket, it would divide the reform vote and, thereby, undercut any realistic chance of victory for free silver. If the People's Party fused with the Democratic Party, it risked losing both its identity and the loyalty of middle-of-the-road Populists who insisted that Populism stood for much more than free silver.

CHARTING A COURSE IN UNCERTAIN POLITICAL WATERS

When Populist delegates gathered for their national nominating convention in St. Louis, difficult decisions had to be made in terms of both the party platform and party candidates. In regard to the platform, the middle-of-the-road faction pushed for a full endorsement of the People's Party platform adopted in 1892. In his account, historian Lawrence Goodwyn claimed that they were successful: "the essential monetary planks . . . were all reaffirmed."[13] However, contrary to his claim, there were some noteworthy changes in the monetary reform planks. First, the platform no longer mentioned the subtreasury plan or any specific distribution scheme whereby money would be loaned by the government directly to the people at a rate not to exceed 2 percent per annum. This change represented a decreased emphasis on specific mechanisms to address the serious problems created by the growing dependency on crop-lien financing in the South. Second, the monetary planks demanded a "safe and sound" currency issued directly by the federal government without the intervention of banks of issue, rather than the "safe, sound, and flexible" currency demand of the Omaha platform of 1892.[14] This slight change in wording is significant. The flexible currency demand was inextricably linked to the call for irredeemable, fiat currency. A monetary system tied to the volume of gold or silver reserves was inherently constrained in terms of its flexibility. Dropping the demand for a flexible currency was evidence of the success of free-silver advocates in toning down the Omaha platform's monetary planks.

One other noteworthy aspect of the Populist platform was its inclusion of a plank that addressed the suffrage restriction campaigns in southern states such as Louisiana: "the People's Party condemns the wholesale system of disfranchisement adopted in some states as unrepublican and undemocratic, and we declare it to be the duty of the several State legislatures to take such action as will secure a full, free, and fair ballot and an honest count."[15] Importantly, the fair election plank placed responsibility for electoral reform on the state legislatures, rather than the federal government. It is amazing that Populists viewed state legislatures as the proper agents for reform, the very legislatures that were pushing for suffrage restriction and that had turned a blind eye to electoral fraud. Thus, while Populists had a fair election plank in their platform, which was absent from both the Republican and Democratic Party platforms, the plank relegated fair election enforcement to state legislatures from which no political observer could have reasonably expected effective enforcement. Thus their strategic framing of the problem of electoral fraud, which had seriously undercut the southern Populist movement in a number of localities, was inherently flawed and guaranteed to be ineffective.[16]

To a large extent, the inability of Populists to effectively frame the electoral fraud problem hurt the third-party movement in the South as much as the practical politics of the free silver-fusion debate that is heavily stressed in most explanations of the movement's decline. Without federal supervision of voter registration and ballot counting in areas where electoral fraud was rampant, the demand for fair elections was without teeth. In the South, and in no southern state was this truer than in Louisiana, Populists could be counted out at election time regardless of how much their support grew.

As for the decision in regard to the party's national ticket, members of the free-silver faction wanted to support the reformed Democratic Party ticket. They fervently believed that the Democratic presidential nominee, William J. Bryan, was the country's best hope for monetary reform and that any decision short of endorsing Bryan would destroy the chances for reform. In contrast, the middle-of-the-road faction wanted to nominate a straight People's Party ticket. They believed that support of the Democratic Party ticket would destroy the third-party movement.[17]

As for the process of determining the party's nominees, the middle-of-the-road advocates understood that their best chance for defeating free-silver fusion with the Democratic Party would not be gained by a direct attack on Bryan. The vice president nominee, William Sewall, was by far the weaker target. Consequently, they moved to change the regular order of nominating a ticket, holding the vice presidential nomination first. They were confident that the convention delegations would not support Sewall. This would make it next to impossible, they believed, for Bryan to accept the People's Party presidential nomination if it should be offered to him. Their motion to select a vice presidential nominee first carried by a vote of 738 to 638, with all but one of the Louisiana delegates in favor of the motion.[18]

The vice presidential nominations proceeded, with the anti-fusionist faction nominating well-known southern Populist Tom Watson. The faction could not have chosen a stronger advocate of Populist reform principles.[19] Strong pro-Watson speeches were made, with Louisiana delegate A. A. Gunby making one of the best-received speeches on Watson's behalf. He stressed that no one had ever accused Watson of "trying to put the new wine of populism into old democratic bottles." Attacking the occupational background of the nominee of the fusionist faction, Sewall, he declared: "I do not understand why this convention should nominate a president of a national bank in order to put down banks. I do not understand . . . why we should nominate a railroad magnate to check the oppression and monopolies of railroads. Nor can I conceive how sensible men could select the greatest corporationist of New England in order to destroy the encroachment of organized corporate greed." Tremendous applause followed Gunby's speech. When the delegates voted on the vice presidential nomination shortly thereafter, Sewall lost badly.[20]

In regard to the all-important presidential nomination, the middle-of-the-road faction did not want the nomination process to begin until convention delegates were informed whether William Jennings Bryan would accept the nomination, given that the convention had selected Watson rather than Sewall for vice president. When the fusionists put forth Bryan's name, the convention turned into "a howling mob" with fistfights breaking out. But in the end, the middle-of-the-road Populists were unsuccessful in stalling the process.[21]

While the anti-fusionists opposed Bryan, they had difficulty finding a well-known Populist to nominate for the presidency. They finally nominated S. F. Norton, a reform editor from Chicago who was committed to revamping the existing redeemable-money financial system. He was an ardent anti-fusionist who supported Populist reform demands in their entirety. On ideological grounds, he was a solid choice. His obscurity relative to Bryan, however, undercut the chances for a "straight" People's Party ticket. Bryan won the nomination by a landslide, with the final count of 1,042 to 321.[22]

Despite the anti-fusionist position of the *Louisiana Populist* during the months preceding the convention, the Louisiana delegation cast its entire vote for Bryan. The unanimous vote, however, disguised the heated debate within the Louisiana delegation. Hardy Brian had strongly argued against fusion: "the men who ran the machine at Chicago and placed the Westerner in nomination, are the same men who have steeped the party in its blackest frauds in the South for the past twenty years." However, once it was clear to him that he had lost the debate, he went along with the majority opinion within the Louisiana delegation in an effort to demonstrate a united front.[23]

In accounting for the unanimous pro-Bryan vote of the Louisiana delegation, Hardy Brian cited patriotism and the biblical story of Solomon, who discovered the truth about two women who claimed the same child as their own only after calling for a sword to divide a child in half: Voters "will see in the patriotic action of the Populists . . . the mother's love that prompted them to yield to others an honor which was their own, in order to save an issue they had protected when all the world beside were its enemies—FREE SILVER."

Despite the explanation for the unanimous pro-Bryan vote of the Louisiana delegation, there was grumbling later by some ardent Louisiana Populists who warned that "when you dance with a bear, watch your partner."[24]

The pro-Bryan vote of the nominating convention—including the vote of the Louisiana delegation—is best understood as a pragmatic political decision. The delegates wanted to endorse the presidential nominee who was most likely to win the election and to push for some type of monetary reform. There was no question that Bryan had a much greater chance for electoral victory than did a presidential nominee on a straight Populist ticket. Furthermore, putting a straight ticket in the field that competed against the Democratic ticket significantly increased the odds of an electoral victory by the gold-standard Republicans, and the one issue on which Populists and free-silver Democrats wholeheartedly agreed was their opposition to the gold standard.

To label the 30 Louisiana delegates or the 1,042 convention delegates who voted for Bryan at the Populist convention as betrayers of true Populism, as historian Lawrence Goodwyn did in his well-known history of the Populist movement, is to gloss over the political realities of the situation. Furthermore, it is a stretch for Goodwyn to argue that the 321 dissenters who refused to support Bryan represented true Populism, while the 1,042 who supported Bryan represented a "shadow" movement.[25] Such an argument is similar to insisting that a small radical faction within the Democratic Party represents the true Democratic spirit, while remaining Democrats are shadow Democrats. More accurately, Bryan dissenters were uncompromising ideological purists afloat in a sea of third-party political pragmatists. While that pragmatism may be criticized, it is nevertheless understandable given the desperate economic times.

FUSION CONFUSION AND THE 1896 NATIONAL ELECTION

The nomination triangle between Bryan, Sewell, and Watson was extremely awkward. Anti-fusionist Populists began a "No Watson, No Bryan" campaign, arguing that the Democratic Party was trying to destroy the People's Party. The chair of the Democratic National Committee, Senator Jones, ridiculed the notion that Sewall would be withdrawn in favor of Watson: "Just as though such a proposition could be considered for a moment by any right thinking man!" He charged that Populists "were not as a rule a credible class," and "were out for nothing but spoil." In probably his harshest public comment directed at southern Populists, he predicted that "in the end they will . . . fuse with the Republicans and vote for McKinley. They will go with the negroes, where they belong."[26]

Fearful of grassroots insurgency, the National Executive Committee of the People's Party refused to rescind Watson's nomination against his wishes. For his part, Watson adamantly refused to withdraw from the race: "We have conceded everything short of extinction of our party. To go into the national campaign with no Populist on the national ticket disbands the party. The Democratic managers know this. . . . It is not so much free silver they want as it is the death of the People's Party." Although the Bryan-Watson Populist ticket remained in the field, Bryan studiously ignored any acknowledgment of or contact with Watson.[27]

Populist leaders at the state level were unsure how to proceed in regard to the Bryan-Sewall-Watson dilemma. The Louisiana People's Party met in a state convention, and a heated discussion ensued. The convention delegates eventually voted to retain flexibility by leaving the final decision up to the members of the Central Committee of the state People's Party.[28]

As Election Day neared, the National Executive Committee of the People's Party finally felt compelled to address rank-and-file Populists through a letter printed in Populist newspapers throughout the nation. The committee stated that it had hoped that "the patriotic action of the People's Party . . . in subordinating the interests of party to the success of the vital issues involved in this campaign, would be met by equally unselfish devotion to a common interest on the part of the Democratic party." The letter went on to say that the committee had hoped that "all the friends of silver could present a solid front against the minions of greed by supporting one ticket, the truly cooperative ticket, Bryan and Watson."[29] Its hope for a cooperative ticket destroyed, the committee outlined two alternative courses of action: insistence on a straight People's Party, Bryan-Watson ticket in every state, which would unfortunately divide the reform vote between the Populist and Democratic tickets and greatly increase the odds of McKinley winning the election, or the arrangement of a formal division of the Electoral College vote between the Bryan-Watson and Bryan-Sewall tickets in every state possible. The latter course of action was the strong preference of the Executive Committee, which argued that it was the best way "to overcome the obstacles and embarrassments which, if the Democratic Party had put the cause first and party second, we would not have encountered."[30]

The members of the Central Committee of the Louisiana People's Party hurriedly followed the advice of the National Executive Committee by arranging a fusion deal with the state Democratic Party. In one of the more generous arrangements arranged by southern Populist leaders, Louisiana Populists secured half of the vice presidential electors. The chair of the National Executive Committee of the People's Party, Senator Butler, congratulated Louisiana on securing such a "good" fusion deal.[31]

From a political standpoint, however, nothing much was gained from the fusion deals in regard to the vice presidential nominees in Louisiana and the other twenty-seven states where Populists were successful in arranging fusion. The Democratic Party in the remaining states refused such arrangements. In large part, the refusals were the result of the People's Party's poor bargaining position in those states. Instead, Democratic leaders relied on the campaign threat that a vote for the Bryan-Watson ticket was a vote for the McKinley-Hobart ticket. Their threats worked. Watson suffered the humiliation of having Populist campaign committees, desperate not to split the reform vote, withdraw the Bryan-Watson ticket from the field whenever formal fusion arrangements could not be secured. Even in his home state of Georgia, mere days before the election, the state Populist committee withdrew the Bryan-Watson ticket.[32]

While the Democratic-Populist presidential candidate lost, Bryan's showing was impressive in many ways. His total popular vote was larger than that of any previously elected president. He received 6.5 million votes (46.8 percent) to McKinley's 7.1 million votes (50.9 percent). He carried twenty-six states, while McKinley won in only twenty-one states. His weakness was in the industrial states; he failed to carry a single industrial state. His strength, as had been expected, was in the western and southern states: he lost only five states west of the Mississippi and only four states south of the Mason-Dixon Line—and in some of these states, he lost by slim margins. Political analysts have computed that a change of about 19,500 votes in these states would have given him an electoral victory.[33]

As for the vice presidential election, Watson only received twenty-seven Electoral College votes, all the result of prearranged fusion deals at the state level. Watson's poor showing reflected the ruin that the Bryan-Sewall-Watson three-way race had brought to the Populist movement.[34]

Looking at the election results from Louisiana, Bryan carried the state as expected. As for the vice presidential race, Louisiana granted four of its eight vice presidential electors to Watson and the other four to Sewall in keeping with the fusion arrangement arranged in the month before Election Day.

Fusion between the Democrats and Populists in Louisiana had been confined to the presidential ticket. Populists had fielded candidates against Democratic incumbents in four of the state's congressional districts. Populist candidates in the Third and Sixth districts did extremely poorly, garnering a mere 195 votes and 924 votes, respectively. Populist candidates in the Fourth and Fifth Congressional districts fared better. Fourth District Populists had chosen B. W. Bailey as their candidate, as they had in the 1894 congressional race. He received 31.5 percent of the vote compared with the 32.6 percent share he had received in 1894, indicating that third-party sentiment in the Fourth District held fairly steady despite the tension over fusion. Fifth Congressional District Populists had nominated Alexis Benoit, who had also served as their candidate in the congressional race in 1894. Benoit received 32 percent of the vote compared to only 23.5 percent in 1894. It is hard to say whether his increased support was due to increased third-party sentiment, or whether there was less electoral fraud than had previously plagued congressional elections in this district as a result of the Democratic-Populist fusion in the presidential race.[35]

By running straight People's Party tickets in the congressional races, Louisiana Populists had tried to maintain their third-party movement. But the question that loomed large was how the People's Party would fare in the future: Was it defunct? Would it regain its distinctive identity?

Three major challenges faced Populists in the aftermath of the elections of 1896. One challenge was to heal the breech between mid-road and fusionist Populists. The second major challenge was the gathering momentum of suffrage restriction efforts that threatened the voter base of the movement. The third challenge arose from the general economic recovery that began in 1898.

FACTIONALISM AND SCHISM

In the aftermath of the election of 1896, middle-of-the-road Populists were determined to wrest control of the party from the fusionists. Their presidential nominee at the People's Party nominating convention in 1896, S. F. Norton, emphatically declared: "We do not believe that there is any possibility of fusion in 1900."[36] Middle-of-the-road Populists, however, faced an immense framing challenge. They had to convince the majority of Populists that fusion with free-silver advocates under the Democratic Party banner was ill-advised in future political campaigns. The *Louisiana Populist* accepted the challenge. It insisted that a single-issue, free-silver campaign in 1900 would be "wrong-headed." To those agitating for such a campaign, it exclaimed: "Mistake! We tried a single issue campaign and failed." It reprinted a letter from one of the members of the National Executive Committee of the People's Party who believed that the Democratic Party would continue the silver fight and that warned: "Two parties cannot exist on the same issue. The greater absorbs the smaller. Therefore, if we remain mere camp followers of another party, disintegration will result."[37]

The alternative to fusion was an aggressive educational campaign on the importance of the Populist principle of fiatism. The *Louisiana Populist* renewed its attack on the "redeemable metal" theory of money, an attack that it had avoided during the election campaigns of 1896 when it had hoped that free-silver forces would ally themselves with the People's Party. It again stressed that the value of money did not have to be, nor should it be, determined by the intrinsic value of the material of the coin or the amount of gold or silver in federal reserves. Rather, it was the number of dollars in circulation that determined the value of money. True financial reform required an irredeemable money supply, the volume of which was controlled by the federal government.[38]

Elaborating further, the *Louisiana Populist* renewed its charge that bimetallism was a flawed financial reform proposal. Although silver coinage would allow for the expansion of the volume of currency, it would be insufficient in volume to solve the nation's economic ills. Economic recovery demanded a volume of currency that was impossible as long as law dictated that currency had to be backed by gold or silver. Furthermore, bimetallism would leave control of the currency supply in the hands of bankers or "money kings" who benefited from a contracted currency supply and high interest rates. This argument rang true to farmers, many of whom were caught in a vicious debt spiral created by the exorbitant interest rates charged on crop-lien loans. The only solution to this financial conundrum was paper money, as full legal tender backed by the federal government. The government could then regulate the volume of currency in regard to the needs of the economy, rather than the availability of gold and silver.[39]

Consistent with its fiatist message, the *Louisiana Populist* published a letter written by George Washburn, a member of the National Executive Committee of the People's Party, which argued that fiatism was *the* major financial reform demand: "We united with the silver forces in the recent campaign—not because we believe free coinage of silver is the solution to the financial problem, but because it would better existing conditions, would meet the least resistance, and become the entering wedge of our main issue, viz., full legal tender paper money, issued and regulated by the government alone. . . . We are not democrats. . . . We simply united for a single campaign. . . . We do not stand for redemption money."[40]

But the mainstream media ignored the middle-of-the-road educational campaign on fiatism, as they had in the past. The editors of major newspapers endorsing the gold standard focused on what they perceived to be the greatest threat—the call for bimetallism. They associated free silver with "cheap money" and insisted that the confidence of the business community in the financial system necessitated an "honest dollar" or "sound money" backed by gold. The editors of major newspapers endorsing bimetallism focused on what they perceived to be the greatest threat—the gold standard. They associated the gold standard with monetary contraction, blaming the contraction for the hard times besetting the nation. Missing in this framing contest in the mainstream media was attention to the call for an irredeemable currency system.[41]

Given that the mainstream media ignored the fiatist perspective on monetary reform, the Populist reform press bore the enormous challenge of educating the public on that perspective. It was a formidable framing challenge, given that its subscriber base was relatively small. It was a challenge that the reform press could not realistically meet.

Seeking to commit the People's Party to an anti-fusionist stance, the National Reform Press Association issued a call for a conference of editors of third-party papers to be held in Memphis in late February 1897. The *Louisiana Populist* urged editors of Populist newspapers in the state to attend. One of the resolutions agreed upon at the convention was that future election campaigns should be waged on the full Populist platform. Another resolution declared: "We strenuously oppose all fusion or entangling alliance with any other political party, and we declare . . . that we will never furl our flag or fight under the banner of either of the two old parties."[42]

Many members of the National Reform Press Association were distrustful of the National Executive Committee of the People's Party, which they held responsible for the fusion debacle. They asked the committee to issue a call for a national convention to discuss the best course of action for the party in the future. But Senator Butler, who currently chaired the committee, did not favor such a convention. Neither did most other members of the committee. They feared that tension between fusion and anti-fusion delegates would result in a formal split of the party.[43]

When the National Executive Committee refused to call a convention, the National Reform Press Association independently issued a convention call for July 4, 1897, in Nashville. A debate concerning the legitimacy of the convention call immediately ensued among Louisiana Populists. The editor of the *Louisiana Populist* initially approved of the Nashville convention and advised sending delegates to represent Louisiana. Other Louisiana Populists, however, opposed sending delegates. They argued that the wait-and-see stance of the National Executive Committee had merit and that Populists should "keep our cool." They also pointed out that of the 102 members of the National Executive Committee that had voiced an opinion, 80 had opposed the calling of a convention.[44]

Hardy Brian, editor of the *Louisiana Populist* and secretary of the Louisiana People's Party, cautioned that ongoing discord within the party would be fatal. He said that it was important to acknowledge that there were honest and sincere men in both the fusion and middle-of-the-road factions. Harmony would prevail "only when [men are] willing to grant to those who hold different views the same high motives for action as each man claims for himself." He advised Populists to "stop abusing those with different views on fusion, who may be led to believe that half a loaf is better than no bread, that of two evils it is wise to choose the lesser." He pointedly stated that "men can be persuaded by argument in kind language who cannot be driven by abuse."[45] In a similar vein, when a prominent Louisiana Populist wrote a letter to the chair of the National Executive Committee, Senator Butler, to express his opposition to fusion, he added: "I am not one of those who believe that either wing of our party is actuated by treacherous motives."[46]

Despite the controversy concerning the Nashville convention, more than six hundred Populists attended. The Committee on Credentials approved 355 of them as voting delegates. Most were from southern states. Despite disagreements among Louisiana Populists on the appropriateness of the Nashville conference, thirteen delegates from Louisiana attended, including A. A. Gunby and B. W. Bailey. The dominance of the South at the convention reflected the strength of anti-fusion sentiment in the South, which derived largely from two factors. First, in the South fusion with the powerful Democratic Party meant absorption and loss of control for Populist leaders. It also meant fusing with a party that in some locales had defrauded the Populists in past elections.[47] In contrast, Populist fusion with the Democratic Party in states such as Kansas, Nebraska, and Colorado meant only a modest loss of control by third-party leaders because the Democratic Party was relatively weak in those states. Second, most southerners had come into the Populist movement through their involvement in the Alliance movement. They had been schooled in the ideology of fiatism since the introduction of the subtreasury plan in 1889. Therefore, they tended to be more skeptical of the claim that free silver was a panacea for the economic ills that they faced. In contrast, in many Western states the ideological difference between Democrat and Populist voters "closely approached the vanishing point."[48] Free silver was the dominant financial reform demand of Populists in these states, rather than fiatism.

The delegates to the Nashville convention took a definitive stance against fusion in future national elections. They also urged greater educational efforts in regard to the full slate of Populist reform principles. But their most important action was the formation of the National Organizing Committee, which was charged with coordinating anti-fusion efforts. It was composed of representatives from each state that had sent delegates to the Nashville convention; Louisiana's representative on the committee was A. A. Gunby.[49] This action in effect created a separate middle-of-the-road national organization that stood ready for independent action should fusionists retain control of the National Executive Committee of the People's Party.

As the congressional elections of 1898 drew near, the National Executive Committee of the People's Party decided that a joint meeting with the anti-fusion National Organizing Committee was necessary. The meeting was scheduled for June 15 in Omaha and, as expected, it was contentious. The National Executive Committee remained under the firm control of those who wanted to retain the option of fusion. It did, however, agree to the creation of a committee of six—three anti-fusionists and three fusionists—to discuss differences and work out a compromise. The end result was the Omaha Contract, which stipulated that the National Executive Committee would not aid fusionists in the upcoming elections. It also declared that the People's Party national nominating convention in 1900 would be called at least thirty days before the Republican Party and Democratic Party nominating conventions.[50]

But the Omaha Contract did not achieve harmony within the party as hoped. Some members of the anti-fusionist National Organizing Committee fervently believed that an early nominating convention was essential to a renewed commitment to Populist principles in their entirety. Consequently, they refrained from voting on the Omaha Contract and independently issued a call for a national convention in Cincinnati on September 4, 1898.[51]

Although the *Louisiana Populist* had been clamoring for a "straight fight in the middle-of-the-road," it rebuked the "fringe element" that had called the Cincinnati convention. Its editor, Hardy Brian, argued that while most southern Populists wanted a straight national ticket in 1900, they were willing to wait patiently until the appropriate time as prescribed in the Omaha Contract.[52]

When the Cincinnati national convention opened, it was clear that the sentiment expressed by the *Louisiana Populist* was not an isolated one. Only twelve states sent delegates. Nevertheless, the convention delegates nominated a straight Populist ticket for the presidential race in 1900. They chose Wharton Barker of Pennsylvania for president and Ignatius Donnelly as vice president. The choice of Barker was odd because he was an obscure figure even within Populist circles. The choice of Donnelly was understandable since he had been instrumental in developing the Farmers' Alliance in Minnesota, had been faithfully at the helm of the People's Party since its inception, and had vehemently opposed fusion in the presidential race of 1896. His advanced age and poor health, however, did not enhance the political attractiveness of the ticket.[53]

The anti-fusionists had been justifiably suspicious of the National Executive Committee. When it convened in February 1900 to set the date and location of the party's nominating convention, a proposal was presented to set the convention for the same time and location as the Democratic Party nominating convention, in violation of the Omaha Contract. Anti-fusionists on the committee argued the proposal was "cowardly and truckling to the Democrats." The proposal was eventually withdrawn, and the national Populist nominating convention was set for May 9 in Sioux Falls, South Dakota.[54]

The reaction of Louisiana Populists to these developments is, unfortunately, unknown. The *Louisiana Populist*—the sole remaining outlet for the views of Louisiana Populists—had ceased publication, a victim of the rapid decline of the Populist movement in Louisiana. The rapidity of its decline was due not only to the ominous developments within the movement at the national level, but to a dramatic contraction of political opportunity within Louisiana because of the successful disfranchisement efforts of the state Democratic Party.

SUFFRAGE RESTRICTION AND POLITICAL OPPORTUNITY

Another major challenge facing the Populist movement in the aftermath of the 1896 election campaigns was the growing push for suffrage restriction. The first successful disfranchisement campaign was in Mississippi in 1890 when Democrats disfranchised most of the state's black voting majority by instituting a literacy requirement. When there was no federal response abrogating that disfranchisement, other southern states became increasingly interested in suffrage restriction.[55]

Democrats in Louisiana had closely followed the suffrage restriction efforts in other southern states. The serious threat created by the Populist-Republican coalition in the state elections of 1896 had increased their interest. The leadership of the Democratic Party was extremely worried about the strong showing of the Populist-Republican fusion ticket in the white-dominated parishes. The Populist taunt that the Democratic Party was a "negro party," due to its dependence on the manipulated vote of black-belt parishes to retain its power, had too much truth to it. The fact that its gubernatorial candidate had failed in 1896 to win in most of the majority-white parishes had stunned party leaders. White supremacy rhetoric, which the party depended upon to retain the loyalty of white voters, was clearly no longer sufficient.

Given the serious challenge to their power, leaders of the Democratic Party in Louisiana renewed their efforts to restrict voting rights. After the defeat in the 1896 state elections of a constitutional amendment to restrict suffrage rights, legislators lost no time in designing another way to curtail voting rights. In the legislative session that followed the 1896 state elections, they passed a bill that put before the voters the question of calling a constitutional convention. Fearing that voters would not approve a new constitution restricting suffrage, legislators attached a proviso to the bill declaring that the new constitution drafted at the convention would become law without being sent to the voters for ratification.[56]

The voting rights of a significant proportion of Louisiana's population were threatened by plans to rewrite the state constitution to allow for voting rights restrictions along the lines of a literacy or education requirement. Louisiana led the nation in the extent of illiteracy among its black population, with

61 percent of its black population under the age of ten reported as illiterate. It was third in the nation in the percent of illiteracy among its white population, with 17 percent of its white population under the age of ten reported as illiterate.[57]

State legislators knew that the odds of getting the constitutional convention bill approved by the present electorate were slim, given the controversial proviso that the new constitution would not require ratification by the people. So they passed a law implementing new voter registration requirements, which would go into effect prior to the vote on the constitutional convention bill. It required all prospective voters to provide certain information, such as birth certificates and proof of residency, to the local registrar's office to avoid being dropped from the voter registration rolls. The local registrars, appointed by the governor and therefore Democrats, were granted total discretion for determining if the information provided by a voter satisfactorily met the requirements. The names of those dropped from the registration list were to be published in the local paper. Unless the purged voter challenged the decision within five days of the publication of his name, the decision was final.[58]

Although the new registration law did not have a property or education qualification, which would have violated the existing state constitution, its clear intent was to reduce the number of uneducated voters of both races. Perhaps the hope was that illiterate voters would be unaware of the new registration law and, therefore, would not file the necessary information with the registrar. The only way that they would become aware of their disfranchisement would be if they read the local paper, an unlikely possibility for illiterate citizens, or if they were informed by others who saw their name in the paper. In rural parishes, communication among the widely dispersed population was such that the likelihood of the latter occurring before the end of the five-day window for objections was improbable.

The new registration law accomplished its purpose. The number of registered voters shrunk from 294,432 on January 1, 1897, to 87,240 on January 1, 1898. The number of blacks registered to vote declined from 130,344 to 12,902, a 90 percent drop. The number of registered whites fell over 50 percent, from 164,088 to 74,133. A Populist activist from Lincoln Parish estimated that third-party strength had been reduced by at least two-thirds. The decline among white voters was at least partly a consequence of political alienation. Some literate small farmers reportedly did not bother with a trip to the registrar's office. Their candidates had been "counted out" through electoral fraud so regularly that they had concluded voting was not worth the effort.[59]

Throughout 1897, the *Louisiana Populist* attacked those pushing for suffrage restriction. It declared: "The whole effort to qualify suffrage in the South under the pretense of white supremacy, is the . . . hand of Plutocracy, clutching at the throats of our laboring and producing classes." It warned its readers that the disfranchisement laws passed in other southern states had disfranchised poor whites, as well as most blacks.[60]

The *Louisiana Populist* also derided the Democratic Party for routinely stuffing ballot boxes and debasing the sacred right of suffrage. It contended that the suffrage restriction campaign of Democrats was a hypocritical and convoluted way to introduce integrity into the election process. It ridiculed the logic of the plan to cure the Democrats' "itch to cheat" on Election Day by denying a significant portion of the state's current electorate their voting rights. It pointedly observed the absurdity of denying up to half of the current electorate in the state their voting rights—citizens who never cast a fraudulent vote or signed a false return, "leaving the ones who did all the corrupt and corrupting things in full possession of the franchise, election machinery, and counts." This made as much sense as protecting people from contagious diseases by killing them. In a similar vein, it declared: "According to this beautiful logic the way to stop lynching is not to hang the inhuman brutes who are guilty of rape, but to hang all the poor helpless girls and the fair, frail women who might unwittingly be the temptation to these fiends."[61]

A more direct manner of addressing election fraud, according to the *Louisiana Populist,* lay in "four words that were also delivered in Sinai: 'Thou Shalt Not Steal.'" If Democrats were truly interested in the integrity of elections, then all that was necessary was that they vigorously prosecute election swindlers.[62]

The *Louisiana Populist* warned its readers that suffrage restriction would not be an effective solution to the electoral fraud. This warning stemmed from its recognition that some Populists reasoned that disfranchising black voters would help the third party. Their reasoning was as follows: if blacks were disenfranchised, Democrats would not be able to manipulate the black vote in the plantation parishes. The manipulated black vote was the basis, to a large extent, of the tremendous power of planters in the Democratic Party. It was used to garner disproportionate influence in nominating conventions of the party and in the state legislature since both the apportionment of convention delegates and the allotment of legislative seats were based on the party vote in the previous election. The manipulated black vote also ensured the Democratic Party of electoral victory whenever it came under serious attack.[63]

The *Louisiana Populist* countered that even if blacks were denied voting rights, Democrats could still steal elections by manipulating the white vote as they had done in the past. It also caustically pointed out that the Democrats' proposal to disfranchise the poor and uneducated was especially unfair since Democrats were to blame for the state's poorly funded and grossly inadequate school system. If uneducated voters were the real problem, then the Democrats should address the root of the problem through improving funding of the state's public education system.[64]

Nowhere was the blaming-the-victim consequence of disfranchising the illiterate voter, to which the *Louisiana Populist* alluded, more true than in Louisiana, where educational funding was pathetically low. In 1886, the state had spent a mere $0.52 per capita versus $18.74 per capita in Massachusetts. The *Farmerville Gazette* complained that the state's public school system was in "deplorable condition," saying it was "little, if any, better than no system at all."[65]

Educational funding was lowest in the rural parishes of Louisiana. In the Fourth Congressional District, where the strength of the LFU and People's Party was greatest, educational funding was only about $0.36 per capita. In Winn Parish, a controversy erupted when the parish government refused to set aside taxes to support local schools. In many parishes, the funding of schools was so low as to make the task of educating most school-aged children impossible. In the Sixth Congressional District parish of St. Landry, the town of Opelousas required teachers to furnish a meeting place at their own expense. Consequently, the schools were extremely crude, with boxes often serving as chairs and facilities overcrowded and poorly ventilated. The four school facilities "if put up and sold at public auction, on liberal terms, including that which, for want of a more appropriate name we must call furniture, would not bring enough to pay for the erection of a decent cow-shed." Some rural communities within the parish were even more unlucky and did not have any public school accommodations.[66]

It is difficult to assess the general feeling among Louisiana Populists about the disfranchisement campaign. There were definitely some Populists who lashed out at the black voter rather than the Democrats who were primarily to blame for election fraud. For example, J. T. Howell, a member of the state executive committee of the People's Party from predominantly black East Baton Rouge Parish, declared that the black voter was "incapable of exercising the franchise for the common good." He argued that it was "essential that white men demand and insist upon his elimination as a factor in our political system."[67]

According to the *Louisiana Populist,* however, the prevailing sentiment at a Populist camp meeting in Monroe in August 1897 was "largely in favor of manhood suffrage as against $$ suffrage." This portrayal is consistent with the suffrage plank in the state People's Party platform, which was approved by the majority of delegates to the state People's Party convention in 1897. The plank explicitly supported voting rights "for every man 21 years old, and of necessary residence, who discharges all the duties of citizenship." Populists also reportedly had strong feelings that any new constitution should be submitted to the vote of the people.[68]

Although state Populist leaders opposed the constitutional convention bill, they knew that it would likely be approved, given the changes in the electorate under the new voter registration law. Therefore, they called upon parish Executive Committees of the party to field Populist nominees for the constitutional convention. They also issued a call for a Populist nominating convention in Monroe for the purpose of nominating a slate of at-large delegates.[69]

One hundred and twenty-four delegates attended the Monroe convention. A debate emerged between two different proposals concerning nominations: one proposal called for a straight Populist ticket—even if that meant all nominees came from north Louisiana. The alternate proposal, advocated by Hardy Brian who chaired the convention, called for a nonpartisan ticket that would include Populists from areas where there was significant third-party support and independent-minded Republicans and Democrats from areas where the third party was weak. The debate between the two proposals was prolonged, with the Committee on Nominations closely divided. Finally convention delegates were polled, and they expressed a preference for a nonpartisan ticket. Their reasoning seemed to be that such a ticket had the best chance of electoral success. In deference to that sentiment, the Committee on Nominations put together a nonpartisan ticket that was subsequently approved by convention delegates.[70]

It was a sad reflection on the condition of the third-party movement in Louisiana that more than six years after its inception it could not nominate a straight ticket that was viable in a statewide election. Most of the non-Populist nominees on the non-partisan ticket were white leaders of the "negro wing" of the Republican Party. The sugar-planter leaders of the Lily-White Republican faction, who had allied themselves with the Populists in the state elections of 1896, generally supported the disfranchisement effort.[71]

Even in its stronghold of the Fourth Congressional District, the People's Party faced challenges to its anti-disfranchisement campaign. Nowhere was the challenge more acute than in Natchitoches Parish, the publishing home of the *Louisiana Populist.* The editor of the *Louisiana Populist,* who had used the columns of the paper repeatedly to lash out at the Democrats' suffrage restriction plans, must have been sorely frustrated by the selection of E. J. Gamble and S. E. Russ as the Populist nominees for parish delegates to the constitution convention. Gamble had publicly declared that voting should be limited to the "intelligent," and that the "ignorant negro vote . . . should be forever eliminated."[72] If elected as a delegate, he promised to work to achieve this end. Also, he publicly declared that poll taxes paid by whites should support white schools only, with black poll tax dollars supporting black schools. Such a distribution of educational funding guaranteed persistently high illiteracy rates among blacks, and therefore their perpetual disfranchisement. The record indicates that Russ, the other Populist nominee, concurred with Gamble's views.[73] Thus, despite the attacks by the *Louisiana Populist* on the disfranchisement efforts, Populists in Natchitoches Parish had nominated two constitutional convention delegates who supported suffrage restriction.

The variation in publicly expressed attitudes of better-known Populists about disfranchisement has led to confusion and disputes among historians. Louisiana historian William Hair claims that Populists stood up for the interests of the black man and opposed disfranchisement. He portrayed Louisiana Populists as being "in favor of fighting wrong to the bitter end."[74] He neglects, however, to mention the attitudes of Louisiana Populists such as Gamble and Russ.

Historians such as C. Vann Woodward, J. Morgan Kousser, and Michael Perman focus in their writings on the resistance to disfranchisement by Populists and poor whites in general. However, in his book *The Disfranchisement Myth,* Glenn Feldman argues that the depictions of "plain-white resistance to disfranchisement have been greatly exaggerated." He bases his assessment on a case study of Alabama, the only state where the suffrage restriction amendment was submitted to the people for ratification. He argues that emotion surrounding the issue of white supremacy in political decisions played an important role in the stance of whites in regard to disfranchisement. While he concedes that the majority of the resistance to disfranchisement came from "plain whites," he stresses that this is very different from arguing that most plain whites opposed disfranchisement.[75]

The historical record of the stance of Populists in Louisiana suggests that Feldman's depiction of the disfranchisement campaign in Alabama may be an apt description of the Louisiana campaign as well. While there were Louisiana Populists that stridently spoke against disfranchisement, there were others that publicly voiced support for suffrage restriction. While scholars may debate the extent to which rank-and-file Populists in Louisiana supported or opposed disfranchisement in 1897, there should be no debate as to whether those who opposed disfranchisement were effective. Only one People's Party candidate, B. W. Bailey from Winn Parish, was elected by the people of Louisiana to serve as a delegate to the constitutional convention that would be making the final decision on suffrage restriction. The constitutional convention was approved, with 36,178 voting in favor and 7,578 voting against it. All thirty-six at-large constitutional convention delegates were Democrats, as were most of the ninety-eight delegates elected to represent the various parishes at the convention. The lopsided Democratic victory was partly the result of the 1897 voter registration law and partly the result of the intimidation created for less-educated voters by the four-foot ballot that had more than a hundred candidate names on it and a time limit of three minutes for completion. The length of the ballot and time limit likely increased the odds of voters choosing to vote a straight ticket, which significantly simplified the process of filling out the ballot.[76]

The fact that the People's Party was only successful in getting one of its delegates elected says much about the weakness of the third-party movement in the state in 1898. The extremely poor showing of the parish Populist tickets and the nonpartisan ticket of at-large delegates was the first clear indication of the decimation of third-party forces in Louisiana in the aftermath of the implementation of the new state voter registration law. The Louisiana Populist movement was in its twilight and its fate would be sealed once suffrage restriction was written into the new constitution, an inevitable outcome given the overwhelming domination of the constitutional convention by Democrats.

The tone of the constitutional convention was set by the opening remarks of E. B. Kruttschnitt, the president of the convention. He stated: "We know that this convention has been called together by the State to eliminate from the electorate the mass of corrupt and illiterate voters who have during the last quarter of a century degraded our politics." He made no reference to the Democratic Party officials who had played such a prominent role in electoral corruption. He had full authority to appoint the members of the convention's standing committees. In his first action at the convention, Populist Bailey offered a resolution that minority political parties should be represented in the appointment of the various standing committees. His resolution was reported on unfavorably by the Committee on Organization and Rules, and convention delegates subsequently supported a motion to postpone indefinitely a vote on the resolution.[77]

The crucial Committee on Suffrage and Elections was composed of twenty-five members, four from each congressional district and one at-large member.[78] Even if Populists had succeeded in dominating the election of convention delegates in the Populist strongholds of the Fourth and Fifth Congressional districts, they would still have been a minority on the committee and relatively powerless to halt the disfranchisement effort. Furthermore, Kruttschnitt would have almost surely given committee appointments to Populists, such as Gamble and Russ, who concurred with Democrats on the need for suffrage restriction.

The Committee on Suffrage and Elections submitted a proposal that would have required voters to demonstrate the ability to read and write in their native language or, as an alternative, own property assessed at $300 or more. They included a "grandfather clause" as a loophole for poor whites: those who had voted prior to 1867, or whose father or grandfather had so voted, were exempted from the literacy requirement.[79] This represented an ingenious attempt to circumvent the Fifteenth Amendment of the U.S. Constitution. Up to now, southern states seeking to disfranchise blacks had used literacy or property qualifications, thereby also restricting the voting rights of many poor whites.

The grandfather clause was extensively debated at the convention. Some delegates objected to it because they believed that the literacy clause should be applied to everyone and favored a straightforward educational or property qualification. Other delegates—including both of Louisiana's U.S. senators—objected to it because they believed it conflicted with the Fifteenth Amendment to the U.S. Constitution, which stated that no state could abridge the right to vote on the basis of race. But the majority of the members of the Committee on Suffrage and Elections supported the grandfather clause, as did most of the convention delegates. The final vote on the grandfather clause was ninety-five in favor, twenty-eight opposed, with eleven delegates absent. Populist delegate Bailey voted against it, asking that the record show that he opposed the disfranchisement proposal as a whole.[80] Although the only Populist candidate to the convention firmly stood his ground on opposing disfranchisement, as the sole representative of Populism at the convention he was utterly irrelevant.

The only other comments in the historical record in regard to Populist sentiment about the suffrage restriction clause being drafted by the convention were by Hardy Brian, editor of the *Louisiana Populist* and chair of the State People's Party Executive Committee. While he criticized the constitutional convention for making "long strides toward destroying the rights of suffrage," he noted that "the great army of tramps, negroes, and dead men who filled up the rolls and furnished names with which to stuff ballot boxes in the cities and the black belt are swept away." In commenting upon the grandfather clause specifically, he declared that if it were the final result of the convention, "the convention will have done well." He further remarked that if all the educated, the property owners, and "the voters of 1868" were given suffrage rights, "we might once more boast of a Democratic form of government in Louisiana."[81] Apparently the disfranchisement of black voters, who represented about half of all the adult male citizens in the state, was not significant enough a matter to make him question the appropriateness of boasting of democracy in Louisiana. This is a far different portrayal of Louisiana Populists than that popularized in William Hair's account in *Bourbonism and Agrarian Protest.*

It is important to note that the grandfather clause did not permanently exempt white illiterates from the new literacy requirement. It gave whites a mere four months to file for an exemption. After that, they were subjected to the same literacy or property requirements as blacks. As the four-month period neared an end, the *Louisiana Populist* urged Populists to take advantage of the grandfather clause and register to vote: "Those who neglect it now will repent later."[82] The editor, Hardy Brian, worried that voting strength in the parish could be cut in half by disfranchisement. His worries were warranted. When the suffrage restriction amendment went into effect and the grandfather clause loophole was closed, the number of registered white voters plummeted.

As indicated in Table 10, white voter registration between 1896 and 1898 dropped 75 percent. The dramatic decline of the white electorate held true for those parishes where the Louisiana Populist movement had its greatest strength: Catahoula, Grant, Jackson, Lincoln, Sabine, Union, Vernon, and Winn parishes. The white electorate in these parishes fell more than 70 percent between 1896 and 1898, from 15,227 to 4,474. This dramatic decline deserves a prominent place in any discussion of the collapse of the Louisiana Populist movement. It is puzzling that in his discussion of the demise of the Populist movement in Louisiana, historian Lawrence Goodwyn ignored the role of white disfranchisement.[83]

TABLE 10
Voter Registration in Louisiana Parishes in 1896 and 1898, by Race

PARISHES	1896 WHITE	1898 WHITE	1896 BLACK	1898 BLACK
Acadia	3,257	545	641	0
Ascension	1,035	1,111	2,298	0
Assumption	2,526	1,645	2,467	0
Avoyelles	2,894	920	2,529	0
Bienville	2,354	413	1,250	0
Bossier	1,427	720	4,624	0
Caddo	2,215	28	4,258	0
Calcasieu	5,725	361	1,526	0
Caldwell	710	145	640	2
Cameron	583	97	82	0
Catahoula	1,585	177	1,195	0
Claiborne	2,110	565	1,940	0
Concordia	400	48	3,437	0
De Soto	2,037	41	2,875	0
East Baton Rouge	2,839	48	5,221	0
East Carroll	386	47	2,635	0
East Feliciana	1,180	26	2,571	0
Franklin	865	220	1,026	0
Grant	1,813	822	912	0
Iberia	2,846	1,204	1,944	0
Iberville	1,800	564	3,466	0
Jackson	1,154	415	496	3
Jefferson	685	579	821	0
Lafayette	626	768	0	0
La Fourche	4,712	2,683	3,282	0
Lincoln	2,470	727	1,431	1
Livingston	1,590	629	350	0
Madison	290	10	2,034	0
Morehouse	892	25	2,888	0
Natchitoches	3,222	316	1,312	0
Orleans	45,907	5,882	14,177	8
Ouachita	1,565	172	2,112	0
Plaquemines	1,888	410	1,974	0
Pointe Coupee	1,333	830	4,254	0
Rapides	6,633	152	3,323	0
Red River	829	77	1,541	0

PARISHES	1896 WHITE	1898 WHITE	1896 BLACK	1898 BLACK
Richland	814	144	1,858	1
Sabine	3,399	903	680	0
St. Bernard	843	284	852	1
St. Charles	558	658	2,138	23
St. Helena	816	163	804	0
St. James	2,051	143	3,160	1
St. John the Baptist	1,557	360	2,646	18
St. Landry	4,686	2,564	3,121	0
St. Martin	2,212	1,151	1,980	1
St. Mary	2,461	343	3,939	0
St. Tammany	1,693	993	1,141	48
Tangipahoa	2,131	363	1,013	1
Tensas	575	304	3,203	1
Terrebonne	2,513	1,851	2,355	0
Union	2,026	280	1,457	0
Vermillion	3,208	1,074	686	0
Vernon	1,311	705	70	0
Washington	1,190	462	420	0
Webster	1,521	791	1,348	0
West Baton Rouge	750	65	1,873	0
West Carroll	306	182	586	0
West Feliciana	700	227	3,802	0
Winn	1,469	445	185	2
TOTAL	153,173	37,877	126,849	111
% CHANGE		-75%		-99%

Source: Report of the Secretary of State, 554 and 558.

Two other important decisions affecting future political opportunity for the third-party or any other reform movement in Louisiana were made by the delegates to the constitutional convention. The first decision concerned whether voter registrars should be elected or appointed. In the past, registrars had been appointed by the governor. This assured the Democrats of a loyal party man should circumstances dictate a need for adjusting the vote count. In a revealing comment, Charles Boatner—an ultra conservative planter who represented the Fifth Congressional District in Congress and whose election in 1894 had been contested because of voting irregularities—stated that there was no longer a need for an appointed, versus elected, registrar "since the classes which have been the object of so much apprehension for many years have been eliminated from our suffrage system."[84] Nevertheless, conservatives successfully pushed for the continued appointment of registrars by the governor. Apparently, they were not willing to take any chance of losing control over who won elections in Louisiana.

The second decision concerned seat apportionment in the state legislature and for state political conventions. The apportionment decision, which was finalized in the last days of the convention, was amazing: While convention delegates had already voted in favor of suffrage restriction that would disfranchise the vast majority of the state's black population, they voted to base apportionment on the total population count.[85] Therefore, the planters who had been deprived of the political benefits of the fraudulent counting or manipulated black vote now gained tremendous political benefit by having the disfranchised black population counted in the apportionment formula. This would allow them to retain their disproportionate and controlling influence in state political conventions and in the state legislature, effectively blocking any nominee for state office or any state legislation that threatened their interests.

If Louisiana Populists still harbored any optimism concerning their possible political influence in the absence of a manipulated black vote, the apportionment decision of the constitution convention effectively killed those fantasies. No decision could have dealt a stronger blow to the Louisiana Populist movement. The *Louisiana Populist* railed against the apportionment decision, saying that Bossier Parish with about 800 to 900 white voters would be apportioned the same number of delegates to state and district political conventions as Natchitoches Parish with its 2,500 to 3,000 white voters. Similar apportionment in terms of seats in the state legislature would make it almost impossible to push any reform legislation through the legislature.[86]

The anger of Populist leaders in Louisiana toward the final outcome of the constitution convention brewed intense resentment toward those who had sympathized with the reform demands of the Populist movement, but remained loyal to the Democratic Party when electing delegates to the constitutional convention. The editor of the *Louisiana Populist* caustically remarked: "Trust in the Democratic party some more. Go on and swallow its promises for the 47th time, it don't cost the party any thing to make them or to break them, and you—well, you be d——d!"[87] The anger was rooted in the realization that the Louisiana Populist movement had been dealt a fatal blow. The *Louisiana Populist* would soon cease publication, a victim of the rapid decline of the Populist movement within the state.

A FRAME CREDIBILITY CRISIS

A number of historians have recognized the role of economic recovery in the demise of the People's Party. These historians note that general economic prosperity was returning by 1898, and they argue that this prosperity swept away much of the discontent that had fueled the rise and growth of Populism.[88] However, the claim that prosperity had a direct, strongly negative effect on the Populist movement is problematic. An alternative explanation fits the available evidence much better: the improving economy played an *indirect* role in the movement's demise by creating credibility problems for the diagnostic frame of the movement. Despite its importance, the frame-credibility problem has not been explored in past writings on the movement's demise.

While the general health of the American economy was improving by the turn of the century in terms of such measures as unemployment and the profitability of the industrial sector of the economy, the "return to prosperity" explanation of the fall of Populism overlooks the important fact that the renewed prosperity did not trickle down to most small farmers, who continued to experience serious economic problems. As a result of persistent economic hardships among many farmers, there remained sufficient discontent to support political dissent. Census data show that farm tenancy steadily increased as more and more farmers lost their farms. Crop prices remained low for wheat and corn farmers, as indicated in Table 11. The average farm price of wheat was lower in 1900 than it had been in 1896. While the average farm price of corn had improved, it was still 30 percent less in 1900 than it had been in 1890. The farm price of cotton also modestly increased, but it still brought only $0.086 per pound in 1900.[89] Given that the cost of producing cotton for many small farmers was about $0.08 per pound, "renewed prosperity" does not accurately describe their economic situation at the turn of the century. Many of them continued to depend on the notorious crop-lien system of financing, with their debt growing more oppressive over time.

TABLE 11

Average Farm Price of Corn, Wheat, and Cotton in the United States, 1890–1900

YEAR	AVG. PRICE OF CORN PER BUSHEL	AVG. PRICE OF WHEAT PER BUSHEL	AVG. PRICE OF COTTON PER POUND
1890	$0.506	$0.838	$0.086
1891	0.406	0.839	0.073
1892	0.394	0.624	0.084
1893	0.365	0.538	0.070
1894	0.457	0.491	0.046
1895	0.253	0.509	0.076
1896	0.215	0.726	0.066
1897	0.263	0.808	0.066
1898	0.287	0.582	0.057
1899	0.303	0.584	0.070
1900	0.357	0.619	0.086

Source: USDA, *Yearbook of Agriculture*, 699, 709, and 754.

The failure of prosperity to reach the farmer was recognized by the Populist press. The *Louisiana Populist* repeatedly criticized the returning-prosperity frame touted by the nation's big daily papers. It argued that the prosperity was chiefly confined to bondholders, monopolists, stock gamblers, and moneylenders. It insisted that most farmers or wage earners were still struggling financially, and that the claim of renewed prosperity was a sham. The *People's Tribune* also complained about the suffering of small farmers in Louisiana, with the agricultural depression worsened by the effects of a terrible drought.[90]

Occasionally, a major daily newspaper lent its credibility to the Populist claims of "sham prosperity." For example, on the eve of the national Populist nominating conventions in 1900, the headline of the *Dallas Morning News* read: "Prosperity of the Trusts." The article recognized the contradiction between prosperity and hard times. It noted the problem of low wages, which it contrasted to the unprecedented profits earned by corporate trusts. The underlying economic problem was diagnosed as an unfair distribution of profits between labor and capital.[91]

Given that hard times persisted for farmers and many wage earners into the twentieth century, the argument that renewed prosperity undercut the Populist movement overstates the extent to which discontent, which had given rise to that movement, had been blunted. The partial economic recovery, however, did play a role in the demise of Populism by calling into question its framing of the economic problems besetting many farmers. Populists had stressed the evils of currency contraction and the economic problems that it allegedly created. They had repeatedly argued that currency contraction was inevitable under the gold standard. They had insisted that without bimetallism, and ultimately a fiat monetary system, the economy was doomed.

The general economic recovery during McKinley's administration challenged that argument, making the economic frame of the Populists vulnerable to criticism. The economic turn-around was in part the consequence of an expanding gold supply. By 1899, the world's gold supply was triple that of 1890. Annual gold production was almost $307 million, compared to $202 million in 1896. The boost in production was the result of two events: the development of a cyanide extraction process that made possible greater extraction of gold from ore and the discovery of new gold fields. Thus, contrary to the claims of Populists and free-silver advocates, the circulating currency had expanded under the gold standard.[92]

A credibility crisis loomed large. The Populist movement, seriously weakened by internal dissension, could not withstand the challenges to its diagnostic frame. While many wage earners and farmers continued to suffer economically, the Populist solution for that suffering appeared faulty. The volume of currency had significantly increased without bimetallism or fiat treasury notes, yet poverty still persisted. An increased per capita circulating currency had not, after all, solved the economic problems that many faced. Most important, the increased volume of currency had done little to lower the interest rates associated with crop-lien loans. Given the uncertainty of future crop prices, merchants continued to charge extremely high interest rates on crop-lien loans, and small farmers continued to struggle to earn a decent livelihood and to hold on to their farms.

Interestingly, scholars exploring the collapse of the Populist movement have failed to incorporate the frame-credibility crisis into their explanation of the rapid demise of the movement. They have also given little attention to the fact that in the media the framing of the problem of low cotton prices, to a large extent, reverted back to the overproduction frame of the late 1870s and early 1880s that the Alliance movement had worked hard to challenge. As indicated in Table 12, the production of cotton had doubled from about 4.5 million bales in the early-to-mid 1870s to more than 8.5 million bales in 1890, and climbed to almost 10.5 million bales in 1900. Newspapers began to

TABLE 12
Acreage Planted in Cotton and Average Cotton Production in the United States, 1866–1900

YEAR	ACREAGE (ACRES)	PRODUCTION (BALES)
1866	6,300,000	2,097,254
1870	8,680,000	4,352,317
1875	10,803,030	4,632,313
1880	15,475,300	6,605,750
1885	18,300,865	6,575,691
1890	20,809,053	8,652,597
1895	20,184,808	7,161,094
1900	–	10,401,453

Source: USDA, *Yearbook of Agriculture,* 754.

clamor about the overproduction of cotton, arguing that cotton prices would not significantly improve until farmers planted less cotton.[93] Missing in these appeals was recognition of a basic agricultural fact that leaders in the Alliance movement had always understood: southern farmers desperately needed cash to pay taxes and to pay off their crop-lien loans. Cotton was the cash crop of the south, with crop-lien loans only extended with cotton as collateral. Telling southern farmers to plant less cotton was akin to telling them that their lives would improve with less cash and without access to loans. It was a message that southern farmers knew was deeply flawed, even if the Alliance's volume-of-currency frame had been found to be faulty as well. Without an effective frame around which farmers could mobilize, disillusionment set in.

ENDINGS: THE ELECTION CAMPAIGN OF 1900

Embittered by the free-silver fusion debate, its southern power base constricted by suffrage restriction efforts, and suffering from its shift to a simple volume-of-currency explanation for economic problems, the People's Party limped into the elections of 1900. On March 9 of that year, the anti-fusion and fusionist factions within the third party held separate national conventions. The anti-fusion convention in Cincinnati was attended by nearly seven hundred delegates. All but five states were represented. The convention proceeded smoothly, and the Barker-Donnelly ticket that had been formed in September 1898 was reaffirmed.[94]

The Sioux Falls convention of the fusionist faction also had about seven hundred delegates. So pervasive was the pro-Bryan sentiment at the convention that the roll-call vote was dispensed with, and Bryan received the presidential nomination by acclamation. The nomination of a vice presidential candidate, however, did not proceed smoothly. One proposal was for the vice presidential nomination to be made by a Conference Committee, composed of one delegate from each state, which would confer with the Democrats on a candidate acceptable to both parties. Another proposal called for the delegates to nominate several candidates, and then let the Democrats choose their favorite. Neither of these proposals was adopted. But the fact that they were seriously discussed reflected the extent to which many fusionist Populists had accepted their party's loss of autonomy and identity. The full extent of this acceptance became clear when they settled on a free-silver Republican, Charles Towne, for vice president. Thus, neither of the candidates on the Sioux Falls People's Party ticket was a Populist.[95]

Following his vice presidential nomination, Towne publicly declared that he had favored the convention proposal advocating the selection of a vice president by a Conference Committee. However, since the majority of delegates had felt differently and extended to him the nomination, he graciously accepted. He also graciously resigned when the delegates to the Democratic nominating convention, meeting in June, refused to select him as their vice presidential nomination, giving him only 89½ votes to Adlai Stevenson's 559½ votes.[96]

Senator Butler, who chaired the National Executive Committee of the People's Party, made no move to call a meeting of the committee to replace Towne after his resignation. Complete fusion with the Democratic ticket was accepted. The ticket selected by the anti-fusionist Populists in Cincinnati would be the only Populist ticket fielded. Reflecting a party in its death throes, it performed very poorly on Election Day, receiving only about fifty thousand votes nationwide.[97] The promise of the Populist movement had clearly dissipated.

Evidence of the pitiful state of the Populist movement in Louisiana had come earlier in the year in the state gubernatorial elections held in April. Donelson Caffery, Jr. had received the gubernatorial nomination of both the People's Party and the Republican Party. The acceptance of his nomination by Louisiana Populists was shocking, given that he was a conservative gold-standard Democrat, albeit a Democrat at odds with the incumbent Foster administration. The Populist-Republican fusion ticket failed to carry a single parish. It was the last People's Party ticket to ever be fielded in Louisiana. The political insurgency among the state's small farmers had been effectively crushed. Democrats ruled supreme, with the economic elite in firm control of the reins of political and economic power.[98]

Conclusion

THE EXPERIENCE OF NINETEENTH-CENTURY Populism varied significantly among the southern states. The movement in Louisiana struggled, both in terms of the size of the Louisiana Farmers' Union (LFU)—an affiliate of the Farmers' Alliance, the vanguard of the Southern Populist movement—and in terms of the clout in state elections of the People's Party, which represented the later stages of nineteenth-century Populism. There is no question that Louisiana Populists faced daunting challenges. To borrow the expression used by one scholar of the Populist movement, their labors were akin to "plowing the oceans."[1]

The weakness of the Populist movement in Louisiana is an interesting issue, both historically and theoretically. Why was the LFU weak, given the intense deprivation of farmers in the state? Why did it struggle, given that it merged organizationally in 1887 with the vibrant Texas Alliance? Why did it have much less mobilization success than the Texas Alliance, its merger partner? Why was the LFU a "rickety" bridge to the third-party movement once the latter emerged in the 1890s?

In this book, such questions have been pursued through the lens of social movement theory. The primary focus of each of the three major social movement theories—political opportunity, mobilization issues, and framing challenges—yielded important insights into the experiences of the Louisiana Populist movement, with the dynamic relationships between political opportunity, mobilization, and framing being of utmost importance. Furthermore, some of the major criticisms that have been lodged against these social movement theories—that they have a strong structural bias and neglect the role of agency; that they ignore the role of emotion; and that they give insufficient attention to the role of geospatial factors in the emergence and growth of movements—were found to be very relevant to the Populist movement. However, the criticisms were readily addressed through expanding the focus of existing movement theories. These theoretical findings will be explicated further as the major analytical insights into the Louisiana Populist movement are recapitulated in the following section.

THE LOUISIANA POPULIST MOVEMENT AND SOCIAL MOVEMENT THEORY

While many aspects of the Louisiana Populist movement come into sharper focus when analyzed through the lens of social movement theory, six findings are central. The first central finding is that the emergence and growth of the LFU during the first phase of the Populist movement was significantly affected by the expansion of political opportunity linked to the end of Reconstruction, the development of a diagnostic frame that effectively countered the "overproduction" frame, and the power of a strategic, self-help frame that was at least initially effectively in mobilizing small farmers.

The second central finding is that the self-help strategic frame limited the mobilization success of the Populist movement. It was of little utility to cotton farmers caught in the debt spiral of crop-lien financing and was irrelevant to agricultural laborers in the sugar-producing parishes. The Colored Farmers' Alliance (CFA) also adopted the self-help frame, even though it was of little utility to most blacks in the agricultural sector. This was a serious deficiency in a state where blacks represented the majority of the population and produced the bulk of the cotton crop.

In regard to the third central finding, a faction within the LFU and CFA shifted its attention to electoral politics when the self-help frame reached the limits of its effectiveness. This shift, however, elicited serious mobilization challenges because the LFU and CFA served as a poor base from which to mobilize voters in the alluvial, plantation parishes and the densely populated parish of Orleans. Efforts to establish new mobilization networks were hampered by the scarcity of resources and the tensions that typified interracial relationships.

The fourth central finding is that the Louisiana Populist movement failed to disseminate an identity frame that transcended racial divisions in Louisiana agriculture. The LFU remained racially segregated and made minimal efforts to coordinate its strategies with the CFA. It also took positions on issues that were at odds with those taken by most blacks. As for the Louisiana People's Party, its effort to court the black vote was short-lived. After 1894, its leaders adopted racist rhetoric, espousing rather than challenging certain tenets of the white supremacy frame of the Democratic Party.

Another central finding is that the mobilization challenges confronting the Louisiana Populist movement during its political phase were inextricably linked to the contraction of political opportunity after the movement became an electoral threat to the Democratic Party. The unfavorable political opportunity was the result of the manipulation of the black vote in the plantation parishes; the control that the planter elite exercised in the state legislature and in nominating conventions; and the failure of Populist leaders to develop an effective strategic frame to address electoral fraud.

The final central finding was that the shift of emphasis within the Louisiana Populist movement in terms of its financial demands—from fiatism and specific income-distribution plans such as the subtreasury proposal to a free-silver emphasis—was the result of a strategic framing decision motivated by political pragmatism. Although the framing shift had major repercussions, it was not the sole factor in the demise of Louisiana Populism. Other key factors were the further contraction of political opportunity resulting from the Democratic Party's successful disfranchisement campaign and the challenge that a general economic recovery beginning in 1898 posed for the movement's framing of the agricultural depression.

Let us turn to a more detailed explication of each of these central findings.

Political Opportunity, Framing, and Mobilization in the Early Experiences of the LFU

The experiences of the LFU highlight the pivotal importance of studying the effects of the broader political system on the opportunity for effective collective action. While crop prices started declining in the 1870s, the political opportunity for mobilizing a widespread protest movement among farmers was limited. Politically, the 1870s were characterized in Louisiana by an intense obsession with the possible Africanization of state politics. As one of only three states where blacks represented the majority of the population, Louisiana had a powerful white supremacy culture that insisted upon white political unity. In state politics, whites stood almost solidly behind the Democratic Party. The paramount political issue of that party, and one that allowed for little attention to other issues, was grabbing power back from the Republican Party and its black allies—a process referred to as Redemption.

Thus, despite the alarming fall of cotton prices in the 1870s, the only acceptable protest frame was to blame economic problems on the tax policies of the Republican Party, consistent with the rhetoric of the Democratic Party. Any other protest frame risked dividing whites politically and undercutting the Democratic Party's efforts to redeem the state from Republicans and their black political allies.

After the end of Reconstruction, the economic plight of small farmers continued to worsen and ultimately gave rise to the LFU. Illustrating the close relationship between the framing choices of a movement and the political opportunity that a movement faces, the small farmers' movement initially operated within a tolerant political climate in large part because it framed the problems of small farmers in such a way that it was not perceived as a threat to the interests of the political and economic elite. The movement focused on self-help strategies, rather than political solutions to agricultural problems. Most LFU members, at least initially, maintained their ties to the Democratic Party. In a state where the leaders of the dominant political party were extremely hostile to any person or group that threatened white unity under the Democratic Party banner, the early strategic framing of the small farmers' movement allowed the movement time to gather some steam without risking a full-scale political assault.

An intricate relationship also existed between the diagnostic frame of the LFU and its mobilization experiences. The most important weakness of the LFU in its infancy was its ineffectiveness in confronting and challenging the leading explanation for the farm crisis—the overproduction argument. Farmers were repeatedly told by politicians that their problems were the result of impersonal market forces. Politicians insisted that there was little they could do other than urge farmers to voluntarily cut back on production. Yet a "grow-less-cotton" solution was problematic. Many farmers had little choice about the percentage of their acreage planted in cotton. Since cotton was the major cash crop of the South, they had to grow enough cotton to pay their tax bills and other expenses. Furthermore, with the declining price of cotton, many needed crop-lien loans to cover expenses and such liens were only extended with cotton as collateral.

Despite the limitations of the grow-less-cotton solution, a bold diagnostic frame that challenged this advice was not forthcoming until the LFU merged with the more vibrant Texas Alliance in 1887. The Alliance was much further along in regard to the development of effective diagnostic and strategic frames. Its leaders had already learned an important lesson: the root causes of the farm crisis had to be framed in a way that would motivate farmers to organize, and strategies had to be promulgated that held out the promise of economic relief.

The LFU gathered momentum by following the lessons learned from its new merger partner in regard to the powerful link between framing and mobilization. After the merger, LFU leaders appointed official lecturers to attack the overproduction explanation of the farm crisis and to promote a rapacious-capitalist diagnostic frame, as well as to educate farmers on the cooperative, self-help strategies of the LFU. Significant growth in the LFU membership followed.

The Effect of Strategic Framing on Mobilization

The link between strategic framing and mobilization is also apparent when looking at the class composition of the LFU, and the Alliance movement in general, whose members were predominantly small farm owners. By strategically framing the farm crisis in a way that focused upon self-help cooperative strategies, the movement limited its appeal primarily to small farm proprietors. Farm communities characterized primarily by sharecropping typically could not raise the capital sufficient to establish local cooperatives. In those rare instances where these communities did form cooperatives, capitalization was insufficient to allow for credit purchases. Therefore sharecroppers dependent on crop-lien loans were unable to trade at the cooperatives. This was a serious obstacle to mobilization, since there was little reason to join the LFU and pay dues if its strategies were irrelevant to one's economic circumstances.

While the early strategic frame of the Populist movement was a handicap for mobilizing sharecroppers in all the southern states, the framing was particularly problematic in Louisiana, which had a farm tenancy rate of almost 60 percent by 1900, one of the highest rates in the South. Thus, the poor fit between the strategic framing of the movement and the needs of sharecroppers was particularly damaging to mobilization efforts in Louisiana, illustrating the effects of geospatial characteristics on social movements. As a result of its early strategic framing choices, the LFU's mobilization success was largely confined to small farm owners residing in the backland parishes of the Fourth, Fifth, and Sixth Congressional districts.

Importantly, Alliance leaders in Texas made a concerted effort to mobilize crop-lien dependent farmers via the joint-note program of the Texas Alliance Exchange. This bold attempt to provide small farmers an alternative to high interest crop-lien loans was, in large part, the reason for the explosive growth of the Alliance in Texas during the late 1880s. Given that the Exchange opened its doors in the fall of 1887, the year that the LFU merged with the Texas Alliance, it is puzzling that there were no discussions of a joint-note program in the LFU.

The failure of the LFU to seize upon the joint-note idea to enhance its appeal to tenant farmers is interesting, given the high rate at which tenancy was growing in Louisiana. The failure to adopt strategies of greater appeal to tenant farmers is all the more puzzling given that tenant farmers produced a majority of the cotton crop in Louisiana. LFU marketing strategies, such as cotton bulking and cotton withholding, were destined to fail without more participation on the part of tenant farmers. By not aggressively courting sharecroppers, the LFU doomed the effectiveness of its strategies for its small farm owner membership. Given this fact, why did it fail to follow the lead of the Texas Alliance in an attempt to appeal to tenant farmers?

At least one plausible answer to this question lies at the intersection of race and class in the agricultural structure of Louisiana. Again illustrating the importance of geospatial factors, in Louisiana more than 70 percent of tenant farmers were black whereas in most southern states the majority of tenant farmers were white. Therefore, any effort to mobilize tenant farmers in Louisiana would of necessity have entailed strong recruitment efforts in the predominantly black parishes. Race was undoubtedly a major factor in strategic framing decisions of the LFU about whether to adjust tactics so as to broaden the appeal of the farmers' movement, to move from a predominantly small farm owner membership to one that included more sharecroppers.

When the CFA emerged in Louisiana, it adopted a diagnostic and strategic frame similar to that of the LFU—that is, it adopted the LFU's diagnosis of the causes of the farm crisis and its proposed strategies for dealing with that crisis: self-help, cooperative strategies. This framing choice came at a cost and illustrates well the close link between the role of agency in framing and its effect on mobilization. As an organization developed to address the economic problems of black farmers, the CFA could have adopted a frame that vilified white planters for exploiting their black tenant farmers. After all, 85 percent of black farmers in Louisiana were tenant farmers. The CFA could have advocated changing the usual fifty-fifty crop split between tenant and landlord to a sixty-forty split that would have been more favorable to struggling tenant farmers. Or it could have aggressively pushed for state or federal regulation of crop-lien interest rates. However, such strategies would have directly and intensely threatened the interests of the planter elite and would have likely invoked a massive backlash against the CFA. Perhaps due to a desire to avoid such a strong backlash, the CFA followed a more conservative path. It limited its appeal primarily to the small minority of black farm owners by adopting the self-help strategic frame of the whites-only Alliance.

It is important to recognize that the potential impact of the CFA on the Alliance movement varied among the major cotton-producing states. If the CFA failed to mobilize widely in Texas, where there were 27,960 blacks per 100,000 whites, the consequences were less damaging than in Louisiana, where there were 100,143 blacks per 100,000 whites.[2] This important fact was overlooked by Lawrence Goodwyn in his influential book on the Populist movement, *Democratic Promise,* in which he explained the weakness of the movement in Louisiana with a vague reference to leadership weakness. He made no mention of geospatial factors that differentially affected the movement in Louisiana.

The failure of the LFU and CFA to broaden their class appeal was a fatal mistake. Without successful mobilization of tenant farmers, white and black, who represented the majority of all farmers in Louisiana, the efforts of the LFU to improve the economic situation of small white farmers were doomed. No significant improvement could occur unless the market price of cotton improved. The LFU, and the Alliance movement in general, had two major strategies prior to 1890 to address directly the decline in cotton prices: cotton bulking and cotton withholding. Without widespread cooperation by cotton farmers, including the black sharecroppers of the alluvial parishes who produced the majority of the state's cotton crop, such strategies were ineffective.

The bifurcated structure of commercial agriculture within Louisiana was also an important factor mediating between the strategic frame of the LFU and CFA and the extent of their mobilization success. In Louisiana, both cotton and sugar were major cash crops. Sugar was the major commercial crop in about 20 percent of the parishes, with cotton produced in insignificant amounts in these parishes. Since the Alliance movement was heavily focused on the problems of cotton farmers, the sugar-producing parishes were left largely untouched by the movement. The major economic complaints of sugar workers were low hourly wages and payment in the form of scrip, neither of which were addressed by the LFU or CFA.

Broadening the appeal of the LFU required a strategic frame that addressed the grievances of all of those who struggled to earn a living from farming, whether from cotton or sugar production. Yet there is no evidence that the LFU ever attempted to bridge the gulf between the cotton-producing and sugar-producing parishes. The failure to make such an attempt lies at least in part in class differences. Given that most of the members of the LFU were small white farm owners, there was an inherent class conflict between its membership and agricultural wage laborers. The last thing small farmers needed as they struggled to make ends meet was an organized effort to increase wages on the part of agricultural wage laborers, such as the day laborers who were used by some small farmers to help harvest cotton. This was clearly evidenced in the strong protest of LFU leaders against the Cotton Pickers League in 1891, when the latter group called for a strike by wage laborers in the cotton fields. It was also evidenced by the silence of LFU leaders during the brutal repression of a major strike in the sugar fields in 1887.

The class tension between the small farm owner membership of the LFU and agricultural laborers was reinforced by race: almost all agricultural wage laborers in Louisiana were black. Therefore any large-scale effort to mobilize across class lines in agriculture meant mobilizing across race lines. Unfortunately, by borrowing the strategic frame of the LFU, the CFA doomed itself to failure in this important task as well.

Identity Framing and Biracial Coalition Formation

While racially tolerant comments by LFU leaders can be found, taken together they do not qualify as a concerted attack on the dominant white supremacy beliefs.[3] Those beliefs were so persuasive that they only could have been significantly weakened by an all-out effort seeking transformational identity framing, not by occasional remarks about the common interests shared by black and white farmers and the need for biracial cooperation. If such a concerted assault on racism had been made by LFU leaders, it would have been impossible to miss in the historical record. The LFU was, from its beginning to its end, a racially segregated organization that did little to coordinate its efforts with the parallel organization of the CFA and made little effort to transform the white versus black racial identity frame of the rural population of the state.

Third-party leaders in Louisiana faced the formidable challenge of generating a transformative identity frame that would undercut the loyalty of white voters to the Democratic Party. Most whites strongly identified with the Democratic Party and its demand for white political unity. The white supremacy frame of the Democratic Party thrived in a political climate where blacks represented the majority of the population and the majority of the registered voters. Only two other states shared this demographic profile, and it is a profile that was at the heart of the effectiveness of the demand for white political unity by Democratic Party leaders in Louisiana. While southern states shared a white supremacy culture, in most of those states a divided white vote did not present a serious political threat to white control of the political system. In Texas, for example, there were less than half a million blacks and more than 1.7 million whites.[4] If white voters in Texas evenly split their vote, each white political contingent would still have more votes than the political contingent supported by blacks even if the latter voted solidly as a block. This was not the case in Louisiana, and as a result the threat of white abandonment of the Democratic Party elicited stronger emotion and produced a much stronger backlash. The strength of this backlash and the geospatial factors that account for that strength are a crucial part of the explanation of the relative weakness of the third-party movement in Louisiana.

Countering the powerful "we" versus "them" racial identity frame of the Democratic Party was a Herculean challenge, especially for a poorly funded third party that faced constant criticism from the mainstream press, which relished retelling "horror tales" of Reconstruction to shore up loyalty to the Democratic Party. The struggles of the third-party movement in Louisiana to meet this challenge illustrate well the importance of the role of emotion and agency in social movement dynamics. Democratic Party leaders incessantly appealed to emotion through the retelling of accounts of political crises during Reconstruction, retellings that typically embellished the threat of the black majority in the state. While voters experienced agency in the sense that they had political choices, they exercised that agency in a cultural and structural context that significantly affected their choices and the outcome of those choices. Emotion, as well as rationality and reason, played a role in their response to what was essentially a framing contest between third-party reform principles and the principle of white political unity under the banner of the Democratic Party.

In defense of the LFU, effectively challenging the racist culture of the times would have entailed challenging beliefs that went to the very core of southern culture. In the terminology of social movement theory, it would have entailed adopting a transformative frame that was antithetical to the prevailing culture. Challenging the white supremacy culture would have called into question the southern interpretation of slavery and the southern response to

Reconstruction—a treasonous stance in the eyes of many southerners whose discussions of the Civil War and Reconstruction were still infused with heated emotion. Thus, the small farmers' movement experienced a no-win situation: Its failure to persistently attack the culture of white supremacy hurt the movement by undermining the biracial coalition that was necessary for its self-help strategies to be effective. Yet any concerted attack by LFU leaders on white supremacy beliefs would have likely cost it dearly among its white constituency.

A transformative identity frame was also undercut by tension between the LFU and the CFA in regard to their positions on the important Lodge election bill. The CFA favored the bill, which called for federal intervention in congressional and presidential elections to ensure that they were conducted in a fair and honest manner. The LFU, as well as the national Alliance organization, stridently opposed the bill on the grounds that it granted too much power to the federal government to intervene in southern politics. Apparently they were more concerned with keeping the federal government out of southern politics than with fair elections and voting rights issues. This stance would prove fatal. When the small farmers' movement turned to politics after 1890, its performance at the polls was undermined by voting rights violations that the Lodge election bill, if passed, may have helped prevent.

In terms of identity framing and the Louisiana People's Party, the CFA was looked to as a possible bridge between the Republican Party and the third party. The national CFA had taken a strong and early interest in the third party and had sent delegates to its founding Cincinnati convention in 1891. Leaders of the CFA in Louisiana followed suit. In fact, the only Louisiana signatures on the call for the Cincinnati convention were those of CFA activists. Subsequently, the leaders of the People's Party in Louisiana had recognized the CFA's political interest in the third party by inviting Superintendent Keys of the state CFA to address the delegates at the convention held to establish a state People's Party organization. Initially, they also explicitly appealed to black voters to abandon their loyalty to the Republican Party.

But in competing for the black vote, Populist leaders faced a daunting challenge. The CFA as an organization had not effectively mobilized blacks throughout the state and served as a poor base from which to appeal to black voters. Therefore, it was an uphill struggle for Populists to gain the loyalty of black voters, a struggle made all the more difficult by the inadequate funding that hampered their campaigns. But that did not stop them from trying, at least initially. Their efforts to transcend the racism of the times, however, were unsuccessful and fleeting. Their gubernatorial candidate in 1892, Robert Tannehill, fared extremely poorly in the predominantly black-populated alluvial parishes and in the black precincts of the backland parishes. Furthermore, in the backland parishes where blacks were a sizeable portion of the populations, most whites stayed loyal to the Democratic Party, perhaps out of fear of dividing the white vote and allowing Republicans to win. Thus, in terms of identity framing, a "we" versus "them" racial mentality prevailed and past party loyalties remained entrenched in parishes where blacks represented more than half of the population.

In response to the poor performance of the third party in parishes with a majority-black population, the leaders of the People's Party in Louisiana reconsidered their call for biracial cooperation and harmony.[5] When the 1894 campaign heated up, they openly declared their support for many of the tenets of the white supremacy frame. They spoke frequently in the third-party press of the "intelligent white man" and spoke of white supremacy as a principle dear to the heart of *all* southern whites, presumably including themselves. They even pushed for white primaries, a political tool eventually to be adopted by southern Democrats to exclude blacks from political influence. The shift in strategic framing in regard to the creation of a biracial political coalition was a result of pragmatic politics and a response to the inverse relationship between percent black and electoral support for the People's Party.

The strategic framing shift from calls for biracial cooperation to calls for white primaries illustrates the importance of a longitudinal approach in the study of social movements. Racial commentary from the early 1890s supports the argument that key leaders of the Louisiana third-party movement were fairly progressive on race issues. Remarks and actions from 1894 to 1896, however, support the argument that they did not significantly differ from the dominant southern culture in their racial attitudes and that earlier tolerant attitudes likely were the result of political expediency. Consequently, the claim of Louisiana historian William Hair that the third party was the only native white political movement to seek "political equality for the Negro" needs qualification.[6] While such a statement applies to the early years of the third-party movement in Louisiana, 1891–1893, a decisive framing shift had taken place by 1894 that makes such a statement patently false.

The strategic framing shift in regard to race was ultimately the result of mobilization dilemmas created by the unsuccessful efforts to create a transformative identity frame that would support the creation of a biracial political alliance. More specifically, the framing shift was the consequence of several factors. First, efforts to attract the black vote were costly in terms of courting the white vote. Second, efforts to court the black vote had been unsuccessful, and third-party leaders recognized that they did not have the resources necessary to campaign effectively in the majority-black parishes. Finally, even if they could improve their electoral support among the black population in the alluvial plantation parishes, getting that vote cast amid serious intimidation and getting it honestly counted were both very big problems.

The Shift to Politics and the Contraction of Political Opportunity

After the limits of the self-help strategic frame were fully realized, a strategic redirection was essential if the Populist movement was to survive. The redirection entailed a shift to politics. The shift to politics was accompanied by an assault on the federal government's monetary policy. Alliance leaders blamed the farm crisis on a contracted money supply created by adherence to the gold standard. They called for a sufficient and flexible currency with money distributed in part through low-interest government land loans and commodity loans, cornerstones of the newly developed subtreasury proposal. The latter was essentially an effort to harness the power of the federal government to address the economic problems faced by most small farmers. If low-interest government loans were available, there would be an alternative to the exorbitant interest rates of crop-lien loans. With low interest rates, farmers could afford to hold their crops off the market if prices were unacceptably low. Cotton withholding would become a viable strategy for addressing excessively low market prices.

The Alliance's subtreasury proposal, and its campaign to promote it, marked the beginning of the second phase of the Populist movement. The subtreasury plan was heatedly condemned by the Democratic Party, not only in Louisiana but throughout the South. A fierce framing contest ensued between subtreasury advocates and foes.

Illustrating the intricate relationship between framing and political opportunity, the strategic framing shift that called for a focus on politics rather than self-help cooperatives immediately elicited a hostile response by the political elite. That hostility was particularly damning in Louisiana because of its highly concentrated power structure. In no other post-Reconstruction state did planters dominate the political process so completely. While oligarchies existed in other locales, the political elite in Louisiana differed in both the extent and degree of control. Their disproportionate power derived mainly from their control over district and state nominating conventions of the Democratic Party and the extraordinary appointive powers of governors in Louisiana.

There was widespread recognition among voters in Louisiana that planters controlled the political process by the manipulation of the black vote in the plantation parishes. With seat apportionment at the Democratic nominating conventions determined by the number of Democratic votes in the previous election, the manipulated vote count assured planters a sufficient number of seats at Democratic nominating conventions to control the selection of party candidates and determine the specifics of the party's platform. Those wanting to confine their reform efforts to pressure-politics within the Democratic Party faced a dilemma: no reform under the banner of the Democratic Party was possible without the approval of the planter elite. Yet the economic self-interest of planters ensured their opposition to major reform proposals, such as the subtreasury plan.

The power of the planter elite over the nominating conventions of the Democratic Party was particularly significant in light of the fact that general elections in Louisiana usually played a minor role in the political process. After Reconstruction ended, Republican chances for success in statewide elections were nominal. The candidate selected by the Democratic Party at its nominating convention was virtually assured victory. Planter control over the gubernatorial selection process was significant because the governor of Louisiana had extraordinary appointive powers over a large number of state-level and parish-level political positions. The extensive gubernatorial appointive powers ensured white political control even in the black-majority parishes.

Furthermore, major reform was doubtful if sectional party loyalties were not successfully circumvented by means of a third party. If farmers north of the Mason-Dixon Line and black southern farmers and agricultural workers remained loyal to the Republican Party and white southern farmers remained loyal to the Democratic Party, there was little hope for enacting major economic reforms.

The logic of a third-party movement notwithstanding, the cautious approach of LFU leaders such as T. S. Adams and J. A. Tetts stalled the process of using the LFU as a bridge to the People's Party. Leaders such as Adams and Tetts feared that an alignment with the third party would be fatal. As southerners, they fully understood that any organization that threatened white political unity would be aggressively attacked. Shifting the strategic frame from seeking political reform through the Democratic Party to reform via a third-party movement would increase the hostility of the political elite toward the small farmers' movement. Therein lay the reason for the ambivalence in choosing between a third-party movement and pressure-politics within the existing political party structure. Ambivalence was rooted in the realization that LFU leaders faced a no-win situation: Shifting the strategic frame to seek reform through a third party would elicit a hostile political reaction, one sufficiently hostile as to risk being fatal. However, retaining the frame of reform through the existing parties risked demobilization given the poor odds of achieving major reform via that route.

The cautious position of the LFU in regard to the third-party movement had a strongly debilitating effect. The third party had sparse resources and its viability to a large extent depended on its ability to bloc-recruit through preexisting organizations. With the LFU hedging in its stance toward the third party, bloc recruitment was hampered.

Any discussion of political opportunity and the Louisiana Populist movement has to give considerable attention to the challenge of electoral fraud. In terms of getting votes counted honestly, the People's Party in Louisiana faced a problem, the intensity of which was unmatched in most southern states. When the third-party movement became a reality, the break in white political unity called forth a level of hostility from the political elite not seen since Reconstruction. Given the strong antipathy to third-party advocates, who were depicted as betrayers of the white race for their willingness to undermine white political unity, Democratic leaders felt justified in their efforts to distort the political process through extensive electoral intimidation and fraud. Louisiana elections routinely resulted in congressional investigations into fraud and other electoral improprieties, with implausible landslide victories in the alluvial plantation parishes and occasionally open admissions of fraud by sanctimonious political leaders convinced that the fraud was in the service of a worthy, higher cause.

In perhaps no other state was the third-party movement subject to a more hostile political climate. It struggled, as in many other states, to respond effectively to the heavy ridicule of its principles and character assassinations of its leaders. But in Louisiana it faced a much greater uphill battle to get the votes it fought so hard for counted as cast. What good would it do if the third party was successful in advocating its frame, if votes were not honestly counted?

Thus, the importance of political opportunity was paramount. A diagnostic or strategic framing success was moot in the presence of a political opportunity structure so hostile that the integrity of the electoral process was significantly compromised. No matter what coalitions the People's Party created to improve its odds of electoral victory, it was all in vain if Democrats had the capability and willingness to manipulate electoral returns to ensure their victory.

The problems of voter intimidation and electoral fraud were prominently highlighted in the state elections of 1896. Political opportunity expanded considerably when wealthy sugar planters deserted the Democratic Party in the state election and forged a coalition between the Republican Party and the People's Party. The wealth of the sugar planters allowed for the dramatic expansion of campaign funding, dwarfing the paltry funding of previous third-party campaigns. Chances for an electoral victory would likely never be more optimal. Yet victory was stolen as a result of electoral improprieties by Democrats, particularly in the alluvial cotton parishes. Opponents of the Democratic Party were ultimately powerless in the face of such actions. It was this fact, more than any other, which destroyed the third-party movement in Louisiana.

It is one of the major ironies of the southern Populist movement that both the Alliance and the People's Party refused to support the only effective way to combat election fraud in the South: federal supervision of elections in districts with a history of electoral fraud allegations. They were unwilling to challenge the hallowed states' rights culture of the South as it related to the political machinery of elections. The emotion attached to the issue of federal versus state control over elections, which was steeped in the politics of Reconstruction, was intense. But without federal supervision of elections, electoral fraud undercut the potential for movement success at the polls.

Framing the Financial Reform Demands of the Movement

The Populist movement had one unquestionable success: it shifted the talk of financial reform to a discussion of the structure of the monetary system. But having done that, Populist leaders found that they had little control over the direction of discussions about monetary policy. Their endorsement of fiatism was given little attention by the mainstream press, and the attention that it received was universally negative. The focus in the major dailies was on the framing contest between monometallist, gold-standard advocates and bimetallist, free-silver supporters.

Given that their fiatist position was largely ignored by the mainstream press and without the resources necessary to mount a strong independent campaign to educate voters, many Populist leaders chose to act expediently. They tried to maximize their political appeal by supporting both bimetallism and fiatism, to a considerable extent a contradictory stance since fiatism asserts that the volume of currency should be based on the needs of the economy, not the availability of gold and/or silver. Populist leaders attempted to resolve the contradiction by claiming that while a fiatist monetary system was ideal, any fiscal policy that expanded the nation's circulating currency was welcome. But such a resolution muddied the monetary reform issue and came at a high cost. As the nation turned its attention to financial reform issues, the reform talk of many Populists and the free-silver advocates within the dominant parties began to take on an ominous similarity.

In his account of the Populist movement, Goodwyn argued that the national leaders of the People's Party sold out the "true" Populists when they shifted their emphasis from fiatism to free silver. But placing the blame solely on national party leaders is wrong. In Louisiana, the shift of emphasis was clearly evident in the Populist press, where attention to free silver as a reform far outweighed attention to fiatism after 1894. By 1896, the only financial plank in the state People's Party platform was the demand for free silver. The call for free silver had become a popular rallying cry among Populists in other southern states as well.

Third-party leaders in the South faced a serious dilemma. There was a chance that they could ride the growing momentum for free silver into political office, if they were willing to shift their financial reform emphasis to free silver. But endorsing free silver as a major reform demand was also risky since any progress made in convincing voters of the evils of the gold standard and the need for currency expansion would aid the free-silver faction of the Democratic Party as much as it did the People's Party. The stronger the free-silver advocates became within the Democratic Party, the greater the chances that they might gain control of the party and, concomitantly, the less attractive abandoning the Democratic Party would become to disgruntled white voters. After all, why endure harassment for forsaking the Democratic Party and for dividing the white vote, if reform was possible through the Democratic Party?

Populist leaders pondered the future of their party. The major demands of the party could only be implemented through legislation at the national level. Yet the third party had fared extremely poorly in the 1894 congressional elections. Furthermore, boding ill for the 1896 presidential election, in a number of major states that were heavily represented in the Electoral College, few Populist candidates were even on the ballot. These states were largely urban with predominantly wage laborers. The People's Party had a weak base from which to try to make inroads in these states since they had been relatively untouched by the Alliance movement, which had mobilized primarily in the small farm communities of heavily rural states. Other possible bases from which to mobilize support among urban laborers, such as labor organizations, were problematic. Leaders of the American Federation of Labor, for example, were hostile to the notion of labor unions becoming involved in partisan politics. The Knights of Labor, though sympathetic to the third-party movement, was struggling for survival. Thus, disseminating the full slate of Populist reform principles among urban wage laborers was a daunting challenge.

While Goodwyn has depicted the free-silver movement as a shadow movement that overpowered the true spirit of Populism that rose from the cooperative struggles of the Alliance movement, his depiction is problematic. In Louisiana, as well as many other states, the Alliance did not serve as a sufficient base for a move into electoral politics. In a winner-takes-all system, electoral victory—or even simply electoral influence—requires that votes be garnered from a wide variety of places. Most of the third-party reform agenda could only be implemented at the national level. Gaining national influence required electoral success in states with large congressional delegations and strong representation in the Electoral College, states that had meager if any Alliance-affiliated organizations to serve as a base for achieving electoral success. As a result of these electoral exigencies, it is inappropriate to label as true Populists only those who came to the third party via the Alliance movement and who maintained a steadfast commitment to fiatism. The third party was, like most political parties in winner-takes-all electoral systems, composed of diverse groups with various sorts of grievances who had to find some middle ground on which to meet.

In effect, a strategic framing contest raged within the diverse constituency of the People's Party. The framing contest was especially acute between middle-of-the road Populists, who were strongly committed to fiatism and wanted to wage a political fight on the full slate of Populist reform demands, and pragmatic Populists, who wanted to focus on the free-silver issue in the elections of 1896 to increase the odds of electoral success. Goodwyn sides with the views of the mid-roaders who, he argues, understood that free silver was not a significant reform. While his support for this faction is understandable, his argument that only middle-of-the road Populists were true Populists and that all other Populists were part of a shadow movement is poorly conceived. This depiction overlooks the heterogeneous nature of the People's Party, a characteristic shared by all political parties in winner-takes-all electoral systems, and the fact that some members of the pragmatic-politics faction of the People's Party such as Hardy Brian had been leaders of the Populist movement since its beginnings when it had focused on self-help, cooperative strategies.

The outcome of the 1896 nominating convention of the third party is best explained by recognizing that the mid-road Populists lost the framing contest that they had engaged in with the pragmatic Populists faction. As the 1896 elections approached, free silver was the only Populist reform demand that had a large following among the general voting populace. While the mid-road Populists called upon the third party to make its fight on the full slate of reform demands, the pragmatic Populists argued that some reform was better than none. One may applaud, as Goodwyn does, the commitment of mid-roaders to more radical reforms. But one must concede the futility of trying to secure those reforms via the ballot box, given the dismal performance of the People's Party in the 1894 congressional elections. To many of the voters who were desperate for economic relief, achievable reform was preferable to a commitment to a full slate of reforms unlikely to ever be implemented.

In explaining the demise of what once had seemed a promising movement, scholars of the Populist movement have focused heavily on the internal problems created by the tension between the free-silver fusionist and mid-road anti-fusionist factions of the People's Party. The strife between these two factions has an important place in explanations of the demise of Populism. It, however, was certainly not the only factor of importance. The collapse of the movement was also a consequence of the dramatic contraction of political opportunity that resulted from the suffrage restriction campaigns in the southern states. The successful disfranchisement campaign in Louisiana virtually destroyed the power base of the Populist movement in that state.

Another important, and hitherto overlooked, factor in the movement's demise is the credibility crisis that arose in regard to its framing of the agricultural crisis. By the mid-1890s the Populist movement had shifted its emphasis from fiatism and calls for specific governmental programs, such as the subtreasury proposal, to a focus on monetary expansion in general. This shift occurred both among the mid-road and free-silver Populist factions. The former faction insisted on the necessity of expanding the monetary supply to meet the needs of the economy without regard to the availability of gold and silver. The latter faction was willing to settle, at least momentarily, for an expansion of the monetary supply through the adoption of bimetallism versus the more restrictive monometallic gold standard. But there was an important common ground between the two factions: Both stressed the evils of currency contraction and the economic hardships that monometallism inextricably imposed. Both factions insisted that the gold standard unavoidably doomed the nation's economy. This diagnostic frame became very vulnerable to criticism when a general economic recovery began in 1898 under the gold-standard policies of the McKinley administration. Due to the discovery of new gold fields and improved techniques for extracting gold from ore, gold production significantly increased. As a result, the volume of circulating currency expanded. Thus in direct contradiction to the claims of Populists, the volume of currency had increased under the gold standard and a general economic recovery was underway.

A credibility crisis ensued. The economic recovery directly challenged the argument of the third party that the gold standard inevitably and unavoidably doomed the economy. Worse yet, many southern farmers who had supported the third party did not benefit from the general economic recovery. This made the framing by Populists of the agricultural crisis suspect. The monetary supply had expanded, yet no significant abatement of their plight occurred. An increased circulating currency had not, after all, solved their economic problems. They continued to suffer from high interest rates on crop-lien loans and low crop prices.

The only Populist proposal that had directly addressed the problem of high crop-lien interest rates, the subtreasury proposal, had been ignored after 1893 in response to harsh criticism by powerful opponents. Populists began treating currency expansion as a panacea for the economic ills of the nation, arguing that once the volume of currency expanded, interest rates would drop and crop prices would rise. When that did not happen, their diagnostic framing of the economic problems besetting the country in general, and farmers more specifically, became highly suspect.

AN INCLUSIVE PERSPECTIVE ON SOCIAL MOVEMENTS

The central theoretical argument of the present study is that the rise and fall of the Louisiana Populist movement is best understood through the lens of a theory of social movements that borrows eclectically from the Resource

Mobilization, Political Process, and Framing perspectives. An inclusive theoretical approach allows for a more complete, nuanced understanding of the dynamics of social movement emergence and development. The importance of the relationships among framing, political opportunity, and mobilization can be seen in each of the central findings of this study.

First, the emergence and growth of the Louisiana Populist movement was significantly affected by the expansion of political opportunity after Reconstruction ended, the development of a diagnostic frame to counter the "overproduction" frame, and a strategic frame that was initially successful in mobilizing small farm owners. Second, the limits of the self-help frame undercut the movement's ability to mobilize tenant farmers and stunted the long-term growth potential of the LFU and the CFA. Third, the shift to an electoral-politics strategic frame elicited serious mobilization challenges because the LFU and the CFA were inadequate bases from which to organize successful political campaigns. Fourth, leaders of the Louisiana Populist movement failed to disseminate an identity frame capable of transcending racial divisions, which undercut their initial efforts to create an enduring biracial political coalition. Fifth, the odds for success by the Louisiana People's Party were significantly reduced by the failure of Populist leaders to develop an effective strategic frame in regard to electoral fraud. Finally, the demise of the Populist movement is best understood by examining the intricate relationships between framing, political opportunity, and mobilization challenges. A credibility problem concerning the diagnostic frame of the movement was accentuated by the crisis created by internal strategic framing disputes and by the contraction of political opportunity resulting from successful suffrage restriction campaigns. An understanding of the rapidity with which the movement demobilized requires a multifaceted explanation that is sensitive to the important roles of framing, political opportunity, and mobilization and to the interplay between these three vital factors. Only with such an explanation can we fully understand the death of the small farmers' dream of economic redemption through the Populist movement.

Notes

PREFACE

1. McMath, *Populist Vanguard,* 165–166.

2. Goodwyn, *Democratic Promise,* 600.

3. Hofstadter, *Age of Reform,* 112.

4. Goodwyn, *Democratic Promise,* 333.

5. Hicks, *Populist Revolt;* Hofstadter, *Age of Reform.*

6. Hair, *Bourbonism and Agrarian Protest,* 241.

7. McNall, *Road to Rebellion,* xiii.

CHAPTER ONE

1. Hair, *Bourbonism and Agrarian Protest.*

2. *Louisiana Populist,* 29 July 1896.

3. McCarthy and Zald, "Resource Mobilization and Social Movements."

4. Ibid.

5. Eisenger, "Conditions of Protest Behavior in American Cities"; Lipsky, *Protest in City Politics;* McAdam, *Political Process and Black Insurgency;* Tarrow, "National Politics and Collective Action"; Tilly, *From Mobilization to Revolution.*

6. Ferree, "Feminist Politics in the U.S. and West Germany"; Jenkins, "Social Movements, Political Representation, and the State"; Joppke, "Social Movements during Cycles of Issue Attention"; Joppke, *Mobilizing Against Nuclear Energy;* Kitschelt, "Political Opportunity Structures and Political Protest"; Kriesi, "The Political Opportunity Structure of New Social Movements."

7. McAdam, *Political Process and Black Insurgency,* 41.

8. Ferree and Miller, "Mobilization and Meaning"; Gamson, Fireman, and Rytina, *Encounters with Unjust Authorities;* Snow, Rochoford, Worden, and Benford, "Frame Alignment Processes."

9. Snow, Rochford, Worden, and Benford, "Frame Alignment Processes."

10. Goodwin and Jasper, *Rethinking Social Movements,* vii.

11. Goodwin and Jasper, "Caught in a Winding, Snarling Vine"; Goodwin and Jasper, *Rethinking Social Movements;* Jasper, "A Strategic Approach to Collective Action"; Kurzman, "The Post-Structuralist Consensus"; Martin and Miller, "Space and Contentious Politics"; Polletta, "Culture is Not Just in Your Head."

12. McAdam, and Paulsen, "Specifying the Relationship Between Social Ties and Activism"; Snow, Zurcher, and Ekland-Olson, "Social Networks and Social Movements."

13. Goodwin and Jasper, *Rethinking Social Movements,* 88

14. Ibid.

15. Snow, Rochford, Worden, and Benford, "Frame Alignment Processes."

16. Cadena-Roa, "Strategic Framing, Emotions, and Superbarrio"; Goodwin, Jasper, and Pollenta, "Return of the Repressed"; Goodwin and Jasper, *Rethinking Social Movement;* Gould, "Life during Wartime"; Kim, "Shame, Anger, and Love in Collective Action."

17. Hoffer, *True Believer;* Kornhauser, *Politics of Mass Society;* Smelser, *Theory of Collective Behavior.*

18. McCarthy and Zald, "Resource Mobilization and Social Movements"; Jenkins and Perrow, "Insurgency of the Powerless."

19. Goodwin, Jasper, and Pollenta, "Return of the Repressed," 71.

20. Aminzade and McAdam, "Emotions and Contentious Politics"; Goodwin and Jasper, "Caught in a Winding, Snarling Vine"; Jasper, "Emotions of Protest"; Kim, "Shame, Anger, and Love in Collective Action."

21. Martin and Miller, "Space and Contentious Politics"; McAdam et al., "Fighting in the Streets"; Rucht, "Impact of National Contexts on Social Movement Structures"; Stillerman, "Space, Strategies, and Alliances in Mobilization"; Waters, "Situating Movements Historically."

22. Martin and Miller, "Space and Contentious Politics."

23. Ibid.

24. Barnes, *Farmers in Rebellion;* Goodwyn, *Democratic Promise.*

25. Barnes, "Strategy Outcome and the Growth of Protest Organizations"; McAdam, "Tactical Innovation and the Pace of Insurgency"; Morris, "Birmingham Confrontation Reconsidered"; Schwartz, *Radical Protest and Social Structure.*

26. Caniglia and Carmin, "Scholarship on Social movement Organizations"; Rucht, "Impact of National Contexts on Social Movement Structures."

27. Oberschall, *Social Conflict and Social Movements,* 14.

28. Jenkins and Perrow, "Insurgency of the Powerless, " 251.

29. Morris, "Black Southern Student Sit-in Movements"; Morris, "Birmingham Confrontation Reconsidered."

30. Haines, "Black Radicalization and the Funding of Civil Rights"; McAdam, *Political Process and Black Insurgency.*

31. Goodwin and Jasper. *Rethinking Social Movements;* Johnson, "Mobilizing the Disabled"; McAdam and Paulsen, "Specifying the Relationship Between Social Ties and Activism"; Morris, "Black Southern Student Sit-in Movements"; Snow, Zurcher, and Ekland-Olson, "Social Networks and Social Movements."

32. Buechler, *Women's Movements in the United States and Beyond;* Staggenborg, "Professionalization and the Formalization in the Pro-Choice Movement."

33. Michels, *Political Parties,* 61–62.

34. Piven and Cloward, *Poor People's Movements.*

35. Barnes, "Organization and Radical Protest"; Lipset, Trow, and Coleman, *Trade Union Democracy;* McAdam, *Political Process and Black Insurgency;* Massad, "Disruption, Organization, and Reform"; Zald and Ash, "Social Movement Organizations."

36. Goodwyn, *Democratic Promise;* Schwartz, *Radical Protest and Social Structure.*

37. Barkan, "Legal Control of the Southern Civil Rights Movement"; Barnes and Connolly, "Repression, the Judicial System, and Political Opportunities"; Buechler, *Women's Movements in the United States;* Haines, "Black Radicalization and the Funding of Civil Rights;" Jasper and Poulsen, "Fighting Back"; Mansbridge, *Why We Lost the ERA;* McAdam, *Political Process and Black Insurgency.*

38. Goodwyn, *Democratic Promise.*

39. McAdam, "Revisiting the U.S. Civil Rights Movement," 205. A focus on threat had already been prominent in the work of some social movement scholars, such as Tilly, *From Mobilization to Revolution.*

40. Goldstone, *Revolution and Rebellion in the Early Modern World;* McAdam, *Political Process and Black Insurgency;* Skocpol, *States and Social Revolution.*

41. Barnes and Connolly, "Repression, the Judicial System, and Political Opportunities"; Kaczorowski, *Politics of Judicial Interpretation.*

42. McAdam, *Political Process and Black Insurgency.*

43. Goodwyn, *Populist Moment;* Martin, *People's Party in Texas.*

44. Benford, "An Insider's Critique"; Goodwin and Jasper, *Rethinking Social Movements;* Goodwin, Jasper, and Polletta, "Return of the Repressed."

45. Benford, "An Insider's Critique"

46. Ibid.; Benford, "Frame Disputes within the Nuclear Disarmament Movement"; Johnson, "Mobilizing the Disabled"; Ryan, *Prime Time Activism.*

47. As quoted in McMath, *Populist Vanguard,* 165.

48. Snow, Rochford, Worden, and Benford, "Frame Alignment Processes."

49. Melucci, "Getting Involved"; Hipsher, "Heretical Social Movement Organizations"; McVeigh, Myers, and Sikkink, "Corn, Klansmen, and Coolidge"; Payerhin, "On Movement Frames and Negotiated Identities."

50. Snow, Rochford, Worden, and Benford, "Frame Alignment Processes."

51. Barnes and Connolly, "Repression, the Judicial System, and Political Opportunities"; Sipress, "'From the Barrel of a Gun'"; Tunnell, *Crucible of Reconstruction;* Vandal, "'Bloody Caddo.'"

52. Kurzman, "Structural Opportunity and Perceived Opportunity in Social Movement Theory"; Noonan, "Women Against the State."

CHAPTER TWO

1. USBC, *Tenth Census of Population.*

2. Not all farms in the alluvial parishes were large plantations. Portions of the river bottoms were poorly suited to plantation life, being cut by bayous into relatively small tracts of land or being too far from river transportation for the large-scale cultivation of commercial crops. The greater the distance of the land from the river banks, the greater the likelihood that small farmer communities would be the norm. Therefore, the alluvial parishes contained a mix of large plantations and smaller farms, but were distinguished by the fact that large plantation estates tilled by tenant farmers were the dominant form of agriculture (Shugg, *Origins of Class Struggle*).

3. USBC, *Eighth Census of Agriculture;* Hair, *Bourbonism and Agrarian Protest.*

4. USBC, *Tenth Census of Population;* Shugg, *Origins of Class Struggle.*

5. Shugg, *Origins of Class Struggle;* Taylor, *Louisiana Reconstructed;* USBC, *Eighth Census of Agriculture;* USBC, *Ninth Census of Agriculture;* White, *Freedmen's Bureau.*

6. White, *Freedmen's Bureau.*

7. Fitzgerald, *Union League Movement;* Oubre, *Forty Acres and a Mule;* Taylor, "Louisiana: An Impossible Task"; White, *Freedmen's Bureau.*

8. Cruden, *The Negro in Reconstruction;* Shugg, *Origins of Class Struggle;* U.S. Senate, *Message on Condition of States Lately in Rebellion;* White, *Freedmen's Bureau.*

9. Hair, *Bourbonism and Agrarian Protest,* 49; White, *Freedmen's Bureau.*

10. Fitzgerald, *Union League Movement; Opelousas Courier,* 30 June 1888; Royce, "Origins of Sharecropping"; *Shreveport Daily Times,* 1 May 1888; Taylor, *Louisiana Reconstructed;* USBC, *Tenth Census of Agriculture.*

11. Peoples, "'Kansas Fever' in North Louisiana"; Royce, "Origins of Sharecropping."

12. U.S. House, *Report on the Industrial Commission on Agriculture,* 776.

13. Peoples, "'Kansas Fever' in North Louisiana;" Schwartz, *Radical Protest and Social Structure; Shreveport Weekly Caucasian,* 6 February 1890 and 6 March 1890.

14. USBC, *Twelfth Census of Agriculture.*

15. The term "backland parishes" is broadly inclusive of all cotton parishes that were not dominated by alluvial land. It includes parishes with primarily oak uplands, piney woods, longleaf pine hills, and pine flatlands. The oak uplands included many types of soils, some of which were close to alluvial land in fertility. The various pine lands were decidedly less fertile than alluvial land.

16. Taylor, *Louisiana Reconstructed.*

17. Shugg, *Origins of Class Struggle;* USBC, *Eighth Census of Agriculture;* USBC, *Ninth Census of Agriculture.*

18. A major obstacle to market access was the lack of a farm-to-market rail network. A primary reason for the underdevelopment of a rail network was planter opposition. Located along major waterways, planters had no need for railroads and did not want to share the necessary expenses of enticing railroads to their area. Furthermore, planters believed that railroad development in the interior of the state would entice more farmers to grow cotton as a cash crop, thereby increasing the cotton supply and lowering cotton prices.

19. Shugg, *Origins of Class Struggle;* USBC, *Eighth Census of Agriculture;* USBC, *Ninth Census of Agriculture;* USBC, *Tenth Census of Agriculture;* USDA, *Yearbook of Agriculture.*

20. Hair, *Bourbonism and Agrarian Protest;* Shugg, *Origins of Class Struggle.*

21. Louisiana Senate, *Senate Journal;* Thornton, "Fiscal Policy and the Failure of Radical Reconstruction."

22. McMath, *Populist Vanguard.*

23. Clark, *Pills, Petticoats, and Plows;* Congressional Quarterly, *Guide to U.S. Elections;* Hair, *Bourbonism and Agrarian Protest;* Schwartz, *Radical Protest and Social Structure;* Shugg, *Origins of Class Struggle;* Sipress, *Revolt of the Smallholders.*

24. Millet, "Agricultural Retardation"; Hair, *Bourbonism and Agrarian Protest.*

25. Millet, "Agricultural Retardation"; Rodrigue, *Reconstruction in the Cane Fields;* Shugg, *Origins of Class Struggle,* 191; USBC, *Tenth Census of Agriculture,* 227.

26. Hair, *Bourbonism and Agrarian Protest;* Millet, "Agricultural Retardation"; Shugg, *Origins of Class Struggle.*

27. Hair, *Bourbonism and Agrarian Protest;* Rodrigue, *Reconstruction in the Cane Fields;* Shugg, *Origins of Class Struggle;* Taylor, *Louisiana Reconstructed;* Taylor, "Louisiana: An Impossible Task."

28. Hair, *Bourbonism and Agrarian Protest,* 88; Rodrigue, *Reconstruction in the Cane Fields.*

29. Hair, *Bourbonism and Agrarian Protest.*

30. Shugg, *Origins of Class Struggle.*

31. Ibid.; USDA, Yearbook of Agriculture.

32. Hair, *Bourbonism and Agrarian Protest;* Rodrigue, *Reconstruction in the Cane Fields.*

33. Hair, *Bourbonism and Agrarian Protest;* USBC, *Tenth Census of Agriculture.*

34. Hair, *Bourbonism and Agrarian Protest.*

35. U.S. House, *Contested Election, Fourth Congressional District of Louisiana;* U.S. House, *Louisiana Contested Elections;* U.S. House, *Denial of Election Franchise.*

36. Rodrigue, *Reconstruction in the Cane Fields.*

37. Dethloff and Jones, "Race Relations in Louisiana"; Shugg, *Origins of Class Struggle in Louisiana;* USBC, *Tenth Census of Agriculture.*

38. Hair, *Bourbonism and Agrarian Protest;* Shugg, *Origins of Class Struggle.*

39. USBC, *Tenth Census of Agriculture,* 58.

40. Dethloff and Jones, "Race Relations in Louisiana"; Hair, *Bourbonism and Agrarian Protest;* Shugg, *Origins of Class Struggle;* White, *Freedmen's Bureau.*

41. Tunnell, *Crucible of Reconstruction;* Louisiana Constitutional Convention, *Debates in the State Constitutional Convention.*

42. Cruden, *The Negro in Reconstruction;* Tunnell, *Crucible of Reconstruction.*

43. Tunnell, *Crucible of Reconstruction.*

44. Shugg, *Origins of Class Struggle;* Taylor, *Louisiana Reconstructed.*

45. Cruden, *The Negro in Reconstruction.*

46. Taylor, "Louisiana: An Impossible Task"; Tunnell, *Crucible of Reconstruction.*

47. Taylor, *Louisiana Reconstructed;* Tunnell, *Crucible of Reconstruction;* USBC, *Ninth Census of Population.*

48. Fitzgerald, *Union League Movement;* Tunnell, *Crucible of Reconstruction.*

49. Fitzgerald, *Union League Movement;* White, *Freedmen's Bureau.*

50. *New Orleans Tribune,* 30 October 1868, as quoted in Warmoth, *War, Politics, and Reconstruction,* 52.

51. Shugg, *Origins of Class Struggle.*

52. Warmoth, *War, Politics, and Reconstruction,* 55.

53. U.S. House, *Denial of Elective Franchise;* Warmoth, *War, Politics, and Reconstruction.*

54. *Planters Banner,* as quoted in Warmoth, *War, Politics, and Reconstruction,* 69. See also Rable, *But There Was No Peace;* Tunnell, *Crucible of Reconstruction;* Tunnell, *Carpetbagger from Vermont;* U.S. House, *Contested Election, Fourth Congressional District;* U.S. House, *Louisiana Contested Elections;* U.S. House, *Denial of Elective Franchise.*

55. U.S. House, *Contested Election, Fourth Congressional District,* 1, 12, and 18–19; Warmoth, *War, Politics, and Reconstruction.*

56. Tunnell, *Crucible of Reconstruction.*

57. Bennett, *Black Power U.S.A;* Gillette, *Retreat from Reconstruction;* Tunnell, *Crucible of Reconstruction;* Warmoth, *War, Politics, and Reconstruction.*

58. Sipress, "'From the Barrel of a Gun'"; Tunnell, *Crucible of Reconstruction;* U.S. House, *Denial of Elective Franchise.*

59. Kaczorowski, *Politics of Judicial Interpretation,*17; Sipress, "'From the Barrel of a Gun'"; Tunnell, *Carpetbagger from Vermont;* U.S. House, *Denial of Elective Franchise.*

60. The Supreme Court ruled that the Fourteenth and Fifteenth amendments limited the federal role to protecting citizens against infringements on their civil and political rights by state officials. Violations of civil rights by individuals were the exclusive domain of the states. In this important ruling, the Court sent a clear message that there would be little federal support to offset the atrocities of the burgeoning white supremacist movement. See Barnes and Connolly, "Repression, the Judicial System, and Political Opportunities for Civil Rights Advocacy"; Kaczorowski, *Politics of Judicial Interpretation;* Lawrence, "Civil Rights and Criminal Wrongs."

61. As quoted in Tunnell, *Carpetbagger from Vermont,* 138.

62. *Alexandria Caucasian,* 4 April 1874, 18 April 1874, and 25 April 1874; *Opelousas Courier,* 23 May 1874.

63. Tunnell, *Crucible of Reconstruction,* 197.

64. Hair, *Bourbonism and Agrarian Protest;* U.S. House, *Denial of Elective Franchise.*

65. For a general discussion of the important role of white violence in undermining Reconstruction and the civil rights movement of the nineteenth century, see Du Bois, *Black Reconstruction in America;* Franklin, *Reconstruction;* Perman, *The Road to Redemption;* Rable, *But There Was No Peace.*

66. Hair, *Bourbonism and Agrarian Protest;* Shugg, *Origins of Class Struggle;* Thornton, "Fiscal Policy and Radical Reconstruction"; U.S. House, *Contested Election, Fourth Congressional District;* U.S. House, *Louisiana Contested Elections;* U.S. House, *Denial of Elective Franchise.*

67. *Alexandria Caucasian,* 18 April 1874, 9 May 1874, and 23 May 1874; Thornton, "Fiscal Policy and Radical Reconstruction"; USDA, *Yearbook of Agriculture;* U.S. House, *Denial of Elective Franchise.*

68. Hair, *Bourbonism and Agrarian Protest.*

69. Buck, *The Granger Movement;* Calvert, *The Southern Grange.*

70. USDA, *Yearbook of Agriculture;* Willis, *The Granger Movement.*

71. *Opelousas Courier,* 4 July 1878, as quoted in Willis, *The Granger Movement,* 38.

72. *New Orleans Daily Picayune,* 19 January 1875, as quoted in Willis, *The Granger Movement,* 45.

73. Calvert, *The Southern Grange,* 49.

74. *Opelousas Journal,* 1 May 1874, as quoted in Thorstad, *Historical and Cultural Geography of the Grange,* 124.

75. USBC, *Tenth Census of Agriculture,* 58; USBC, *Twelfth Census of Agriculture,* 48.

76. There was an unsuccessful attempt to revitalize the Grange in the 1880s. See *Proceedings of the Third Annual Session of the Louisiana State Grange; Proceedings of the Fifth Annual Session of the Louisiana State Grange.*

CHAPTER THREE

1. Anti-monopoly comments filled the newspaper affiliated with the small farmers' movement. It is clear, however, from the context that they did not use the term "monopoly" to imply that one firm controlled a particular product market, but rather that there was inadequate competition, and sometimes overt collusion, among businesses in many product markets. Their use of the term is more consistent with what economists today refer to as oligopolies.

2. Louisiana Senate, *Official Journal of the Senate of the State of Louisiana.*

3. *Bienville News,* as quoted in *Opelousas Courier,* 14 April 1888; see also *Opelousas Courier,* 7 April 1888.

4. *Colfax Chronicle,* 16 January 1886, 27 February 1886, and 27 April 1889; *Shreveport Daily Times,* 15 February 1887; Thornton, "Fiscal Policy and the Failure of Radical Reconstruction"; *Winn Parish Democrat,* 11 September 1888 and 25 October 1889.

5. *Louisiana Populist,* 14 December 1894.

6. Hair, *Bourbonism and Agrarian Protest;* Shugg, *Origins of Class Struggle;* USBC, *Ninth Census of Agriculture;* USBC, *Tenth Census of Agriculture;* USBC, *Eleventh Census of Agriculture.*

7. McMath, *American Populism.*

8. Hair, *Bourbonism and Agrarian Protest.*

9. Ibid.; USBC, *Tenth Census of Agriculture.*

10. Dunning, *Farmers' Alliance History and Agricultural Digest;* Hair, *Bourbonism and Agrarian Protest;* Morgan, *History of the Wheel and the Alliance.*

11. *Colfax Chronicle,* 5 March 1887; *National Economist,* 30 August 1890.

12. Barnes, *Farmers in Rebellion.*

13. Ibid.; Garvin and Daws, *History of the National Farmers' Alliance,* 38–39.

14. *Southern Mercury,* 11 September 1888; *National Economist,* 25 May 1889 and 7 September 1889.

15. *Colfax Chronicle,* 11 August 1888; *Opelousas Courier,* 4 August 1888; *National Economist,* 25 May 1889.

16. *Colfax Chronicle,* 3 September 1887, 7 July 1888, 27 July 1889, 22 February 1890, 8 March 1890, 30 March 1890, and 2 August 1890; *Shreveport Daily Times,* 12 July 1887; *St. Landry Clarion,* 27 June 1891 and 1 August 1891. For a similar view of the role of social events in the Alliance movement, see Goodwyn, *Populist Moment;* McNall, *Road to Rebellion.*

17. Berger and Luckmann, *Social Construction of Reality.*

18. USBC, *Ninth Census of Agriculture;* USBC, *Tenth Census of Agriculture;* USBC, *Eleventh Census of Agriculture.*

19. USDA, *Yearbook of Agriculture,* 754.

20. *Alexandria Caucasian,* 16 May 1874; *Colfax Chronicle,* 9 January 1886, 31 July 1886 25 September 1886, and 5 March 1887; *Shreveport Weekly Caucasian,* 10 October 1895; *St. Landry Clarion,* 11 March 1893 and 1 July 1893; *St. Landry Democrat,* 4 February 1893.

21. *Southern Mercury,* 4 April 1890; USBC, *Twelfth Census of Agriculture,* 407.

22. U.S. Senate, *Report on the Condition of Cotton Growers.*

23. *Texas Advance,* 28 October 1893; see also ibid., 30 June 1894.

24. *Southern Mercury,* 11 April 1895.

25. As quoted in the *National Economist,* 30 August 1890; see also ibid., 7 September 1889; *Shreveport Weekly Caucasian,* 6 February 1890; and *Southern Mercury,* 7 February 1895, 7 March 1895, and 16 May 1895.

26. As quoted in Winkler, *Platforms of Political Parties in Texas,* 235.

27. Reprinted in *Shreveport Daily Times,* 17 October 1886.

28. Garvin and Daws, *History of the National Farmers' Alliance,* viii.

29. *Shreveport Weekly Caucasian,* 27 March 1890; see also *Shreveport Daily Caucasian,* 9 November 1889.

30. Clark, *Pills, Petticoats, and Plows;* Congressional Quarterly, *Guide to U.S. Elections;* Schwartz, *Radical Protest and Social Structure;* Suarez, "Bargains, Bills, and Bankruptcies"; Woodward, *Origins of the New South.*

31. *Shreveport Daily Caucasian,* 19 October 1889.

32. *Colfax Chronicle,* 4 December 1886 and 11 December 1886; *Shreveport Daily Times,* 30 November 1886, 2 December 1886, and 5 December–9 December 1886.

33. *Shreveport Daily Times,* 20 April 1887; see also ibid., 30 January 1887; *Colfax Chronicle,* 16 July 1887 and 22 October 1887.

34. *Colfax Chronicle,* 12 January 1889.

35. Barnes, *Farmers in Rebellion; Colfax Chronicle,* 16 August 1890; Schwartz, *Radical Protest and Social Structure.*

36. Barnes, *Farmers in Rebellion.*

37. *Colfax Chronicle,* 23 August 1888, 14 December 1889, 1 March 1890, and 28 June 1890; *Southern Mercury,* 7 March 1889.

38. *Colfax Chronicle,* 6 October and 20 October 1888; *National Economist,* 13 April 1889 and 16 November 1889; *Southern Mercury,* 17 January 1887.

39. *Opelousas Courier,* 20 July 1889.

40. Goodwyn, *Democratic Promise.*

41. Barnes, *Farmers in Rebellion.*

42. *Southern Mercury,* 9 April 1889.

43. *Colfax Chronicle,* 13 February 1892 and 23 April 1892; *Opelousas Courier,* 31 January 1891 and 11 April 1891; *Shreveport Weekly Caucasian,* 6 February 1890.

44. Census data on farm ownership and tenancy were first collected in the agricultural census of 1880. The adequacy of the data is an issue. Tracts of land owned by a single planter, but worked by different tenants, were recorded as different farms, and census enumerators failed to ascertain who owned the land. Twenty farms operated by twenty tenant farmers could have one, five, ten, or even twenty different owners. Consequently, the data are problematic when discussing farm ownership. In regard to tenancy data, the census takers in 1880 and 1890 reported most blacks in the cotton parishes as agricultural laborers. This changed in 1900, when the accuracy of the tenancy count improved. To compare 1880, 1890, and 1900 data on tenancy risks overstating the increase in tenancy in Louisiana. Consequently, I rely solely on data from the census of 1900 when discussing tenancy rates.

45. Goodwyn, *Democratic Promise.*

46. Schwartz, *Radical Protest and Social Structure.*

47. *Colfax Chronicle,* 5 October 1889.

48. Ibid., 27 September 1890.

49. Ibid., 9 March 1889 and 12 October 1889; *Shreveport Daily Caucasian,* 23 October 1889; *Weekly Pelican,* 8 October 1887.

50. U.S. Senate Report, *Report on the Condition of Cotton Growers.*

51. Barnes, *Farmers in Rebellion;* McMath, *Populist Vanguard.*

52. USBC, *Tenth Census of Agriculture,* 227.

53. *Louisiana Populist,* 7 September 1894; USDA, *Yearbook of Agriculture,* 754; U.S. Senate Report, *Report on the Condition of Cotton Growers.*

54. Garvin and Daws, *History of the National Farmers' Alliance.*

55. Barnes, *Farmers in Rebellion;* Macune, "*Farmers Alliance Narrative.*"

56. Macune, "*Farmers Alliance Narrative.*"

57. Ousley, "A Lesson in Co-operation," 822.

58. Macune, "*Farmers Alliance Narrative*"; Ousley, "A Lesson in Co-operation."

59. Barnes, *Farmers in Rebellion.*

60. Ibid.

61. *Southern Mercury,* 31 May 1888.

62. *National Economist,* 25 May 1889; *Southern Mercury,* 4 September 1888 and 9 January 1890.

63. Ousley, "A Lesson in Co-operation"; *Southern Mercury,* 3 May 1888, 31 May 1888, 7 June 1888, and 5 July 1888.

64. Goodwyn, *Democratic Promise.*

65. *Southern Mercury,* 7 February 1889 and 4 September 1890; Barnes, *Farmers in Rebellion.*

66. A crucial issue concerns the reasons for the poor capitalization of the Texas Alliance Exchange While Goodwyn (*Democratic Promise*) posits an impoverishment explanation, a more complete explanation is found in Barnes's work on the Texas Alliance (*Farmers in Rebellion,* 80–99).

67. *Colfax Chronicle,* 8 September and 15 September 1888; *Opelousas Courier,* 3 November 1888.

68. U.S. House, *Investigation of Cotton Bagging Trust.*

69. *Colfax Chronicle,* 11 August 1888, 8 September 1888, 22 September 1888, 29 September 1888, and 6 October 1888; *Opelousas Courier,* 11 August 1888 and 22 September 1888.

70. *Colfax Chronicle,* 15 September 1888.

71. Ibid., 11 August 1888, 15 September 1888, and 29 September 1888; *Opelousas Courier,* 8 September 1888; *National Economist,* 13 April 1889, 15 June 1889, and 27 July 1889; *Southern Mercury,* 30 May 1889, 10 July 1890, and 17 July 1890.

72. *Southern Mercury,* 1 August 1888, 8 August 1888, 18 September 1888, 25 September 1888, 9 October 1888, and 16 October 1888.

73. *National Economist,* 26 July 1890; *Shreveport Daily Caucasian,* 28 January 1890.

74. *National Economist,* 13 April 1889 and 27 April 1889.

75. *Colfax Chronicle,* 17 August 1889.

76. Ibid., 11 May 1889, 18 May 1889, 13 July 1889, 7 September 1889, 14 September 1889; *Opelousas Courier,* 8 June 1889.

77. *National Economist,* 21 September 1889 and 16 November 1889; *Opelousas Courier,* 8 June 1889 and 29 September 1889; *Shreveport Weekly Caucasian,* 30 June 1890.

78. *National Economist,* 8 June 1889, 17 August 1889, and 16 November 1889; *Opelousas Courier,* 8 June 1889; *Shreveport Daily Caucasian,* 19 October 1889 and 28 January 1890; *Winn Parish Democrat,* 25 October 1889.

79. *Colfax Chronicle,* 24 August 1889; *Opelousas Courier,* 29 September 1888; *Shreveport Daily Caucasian,* 19 October 1889; *Shreveport Weekly Caucasian,* 24 October 1889.

80. *Colfax Chronicle,* 24 August 1889.

81. *Cotton Belt,* 24 August 1889; see also the Morehouse Parish LFU resolution reported in *National Economist,* 26 July 1890.

82. *National Economist,* 15 June 1889 and 26 July 1890; *Southern Mercury,* 6 June 1889.

83. As quoted in McMath, *Populist Vanguard,* 57 (italics in the original).

84. Goodwyn, *Democratic Promise.*

85. Schwartz, *Radical Protest and Social Structure,* 244.

86. Ibid., 245–246.

87. USBC, *Twelfth Census of Agriculture,* 408–409.

88. Hicks, *The Populist Revolt;* McMath, *Populist Vanguard.*

89. The 1890 schedules were destroyed by fire and, therefore, unavailable for use in this analysis.

90. As quoted in the *Colfax Chronicle* 18 June 1887; see also ibid., 5 March 1887.

91. Hair, *Bourbonism and Agrarian Protest,* 167.

92. *Colfax Chronicle,* 4 February 1888, 7 July 1888, 13 July1889, 11 January 1890, 2 August 1890, 16 August 1890, 20 September 1890, 1 November 1890, 8 November 1890, and 29 November 1890; *Shreveport Daily Times,* 25 November 1886 and 7 April 1888.

93. Rodrigue, *Reconstruction in the Cane Fields.*

94. *National Economist,* 14 March 1889.

95. *Southern Mercury,* 10 April 1890; see also *Colfax Chronicle,* 12 March 1887.

CHAPTER FOUR

1. Abramowitz, "The Negro in the Populist Movement."

2. Goodwyn, *Democratic Promise.*

3. *Beeville Bee,* 31 January 1889; *Constitution of the Colored Farmers National Alliance; National Economist,* 2 November 1889 and 14 December 1889; Rogers, "The Negro Alliance in Alabama"; *Southern Mercury,* 10 May 1888 and 13 February 1890.

4. *Beeville Bee,* 31 January 1889; *National Economist,* 14 March 1889; *Southern Mercury,* 14 February 1889.

5. *National Economist,* 14 March 1889.

6. Ibid.

7. Ibid.

8. *Winn Parish Democrat,* 8 March 1889.

9. *Constitution of the Colored Farmers National Alliance;* Hair, *Bourbonism and Agrarian Protest.*

10. *National Economist,* 2 November 1889 and 25 January 1890.

11. *Opelousas Courier,* 11 July 1891.

12. *Constitution of the Colored Farmers National Alliance;* Rogers, "The Negro Alliance in Alabama."

13. USBC, *Twelfth Census of Population.*

14. For a similar argument, see Rogers, "The Negro Alliance in Alabama,"38–44.

15. USBC, *Twelfth Census of Agriculture.*

16. Goodwyn, *Democratic Promise,* 333–334.

17. Others claimed that good cotton pickers averaged 200 to 225 pounds of cotton per day (*Ft. Worth Gazette,* 12 September 1891); Calvert, *The Southern Grange.*

18. *Ft. Worth Gazette,* 7 September 1891; Gaither, *Blacks and the Populist Revolt;* Shapiro, "Populists and the Negro."

19. *Ft. Worth Gazette,* 7 September 1891.

20. Ibid., 12 September 1891; *National Economist,* 15 November 1890; *Shreveport Weekly Caucasian,* 22 March 1890.

21. *Houston Daily Post,* 16 April 1892; see also Arnett, *Populist Movement in Georgia.*

22. Shapiro, "Populists and the Negro."

23. Abramowitz, "The Negro in the Populist Movement."

24. Ibid.; Lewis, "Political Mind of the Negro"; Shapiro, "Populists and the Negro"; *Weekly Pelican,* 12 January 1890, 9 February 1890, and 16 February 1890.

25. Hair, *Bourbonism and Agrarian Protest,* 78.

26. *New Orleans Democrat,* as quoted in Hair, *Bourbonism and Agrarian Protest,* 81.

27. U.S. Senate, *Denial of Elective Franchise at Election of 1878.*

28. *Shreveport Daily Caucasian,* 17 October 1889; see also ibid., 6 December 1889, 7 December 1889, 26 December 1889, and 1 March 1890.

29. Ibid., 18 December 1889.

30. *New Orleans Daily Picayune,* as quoted in the *Shreveport Daily Caucasian,* 17 October 1889.

31. *New Orleans Daily States,* as quoted in the *Opelousas Courier,* 9 August 1890.

32. Godeke, *Analysis of the Lodge "Force" Bill; Opelousas Courier,* 20 December 1890; *St. Landry Clarion,* 14 February 1891 and 2 January 1892.

33. *Proceedings of the National Farmers' Alliance and Colored Farmers National Alliance,* 15–16; see also Abramowitz, "The Negro in the Populist Movement"; Shapiro, "Populists and the Negro."

34. Godeke, *Analysis of the Lodge "Force" Bill.*

35. Abramowitz, "The Negro in the Populist Movement"; *National Economist,* 7 March 1891; Rogers, "The Negro Alliance in Alabama."

36. *St. Landry Clarion,* 20 December 1890 and 17 January 1891. Although Republicans controlled Congress when the Lodge bill was introduced, Democrats successfully defeated the bill by filibustering. The honest elections, voting rights protections in the bill would not be forthcoming for another three-quarters of a century when Congress passed the Voting Rights Act of 1965 (Godeke, *Analysis of the Lodge "Force" Bill*).

37. Historians have commented on the tendency of whites in Louisiana to use violence to control blacks. Vandal ("Bloody Caddo") calculated that during Reconstruction, no less than 30 percent of whites in Caddo Parish between the ages of eighteen and forty-five were involved in black homicides, with about one-third of those whites involved in multiple homicides. In white-on-black homicides where the occupation of the perpetrators was known, 21 percent were small farmers and 44 percent were planters. Thus, while planters were more often involved in violence against blacks, small farmers were not indifferent to calls to defend white supremacy norms against recalcitrant blacks. In "Black Violence in Post-Civil War Louisiana," Vandal reports that the Red River Delta area within the Fourth Congressional District was infamous for its violence: While it contained only 13 percent of the rural population of Louisiana, 61 percent of white-against-black homicides occurred there. According to historian Joel Sipress, in the violent conflict in 1873 known as the Colfax Massacre, which took place in Grant Parish in the Fourth Congressional District, white moderates united with conservative extremists to destroy black political power ("From the Barrel of a Gun").

38. *Shreveport Daily Caucasian,* 3 December 1889 and 28 November 1889, respectively.

39. Ibid., 30 October 1889 and 2 November 1889; see also ibid., 7 November 1889 and 17 January 1890.

40. Ibid., 30 October 1889.

41. Ibid., 7 December 1889.

42. Ibid., 4 November 1889; see also 22 October 1889, 24 October 1889, 29 October 1889, 26 December 1889, 1 January 1890, 4 January 1890, 12 February 1890, and 26 February 1890.

43. Ibid., 31 December 1889 and 28 January 1890.

44. Ibid., 27 December 1889 and 31 December 1889.

45. Ibid., 28 November 1889.

46. Ibid., 25 November 1889.

47. New Orleans *Daily States,* as quoted in Hair, *Bourbonism and Agrarian Protest,* 26.

48. *Shreveport Daily Caucasian,* 16 November 1889, 27 December 1889, and 30 January 1890.

49. Ibid., 25 November 1889.

50. *Shreveport Weekly Caucasian,* 28 November 1889.

51. *Shreveport Daily Caucasian,* 30 November 1889; for similar statements, see ibid., 14 November 1886, 21 November 1886, 10 October 1889, 24 October 1889, 28 October 1889, 19 November1889, and 23 November 1889, 23 January 1890, 20 February 1890, and 25 February 1890.

52. Ibid., 14 January 1890; see also ibid., 4 November 1889, 29 November 1889, 30 November 1889, 21 December 1889, 27 December 1889, and 20 February 1890.

53. *Shreveport Weekly Caucasian,* 20 February 1890; see also the *Shreveport Daily Caucasian,* 6 February 1890 and 10 February 1890.

54. Hair, *Bourbonism and Agrarian Protest; Shreveport Daily Caucasian,* 21 November 1886, 18 November 1889, 22 November 1889, and 3 December 1889; *Shreveport Weekly Caucasian,* 13 February 1890.

55. *Southern Mercury,* 10 April 1890.

56. *Colfax Chronicle,* 13 July 1889.

57. Ibid., 22 March 1890. Goodwyn, however, was politically conservative. He broke with the LFU when it shifted its primary focus from self-help strategies to a reform-through-politics strategic frame.

58. *Shreveport Weekly Caucasian,* 20 February 1890.

59. *Shreveport Daily Caucasian,* 8 August 1895.

60. Ibid., 8 January 1890; *Shreveport Weekly Caucasian,* 30 January 1890.

61. *Shreveport Daily Caucasian,* 8 March 1890.

62. Ibid., 3 December 1889.

63. Sipress, "A Narrowing of Vision."

64. *United States of America v. C. C. Nash, Cruickshank (sic), et. al.*

65. *Colfax Chronicle,* 17 March 1888 and 13 September 1888. One reviewer pointed out that given the sheer number of whites that participated in the Colfax Massacre, it might have been difficult for anyone, black or white, to avoid business transactions with them all. However, Nash was identified as one of the leaders of the massacre and was among only nine whites indicted by the federal government for the murders. It is important to note, however, that he served on a parish landlord committee in December 1886 and January 1887 that negotiated with black tenant farmers who had threatened to strike. This time he served as a voice of moderation. To what extent this may have altered his reputation among local blacks is unclear.

66. *St. Landry Clarion,* 27 July 1891, 8 August 1891, and 15 August 1891.

67. Ibid., 15 November 1890.

68. *New Orleans Picayune,* 24 April 1891, as quoted in the *Opelousas Courier,* 2 May 1891 and 25 April 1891.

69. *St. Landry Clarion,* 2 May 1891 and 27 June 1891; see also *Louisiana Populist,* 17 June 1898; *Opelousas Courier,* 2 May 1891 and 9 May 1891.

70. *St. Landry Clarion,* 25 April 1891.

71. *Opelousas Courier,* 2 May 1891.

72. Ibid.

73. *Acadia Sentinel,* as quoted in the *Opelousas Courier,* 18 April 1891.

74. *Baton Rouge Advocate,* as quoted in the *Opelousas Courier,* 9 May 1891.

75. *Opelousas Courier,* 18 April 1891 and 2 May 1891.

76. Ibid., 11 July 1891; *St. Landry Clarion,* 16 July 1892.

77. Hair, *Bourbonism and Agrarian Protest,* 94.

78. *National Economist,* 31 May 1890.

79. Ayers, *Promise of the New South;* Kantrowitz, *Ben Tillman and the Reconstruction of White Supremacy;* Woodward, *Origins of the New South;* Woodward, *Tom Watson.*

80. Snow, Rochford, Worden, and Benford, "Frame Alignment Processes."

CHAPTER FIVE

1. *Colfax Chronicle,* 17 August 1889, and *Opelousas Courier,* 17 March 1888, respectively.

2. *Shreveport Weekly Caucasian,* 13 February 1890; see also *Opelousas Courier,* 2 August 1890, 24 January 1891, and 3 September 1892.

3. Barnes, *Farmers in Rebellion;* Macune, "Farmers Alliance Narrative"; *National Economist,* 3 May 1890; *Shreveport Daily Caucasian,* 6 December 1889.

4. *National Economist,* 14 December 1889.

5. Winkler, *Platforms of Political Parties in Texas,* 235–237.

6. Palmer, *Man Over Money.*

7. Unger, *Greenback Era,* 265.

8. *Colfax Chronicle,* 4 January 1890; *Farmers' Vidette,* 12 February 1891, as quoted in *National Economist,* 7 March 1891; Macune, "Farmers Alliance Narrative"; Palmer, *Man Over Money; Shreveport Weekly Caucasian,* 27 March 1890; *St. Landry Clarion,* 9 May 1891.

9. *Colfax Chronicle,* 22 March 1890; Tracy, "The Subtreasury Plan"; *National Economist,* 19 April 1890.

10. *National Economist,* 3 April 1890; Tracy, "The Subtreasury Plan"; USBC, *Eleventh Census of Agriculture,* 148–149.

11. Macune, "Farmers Alliance Narrative."

12. *Shreveport Weekly Caucasian,* 13 March 1890.

13. Ibid., 30 January 1890; see also 13 February 1890, 20 February 1890, and 13 March 1890; *Shreveport Daily Caucasian,* 18 February 1890.

14. *Shreveport Weekly Caucasian,* 20 February 1890 and 13 March 1890.

15. *St. Landry Clarion,* 27 June 1891.

16. *National Economist,* 24 May 1890 and 23 August 1890; see also Tindall, *South Carolina Negroes.*

17. Report of the Secretary of State, 551; USBC. *Eleventh Census of Population,* 782.

18. *Colfax Chronicle,* 6 September 1890; *National Economist,* 30 August 1890.

19. *St. Landry Clarion,* 20 December 1890, and *Shreveport Weekly Caucasian,* 14 November 1889, respectively.

20. *Shreveport Daily Caucasian,* 10 February 1890.

21. *Opelousas Courier,* 28 September 1889; see also ibid., 10 March 1888, 24 March 1888, 7 April 1888, and 14 April 1888.

22. Ibid., 14 December 1889.

23. *Weekly Pelican,* 23 July 1887; see also ibid., 15 January 1887 and 22 August 1887; Goodwyn, *Democratic Promise;* Hair, *Bourbonism and Agrarian Protest;* Rodrigue, *Reconstruction in the Cane Fields.*

24. *Weekly Pelican,* 8 October 1887, 1 December 1888, 29 December 1888, 26 January 1889, 2 March 1889, 9 March 1889, and16 March 1889.

25. *Colfax Chronicle,* 8 November 1890; *Opelousas Courier,* 10 March 1888; *Shreveport Daily Times,* 17 December 1886 and 9 February 1887.

26. *Weekly Pelican,* 12 February 1887; see also 2 April 1887 and 23 July 1887.

27. Ibid., 22 October 1887; see also 5 November 1887.

28. Hair, *Bourbonism and Agrarian Protest.*

29. *Colfax Chronicle,* 6 September 1890 and 4 July 1891. Goodwyn's strident stance against the subtreasury was atypical for the Grant Parish LFU and reflected the fact that he was much more fiscally conservative than other members of the parish LFU.

30. *Shreveport Daily Caucasian,* 2 February 1890.

31. *Shreveport Weekly Caucasian,* 20 February 1890, and *Southern Mercury,* 3 May 1888, respectively.

32. *Shreveport Daily Caucasian,* 11 February 1890; see also *National Economist,* 28 June 1890.

33. *Shreveport Weekly Caucasian,* 20 February 1890.

34. *Colfax Chronicle,* 6 September 1890; see also *Shreveport Daily Caucasian,* 30 January 1890.

35. *Colfax Chronicle,* 16 August 1890.

36. Ibid., 30 August 1890.

37. Ibid., 30 August 1890.

38. *National Economist,* 4 October 1890; see also *Colfax Chronicle,* 23 August 1890, 30 August 1890, and 20 September 1890.

39. *Colfax Chronicle,* 27 January 1883; Hair, 1969. *Bourbonism and Agrarian Protest*: 50; *St. Landry Clarion.* 8 November 1890.

40. *Colfax Chronicle,* 20 September 1890.

41. Ibid., 4 October 1890.

42. Ibid.

43. Ibid., 17 August 1889 and 4 October 1890; *National Economist,* 7 September 1889; *Opelousas Courier,* 11 October 1890; *St. Louis Daily Globe-Democrat,* 5 December 1889.

44. *Colfax Chronicle,* 4 October 1890. See also ibid., 18 October 1890, and 8 November 1890.

45. *New Orleans Times-Democrat,* quoted in *National Economist,* 4 October 1890.

46. *Colfax Chronicle,* 11 October 1890; see also 25 October 1890.

47. Ibid., 11 October 1890.

48. Ibid., 8 November 1890.

49. Hair, *Bourbonism and Agrarian Protest; Report of the Secretary of State.*

50. Hair, *Bourbonism and Agrarian Protest.*

51. Ibid.; *Report of the Secretary of State.*

52. *Colfax Chronicle,* 12 September 1891 and 28 March 1891; *New Orleans Times-Democrat,* as quoted in *Colfax Chronicle,* 3 October 1891.

53. As quoted in the *Colfax Chronicle,* 27 December 1890.

54. *Colfax Chronicle,* 25 July 1891; ibid., 13 September 1890; *Shreveport Daily Caucasian,* 27 March 1890, and *Colfax Chronicle,* 23 August 1890, respectively.

55. *Opelousas Courier,* 20 December 1890.

56. *Shreveport Daily Caucasian,* 27 March 1890.

57. *Opelousas Courier,* 14 March 1891. See also *Colfax Chronicle,* 28 February 1891, 1 August 1891, and 28 March 1891; *Opelousas Courier,* 21 March 1891, 13 June 1891, 17 October 1891, and 6 August 1892.

58. *New Orleans Picayune,* as reprinted in *Colfax Chronicle,* 5 September 1891; *Opelousas Courier,* 14 March 1891 and 29 August 1891; *Colfax Chronicle,* 6 September 1890.

59. Hair, *Bourbonism and Agrarian Protest.*

60. *National Economist,* 15 November 1890.

61. *Proceedings of the Annual Session of the Supreme Council of the National Farmers Alliance,* 5; *St. Landry Clarion,* 6 June 1891.

62. Macune, "Farmers Alliance Narrative."

63. *National Economist,* 30 May 1891.

64. *Colfax Chronicle,* 6 September 1890; *St. Landry Clarion,* 20 December 1890, 14 March 1891, 16 March 1891, and 2 May 1891.

65. *Colfax Chronicle,* 6 September 1890; *Shreveport Weekly Caucasian,* 27 March 1890; *St. Landry Clarion,* 2 May 1891 and 9 May 1891.

66. *Colfax Chronicle,* 6 September 1890.

67. Barnes, *Farmers in Rebellion.*

68. *Colfax Chronicle,* 6 September 1890.

69. *The Pelican Banner,* as quoted in *National Economist,* 2 August 1890.

70. *St. Landry Clarion,* 20 December 1890; see also ibid., 28 February 1891 and 24 December 1892.

71. *National Economist,* 18 April 1891.

72. Barnes, *Farmers in Rebellion; Colfax Chronicle,* 21 February 1891.

73. Ibid., 20 August 1890 and 22 August 1891; *Opelousas Courier,* 6 August 1892; *Shreveport Weekly Caucasian,* 20 February 1890; *St. Landry Clarion,* 25 July 1891.

74. *Opelousas Courier,* 8 August 1891.

75. Schwartz, *Radical Protest and Social Structure.*

76. Hair, *Bourbonism and Agrarian Protest.*

77. There are countless citations that support this claim. But some of the most dramatic examples are found in the *Colfax Chronicle,* 22 March 1891, 11 April 1891, and 11 July 1891; *Opelousas Courier,* 28 September 1889, 4 April 1891, and 31 October 1891; *Shreveport Daily Caucasian,* 6 December 1889, 10 February 1890, and 27 March 1894; *Shreveport Daily Times,* 5 December 1886, 15 December 1886, and 9 February 1887.

78. *Opelousas Courier,* 4 April 1891.

79. *Alexandria Times,* as quoted in *Opelousas Courier,* 4 April 1891; see also *Colfax Chronicle,* 26 July 1890.

80. *Shreveport Daily Caucasian,* 10 April 1894.

81. *New Orleans Times-Democrat,* as quoted in *Opelousas Courier,* 31 October 1891; see also *Opelousas Courier,* 7 April 1888, 5 April 1890, and 31 May 1890.

82. *National Economist,* 30 August 1890.

83. *Shreveport Daily Caucasian,* 27 April 1894; see also *Colfax Chronicle,* 11 July 1891 and 18 July 1891; *opelousas Courier,* 12 September 1891.

84. In antebellum Louisiana, large planters had dominated the party. They controlled the state senate because the senatorial seat allocations were based on total population, including slaves. The Senate had veto power over legislation passed in the lower chamber, so reforms that threatened the interests of the large planters were doomed. When the state constitution was amended in 1852 to extend the total population basis of representation to the lower chamber, the power of the planter elite was complete. No other state gave large slaveholders more power. While their power was muted during Reconstruction, after the end of Reconstruction they moved quickly to reinstate their power base (Hair, *Bourbonism and Agrarian Protest;* Shugg, *Origins of Class Struggle*).

85. *Colfax Chronicle,* 12 June 1886 and 9 August 1890; Hair, *Bourbonism and Agrarian Protest; Shreveport Daily Times,* 8 June 1886.

86. *Shreveport Daily Times*, 15 April 1887, 20 April 1887, and 8 October 1886. The fact that planter control and electoral fraud were sensitive issues in Louisiana politics was reflected in the frequent coverage of this topic in newspapers. Additional discussion can be found in the *Shreveport Daily Times*, 24 August 1886, 10 September 1886, 9 January 1887, 30 January 1887, 8 February 1887, 26 February 1887, and 13 March 1887; *St. Landry Clarion*, 2 January 1892; *Colfax Chronicle*, 22 February 1891.

87. *Shreveport Daily Times*. 19 November 1886.

88. *Louisiana Journal*, as quoted in *Shreveport Daily Times*, 19 November 1886; see also ibid., 26 February 1887.

89. *Report of the Secretary of State*, 552–553; *Shreveport Daily Times*, 19 November 1886.

90. *Abbeville Meridional* as quoted in the *Shreveport Daily Times*, 8 February 1887.

91. Hair, *Bourbonism and Agrarian Protest*.

92. *Natchitoches People's Vindicator*, 26 October 1878, as quoted in Hair, *Bourbonism and Agrarian Protest*, 61.

93. Hair, *Bourbonism and Agrarian Protest*, 113–114.

94. *Morehouse Clarion*, as quoted in *Shreveport Daily Times*, 16 December 1886.

95. *Shreveport Daily Times*, 19 April 1888; see also *Opelousas Courier*, 14 January 1888, 21 January 1888, and 4 February 1888.

96. *Shreveport Daily Times*, as quoted in *Opelousas Courier*, 25 February 1888.

97. *St. Landry Democrat*, 13 January 1894; see also *Colfax Chronicle*, 22 May 1886, 4 September 1887, and 3 March 1894; *Shreveport Daily Caucasian*, 29 April 1894 and 15 May 1894; *St. Landry Democrat*, 26 August 1893.

98. *National Economist*, 15 June 1889.

CHAPTER SIX

1. Hair, *Bourbonism and Agrarian Protest*; Hicks, *Populist Revolt*.

2. Hicks, *Populist Revolt*; McMath, *American Populism*.

3. Goodwyn, *Populist Moment*; McMath, *Populist Vanguard*.

4. Goodwyn, *Populist Moment*, 180.

5. *National Economist*, 13 December 1890 and 30 January 1891.

6. *Colfax Chronicle*, 3 January 1891; *Southern Mercury*, 13 March 1890.

7. *Southern Mercury*, 20 February 1890.

8. Hicks, *Populist Revolt*.

9. *Colfax Chronicle*, 10 January 1891 and 31 January 1891; *National Economist*, 16 November 1889.

10. Hicks, *Populist Revolt*.

11. *Colfax Chronicle*, 11 July 1891; Hair, *Bourbonism and Agrarian Protest*, 212.

12. Abramowitz, "The Negro in the Populist Movement"; *National Economist*, 5 March 1892.

13. *Colfax Chronicle*, 6 June 1891; *National Economist*, 30 May 1891.

14. *National Economist*, as quoted in *St. Landry Clarion*, 6 June 1891; *National Economist*, 9 May 1891.

15. *Farmers Vidette*, as quoted in *Colfax Chronicle*, 25 July 1891.

16. *Colfax Chronicle*, 20 June 1891; see also 1 August 1891.

17. Ibid., 27 June 1891 and 18 July 1891.

18. *Ft. Worth Gazette*, 2 July 1891 and 21 July 1891; Hair, *Bourbonism and Agrarian Protest*.

19. *St. Landry Clarion,* 6 June 1891.

20. *Opelousas Courier,* 8 August 1891.

21. Ibid.

22. *Colfax Chronicle,* 31 January 1891 and 13 June 1891.

23. Hair, *Bourbonism and Agrarian Protest,* 29.

24. *Colfax Chronicle,* 11 July 1891 and 18 July 1891.

25. *Shreveport Weekly Caucasian,* 20 March 1890.

26. *Shreveport Daily Caucasian,* 28 January 1890; *Shreveport Weekly Caucasian,* 30 January 1890 and 20 March 1890; *St. Landry Clarion,* 11 October 1890, 6 December 1890, and 18 July 1891.

27. *Colfax Chronicle,* front page of every issue from mid-October 1891–April 1892; *Opelousas Courier,* 8 March 1890 and 26 April 1890; *St. Landry Democrat,* 14 March 1891.

28. *Opelousas Courier,* 20 September 1890; see also ibid., 3 May 1890, 17 May 1890, 9 August 1890, 13 September 1890, 27 September 1890, 20 December 1890, 28 February 1891, 27 June 1891, 5 August 1891, 15 September 1891, and 26 September 1891.

29. *Colfax Chronicle,* 13 December 1890, 20 December 1890, and 27 December 1890.

30. LFU column, *Shreveport Weekly Caucasian,* 20 March 1890.

31. *Colfax Chronicle,* 20 June 1891; *Ft. Worth Gazette,* 21 July 1891; *National Economist,* 26 September 1891; *St. Landry Clarion,* 3 January 1891, 16 May 1891, 30 May 1891, and 6 June 1891.

32. *Colfax Chronicle,* 15 August 1891; *Ft. Worth Gazette,* 7 August 1891; *National Economist,* 5 September 1891; *Opelousas Courier,* 8 August 1891 and 15 August 1891.

33. Reprinted in *Colfax Chronicle,* 8 August 1891 and *St. Landry Clarion,* 8 August 1891.

34. *Colfax Chronicle,* 15 August 1891; *St. Landry Clarion,* 26 September 1891, 10 October 1891, 17 October 1891, 7 November 1891, and 21 November 1891.

35. *Louisiana Populist,* 26 July 1895; see also *Colfax Chronicle,* 22 August 1891.

36. *Colfax Chronicle.,* 15 August 1891.

37. Ibid., 22 August 1891.

38. Reprinted in the *National Economist,* 24 October 1891.

39. As reported in *Shreveport Weekly Caucasian,* 20 December 1890.

40. *National Economist,* 5 September 1891.

41. Ibid., 19 September 1891.

42. *Colfax Chronicle,* 22 August 1891; see also ibid., 3 October 1891, 10 October 1891, 7 November 1891, 14 November 1891, and 2 January 1892; *St. Landry Clarion,* 10 October 1891, 7 November 1891, and 17 November 1891.

43. *National Economist,* 17 October 1891; see also ibid., 26 September 1891 and 31 October 1891.

44. Ibid., 26 September 1891 and 31 October 1891.

45. *Colfax Chronicle,* 17 October 1891 and 24 October 1891; *National Economist,* 17 October 1891; *Opelousas Courier,* 17 October 1891.

46. *Opelousas Courier,* 31 October 1891; see also ibid., 26 September 1891 and 10 October 1891.

47. Hair, *Bourbonism and Agrarian Protest; Opelousas Courier,* 5 October 1889 and 7 December 1889; *Shreveport Daily Caucasian,* 29 October 1889; *Shreveport Weekly Caucasian,* 31 October 1889; *St. Landry Clarion,* 14 March 1892.

48. *Colfax Chronicle,* 7 March 1891 and 28 November 1891; Hair, 1969. *Bourbonism and Agrarian Protest;* Rodrigue, *Reconstruction in the Cane Fields;* Rodrigue, "Labor Militancy and Black Grassroots Political Mobilization"; *Shreveport Daily Times,* 8 February 1887; *St. Landry Clarion,* 26 December 1891.

49. *Colfax Chronicle,* 28 November 1891; USBC, *Eleventh Census of Population,* 782.

50. *Opelousas Courier,* 9 January 1892 and *New Orleans Daily States,* as quoted in *Opelousas Courier,* 7 November 1891, respectively.

51. Ibid., 21 November 1891.

52. *The Ocala Demand,* as quoted in *Opelousas Courier,* 9 January 1892.

53. *Opelousas Courier,* 9 January 1892; *St. Landry Clarion,* 26 December 1891.

54. *Opelousas Courier,* 14 November 1891; see also ibid., 7 November 1891 and 28 November 1891; *Baton Rouge Advocate,* as quoted in ibid., 31 October 1891.

55. Ibid., 19 March 1892.

56. *National Economist,* 17 October 1891.

57. *Colfax Chronicle,* 26 September 1891; Hair, *Bourbonism and Agrarian Protest.*

58. Hair, *Bourbonism and Agrarian Protest; National Economist*, 17 October 1891.

59. *National Economist,* 17 October 1891.

60. Ibid., 17 October 1891; also excerpted in the *New Orleans Daily Picayune,* 4 October 1891, as quoted in Hair, *Bourbonism and Agrarian Protest,* 218.

61. *Colfax Chronicle,* 10 January 1891 and 31 January 1891; *National Economist,* 16 November 1889.

62. Carlton, "The Politics of the Convict Lease System in Louisiana."

63. *National Economist,* 17 October 1891.

64. *Daily Picayune,* 5 October 1891, as quoted in Hair, *Bourbonism and Agrarian Protest,* 219.

65. *Colfax Chronicle,* 17 October 1891.

66. Hicks, *Populist Revolt.*

67. Goodwyn, *Populist Moment;* Hicks, *Populist Revolt;* McMath, *American Populism.*

68. *Winnfield Comrade,* as quoted in Hair, *Bourbonism and Agrarian Protest,* 222.

69. Hair, *Bourbonism and Agrarian Protest.*

70. *Colfax Chronicle,* 17 August 1889; *National Economist,* 19 September 1891.

71. *New Orleans Daily States,* as quoted in *Opelousas Courier,* 2 January 1892; see also *Opelousas Courier,* 18 June 1892.

72. Hair, *Bourbonism and Agrarian Protest.*

73. *Colfax Chronicle,* 19 March 1892; *Opelousas Courier,* 20 February 1892 and 27 February 1892; *St. Landry Clarion,* 19 March 1892.

74. *Colfax Chronicle,* 9 April 1892; *Opelousas Courier,* all issues in April 1892; *St. Landry Clarion,* 26 March 1892 and 9 April 1892.

75. *Colfax Chronicle,* 30 April 1892.

76. Ibid.; Hair, *Bourbonism and Agrarian Protest; Opelousas Courier,* 19 March 1892; Sipress, *Revolt of the Smallholders.*

77. *Report of the Secretary of State,* 562.

78. *New Orleans Times-Democrat* and the *New Orleans Daily Picayune,* respectively, as quoted in the *Opelousas Courier,* 23 April 1892 and 18 June 1892.

79. *Colfax Chronicle,* 30 April 1892; Hair, *Bourbonism and Agrarian Protest.*

80. Hair, *Bourbonism and Agrarian Protest; Opelousas Courier,* 14 May 1892.

81. Barnes, *Farmers in Rebellion.*

82. Hair, *Bourbonism and Agrarian Protest.*

83. *Colfax Chronicle,* 7 February 1891 and 23 April 1892; Sipress, *Revolt of the Smallholders,* 79.

84. *Opelousas Courier,* 23 April 1892; *St. Landry Clarion,* 23 April 1892; *Report of the Secretary of State,* 562.

85. *Report of the Secretary of State,* 562.

86. Ibid.

87. Barnes, *Farmers in Rebellion;* Goodwyn, *Democratic Promise;* Hicks, *Populist Revolt;* McNall, *Road to Rebellion;* Woodward. *Tom Watson.*

88. Hair, *Bourbonism and Agrarian Protest.*

89. *Colfax Chronicle,* 7 August 1886; Hair, *Bourbonism and Agrarian Protest; Shreveport Daily Times,* 10 December 1886; *St. Landry Clarion,* 3 September 1892.

90. McLaurin, *Knights of Labor in the South;* Rodrigue, *Reconstruction in the Cane Fields;* Rodrigue, "Labor Militancy and Black Grassroots Political Mobilization."

91. Rodrigue, *Reconstruction in the Cane Fields;* Rodrigue, "Labor Militancy and Black Grassroots Political Mobilization."

92. *Colfax Chronicle,* 20 June 1891.

93. USBC, *Eleventh Census of Population.*

CHAPTER SEVEN

1. *Colfax Chronicle,* 30 April 1892.

2. Ibid., 14 May 1892.

3. Ibid., 7 March 1891 and 16 July 1892; *Opelousas Courier,* 28 July 1888 and 3 November 1888; *Shreveport Daily Caucasian,* 7 November and 12 November 1889.

4. *St. Landry Clarion,* 30 May 1891; *Weekly Caucasian,* 20 February 1890.

5. *Opelousas Courier,* 28 May 1892.

6. Barnes, *Farmers in Rebellion;* Laughlin, *History of Bimetallism; Shreveport Weekly Caucasian,* 6 March 1890; *St. Landry Clarion,* 23 April 1892.

7. *St. Landry Clarion,* 6 June 1891.

8. Ibid., 15 October 1892.

9. *Colfax Chronicle,* 18 June 1892 and 2 July 1892; *Opelousas Courier,* 18 June 1892; *St. Landry Clarion,* 15 October 1892.

10. *Colfax Chronicle,* 10 September 1892; Hicks, *Populist Revolt.*

11. Ibid., 23 July 1892; Hair, *Bourbonism and Agrarian Protest.*

12. Hair, *Bourbonism and Agrarian Protest.*

13. *Colfax Chronicle,* 15 October 1892; see also ibid., 23 July 1892, 30 July 1892, 6 August 1892, and 20 August 1892.

14. Ibid., 30 July 1892, 3 September 1892, and 5 November 1892.

15. *St. Landry Clarion,* 15 October 1892; *Baton Rouge Advocate,* as quoted in Hair, *Bourbonism and Agrarian Protest,* 232.

16. *Louisiana Populist,* 2 November 1892.

17. *St. Landry Clarion,* 13 August 1892.

18. Ibid., 27 August 1892.

19. *Baton Rouge Daily Advocate,* 6 October 1892, as quoted in Hair, *Bourbonism and Agrarian Protest,* 228; *New Orleans Daily States,* as quoted in *Colfax Chronicle,* 13 August 1892.

20. Hair, *Bourbonism and Agrarian Protest; St. Landry Clarion,* 22 October 1892.

21. *Colfax Chronicle,* 22 October 1892; Hair, *Bourbonism and Agrarian Protest; St. Landry Clarion,* 22 October 1892.

22. *Colfax Chronicle,* 5 November 1892; *St. Landry Clarion,* 22 October 1892.

23. *Winnfield Comrade,* as quoted in *Colfax Chronicle,* 29 October 1892.

24. *Report of the Secretary of State,* 552–553, 575–576. The exception was the rare occasion when there was a split in the Democratic Party, such as occurred between the anti-lottery and pro-lottery factions in the gubernatorial election of 1892. But the lapse was momentary, with control and manipulation of the election machinery soon reinstated.

25. Precinct election returns are from *Colfax Chronicle,* 23 April 1892 and 12 November 1892.

26. *Report of the Secretary of State,* 587; *St. Landry Clarion,* 24 December 1892.

27. Goodwyn, *Democratic Promise.*

28. Hicks, *Populist Revolt,* 113.

29. *Colfax Chronicle,* 20 August 1892, 27 August 1892, and 3 September 1892; *Opelousas Courier,* 23 July 1892; *St. Landry Clarion,* 23 July 1892. The rickety-bridge metaphor for the relationship between the Alliance and People's Party was true for a number of other states as well. In only five southern states did the Populist presidential vote in 1892 amount to more than one-half of the reported membership of the state Alliance (McMath, *Populist Vanguard).*

30. McMath, *Populist Vanguard.*

31. Goodwyn, *Democratic Promise;* Hicks, *Populist Revolt;* McMath, *Populist Vanguard.*

32. Rezneck, "Unemployment, Unrest, and Relief in the United States."

33. Ibid.; see also Hicks, *Populist Revolt;* Koenig, *Bryan.*

34. Hicks, *Populist Revolt.*

35. *Shreveport Daily Caucasian,* 5 April 1894, 11 April 1894, 20 April 1894, and 23 April 1894.

36. U.S. Senate, *Report on the Condition of Cotton Growers,* 349–351.

37. *Louisiana Populist,* 24 August 1894, 28 September 1894, 9 November 1894, 16 November 1894, and 14 December 1894; *Winnfield Comrade,* 13 December 1894.

38. *Louisiana Populist,* 9 November 1894.

39. Ibid., 7 December 1894.

40. *Shreveport Daily Caucasian,* 2 February 1894.

41. *Colfax Chronicle,* 24 March 1894, 28 July 1894, and 17 November 1894; *Shreveport Daily Caucasian,* 6 May 1894 and 24 June 1894; *St. Landry Democrat,* 19 August 1893.

42. *Colfax Chronicle,* 20 October 1894; *Shreveport Daily Caucasian,* 2 February 1894, 6 March 1894, 26 March 1894, 1 April 1894, 13 April 1894, 15 April 1894, 1 June 1894, and 21 June 1894.

43. *Shreveport Progress,* as quoted in *Colfax Chronicle,* 15 September 1894; *St. Landry Clarion,* 11 February 1893.

44. *Louisiana Populist,* 26 October 1894.

45. Hair, *Bourbonism and Agrarian Protest.*

46. *Winnfield Comrade,* 13 December 1894.

47. *Louisiana Populist,* 5 October 1894.

48. *Colfax Chronicle,* 2 September 1893 and 26 May 1894.

49. The shift to a free-silver focus is best viewed as a pragmatic political decision based on the challenges of generating commitment to the controversial principle of fiatism. This is consistent with the view adopted by historian Joel Sipress in his article on the role that Hardy Brian, the editor of the *Louisiana Populist,* played in shifting the focus of the Louisiana Populist movement (Sipress, "The Narrowing of Vision").

50. *Colfax Chronicle,* 28 July 1894.

51. Ibid.; see also ibid., 11 August 1894 and 25 August 1894.

52. Hair, *Bourbonism and Agrarian Protest,* 231.

53. *Louisiana Populist,* 24 April 1894.

54. Ibid., 24 August 1894.

55. Ibid., 31 August 1894.

56. Woodward, *Burden of Southern History,*156.

57. McMath, "C. Vann Woodward and the Burden of Southern Populism," 756.

58. *Louisiana Populist,* 19 October 1894 and 2 November 1894.

59. Ibid., 7 September 1894.

60. *Shreveport Daily Caucasian,* 8 August 1895.

61. *Colfax Chronicle,* 1 September 1894; *Louisiana Populist,* 16 November 1894.

62. Hair, *Bourbonism and Agrarian Protest; Louisiana Populist,* 9 November 1894.

63. *Louisiana Populist,* 16 November 1894 and 7 December 1894; *Report of the Secretary of State,* 575, 577; USBC, *Eleventh Census of Population,* 782.

64. *Shreveport Progress,* as quoted in Hair, *Bourbonism and Agrarian Protest,* 242.

65. Hair, *Bourbonism and Agrarian Protest; Louisiana Populist,* 16 November 1894, 7 December 1894, 21 December 1894, 28 December 1894, and 16 August 1895; *Report of the Secretary of State,* 554, 577; U.S. House, *Digest of Contested Election Cases,* 519–526.

66. *Report of the Secretary of State,* 577.

67. Hair, *Bourbonism and Agrarian Protest.*

68. *Report of the Secretary of State,* 577–578.

69. Congressional Quarterly, *Guide to U.S. Elections,* 672–676.

70. McMath, *American Populism;* Voss, *The Making of American Exceptionalism.*

71. *Louisiana Populist,* 23 November 1894.

CHAPTER EIGHT

1. Hair, *Bourbonism and Agrarian Protest*

2. See the *New Orleans Daily States,* as quoted in *Opelousas Courier,* 28 September 1889 and 8 February 1890; *Opelousas Courier,* 30 April 1892; *Shreveport Daily Caucasian,* 30 October 1889, 2 November 1889, 6 January 1890, and 17 January 1890; and the *Shreveport Daily Times,* 4 February 1887.

3. *Weekly Pelican,* 29 December 1888.

4. *Shreveport Daily Caucasian,* 15 April 1894, 29 April 1894, 9 May 1894, and 13 May 1894; *Winnfield Comrade,* 13 December 1894.

5. Hair, *Bourbonism and Agrarian Protest; Shreveport Daily Caucasian,* 13 May 1894.

6. Hair, *Bourbonism and Agrarian Protest,* 235.

7. *Report of the Secretary of State,* 554; *Shreveport Daily Caucasian,* 25 June 1894; USBC, *Eleventh Census of Population,* ciii.

8. *Colfax Chronicle,* 14 March 1896; *Louisiana Populist,* 19 October 1894, 26 October 1894, 22 November 1895, and 28 February 1896; Uzee, "The Republican Party in the Louisiana Election of 1896."

9. *Louisiana Populist,* 25 October 1895; for similar statements, see ibid., 22 March 1895, 6 September 1895, 22 November 1895, and 20 December 1895.

10. Ibid., 1 November 1895.

11. Ibid., 13 September 1895.

12. *New Orleans Times-Democrat* as quoted in *Shreveport Daily Caucasian,* 17 June 1894; see also *Shreveport Daily Caucasian,* 19 December 1895.

13. *Louisiana Populist,* 17 May 1895; see also the criticism in the *Shreveport Daily Caucasian,* 24 June 1895 and 25 June 1895, as well as the *New Orleans Picayune,* as reported in the *Shreveport Daily Caucasian,* 22 July 1895.

14. *Colfax Chronicle,* 24 August 1895 and 28 December 1895; *Shreveport Weekly Caucasian,* 8 August 1895 and 15 August 1895.

15. *Shreveport Daily Caucasian,* 23 July 1895; see also 26 July 1895 and 4 August 1895.

16. *Colfax Chronicle,* 7 July 1895 and 4 January 1896. The *Colfax Chronicle*'s stance on the suffrage amendment was misrepresented by historian William Hair who claimed that the *Chronicle* opposed the amendment (*Bourbonism and Agrarian Protest,* 236).

17. *New Orleans Daily States,* as quoted in *Shreveport Weekly Caucasian,* 15 August 1895; see also *Shreveport Daily Caucasian,* 21 July 1895.

18. *New Orleans Daily States,* as quoted in *Shreveport Daily Caucasian,* 19 December 1895.

19. *Shreveport Daily Caucasian,* 27 August 1895.

20. Ibid., 18 July 1895.

21. Ibid., 11 July 1895, 29 July 1895, 5 September 1895, and 18 December 1895.

22. Ibid., 2 September 1895.

23. Hair, *Bourbonism and Agrarian Protest.*

24. *Louisiana Populist,* 22 March 1895.

25. Ibid., 25 January 1895.

26. Ibid., 22 February 1895; see also ibid., 1 March 1895, 19 April 1895, and 6 September 1895.

27. Ibid., 8 March 1895; see also ibid., 29 March 1895, 23 August 1895, and 6 September 1895; *Shreveport Daily Caucasian,* 8 August 1895.

28. Goodwyn, *Democratic Promise,* 182.

29. This view is also expressed in Sipress, "A Narrowing of Vision."

30. Ibid.

31. Ibid., 3.

32. Ibid., 5.

33. Uzee, "The Republican Party in the Louisiana Election of 1896."

34. Hair, *Bourbonism and Agrarian Protest;* Uzee, "The Republican Party in the Louisiana Election of 1896."

35. *Colfax Chronicle,* 24 August 1895; *Louisiana Populist,* 6 December 1895.

36. As quoted in the *Colfax Chronicle,* 8 February 1896; see also ibid., 18 January 1896 and 1 February 1896.

37. Ibid., 11 January 1896.

38. Ibid., 15 February 1896.

39. Hair, *Bourbonism and Agrarian Protest.*

40. *Colfax Chronicle,* 11 January 1896; *Louisiana Populist,* 8 January 1896.

41. Ibid., 17 January 1896.

42. Hair, *Bourbonism and Agrarian Protest;* Uzee, "The Republican Party in the Louisiana Election of 1896."

43. *Colfax Chronicle,* 22 February 1896, 29 February 1896, 14 March 1896, 28 March 1896, 4 April 1896, and 18 April 1896; *Louisiana Populist,* 28 February 1896.

44. *Colfax Chronicle,* 4 April 1896.

45. Ibid., 29 February 1896.

46. Ibid., 21 March 1896; Hair, *Bourbonism and Agrarian Protest.*

47. *Louisiana Populist,* 10 April 1896.

48. *Colfax Chronicle,* 29 February 1896, 14 March 1896, 18 April 1896, and 28 December 1896; Hair, *Bourbonism and Agrarian Protest,* 256.

49. *Natchitoches Enterprise,* as quoted in *Louisiana Populist,* 21 February 1896.

50. *Colfax Chronicle,* 21 March 1896 and 28 March 1896.

51. *Colfax Chronicle,* 29 February 1896, 4 April 1896, and 18 April 1896, respectively.

52. *Shreveport Daily Caucasian,* 5 August 1895; see also ibid., 9 July 1895 and 14 July 1895.

53. Reports of barbecues and picnics organized by Populists were frequently reported in newspapers that closely followed the third-party movement. See *Colfax Chronicle,* 29 February 1896, 21 March 1896, and 28 March 1896; *Louisiana Populist,* 14 June 1895, 28 June 1895, 12 July 1895, 19 July 1895, 9 August 1895, and 16 August 1895.

54. Hair, *Bourbonism and Agrarian Protest,* 281–283.

55. *Louisiana Populist,* 21 February 1896.

56. Ibid., 13 March 1896.

57. *Colfax Chronicle,* 28 March 1896; Hair, *Bourbonism and Agrarian Protest.*

58. USBC, *Eleventh Census of Population,* ciii.

59. *Colfax Chronicle,* 20 February 1886 and 4 January 1896.

60. *Lake Providence Banner-Democrat,* 7 March 1896 and 28 March 1896, as quoted in Hair, *Bourbonism and Agrarian Protest,* 259.

61. Hair, *Bourbonism and Agrarian Protest.*

62. *Iberville South* and *New Orleans Daily States,* as quoted in Hair, *Bourbonism and Agrarian Protest,* 257; Rodrigue, "Labor Militancy and Black Grassroots Political Mobilization."

63. Hair, *Bourbonism and Agrarian Protest.*

64. *Shreveport Daily Caucasian,* 2 August 1895 and 7 August 1895.

65. *Shreveport Weekly Caucasian,* 15 August 1895.

66. *Colfax Chronicle,* 11 April 1896; Hair, *Bourbonism and Agrarian Protest.*

67. Hair, *Bourbonism and Agrarian Protest,* 262.

68. Ibid.

69. *Shreveport Evening Judge,* 15 December 1896.

70. *Louisiana Populist,* 20 March 1896.

71. *Colfax Chronicle,* 25 April 1896; Hair, *Bourbonism and Agrarian Protest,* 263.

72. *Louisiana Populist,* 1 May 1896; see also ibid., 15 May 1896 and 29 May 1896.

73. *Report of the Secretary of State,* 554; USBC, *Twelfth Census of Population,* 187; Uzee, "The Republican Party in the Louisiana Election of 1896."

74. *Louisiana Populist,* 8 May1896.

75. Hair, *Bourbonism and Agrarian Protest.*

76. *Colfax Chronicle,* 25 April 1896 and 9 May 1896.

77. *Baton Rouge Daily Advocate,* as quoted in Hair, *Bourbonism and Agrarian Protest,* 265.

78. Hair, *Bourbonism and Agrarian Protest;* Uzee, "The Republican Party in the Louisiana Election of 1896."

79. *Louisiana Populist,* 8 May 1896.

80. Hair, *Bourbonism and Agrarian Protest.*

81. Ibid., 266–267; *Louisiana Populist,* 12 June 1896.

82. Hair, *Bourbonism and Agrarian Protest.*

83. *Louisiana Populist,* 12 June 1896.

CHAPTER NINE

1. *Colfax Chronicle,* 6 June 1896; Hair, *Bourbonism and Agrarian Protest.*

2. Election fraud was not unique to Louisiana politics, but rather was a political factor in many southern states and was a serious challenge to the southern Populist movement in general. See Hyman, *The Anti-Redeemers;* Kantrowitz, *Ben Tillman and the Reconstruction of White Supremacy;* Shaw, *The Wool-Hat Boys.*

3. *Louisiana Populist,* 3 January 1896.

4. Ibid., 19 April 1895, 2 May 1895, and 6 March 1896, respectively. Other southern Populist leaders similarly railed against limiting reform demands to free silver. Georgia Populist Tom Watson strongly urged Populists to stay in the "middle-of-the-road" and to refuse to compromise principles in order to cooperate or fuse with either of the old parties (Woodward, *Tom Watson*). The *Southern Mercury,* the mouthpiece of the People's Party in Texas, warned that trimming reform demands to the single reform of free silver would be fatal to the party (*Southern Mercury,* 31 January 1895, 14 February 1895, 9 May 1895, 31 October 1895, and 23 January 1896).

5. As quoted in Argersinger, *Populism and Politics,* 209.

6. *Louisiana Populist,* 20 March 1896.

7. Barnes, *Farmers in Rebellion;* Goodwyn, *Populist Moment;* Hicks, *Populist Revolt;* see *Louisiana Populist,* 2 August 1895, for a letter to the editor expressing similar expectations.

8. *Houston Daily Post,* 19 June 1896.

9. Koenig, *Bryan.*

10. Ibid.

11. Hicks, *Populist Revolt.*

12. Koenig, *Bryan.*

13. Goodwyn, *Democratic Promise,* 482.

14. Johnson, *National Party Platforms.*

15. Clanton, *Congressional Populism,* 113.

16. The details of the fair election plank were reminiscent of the oppositional stance of the LFU, and the Alliance movement in general, to the Lodge election bill of 1890. This bill, which called for federal intervention to address electoral improprieties, had been strongly condemned by the Alliance for giving the federal government powers that belonged to the states. Thus, the Alliance seemed more committed to a states' rights ideology when it came to elections than to the democratic ideal of fair elections.

17. Goodwyn, *Democratic Promise;* Hicks, *Populist Revolt.*

18. Goodwyn, *Populist Moment*; *Houston Daily Post,* 25 July 1896; Sipress, "A Narrowing of Vision"; *Southern Mercury,* 30 July 1896.

19. Illustrative of his commitment to the Populist movement was an oft-repeated tale of his behavior after being elected to Congress. He introduced bills on nearly every plank of the Alliance platform. Frustrated over the subtreasury bill languishing in committee in 1891, he asked for the unanimous consent required to force the Committee on Ways and Means to report on it. When such consent was not given, he thereafter objected to every request for unanimous consent. Finally, members of the House relented and granted his request. However, the committee report on the subtreasury

was not presented until the final day of the session and almost no discussion occurred prior to its defeat (Hicks, *Populist Revolt;* Woodward, *Tom Watson*).

20. *Louisiana Populist,* 7 August 1896.

21. Goodwyn, *Populist Moment,* 260.

22. Ibid.; *Houston Daily Post,* 26 July 1896; *Southern Mercury,* 30 July 1896.

23. *Louisiana Populist,* 7 August 1896.

24. Ibid.; *Monroe Bulletin,* quoted in *Louisiana Populist,* 9 October 1896.

25. Goodwyn, *Democratic Promise.*

26. Woodward, *Tom Watson,* 310.

27. As quoted in ibid., 311; see also Kantrowitz, *Ben Tillman and the Reconstruction of White Supremacy*; Woodward, *Tom Watson.*

28. *Louisiana Populist,* 4 September 1896.

29. Ibid., 23 October 1896.

30. Ibid.

31. Hair, *Bourbonism and Agrarian Protest.*

32. Shaw, *The Wool-hat Boys;* Woodward, *Tom Watson.*

33. Bryan's explanation for his loss was that he had suffered from the unpopularity of the incumbent Democratic administration of Cleveland. He argued that workers in the industrial states, angered by the high unemployment rate, had abandoned the Democratic Party and latched onto McKinley's promise of prosperity. A more complete explanation of his loss, however, must include the major resource differences between the lavishly funded Republican campaign and the relatively modest funding of Bryan's campaign. The Republicans ran an extremely well-funded campaign, which represented the first time in American politics that big money entered a presidential race. Ohio industrialist Mark Hanna, who ran the campaign, raised unprecedented sums of money to advocate for "sound money" redeemable in gold and to renounce bimetallism. The vast majority of the newspapers in the Northeast adopted the "sound-money, honest dollar" stance, which created an almost insurmountable challenge to the Populist-Democratic campaign in a region that carried a formidable influence in the Electoral College. Also, the Bryan-Sewall-Watson fiasco was a major problem. Denied the option of voting for the Bryan-Watson ticket, some Populists opted to stay home from the polls (Koenig, *Bryan;* Woodward, *Tom Watson*).

34. Hicks, *Populist Revolt,* 375.

35. Hair, *Bourbonism and Agrarian Protest,* 271. Interesting, the total vote count of about 15,000 in each of these congressional districts was significantly lower than it had been in the 1894 congressional races. There was almost an 18 percent decline in voter turnout in the Fourth Congressional District, and a 22 percent decline in the Fifth Congressional District. It is impossible to say what role Populist disaffection with the fusion mess may have played in the decline. Also, particularly in the Fifth Congressional District where the 1894 congressional election results had been invalidated due to electoral fraud, another factor may have been less "counting out" of Populist votes out of concern that fraud would invalidate the election again.

36. *Louisiana Populist,* 17 September 1897.

37. Ibid., 22 January 1897.

38. Ibid., 15 January 1897, 22 January 1897, 29 January 1897, 5 February 1897, 9 April 1897, 16 April 1897, 28 May 1897, 17 September 1897, 24 September 1897, and 4 February 1898.

39. Ibid., 12 February 1897, 12 March 1897, 19 March 1897, 25 June 1897, and 23 December 1898; see also *People's Tribune,* 20 March 1897.

40. *Louisiana Populist*, 22 January 1897, see also the 15 January 1897 issue.

41. Hicks, *Populist Revolt;* Goodwyn, *Democratic Promise.* A search of the historical abstracts of the *New York Times* from 1896 to 1900, using the search words of fiatism and irredeemable currency, found only a handful of articles commenting upon fiatism. All of those articles contrasted fiatism to "sound money," a term reserved exclusively for redeemable currency (*New York Times: Proquest Historical Newspapers).*

42. *Louisiana Populist*, 29 January 1897 and 12 March 1897.

43. Hicks, *Populist Revolt.*

44. *Louisiana Populist*, 7 May 1897, 14 May 1897, and 21 May 1897.

45. Ibid., 4 June 1897 and 22 October 1897.

46. Ibid., 25 June 1897.

47. Ibid., 9 July 1897 and 16 January 1897.

48. Hicks, *Populist Revolt*, 390–391.

49. *Louisiana Populist*, 9 July 1897 and 16 July 1897.

50. Hicks, *Populist Revolt.*

51. Ibid.

52. *Louisiana Populist*, 27 August 1898, 9 September 1898, and 17 September 1898.

53. Hicks, *Populist Revolt.*

54. Barnes, *Farmers in Rebellion*, 192.

55. Kantrowitz, *Ben Tillman and the Reconstruction of White Supremacy;* Kousser, *The Shaping of Southern Politics.*

56. *Colfax Chronicle*, 2 May 1896 and 9 May 1896.

57. USBC, *Twelfth Census of Population*, ciii.

58. Hair, *Bourbonism and Agrarian Protest;* Kousser, *The Shaping of Southern Politics.*

59. Hair, *Bourbonism and Agrarian Protest*; *Official Journal of the Constitutional Convention*, no pagination.

60. *Louisiana Populist*, 27 August 1897

61. Ibid., 3 September 1897 and 19 November 1897, respectively.

62. Ibid., 3 September 1897; see also ibid., 1 January 1897, 9 April 1897, and 3 September 1897.

63. *Shreveport Weekly Caucasian*, 15 August 1895; *Winnfield Comrade*, 25 June 1896, as quoted in *Colfax Chronicle*, 4 July 1896.

64. *Louisiana Populist*, 3 September 1897 and 24 December 1897.

65. As quoted in *Opelousas Courier*, 6 July 1889; see also *Shreveport Daily Caucasian*, 15 March 1894.

66. *Opelousas Courier*, 6 July 1889; see also *Colfax Chronicle*, 13 February 1886, 20 February 1886, 10 July 1886, and 16 May 1891; *Louisiana Populist*, 3 September 1897; *Opelousas Courier*, 14 November 1891; *Shreveport Daily Caucasian*, 25 November–26 November 1889 and 14 January–17 January 1894; *St. Landry Clarion*, 1 November 1890.

67. *Winnfield Comrade*, 25 June 1896 as quoted in *Colfax Chronicle*, 4 July 1896. See also *Colfax Chronicle*, 30 May 1896; *Louisiana Populist*, 17 June 1898; *Shreveport Weekly Caucasian*, 15 August 1895.

68. *Louisiana Populist*, 27 August 1897, 15 October 1897, and 17 December 1897.

69. Ibid., 13 August 1897 and 3 September 1897.

70. Ibid., 26 November 1897.

71. Ibid.; Hair *Bourbonism and Agrarian Protest.*

72. *Louisiana Populist*, 26 November 1897 and 3 December 1897.

73. Ibid., 17 September 1897, 10 December 1897, 24 December 1897, and 19 August 1898.

74. Hair, *Bourbonism and Agrarian Protest*, 27.

75. Feldman, *Disfranchisement Myth*, 1; Kousser, *The Shaping of Southern Politics;* Perman, *Struggle for Mastery;* Woodward, *Origins of the New South.* Woodward, however, modified his original interpretation in later writings. In his book *The Strange Career of Jim Crow,* he argued that poor whites were more responsible for the success of the disfranchisement campaigns in the South than he had once thought.

76. Kousser, *The Shaping of Southern Politics; Louisiana Populist,* 11 February 1898.

77. *Official Journal of the Constitutional Convention,* no pagination.

78. Ibid.

79. Ibid.

80. *Louisiana Populist,* 25 March 1898; *Official Journal of the Constitutional Convention,* no pagination.

81. *Louisiana Populist,* 18 February 1898, 4 March 1898, and 11 March 1898, respectively.

82. Ibid., 5 August 1898, 12 August 1898, and 19 August 1898.

83. Goodwyn, *Populist Moment,* 194–196.

84. *Official Journal of the Constitutional Convention.*

85. Ibid.

86. *Louisiana Populist,* 20 May 1898.

87. Ibid., 20 May 1898.

88. Barr, *Reconstruction to Reform;* Durden, *Climax of Populism;* Hicks, *Populist Revolt;* Koenig, *Bryan;* Martin, *People's Party in Texas;* Tindall, "The People's Party."

89. USDA, *Yearbook of Agriculture,* 754.

90. *Louisiana Populist,* 10 December 1897, 22 April 1898, 30 September 1898, 21 October 1898, 30 December 1898, 6 January 1899, and 10 March 1899; *People's Tribune,* 6 February 1897 and 20 March 1897.

91. *Dallas Morning News,* 2 May 1900.

92. Arnett, *Populist Movement in Georgia;* Hicks, *Populist Revolt.* Fiatists, however, were correct that the problem of inadequate gold production—as well as problems of excessive redemption of paper money and government notes for gold and gold hoarding—would never have been problems under an irredeemable, fiat currency system. Furthermore, Populist criticisms of redeemable currency were remarkable insights, well before the time when most economists would voice such criticisms and when the United States would finally abandon the gold standard. The prevalence of the gold standard internationally lasted until the economic depression of the 1930s. Between 1931 and 1934, the governments of most countries abandoned the gold standard. In 1933, the United States adopted a "modified" gold standard—the value of a dollar was still measured in ounces of gold, but paper currency and government notes could not be redeemed for gold. By the mid-1970s gold had ceased to serve as a standard in the international monetary system. Congress formally removed the United States from the gold standard in 1978. By 1980, no major currency in the world was redeemable in gold ("Gold Standard," http://encarta.com).

93. *The New York Times,* 29 September 1896, 17 March 1897, 30 June 1897, 26 November 1897, 30 January 1898, 14 May 1898, and 26 February 1899.

94. Hicks, *Populist Revolt.*

95. Barnes, *Farmers in Rebellion;* Hicks, *Populist Revolt.*

96. Hicks, *Populist Revolt.*

97. Ibid.

98. Hair, *Bourbonism and Agrarian Protest.*

CONCLUSION

1. McNall, *Road to Rebellion,* 302.

2. USBC, *Twelfth Census of Population,* ciii.

3. Gerteis examined the "movement narratives" of the Alliance movement in regard to race. He concluded that racial attitudes in the Alliance movement were "deeply ambivalent" (*Class and the Color Line,* 158). But he claimed that where the desire for racial inclusion existed, it was genuine. His conclusion, gleaned from a content analysis of *National Economist* articles from 1891 to 1893, does not fit the movement narratives of the LFU very well—narratives that occasionally expressed a willingness to support racial cooperation as long as the CFA remained a separate organization, but more frequently expressed an unshakeable belief in the superiority of whites and the desire for whites to retain political power in local and state politics.

4. USBC, *Eleventh Census of Population,* ciii

5. Gerteis draws attention to the "linear trend away from white Populists' early optimism about the prospects of interracial coalition" (*Class and the Color Line,* 168). His observation is consistent with mine: There was a notable shift in strategic framing in regard to creating a biracial political coalition. The shift began after the congressional elections of 1892 and gained more steam after the congressional elections of 1894.

6. Hair, *Bourbonism and Agrarian Protest,* 241.

Bibliography

CONTEMPORARY ACCOUNTS AND DOCUMENTS

Constitution of the Colored Farmers National Alliance and Co-operative Union of the United States. J. J. Pastoriza, Printer, Houston, Texas. Tennessee State Library and Archives, 1889.

Dunning, Nelson. *The Farmers' Alliance History and Agricultural Digest.* Alliance Publishing Co., 1891.

Garvin, W. L., and S. O. Daws. *History of the National Farmers' Alliance and Co-operative Union of America.* J. N. Rogers and Co., 1887.

Macune, Charles. "Farmers Alliance Narrative." Personal Memoirs, Barker Texas History Archives, University of Texas at Austin, 1920.

Morgan, W. Scott. *History of the Wheel and Alliance, and the Impending Revolution.* Self-published, 1889.

Ousley, Clarence. "A Lesson in Co-operation." *Popular Science Monthly* 36 (1890): 821–828.

Proceedings of the Annual Session of the Supreme Council of the National Farmers Alliance and Industrial Union. Washington, D.C.: The National Economist Publishing Co., 1891.

Proceedings of the Third Annual Session of the Louisiana State Grange, Patrons of Husbandry. New Orleans. Special Collections Department, William R. Perkins Library, Duke University, 1885.

Proceedings of the Fifth Annual Session of the Louisiana State Grange. Printed at the Office of the *Independent,* Amite City, La., 1887.

Proceedings of the National Farmers' Alliance and Industrial Union and the Colored Farmers National Alliance and Co-operative Union. Printed by the National Farmers' Alliance and Industrial Union. YA Pamphlet Collection, Library of Congress, 1891.

Tracy, Harry. "The Subtreasury Plan." Appendix to James "Cyclone" Davis, *A Political Revelation.* Dallas, Tex., 1894.

NEWSPAPERS

Alexandria Caucasian. Hill Memorial Archives, Louisiana State University.
Beeville Bee. Barker Texas History Archives, University of Texas at Austin.
Colfax Chronicle. Hill Memorial Archives, Louisiana State University.
Cotton Belt. Barker Texas History Archives, University of Texas at Austin.
Dallas Morning News, Texas State Library Archives, Austin.
Ft. Worth Gazette, Texas State Library Archives, Austin.
Galveston Daily News, Texas State Library Archives, Austin.
Houston Daily Post, Texas State Library Archives, Austin.
Louisiana Populist. Hill Memorial Library, Louisiana State University.
National Economist. Library of Congress Archives, Washington, D.C.
New York Times. Coe Library, University of Wyoming.
New York Times: Proquest Historical Newspapers, 1851-2005; electronic database.
Opelousas Courier. Hill Memorial Library, Louisiana State University.
People's Tribune, Hill Memorial Library, Louisiana State University.
Shreveport Daily Caucasian. Hill Memorial Archives, Louisiana State University.
Shreveport Daily Times. Hill Memorial Archives, Louisiana State University.
Shreveport Evening Judge, Hill Memorial Archives, Louisiana State University.
Shreveport Weekly Caucasian. Hill Memorial Archives, Louisiana State University.
Southern Mercury. Barker Texas History Archives, University of Texas at Austin.
St. Landry Clarion. Hill Memorial Library, Louisiana State University.
St. Landry Democrat. Hill Memorial Library, Louisiana State University.
St. Louis Globe-Democrat. Barker Texas History Archives, University of Texas at Austin.
Texas Advance. Barker Texas History Archives, University of Texas at Austin.
Weekly Pelican. Hill Memorial Archives, Louisiana State University.
Winn Parish Democrat. Hill Memorial Library, Louisiana State University.
Winnfield Comrade. Hill Memorial Library, Louisiana State University.

STATE AND FEDERAL GOVERNMENT DOCUMENTS

Louisiana Constitutional Convention. *Debates in the State Constitutional Convention for the Revision and Amendment of the Constitution of the State of Louisiana, 1864.* Microfilm, Louisiana State Archives, 1864.

Louisiana Senate. *Senate Journal, 1877.* Newsprint, Louisiana State Archives, 1877.

———. *Official Journal of the Senate of the State of Louisiana.* Louisiana State Archives, 1882.

Official Journal of the Constitutional Convention of the State of Louisiana, Newsprint, Louisiana State Archives, 1878.

Report of the Secretary of State to his Excellency W. W. Heard, Governor of the State of Louisiana, 1902.

United States of America v C. C. Nash, Cruickshank (sic), et al. Microfilm, Texas State University, 1874.

USBC (U.S. Bureau of the Census). *Eighth Census of Agriculture.* Government Printing Office, 1860.

———. *Ninth Census of Agriculture.* Government Printing Office, 1870.

———. *Ninth Census of Population.* Government Printing Office, 1870.

———. *Tenth Census of Agriculture.* Government Printing Office, 1880.

———. *Tenth Census of Population.* Government Printing Office, 1880.

———. *Eleventh Census of Agriculture.* Government Printing Office, 1890.

———. *Eleventh Census of Population.* Government Printing Office, 1890.

———. *The Compendium of the Eleventh Census.* Government Printing Office, 1890.

———. *Twelfth Census of Agriculture.* Government Printing Office, 1900.

———. *Twelfth Census of Population.* Government Printing Office, 1900.

USDA (U.S. Department of Agriculture). *Yearbook of Agriculture, 1901.* Government Printing Office, 1902.

U.S. House. *Contested Election, Fourth Congressional District of Louisiana.* H. Miscellaneous Doc. 32, 41st Cong., 2d sess., serial set 1402, vol. 1, Government Printing Office, 1869.

———. *Louisiana Contested Elections.* H. Miscellaneous Doc. 154, 41st Cong., 2d sess., serial set 1435, vol. 5, Government Printing Office, 1870.

———. *Denial of Elective Franchise in Election of 1874, Louisiana.* H. Rept. 261, 43rd Cong., 2nd sess., serial set 1660, vol. 5, Government Printing Office, 1875.

———. *Testimony Taken in Investigation of Whiskey and Cotton Bagging Trusts.* H. Rept. 4165, 50th Cong., 2d sess., serial set 2675, Government Printing Office, 1889.

———. *Digest of Contested Election Cases in the House of Representatives from the First to the Fifty-Sixth Congress, 1789-1901.* H. Doc. 510, 56th Cong., 2d sess., serial set 4172, Government Printing Office, 1901.

———. *Report on the Industrial Commission on Agriculture and Agricultural Labor.* H. Doc. 179, 57th Cong., 1st sess., serial set 4340, Government Printing Office, 1901.

U.S. Senate. *Message of the President on Condition of States Lately in Rebellion.* S. Doc. 24, 39th Cong., 1st sess., serial set 1237, vol. 1, Government Printing Office, 1865.

———. *Denial of Elective Franchise at Election of 1878, Louisiana.* S. Rept. 855, 45th Cong., 3rd session, serial set 1840, Government Printing Office, 1879.

———. *Report of the Committee of Agriculture and Forestry on Condition of Cotton Growers in the United States.* S. Rept. 986, 53rd Cong., 3rd sess., serial set 3290, vol. 1, Government Printing Office, 1907 [1894–1895].

SECONDARY SOURCES

Abramowitz, Jack. "The Negro in the Populist Movement." A Bobbs-Merrill Reprint in Black Studies. Reprinted from *The Journal of Negro History* 38 (1953): 257–289.

Aminzade, Ron, and Doug McAdam. "Emotions and Contentious Politics." *Mobilization: An International Journal* 7, no. 2 (2002): 107–109.

Amundson, Richard. "Oakley Plantation: A Post-Civil War Venture in Louisiana Sugar." *Louisiana History* 9, no. 1 (1968): 21–42.

Argersinger, Peter. *Populism and Politics.* University Press of Kentucky, 1974.

Arnett, Alex. *The Populist Movement in Georgia.* AMS Press, 1967.

Ayers, Edward. *The Promise of the New South.* Oxford University Press, 1992.

Barkan, Steven. "Legal Control of the Southern Civil Rights Movement." *American Sociological Review* 49 (1984): 552–565.

Barnes, Donna. *Farmers in Rebellion: The Rise and Fall of the Southern Farmers Alliance and People's Party in Texas.* University of Texas Press, 1984.

———. "Strategy Outcome and the Growth of Protest Organizations: A Case Study of the Southern Farmers Alliance." *Rural Sociology* 52, no. 2 (1987): 164–186.

———. "Organization and Radical Protest: An Antithesis?" *The Sociological Quarterly* 28, no. 4 (1987): 575–594.

Barnes, Donna, and Catherine Connolly. "Repression, the Judicial System, and Political Opportunities for Civil Rights Advocacy during Reconstruction." *The Sociological Quarterly* 40, no. 2 (1999): 327–345.

Barr, Alwyn. *Reconstruction to Reform: Texas Politics, 1876–1906.* University of Texas Press, 1971.

Benford, Robert. "Frame Disputes within the Nuclear Disarmament Movement." *Social Forces* 71 (1993): 677–701.

———. "An Insider's Critique of the Social Movement Framing Perspective." *Sociological Inquiry* 67 (1997): 409–430.

Bennett, Lerone. *Black Power U.S.A.: The Human Side of Reconstruction, 1867–1877.* Johnson Publishing Co., 1967.

Berger, Peter, and Thomas Luckmann. *The Social Construction of Reality.* Doubleday and Co., 1966.

Brockett, Charles. "The Structure of Political Opportunities and Peasant Mobilization in Central America." *Comparative Politics* 23 (1991): 253–274.

Buck, Solon. *The Granger Movement: A Study of Agricultural Organization and Its Political, Economic and Social Manifestations, 1870–1880.* University of Nebraska Press, 1913.

Buechler, Steven. *Women's Movements in the United States: Women Suffrage, Equal Rights, and Beyond.* Rutgers University Press, 1990.

Cadena-Roa, Jorge. "Strategic Framing, Emotions, and Superbarrio—Mexico City's Masked Crusader." *Mobilization: An International Journal* 7, no. 2 (2002): 201–218.

Calvert, Robert. "The Southern Grange." Ph.D. dissertation, University of Texas at Austin, 1970.

Caniglia, Beth, and JoAnn Carmin. "Scholarship on Social movement Organizations: Classic Views and Emerging Trends." *Mobilization: An International Journal* 10, no. 2 (2005): 201–212.

Carlton, Mark. "The Politics of the Convict Lease System in Louisiana, 1896–1901." *Louisiana History* 8, no. 1 (1967): 5–25.

Clanton, Gene. *Congressional Populism and the Crisis of the 1890s.* University Press of Kansas, 1998.

Clark, Thomas. *Pills, Petticoats, and Plows: The Southern Country Store.* Bobbs-Merrill Co., 1944.

Congressional Quarterly. *Guide to U.S. Elections.* Congressional Quarterly, Inc., 1975.

Cruden, Robert. *The Negro in Reconstruction.* Prentice-Hall, 1969.

Dethloff, Henry, and Robert Jones. "Race Relations in Louisiana." *Louisiana History* 9, no. 4 (1968): 301–323.

Du Bois, W. E. B. *Black Reconstruction in America, 1860–1880.* Atheneum, 1935 [1969].

Durden, Robert. *The Climax of Populism.* University of Kentucky Press, 1965.

Eisenger, Peter. "The Conditions of Protest Behavior in American Cities." *American Political Science Review* 67 (1973): 11–28.

Feldman, Glenn. *The Disfranchisement Myth: Poor Whites and Suffrage Restriction in Alabama.* University of Georgia Press, 2004.

Ferree, Myra. "Feminist Politics in the U.S. and West Germany." In *The Women's Movements of the United States and Western Europe,* edited by Mary Katzenstein and Carol Mueller. Temple University Press, 1987.

Ferree, Myra, and Frederick Miller. "Mobilization and Meaning: Toward an Integration of Social Psychological and Resource Perspectives on Social Movements." *Sociological Inquiry* 55 (1985): 36–61.

Fireman, Bruce, and William Gamson. "Utilitarian Logic in the Resource Mobilization Perspective." In *The Dynamics of Social Movements,* edited by Mayer Zald and John McCarthy. Winthrop Publishers, 1979.

Fitzgerald, Michael. *The Union League Movement in the Deep South: Politics and Agrarian Change During Reconstruction.* Louisiana State University Press, 1989.

Franklin, John Hope. *Reconstruction: After the Civil War.* University of Chicago Press, 1961.

Gaither, Gerald. *Blacks and the Populist Revolt: Ballots and Bigotry in the "New South."* University of Alabama Press, 1977.

Gamson, William, Bruce Firman, and Steven Rytina. *Encounters with Unjust Authorities.* Dorsey Press, 1982.

Gerteis, Joseph. *Class and the Color Line: Interracial Class Coalition in the Knights of Labor and the Populist Movement.* Duke University Press, 2007.

Geschwender, James. "Social Structure and the Negro Revolt: An Examination of Some Hypotheses." *Social Forces* 43 (1964): 250–256.

———. "Continuities in Theories of Status Inconsistency and Cognitive Dissonance." *Social Forces* 46 (1967): 165–167.

Gillette, William. *Retreat from Reconstruction.* Louisiana State University Press, 1979.

Godeke, Dan. "Analysis of the Lodge 'Force' Bill of 1890." Master's thesis, Southern Illinois University, 1965.

"Gold Standard." *http://encarta.com*; accessed in 2009 before Microsoft discontinued the online version.

Goldstone, Jack. *Revolution and Rebellion in the Early Modern World.* University of California Press, 1991.

Goodwin, Jeff, and James Jasper. "Caught in a Winding, Snarling Vine: The Structural Bias of Political Process Theory." *Sociological Forum* 14 (1999): 27–54.

———. *Rethinking Social Movements: Structure, Meaning, and Emotion.* Rowman and Littlefield Publishers, Inc., 2004.

Goodwin, Jeff, James Jasper, and Francesca Pollenta. "The Return of the Repressed: The Fall and Rise of Emotions in Social Movement Theory." *Mobilization: An International Journal* 5, no. 1 (2000): 65–83.

Goodwyn, Lawrence. *Democratic Promise: The Populist Movement in America.* Oxford University Press, 1976.

———. *The Populist Moment: A Short History of the Agrarian Revolt in America.* Oxford University Press, 1978.

Gould, Deborah. "Life during Wartime: Emotions and the Development of Act Up." *Mobilization: An International Journal* 7, no. 2 (2002): 177–200.

Gurr, Ted. *Why Men Rebel.* Princeton University Press, 1970.

Haines, Herbert. "Black Radicalization and the Funding of Civil Rights: 1957–1970." *Social Problems* 32 (1984): 31–43.

Hair, William. *Bourbonism and Agrarian Protest: Louisiana Politics, 1877–1900.* Louisiana State University Press, 1969.

Handler, Joel. *Social Movements and the Legal System: A Theory of Law Reform and Social Change.* Academic Press, 1978.

Hicks, John. *The Populist Revolt: A History of the Farmers' Alliance and the People's Party.* University of Nebraska Press, 1961 [1931].

Hipsher, Patricia. "Heretical Social Movement Organizations and their Framing Strategies." *Sociological Inquiry* 77, no. 2 (2007): 241–263.

Hoffer, Eric. *The True Believer: Thoughts on the Nature of Mass Movements.* The New American Library, 1951.

Hofstadter, Richard. *The Age of Reform: From Bryan to F. D. R.* Knopf, 1955.

Hyman, Michael. *The Anti-Redeemers: Hill-Country Political Dissenters in the Lower South from Redemption to Populism.* Louisiana State University, 1990.

Jasper, James. "The Emotions of Protest: Affective and Reactive Emotions in and around Social Movements." *Sociological Forum* 13 (1998): 397–424.

———. "A Strategic Approach to Collective Action: Looking for Agency in Social-Movement Choices." *Mobilization: An International Journal* 9, no. 1 (2004): 1–16.

Jasper, James, and Jane Poulsen. "Fighting Back: Vulnerabilities, Blunders, and Counter-mobilization by the Targets in Three Animal Rights Campaigns." *Sociological Forum* 8 (1993): 639–657.

Jenkins, J. Craig. "Social Movements, Political Representation, and the State: An Agenda and Comparative Framework." In *The Politics of Social Protest: Comparative Perspectives on States and Social Movements,* edited by J. Craig Jenkins and Bert Klandermas. University of Minnesota Press, 1995.

Jenkins, J. Craig, and Charles Perrow. "Insurgency of the Powerless: Farm Worker Movements (1946–1972)." *American Sociological Review* 42 (1977): 249–268.

Johnson, Donald B., ed., *National Party Platforms.* Vol. 1. University of Illinois Press, 1956.

Johnson, Roberta. "Mobilizing the Disabled." In *Waves of Protest: Social Movements Since the Sixties,* edited by Jo Freeman and Victoria Johnson. Rowman and Littlefield Publishers, 1999.

Joppke, Christian. "Social Movements during Cycles of Issue Attention: The Decline of the Anti-nuclear Energy Movements in West Germany and the USA." *British Journal of Sociology* 42 (1991): 43–60.

———. *Mobilizing Against Nuclear Energy: A Comparison of West Germany and the United States.* University of California Press, 1993.

Kaczorowski, Robert. *The Politics of Judicial Interpretation: The Federal Courts, Department of Justice and Civil Rights, 1866–1876.* Oceana Publications, 1985.

Kantrowitz, Stephen. *Ben Tillman and the Reconstruction of White Supremacy.* University of North Carolina Press, 2000.

Kim, Hyojoung. "Shame, Anger, and Love in Collective Action: Emotional Consequences of Suicide Protest in South Korea, 1991." *Mobilization: An International Journal* 7, no. 2 (2002): 150–176.

Kitschelt, Herbert. "Political Opportunity Structures and Political Protest: Anti-Nuclear Movements in Four Democracies." *British Journal of Political Science*16 (1986): 57–85.

Koenig, Louis. *Bryan: A Political Biography of William Jennings Bryan.* G. P. Putnam's Sons, 1971.

Kornhauser, William. *The Politics of Mass Society.* Free Press, 1959.

Kousser, J. Morgan. *The Shaping of Southern Politics: Suffrage Restriction and the Establishment of the One-Party South, 1880–1910.* Yale University Press, 1974.

Kriesi, Hanspeter. "The Political Opportunity Structure of New Social Movements: Its Impact on Their Mobilization." In *The Politics of Social Protest: Comparative Perspectives on States and Social Movements,* edited by J. Craig Jenkins and Bert Klandermas. University of Minnesota Press, 1995.

Kriesi, Hanspeter, Ruud Koopmans, Jan W. Duyvendak, and Marco Giugni. "New Social Movements and Political Opportunities in Western Europe." *European Journal of Political Research* 22 (1992): 219–244.

Kurzman, Charles. "Structural Opportunity and Perceived Opportunity in Social Movement Theory: The Iranian Revolution of 1979." *American Sociological Review* 61 (1996): 153–170.

———. "The Post-Structuralist Consensus in Social Movement Theory." In *Rethinking Social Movements: Structure, Meaning, and Emotions,* edited by Jeff Goodwin and James Jasper. Rowman and Littlefield Publishers, 2004.

Laughlin, J. Laurence. *The History of Bimetallism in the United States.* Appleton and Co., 1892.

Lawrence, Frederick. "Civil Rights and Criminal Wrongs: The Mens Rea of Federal Civil Rights Crimes." *Tulane Law Review* 67 (1993): 2113–2229.

Lewis, Elsie. "The Political Mind of the Negro, 1865–1900." *The Journal of Southern History* 21 (1955): 189–202.

Lipset, Seymour, Martin Trow, and James Coleman. *Trade Union Democracy.* Free Press, 1956.

Lipsky, Michael. *Protest in City Politics.* Rand McNally, 1970.

Mansbridge, Jane. *Why We Lost the ERA.* University of Chicago Press, 1986.

Martin, Deborah, and Byron Miller. "Space and Contentious Politics." *Mobilization: An International Journal* 8, no. 2 (2003): 143–156.

Martin, Roscoe. *The People's Party in Texas: A Study in Third-Party Politics.* University of Texas Press, 1933.

Massad, Timothy. "Disruption, Organization, and Reform: A Critique of *Poor People's Movements,*" *Dissent* 27 (1980): 81–90.

McAdam, Doug. *Political Process and the Development of Black Insurgency, 1930–1970.* University of Chicago Press, 1982.

———. "Tactical Innovation and the Pace of Insurgency." *American Sociological Review* 48 (1983): 735–754.

———. "Conceptual Origins, Current Problems, Future Directions." In *Comparative Perspectives on Social Movements: Political Opportunities, Mobilizing Structures, and Cultural Framings,* edited by Doug McAdam, John McCarthy, and Mayer Zald. Cambridge University Press, 1996.

———. "Revisiting the U.S. Civil Rights Movement: Toward a More Synthetic Understanding of the Origins of Contention." In *Rethinking Social Movements: Structure, Meaning, and Emotions*, edited by Jeff Goodwin and James Jasper. Rowman and Littlefield Publishers, 2004.

McAdam, Doug, and Ronnelle Paulsen. "Specifying the Relationship Between Social Ties and Activism." *American Journal of Sociology* 99 (1993): 640–667.

McAdam, Doug, John McCarthy, and Mayer Zald. *Comparative Perspectives on Social Movements: Political Opportunities, Mobilizing Structures, and Cultural Framings*. Cambridge University Press, 1996.

McAdam, Doug, Robert Sampson, Simon Weffer, and Heather MacIndoe. "'There Will be Fighting in the Streets': The Distorting Lens of Social Movement Theory." *Mobilization: An International Journal* 10, no. 1 (2005): 1–18.

McCarthy, John, and Mayer Zald. "Resource Mobilization and Social Movements: A Partial Theory." *American Journal of Sociology* 82, no. 6 (1977): 1212–1241.

McCormack, Thelma. "The Motivation of Radicals." In *Collective Behavior*, edited by R. Turner and L. Killian. Prentice-Hall, 1957.

McLaurin, Melton A. *Knights of Labor in the South*. Greenwood Press, 1978.

McMath, Robert. *Populist Vanguard: A History of the Southern Farmers' Alliance*. University of North Carolina Press, 1975.

———. *American Populism: A Social History, 1877–1898*. Hill and Wang, 1993.

———. "C. Vann Woodward and the Burden of Southern Populism." *The Journal of Southern History* 67, no. 4 (2001): 741–768.

McNall, Scott. *The Road to Rebellion: Class Formation and Kansas Populism, 1865–1900*. University of Chicago Press, 1988.

McPhail, Clark. "Civil Disorder Participation: A Critical Examination of Recent Research." *American Sociological Review* 38 (1971): 721–735.

McVeigh, Rory, Daniel Myers, and David Sikkink. "Corn, Klansmen, and Coolidge: Structure and Framing in Social Movements." *Social Forces* 83, no. 2 (2004): 653–690.

Melucci, Alberto. "Getting Involved: Identity and Mobilization in Social Movements." In *From Structure to Action: Comparing Social Movement Research Across Cultures. International Social Movement Research* 1 (1988): 329–348, edited by Bert Klandermans, Hanspeter Kriesi, and Sidney Tarrow. JAI Press.

Meyer, David, and Susan Staggenborg. "Movements, Countermovements, and the Structure of Political Opportunity." *American Journal of Sociology* 101, no. 6 (1996): 1628–1660.

Michels, Robert. *Political Parties: A Sociological Study of the Oligarchical Tendencies of Modern Democracy*. Free Press, 1915 [1962].

Millet, Donald. "Some Aspects of Agricultural Retardation in Southwest Louisiana, 1865–1900." *Louisiana History* 11 (1970): 37–61.

Morris, Aldon. "Black Southern Student Sit-in Movements: An Analysis of Internal Organization." *American Sociological Review* 45 (1981): 744–767.

———. *The Origins of the Civil Rights Movement: Black Communities Organizing for Change.* Free Press, 1984.

———. "Birmingham Confrontation Reconsidered: An Analysis of the Dynamics and Tactics of Mobilization." *American Sociological Review* 58 (1993): 621–636.

Morrison, Denton, and Allan Steeves. "Deprivation, Discontent, and Social Movement Participation: Evidence on a Contemporary Farmers Movement." *Rural Sociology* 32 (1967): 414–434.

Mottl, Tahi. "The Analysis of Countermovements." *Social Problems* 27 (1980): 620–635.

Mueller, Edward. "A Test of a Partial Theory of Potential for Political Violence." *American Political Science Review* 66 (1972): 928–959.

Noonan, Rita. "Women Against the State: Political Opportunities and Collective Action Frames in Chile's Transition to Democracy." In *Social Movements: Readings on Their Emergence, Mobilization, and Dynamics,* edited by Doug McAdam and David Snow. Roxbury Publishing Co., 1997.

Oberschall, Anthony. *Social Conflict and Social Movements.* Prentice-Hall, 1973.

Orum, Anthony. *Black Students in Protest: A Study of the Origins of the Black Student Movement.* American Sociological Association, Rose Monograph Series, 1972.

Oubre, Claude. *Forty Acres and a Mule: The Freedmen's Bureau and Black Land Ownership.* Louisiana State University Press, 1978.

Palmer, Bruce. *Man over Money: The Southern Populist Critique of American Capitalism.* University of North Carolina Press, 1980.

Payerhin, Marek. "On Movement Frames and Negotiated Identities: The Case of Poland's First Solidarity Congress." *Social Movement Studies* 5, no. 2 (2006): 91–115.

Peoples, Morgan. "'Kansas Fever' in North Louisiana," *Louisiana History* 11, no. 2 (1970): 121–135.

Perman, Michael. *The Road to Redemption: Southern Politics, 1869–1879.* University of North Carolina Press, 1984.

———. *The Struggle for Mastery: Disfranchisement in the South, 1888–1908.* University of North Carolina Press, 2001.

Petersen, Svend. *A Statistical History of American Presidential Elections.* Frederick Ungar Publishing Co., 1963.

Petras, James, and Maurice Zeitlin. "Miners and Agrarian Radicalism." *American Sociological Review* 32 (1967): 578–586.

Piven, Frances Fox, and Richard Cloward. *Poor People's Movements: Why They Succeed, How They Fail.* Vintage Books, 1977.

Polletta, Francesca. "Culture is Not Just in Your Head." In *Rethinking Social Movements: Structure, Meaning, and Emotions,* edited by Jeff Goodwin and James Jasper. Rowman and Littlefield Publishers, 2004.

Portes, Alejandro. "On the Logic of Post-Factum Explanations: The Hypothesis of Lower-Class Frustration as the Cause of Leftist Radicalism." *Social Forces* 50 (1971): 26–44.

Rable, George. *But There Was No Peace: The Role of Violence in the Politics of Reconstruction.* University of Georgia Press, 1984.

Rezneck, Samuel. "Unemployment, Unrest, and Relief in the United States during the Depression of 1893–97." *Journal of Political Economy* 41 (1953): 324–345.

Rodrigue, John. *Reconstruction in the Cane Fields: From Slavery to Free Labor in Louisiana's Sugar Parishes, 1862–1880.* Louisiana State University Press, 2001.

———. "Labor Militancy and Black Grassroots Political Mobilization in the Louisiana Sugar Region, 1865–1868." *The Journal of Southern History,* 67, no. 1 (2001): 115–142.

Rogers, William. "The Negro Alliance in Alabama." *The Journal of Negro History* 45 (1960): 38–44.

Royce, Edward. "The Origins of Sharecropping: Explaining Social Change." *Current Perspectives in Social Theory* 6 (1985): 279–299.

Rucht, Dieter. "The Impact of National Contexts on Social Movement Structures: A Cross-movement and Cross-national Comparison." In *Comparative Perspectives on Social Movements: Political Opportunities, Mobilizing Structures, and Cultural Framings,* edited by Doug McAdam, John McCarthy, and Mayer Zald. Cambridge University Press, 1996.

Ryan, Charlotte. *Prime Time Activism.* South End Press, 1991.

Schwartz, Michael. *Radical Protest and Social Structure: The Southern Farmers Alliance and Cotton Tenancy.* Academic Press, 1976.

Schwartz, Michael, and Paul Shuva, "Resource Mobilization versus the Mobilization of People: Why Consensus Movements Cannot Be Instruments of Social Change." In *Frontiers in Social Movement Theory,* edited by Aldon Morris and Carol Mueller. Yale University Press, 1992.

Selznick, Phillip. "Institutional Vulnerability in Mass Society." In *Protest, Reform, and Revolt,* edited by Joseph Gusfield. Wiley and Sons, 1970.

Shapiro, Herbert. "The Populists and the Negro: A Reconsideration." In *The Making of Black America,* edited by August Meier and Elliott Rudwick. Reprinted in the Bobbs-Merrill Reprint Series in Black Studies, 1969.

Shaw, Barton. *The Wool-Hat Boys: Georgia's Populist Party.* Louisiana State University Press, 1984.

Shugg, Roger. *Origins of Class Struggle in Louisiana: A Social History of White Farmers and Laborers During Slavery and After, 1840–1875.* Louisiana State University Press, 1939.

Sipress, Joel. "The Revolt of the Smallholders: Origins of Populism in Grant Parish, Louisiana, 1860–1892." Master's thesis, University of North Carolina at Chapel Hill, 1989.

———. "From the Barrel of a Gun: The Politics of Murder in Grant Parish." *Louisiana History* 42 (2001): 303–321.

———. "A Narrowing of Vision: Hardy L. Brian and the Fate of Louisiana Populism." *The Journal of the Gilded Age and Progressive Era* 7, no. 1 (2008): electronic access, no pagination.

Skocpol, Theda. *States and Social Revolution.* Cambridge University Press, 1979.

Smelser, Neil. *Theory of Collective Behavior.* Free Press, 1963.

Snow, David, Louis Zurcher, and Sheldon Ekland-Olson. "Social Networks and Social Movements: A Microstructural Approach to Differential Recruitment." *American Sociological Review* 45 (1980): 787–801.

Snow, David, E. Burke Rochford, Steven Worden, and Robert Benford. "Frame Alignment Processes, Micromobilization, and Movement Participation." *American Sociological Review* 51 (1986): 464–481.

Snyder, David, and Charles Tilly. "Hardship and Collective Violence in France, 1830 to 1960." *American Sociological Review* 37 (1972): 520–532.

Staggenborg, Suzanne. "The Consequences of Professionalization and the Formalization in the Pro-Choice Movement." *American Sociological Review* 53 (1988): 585–606.

Stillerman, Joel. "Space, Strategies, and Alliances in Mobilization: The 1960 Metalworkers' and Coal Miners' Strike in Chile." *Mobilization: An International Journal* 8, no. 1 (2002): 65–85.

Suarez, Raleigh. "Bargains, Bills, and Bankruptcies: Business Activity in Rural Antebellum Louisiana." *Louisiana History* 7, no. 3 (1966): 189–206.

Tarrow, Sidney. "National Politics and Collective Action: Recent Theory and Research in Western Europe and the United States." *Annual Review of Sociology* 14 (1988): 421–440.

———. "States and Opportunities: The Political Structuring of Social Movements." In *Comparative Perspectives on Social Movements: Political Opportunities, Mobilizing Structures, and Cultural Framing,* edited by Doug McAdam, John McCarthy, and Mayer Zald. Cambridge University Press, 1996.

Taylor, Joe Gray. *Louisiana Reconstructed, 1863–1877.* Louisiana State University Press, 1974.

———. *Louisiana: A Bicentennial History.* W. W. Norton and Co., 1976.

———. "Louisiana: An Impossible Task." In *Reconstruction and Redemption in the South.* Louisiana State University Press, 1980.

Thornton, J. Mills. "Fiscal Policy and the Failure of Radical Reconstruction in the Lower South." In *Region, Race, and Reconstruction: Essays in Honor of C. Vann Woodward,* edited by J. Morgan Kousser and James McPherson. Oxford University Press, 1982.

Thorstad, Linda. "The Historical and Cultural Geography of the Grange in Minnesota and Louisiana 1870–1880." Ph.D. dissertation, Louisiana State University, 1999.

Tilly, Charles. *From Mobilization to Revolution.* Addison-Wesley, 1978.

Tindall, George B. *South Carolina Negroes, 1877–1900.* University of South Carolina Press, 1952.

———. "The People's Party." In *History of U.S. Political Parties,* edited by Arthur Schlesinger. Chelsea House Publishers, 1973.

Tunnell, Ted. *Crucible of Reconstruction: War, Radicalism and Race in Louisiana, 1862–1877.* Louisiana State University, 1984.

———. *Carpetbagger from Vermont: The Autobiography of Marshall Harvey Twitchell.* Louisiana State University Press, 1989.

Unger, Irwin. *The Greenback Era: A Social and Political History of American Finance, 1865–1879.* Princeton University Press, 1964.

Uzee, Philip. "The Republican Party in the Louisiana Election of 1896," *Louisiana History* 2, no. 3 (1961): 332–344.

Vandal, Gilles. "'Bloody Caddo': White Violence against Blacks in a Louisiana Parish, 1865–1876." *Journal of Social History* 25, no. 2 (1991): 373–388.

———. "Black Violence in Post-Civil War Louisiana." *The Journal of Interdisciplinary History* 25, no. 1 (1994): 45–64.

Voss, Kim. *The Making of American Exceptionalism: The Knights of Labor and Class Formation in the Nineteenth Century.* Cornell University Press, 1993.

———. "The Collapse of a Social Movement: The Interplay of Mobilizing Structures, Framing, and Political Opportunities in the Knights of Labor." In *Comparative Perspectives on Social Movements,* edited by Doug McAdam, John McCarthy, and Mayer Zald. Cambridge University Press, 1996.

Warmoth, Henry Clay. *War, Politics, and Reconstruction: Stormy Days in Louisiana.* Macmillan Co., 1930.

Waters, Sarah. "Situating Movements Historically: May 1968, Alain Touraine, and New Social Movement Theory." *Mobilization: An International Journal* 13, no. 1 (2008): 63–82.

White, Howard. *The Freedmen's Bureau in Louisiana.* Louisiana State University Press, 1970.

Willis, Curley Daniel. "The Granger Movement in Louisiana." Master's thesis, Louisiana State University, 1935.

Wilson, John. *Introduction to Social Movements.* Basic Books, 1973.

Winkler, Ernest. *Platforms of Political Parties in Texas.* University of Texas Press, 1916.

Woodward, C. Vann. *Origins of the New South, 1877–1913.* Louisiana State University Press, 1951

———. *Tom Watson: Agrarian Rebel.* Oxford University Press, 1963 [1938].

———. *The Strange Career of Jim Crow.* Oxford University Press, 1966.

———. *The Burden of Southern History.* Louisiana State University Press, 1993.

Zald, Mayer, and Roberta Ash. "Social Movement Organizations: Growth, Decay, and Change." *Social Forces* 44 (1966): 327–341.

Index